FAULKNER'S REVISION OF *ABSALOM, ABSALOM!*

Faulkner's Revision of *Absalom, Absalom!*

A Collation of the Manuscript and the Published Book

by GERALD LANGFORD

UNIVERSITY OF TEXAS PRESS

AUSTIN AND LONDON

International Standard Book Number 0-292-70113-6
Library of Congress Catalog Card Number 79-157252
© 1971 by Gerald Langford

Typesetting by Beljan, Ann Arbor, Michigan
Printed by Malloy Lithographing, Inc., Ann Arbor, Michigan
Bound by Universal Bookbindery, Inc., San Antonio, Texas

In memory of John Cook Wyllie

CONTENTS

ACKNOWLEDGMENTS

Grateful acknowledgment is made to Random House, Inc., for permission to quote from *Absalom, Absalom!*, by William Faulkner. Copyright 1936 and renewed 1964 by Estelle Faulkner and Jill Faulkner Summers.

Thanks are due also to Yale University Press for permission to quote from *William Faulkner: The Yoknapatawpha Country*, by Cleanth Brooks (copyright 1963 by Yale University).

* * *

To the Research Institute of The University of Texas at Austin, I am indebted for granting me a semester's leave from teaching duties during my work on this project.

To Mrs. Denise Ronan, who worked as my research assistant in the first stage of the undertaking, I wish also to express my indebtedness for a tentative transcript which she made of the difficult handwritten manuscript of *Absalom, Absalom!* Mrs. Ronan's work proved a valuable timesaver in my preliminary evaluation of the problems and possibilities of this study.

G. L.

FAULKNER'S REVISION OF *ABSALOM, ABSALOM!*

Introduction

As one of the major achievements in twentieth-century fiction, William Faulkner's *Absalom, Absalom!* would be an instructive work in which to study the writer's revisions even if these were confined to matters of word choice and sentence structure. Some of the revisions, however, are structural, and it is particularly interesting to learn that, while writing and reworking the novel, Faulkner altered in several ways his original design. Most notably, he changed his mind about having it known from the beginning that Charles Bon was Sutpen's part-Negro son, and he developed Quentin Compson into the pivotal figure of the story instead of leaving him, as he was in the first version, merely one of the four narrators who pieced together the Sutpen chronicle. To trace the process of such revision is to experience a sharp focusing of the dominant theme of the novel, and to witness a demonstration of how the meaning of a fictional work can shape its structure and thus stand revealed by what has become the outward and visible sign, or form, of that meaning.

At the opposite end of a scale of importance, the value of a study of Faulkner's original manuscript is illustrated by a recent article about the presumably deliberate errors and inconsistencies in the novel.[1] Familiar with only the published text, the writer of the article discusses the tendency of the several narrators, "like most tellers of stories, to exaggerate or to use round numbers. Generally, the reports agree that Miss Rosa lived in hate of Sutpen for forty-three years, but at least twice the figure is rounded off to forty-five." In the manuscript the figure is regularly forty-five; it would seem clear that, in revising, Faulkner simply missed making the change once or twice (see, for example, book 11/1).[2] Again, according to the article, "a few inconsistencies remain puzzling and inexplicable. Only a careless and unintentional mistake or some kind of incredible subtlety, it seems, could explain Quentin's memory of how he heard '*Mrs* Coldfield's feet . . . approaching along the upper hall' as she returned from seeing the sick Henry Sutpen at the end of the novel (p. 370). The *Mrs* is the more amazing because of Miss Rosa's old-maidish lifetime of hate and virginity."

[1] Floyd C. Watkins, "What Happens in *Absalom, Absalom!?*" *Modern Fiction Studies* 13 (Spring 1967): 79–87; see 85 and 86.

[2] References in this Introduction are to page/line in both the Ms. and the published book.

Since the word is *Miss* in the manuscript, the change seems to be merely a typographical error. Other matters discussed in the article include the suggestion that subtle characterization may perhaps be found in various inconsistencies in the dating of events by Miss Rosa and Mr. Compson—errors which, as we shall notice, seem clearly the unintentional result of Faulkner's reworking of his original chronology.

As was his general practice, Faulkner wrote *Absalom, Absalom!* in longhand, making some changes as he went along and making more changes as he produced a typescript and corrected the galley proofs. It is the first version and the final version with which we are here concerned. The original manuscript, located in the Humanities Research Center of The University of Texas at Austin, is a meticulously neatly written volume of 175 pages. Because of one omission and two letter-numbered insertions, Faulkner's own final page number is 172. To facilitate use of the manuscript, the library has had the pages correctly pencil-numbered, and references in the following collation are to this new pagination, with Faulkner's numbers included within brackets. References to the published book are to the Modern Library Edition (New York, 1951).

A formidable barrier to the study of Faulkner's manuscripts is the tiny handwriting, which is difficult enough when words are spelled out normally but which also incorporates a kind of private shorthand. Often the context alone makes it possible to distinguish between *they* and *them*, for example, both of which may appear simply as *th*. At the end of a word *le* is written the same as *te*; the letter *c* designates both *c* and *s*; *f* is often indistinguishable from *g* and *j*; both *is* and *was* are indicated by a scrawl that looks like *us*; a final *ing* is indicated by a trailing line that is sometimes too abbreviated to be detected; *negro* is barely, if at all, differentiated from *nigger*; and some words are regularly shortened (for example, *Je* followed by three indecipherable letters means *Jefferson*). In the collation, therefore, question marks in brackets follow doubtful words, and occasionally an obdurate cipher is omitted in favor of the bracketed label *illegible word*. Revisions that are simply eliminations of careless repetition or clarifications of tense sequence, pronoun reference, and the like are omitted, as are such negligible changes as from *dresses that* to *dresses which*, or from *as though* to *as if*; and changes of punctuation within sentences have been omitted except when the sense of the statement is changed. All changes of end punctuation, however, are included in the collation. The obvious errors in the published book are designated *sic*.[3]

According to the first page of the manuscript, Faulkner began writing

[3]11/1; 18/33 (several repetitions of this inconsistency in the use of the apostrophe will not be enumerated); 23/33; 49/12; 78/22; 106/28; 118/5, 30; 126/6, 12; 130/12; 133/7; 140/14; 141/33; 154/19; 155/22; 169/25; 176/13, 21; 180/14; 181/27; 183/18; 192/15; 201/21; 210/1; 232/24; 246/33; 253/30; 255/27; 264/27; 266/12, 27; 267/29; 276/2; 277/20; 278/23; 283/5; 291/15; 295/12; 330/20; 335/23; 351/16; 358/3; 369/31; 370/21.

Absalom, Absalom! on March 30, 1935, and Chapter V is dated October 15, 1935, so that the writing of the first 58 pages required six and a half months—an average of 2 handwritten pages a week unless Faulkner wrote in interrupted spurts. The final page of the manuscript is dated January 31, 1936; thus the last 117 pages were written in three and a half months— an average of one and a quarter pages a day. The rapid outpouring of this latter portion of the novel is indicated in other ways, too. Like most "first drafts," the present manuscript is a composite of reworked passages and other passages written probably only once: this fact is revealed, first, by Faulkner's preservation in the manuscript of various cancelled passages followed by reworked versions, and second, by his economical practice of simply pasting in, instead of copying over, passages clipped from pages written earlier or later than the pages on which they appear.[4] In the first five chapters there are sixty-four pasted-in passages; in the last four chapters (over half of the novel) there are forty. Moreover, Faulkner's numbering of pages 1–58 involves twenty-eight changes of page number caused by the shifting of pages back and forth in the process of organizing the sequence of the story; there are only seven changes in the numbering of pages 59–172.[5] Noteworthy for a study of the organization of the manuscript is a system whereby, in order to keep a word count, Faulkner inserted a marginal number every ten lines. Repeated in cycles of six, these numbers mark off sections of roughly 200 words each, or 1,200 words for each cycle, compared with a page of roughly 300 words as the book was printed.

Considering the manuscript version of the novel as a whole and comparing it with the published book, one might begin to organize his findings by noting that Faulkner's revisions caused several inconsistencies which confuse one of the main issues in the story. Cleanth Brooks unwittingly calls attention to this confusion when he takes Ilse Dusoir Lind to task for stating that General Compson told Quentin something he had not divulged to Quentin's father—the fact that Charles Bon was Sutpen's son.[6] In attempting to disprove Miss Lind's statement, Mr. Brooks writes:

---

[4]Pasted-in passages are indicated in the collation. Beneath four of these later additions there are passages, more or less decipherable, which had been written on the pages as they originally stood: see Ms. 51/1–7; 66/9–11; 79/13–20; 137/10–11.

[5]The following manuscript pages show renumbering (page numbers added by the library are included in italics when they differ from Faulkner's numbers): 5 6; 8 9; 9 10; 12 5 13; 13 5 13 6 14; 14 6 14 7 15; 15 7 15 8 16; 16 8 16 9 17; 17 9 17 10 18; 18 10 18 11 19; 19 12 20; 20 13 21; 21 14 22; 22 15 23; 23 16 24; 5 24 25; 35 34 35; 36 35 36; 34 36 37; 38 39 40 41; 40 41 42; 412 43; 423 44; 44 424 45; 48 (written over an illegible number) 48 49; 46 50 51; 534 55; 56 55 56; 66 65 66; 79 76 77; 810 81; 88 867 88; 878 89; 134 136 137; 142 141 142.

[6]See "The Design and Meaning of *Absalom, Absalom!*" by Ilse Dusoir Lind, *PMLA* (December 1955): 887–912; reprinted in *William Faulkner: Three Decades of Criticism,* edited by Frederick J. Hoffman and Olga W. Vickery, pp. 278–304 (East Lansing: Michigan State University Press, 1960).

But nowhere in this novel is there any account of General Compson's telling Quentin anything. When the novel opens on a September afternoon in 1909, General Compson has long been dead. Moreover, there is in the novel no cutback to a scene in which Quentin has a conversation with his grandfather. One cannot say that the notion that Quentin was given the Sutpen secret by his grandfather is completely impossible. If we are to trust the genealogy of the Compson family published by Faulkner in the Modern Library edition of *The Sound and the Fury*, General Compson did not die until 1900, and since Quentin was born in 1890, the old man in his late eighties conceivably could have confided the secret to his ten-year-old grandson. But this theory is a highly improbable way of accounting for the facts. Actually, if one will look at pages 181 and 266–74, he will find that Quentin must have learned the secret of Bon's birth on his night visit to Sutpen's Hundred with Miss Rosa, that he did tell his father about it, and that this knowledge altered his father's view of the meaning of the story.[7]

Curiously, Mr. Brooks does not notice that his argument is undermined by one of Quentin's statements. Quentin tells Shreve that, until he himself supplied the key information, his father was ignorant of certain facts because "Grandfather didn't tell him all of it either, like Sutpen never told Grandfather quite all of it" (Book 266/19–21). How could Quentin be aware that General Compson knew things he had not passed on to Mr. Compson unless the old man told him so? At this stage, then, Miss Lind seems correct in stating that, without Mr. Compson's knowledge, the old man told the boy that Bon was Sutpen's son. Moreover, as we shall see presently, Quentin somehow learned of his grandfather's surmise that Bon had Negro blood.

Mr. Brooks goes on to remind us that on page 61 Mr. Compson could not know any of the truth about Bon because in telling Quentin that Clytie was Sutpen's daughter he does not include Bon in the list of Sutpen's children; whereas on page 265 Quentin tells Shreve: "Father said he probably named him himself." Here, Mr. Brooks points out, Quentin's father suddenly knows that Bon was Sutpen's son and seems to know also about the Negro blood, for he tells Quentin that Sutpen's conscience would not allow his first wife and child any place in his design "even though he could have closed his eyes and, if not fooled the rest of the world as they [his wife's parents] had fooled him, at least have frightened any man out of speaking the secret aloud" (p. 266/1–4).

> Naturally [Mr. Brooks observes] Shreve seizes upon the discrepancy between Mr. Compson's former ignorance and present knowledge, and protests to Quentin: "Your father . . . seems to have got an awful lot of delayed information awful quick, after having waited forty-five years." Quentin concedes that his father had got new information, information that could not have come from General Compson, since, as Quentin remarks, "Sutpen never told Grandfather quite all of it." Then Quentin makes the

---

[7]Cleanth Brooks, *William Faulkner*: *The Yoknapatawpha Country* (New Haven: Yale University Press, 1963), pp. 436–438.

surprising disclosure that it was he who supplied the information and that he gained it on the evening on which he and Miss Rosa went out to Sutpen's Hundred. (See also Quentin's remark on p. 181.) ... The author makes it very plain that what Quentin learned at Sutpen's Hundred constituted information that his father had never had and that for the first time made sense, to Mr. Compson, of the conversation between Sutpen and General Compson so many years before.

Unfortunately the issue is not so clear-cut as Mr. Brooks would have it. That Quentin's father does not know in Chapter IV that Bon was Sutpen's son is, of course, even clearer than Mr. Brooks indicates. Quentin is told by his father that Henry killed Bon "apparently for the very identical reason which four years ago he quitted home to champion, ... Yes, granted that, even to the unworldly Henry, let alone the more travelled father, the existence of the eighth part negro mistress and the sixteenth part negro son, granted even the morganatic ceremony ... was reason enough [to forbid Bon's marriage to Judith] ... It's just incredible. It just does not explain" (Book 100/10, 19, 28). The confusion arises when—despite this profession of ignorance and despite what Quentin tells Shreve in the passage cited by Mr. Brooks—Mr. Compson's later knowledge turns out to be knowledge or at least surmise which he is bound to have had all along. When Quentin quotes General Compson's account of the information which had been withheld from Sutpen by his first wife's family ("concealed it so well that it was not until after the child was born that I discovered that this factor existed," as Sutpen had put it), Shreve interrupts:

"Your old man," Shreve said. "When your grandfather was telling this to him, he didn't know any more what your grandfather was talking about than your grandfather knew what the demon was talking about when the demon told it to him, did he? And when your old man told it to you, you wouldn't have known what anybody was talking about if you hadn't been out there and seen Clytie. Is that right?" (Book 274/22-28)

In other words, General Compson did tell Quentin's father what Sutpen had told him, and it is difficult to follow Shreve's conclusion that General Compson did not understand what Sutpen was talking about. Quentin has just explained that his grandfather did not understand "what choice he was talking about even, what second choice he was faced with until the very last word he spoke before he got up and put on his hat and shook Grandfather's left hand and rode away" (Book 272/26-29). This last word was the "factor" which was concealed from him until after the birth of the child to whom General Compson assumed he had given the name Bon. At this point, then, General Compson suddenly understood the choice which confronted Sutpen when Judith fell in love with Bon. As Sutpen had put it:

". . . either I destroy my design with my own hand, which will happen if I am forced to play my last trump card, or do nothing, let matters take the course which I know they will take and see my design complete itself quite normally and naturally and successfully to the public eye, yet to my own in such fashion as to be a mockery and a betrayal of that little boy who approached that door fifty years ago and was turned away . . ." (Book 274/5–12)

It seems reasonably clear at this point that General Compson guessed—and passed on to Quentin's father—the fact that Bon was Sutpen's part-Negro son. Yet on page 100, as we have seen, Mr. Compson says he is bewildered by Sutpen's action in forbidding Judith's marriage to Bon.

Inadvertently again, Mr. Brooks calls attention to a further inconsistency in his discussion of the passage already cited as revealing Mr. Compson's suddenly acquired knowledge. The passage in full is as follows:

"Father said he probably named him himself. Charles Bon. Charles Good. He didn't tell Grandfather that he did, but Grandfather believed he did, would have. That would have been a part of the cleaning up, just as he would have done his share toward cleaning up the exploded caps and musket cartridges after the seige if he hadn't been sick (or maybe engaged); he would have insisted on it maybe, the conscience again which could not allow her and the child any place in the design even though he could have closed his eyes and, if not fooled the rest of the world as they had fooled him, at least have frightened any man out of speaking the secret aloud—the same conscience which would not permit the child, since it was a boy, to bear either his name or that of its maternal grandfather, yet which would also forbid him to do the customary and provide a quick husband for the discarded woman and so give his son an authentic name. He chose the name himself, Grandfather believed, just as he named them all—the Charles Goods and the Clytemnestras and Henry and Judith and all of them—that entire fecundity of dragons' teeth as father called it . . ." (Book 265/26 to 266/13)

As Mr. Brooks reads the passage, Quentin is here quoting his father, and the statement "rather clearly implies that Mr. Compson knows that the impediment is a trace of Negro blood. . . . information that could not have come from General Compson, since, as Quentin remarks, 'Sutpen never told Grandfather quite all of it.' " Rather, Mr. Brooks argues, it was clearly Quentin who supplied the information to his father after his interview with Henry Sutpen. This seems a decidedly questionable reading of the passage. If Quentin is quoting his father, then what he is quoting is his father's paraphrase of General Compson's surmise. Thus Mr. Compson's awareness of the truth about Bon could not have come entirely from Quentin. So what are we to make of Quentin's statement to Shreve that his father had not known about Bon until he, Quentin, told him? It is possible, of course, that Mr. Brooks is wrong in assuming that in the quoted passage Quentin is paraphrasing what his father has told him. Beginning with the statement "That would have been a part of the cleaning up," Quentin might seem to be speculating on the basis of knowledge which he says he was the first to discover. Only, as we have seen, he could not have been the discoverer of the truth about a situation which his grandfather had understood and discussed with both his father and himself.

Such inconsistencies, the manuscript reveals, are the result of Faulkner's change of plan during the writing of the novel. Apparently the original idea was that the truth about Bon should be known from the beginning. In Chapter II of the manuscript, Mr. Compson's reference to Sutpen's life in Haiti included two statements (here italicized) which were cut in revision:

> [Sutpen] set out into the world which even in theory he knew nothing about and with a fixed goal in his mind which ~~men of 30 often do not~~ most men do not set up until ~~after 30~~ the blood begins to slow at 30 or more, and then only because the image to them represents peace and indolence or at least a crowning of ~~ambi~~ vanity *instead of the vindication of a past affront in the person of a son* ~~not yet even begotten the~~ *whose seed* ~~of whose~~ *was not yet, and would not be for years yet, planned.* —that same alertness which he had to wear day and night without changing or laying aside, (like the clothing which without doubt and for a time at least he had to sleep in as well as live in) and in a country and among a people now whose very language he had to learn *and where because of this he was to make that mistake which if he had acquiesced to it would not have been even an error and which, since he refused to be stopped by it, became his doom* —that ~~alertness unsleeping~~ unsleeping care which must have known that it could permit itself but one mistake. (Ms. 22/26–34)

Here Mr. Compson sounds as if he understood the whole Sutpen story. He could hardly have attributed Sutpen's "doom" to the marriage in Haiti unless he knew that it was the son born of that union who, many years after being repudiated, was to reappear and threaten to marry Sutpen's daughter by a second marriage. Moreover, the words he used ("because of this he was to make that mistake . . .") can only mean that he was also aware of that crucial fact which Sutpen misunderstood because of his imperfect grasp of the language. Bon's Negro blood was clearly a threat to the establishment of a dynasty in the antebellum South, and in trying to block the marriage Sutpen ran the risk that finally came to pass when he lost his only heir as the price of stopping Bon. Thus the mistake he made in his first marriage did indeed become his doom when he refused to be stopped by it.

In writing Chapter IV Faulkner suddenly changed his original plan. The manuscript preserves the following cancelled passage as part of Mr. Compson's account of Henry's break with his father:

> Because what else could he (Henry) have hoped to find in New Orleans, if not the truth, not what his father had told him, what he had denied and refused
> ~~Because to believe that Sutpen did not tell him that night is simply incredible. Even granting that that is not reason enough for Henry to have repudiated his father, even granted that that is drawing[?] things[?] a little too~~ what else [sic] could Sutpen have told him, what other reason for his

refusal to permit the marriage to accept even tho, despite himself, he must actually have believed? (Ms. 39/18–22)

In this passage and in a reworking of it a few pages later (Ms. 45/9–14), Mr. Compson did not understand why Sutpen forbade the marriage. After speculating that Sutpen's reason for forbidding the marriage was the fact of Bon's eighth-part Negro mistress and the sixteenth-part Negro son, he now expressed bewilderment: "It's just incredible. It just does not explain. ~~to~~ ⟨now.⟩[8] Or perhaps that's it. ~~Perhaps~~ They dont explain and we are not supposed to know" (Ms. 45/13–14).

Having thus decided to make Mr. Compson ignorant of the fact that Bon was Sutpen's son, Faulkner apparently began to have doubts about this change. On the following page he inserted in Mr. Compson's recital a parenthetical remark (cut in revision) which seems to suggest an awareness that Sutpen's discovery of the octoroon mistress was only a pretext for his forbidding the marriage:

It was his [Bon's] only chance, though of course neither he nor Judith could have known this, since Sutpen (granted that the following Xmas, the moment when Sutpen was to absolutely forbid the marriage was in the cards) tho but two weeks absent from home, had already ~~discovered~~ found out about the octoroon mistress and the child in New Orleans." (Ms. 46/26–29)

Forbidding the marriage could not have been "in the cards" unless Sutpen's stand in the matter was caused by something other than what he discovered in New Orleans.

In Chapter VII Faulkner plainly restored Mr. Compson's knowledge that Bon was Sutpen's son, for here Quentin quoted his father's comment on the names Sutpen chose for his offspring:

. . . the Charles Goods and the Clytemnestras and Henry and Judith and all of them—that entire fecundity of dragon teeth, as father called it. And father said ~~how he~~ how he must have stood there on the front gallery that afternoon and waited for Henry and the friend Henry had been writing home about all fall to come up the drive and ~~they did~~ that maybe ~~after~~ even after Henry wrote the name in the letter Sutpen probably told himself it couldn't be, that there was a limit even to irony where it became just harmless coincidence, . . ." (Ms. 120/14–18)

This had to be Mr. Compson's long-standing knowledge, for the manuscript does not contain the passages Faulkner added in revision to make Quentin the source of his father's knowledge (Book 181/22–24 and 266/14–27).

Two additional passages make the original intention still clearer. In Quentin's summary (derived from his father) of General Compson's account of the remarks Sutpen made about his first marriage, Faulkner first wrote,

[8]For typographical convenience, angle brackets are used to indicate interlinear insertions in the Ms.

but at a later time cancelled, a statement in which Bon was called Judith's half-brother:

> He had been tricked by it [his first marriage] himself, but he had got out without asking or receiving help from anyone; let anyone else who might be so imposed on do the same.) ~~and-so-he-(Grandfather)-believed~~ that ~~he knew all that Sutpen could know~~ knew: ~~that Bon might decide at any moment to defy Henry and come to Judith, and~~ that ~~when he did so Judith would marry him half-brother or-no~~—sitting there and moralizing . . . (Ms. 122/20–23)

Faulkner also wrote, but at some later time cancelled, a statement by Quentin that Sutpen told General Compson about Bon's Negro blood.

> "Yes," Quentin said. "Sitting in Grandfather's office that p.m. ~~and telling him how he never found out until after Bon was born that the mother that they had told him was a Spaniard had some nigger blood. Yes. Sitting there~~ with his head kind of flung back a little, explaining to Grandfather . . . (Ms. 130/7–8)

It seems clear enough that Faulkner began with one intention, changed his mind, but then returned to his original intention. In revising the novel he changed his mind again but failed to alter several passages which indicate that the truth about Bon had been at least surmised all along.

In line with this alteration of the course of the story, Faulkner upgraded Quentin's role in the revised version. In spite of the inconsistencies outlined above, it is clear that Quentin is meant to become the discoverer of the fact which enables his father and himself to understand the events over which they have puzzled so long. To heighten Quentin's key role, Faulkner made several changes in the viewpoint of narration, the effect being to keep our attention focused on the boy as he and Shreve reconstruct the story in Chapters VI, VII, and VIII. These revisions are most notable in Chapter VI, where Shreve takes over the narration after Quentin has been briefly reminded of his trip to Sutpen's Hundred with Miss Rosa. In the manuscript Shreve's narration continued unbroken for the rest of the chapter. In revision Faulkner eliminated most of Shreve's recital, substituting a presentation of the events through several shifts to Quentin's reverie. As will be illustrated below, these changes relegate Shreve to the background and move Quentin forward to create the effect of a multidimensional stage: Quentin now stands front center, resisting vainly as the reality of the present is usurped repeatedly by the obsessive ghosts of the past.

To facilitate the location of these and other matters of interest to a student of the novel, perhaps the most helpful procedure will be to survey, chapter by chapter, the more notable changes recorded in the collation.

CHAPTER I

The September afternoon of Quentin's visit to Miss Rosa's house was dated 1910 in the manuscript (Ms. 1/10), instead of 1909 as in the book.

Thus, when Faulkner began writing *Absalom, Absalom!*, he had forgotten that in *The Sound and the Fury* Quentin enters Harvard in the fall of 1909 and commits suicide in June 1910. (Though the corrected date is given in the Genealogy appended to the book, the Chronology preserves the original error by listing 1910 as the year when "Rosa Coldfield and Quentin find Henry Sutpen hidden in the house.") This correction necessitated other changes. Rosa's sitting room had had its blinds closed for forty-five years in the manuscript, and Rosa had worn black for forty-five years (Ms. 1/3, 10), instead of forty-three in both instances in the book (but see Book 11/1, where Faulkner neglected to make the change; see also 14/19, 21, 28). Forty-five subtracted from 1910 gives a date of 1865 for Sutpen's outrageous proposal to Rosa, and later in the manuscript Sutpen's return from the war was so dated (Ms. 25/41), though at one point the manuscript is inconsistent (Rosa "died young of outrage in 1866 one summer": Ms. 80/29). The change from 1910 to 1909 places the proposal in 1864, which is too early to bring Sutpen home from the war; hence the additional change from forty-five to forty-three, which brings Sutpen home in 1866 (see Book 61/13).

The number of years Judith had been dead is changed from twenty in the manuscript (Ms. 4/7) to twenty-five in the book so as to accord with the dating of her death in 1884 (see Genealogy). Again, Rosa said in the manuscript that she had had twenty-two years in which to watch Sutpen (Ms. 5/21); then she changed it to twenty (Ms. 5/31). It is twenty in the book, but neither figure is correct according to the later statement that she was born in 1845 (Ms. 25/4 and Book 59/9), a date which would have given her twenty-one years in which to watch Sutpen before agreeing to marry him in 1866. Finally, Rosa said in the manuscript that she was two years younger than Judith and four years younger than Henry (Ms. 7/21–22), figures which are changed in the book to four and six.

More significant than such arithmetical matters is the kind of omissions Faulkner made in revising. For example, the paragraph which in the book ends with the single statement about Rosa's career as a poetess (Book 11/5–19) is extended in the manuscript to include a summary of her family history:

> . . . undefeat; and these from a woman whose family's martial[?] background as both town and county knew consisted of the father who, a conscientious objector on religious grounds, had starved himself to death ~~hidden~~ (some said, walled up) in the attic of his house, hidden there from Confederate provost marshals ~~while the same daughter~~ and fed secretly at night by the same daughter who now celebrated the lost cause's unregenerate[?] vanquished in verse, and the nephew who, ~~missing from home for 3 years, returned~~ served 3 years in the same company with his sister's fiance and then shot the fiance to death before the gate to the house where his sister waited in her wedding gown on the eve of the wedding and then fled, ~~none~~ vanished, none knew where. (Ms. 3/4–12)

To retain this passage would be to introduce, too early and in too concentrated a form, characters and events better understood when introduced piecemeal in more appropriate contexts (see Book 11/31; 15/17–23; 22/12).

Again, the statement in the book that the men of Jefferson did not tell their womenfolks what Sutpen was doing (Book 18/11) went on in the manuscript to include a remark about General Compson, who is not a functional character in the present scene:

> . . . by at least shielding him in it by not telling their womenfolk about it if by no more; doubtless the reason that your grandfather was the only one who admitted to having offered him money on his own signature was because your grandfather was at least that rare type of man whose life was too open and unable to even conceal his mistakes. I had had all my life to watch him in, . . . (Ms. 5/25–26)

For a final, different sort of example, Faulkner cut the second of the following two passages, which involve needless repetition:

> 'Protect her, at least. At least save Judith'—a child, yet whose child's vouchsafed innocence could answer what the mature wisdom of her elders apparently had not: 'Protect her? From whom and from what? He has already given them life; he does not need to harm them further. It is from themselves that they need protection.' (Ms. 8/39–42)

> . . . conviction ~~that~~ (that same instinctive knowledge which ~~had~~ enabled me to tell Ellen that it was not from him that Judith would need protection) . . . (Ms. 11/19–20)

Such a tightening of the narrative is observable even in the handling of words and phrases. A few examples of omissions from the manuscript wording (here italicized) will suffice:

amazed *outraged* voice (Ms. 1/14)

intervals *of self-confounding unsurprise* like a stream (Ms. 1/23)

had already established (*even if not affirmed*) herself (Ms. 3/2)

the skeleton . . . still in the closet. *Or more than that, even.* (Ms. 3/34)

man to *apparently* ~~find~~ ⟨discover⟩ ~~papa and~~ discover *not only* Ellen *but papa too*, in church. (Ms. 7/12)

with ~~that~~ triumph *while papa and Ellen talked* (Ms. 11/27)

palmlifted *like a racing* [?] *banner*, the horseman would sit (Ms. 1/31)

in the *dim* gloom (Ms. 2/35).

There are as many additions made in revision as there are omissions, and the effect is consistently to heighten or clarify the passages involved.

Not content with the statement in the manuscript that "the dead man himself would appear" (Ms. 1/15), Faulkner first added in the margin "as tho by outraged recapitulation evoked," and then in revision changed the first statement to read: "the long-dead object of her impotent yet indomitable frustration would appear" (Book 7/24–25): changes which deepen the texture of the statement by fusing the dead man and the effect he has had on Rosa. A comparable effect is found in the added statement describing Sutpen's ghost: ". . . (mused, thought, seemed to possess sentience, as if, though dispossessed of the peace—who was impervious anyhow to fatigue—which she declined to give it, it was still irrevocably outside the scope of her hurt or harm) . . ." (Book 13/22–25); moreover, by lengthening and complicating the sentence, Faulkner helped to create a main effect of the style throughout the book—that of a tentative probing ever deeper into the labyrinth of the past.

Suspense about Rosa's nocturnal mission is heightened by two added references to Quentin at home (here italicized):

("But why tell me about it?" he said to his father that evening, *when he returned home, after she had dismissed him at last with his promise to return for her in the buggy;* "why tell me about it? . . . (Book 12/14–17)

. . . "Do you want to know the real reason why she chose you?" *They were sitting on the gallery after supper, waiting for the time Miss Coldfield had set for Quentin to call for her.* (Book 12/25–28)

A similar device is created by the addition of two comments on Sutpen: the backward-looking statement that his name was one "which nobody ever heard before, knew for certain was his own any more than the horse was his own or even the pistols" (Book 14/32 to 15/1) and the forward-looking suggestion that he needed to make his position impregnable "even against the men who had given him protection on that inevitable day and hour when even they must rise against him in scorn and horror and outrage; . . ." (Book 15/7–10).

One of the most instructive features of the manuscript is its preservation of a number of reworked passages in which Faulkner can be observed feeling his way toward an effect that came clear only gradually through a process of manipulating and reordering and amplifying his materials. The first such passage (Ms. 7/34 ff.) is composed of six attempts at the section of Rosa's recital occupying pages 22–23 in the book. The chief difficulty confronting Faulkner here seems to have been the problem of transitions. In his first attempt to write the passage he seems to have been uncertain how to order and connect the two episodes from Rosa's childhood. He first wrote her reply to the dying Ellen, then cancelled it and considered substituting an account of Sutpen's Sunday morning races to church:

[Quentin visualized Rosa's] air Cassandralike and humorless and profoundly and sternly prophetic out of all proportion even to the actual years even

14

of a child who had never been young. "Because I was born too late. I was born a woman and hence a fool too, but at least mine was that vouchsafed instinct of innocence which, when Ellen, dying, had only me to turn to and say 'Protect her, at least. Protect Judith at least', could answer: 'Protect her? From whom and from what? He has already given them life: he does not need to harm them any ~~more~~ further'. It is from themselves that they need protection'. 22 years too late: a child to whom out of the overheard talk of grown people my own sister's and my nephew's and niece's and their father's faces had come to be like the faces in an ogre tale between supper and bed.—

---

a child who was to remember the 4 faces as seen for the first time in her life on that first Sunday [MARGIN: in the carriage] when the town realized that he had turned the road to town into a race course. (Ms. 7/35–43)

In a second attempt Faulkner moved the ogre-tale comparison forward to serve as an introduction to both episodes, and he reversed the order of presenting the Sunday races and Rosa's reply to Ellen, as if to try a chronological telling:

> . . . proportion to the actual years even of a child who had never been young. "Because I was not there. I was born too late. 22 years too late: a child to whom out of the overheard talk of grown people my own sister's and nephew's and niece's faces had grown to be like the faces in an ogre tale between supper and bed [MARGIN: long before ~~she~~ ⟨I⟩ was old enough or big enough to go out there and play with them]—a child who was to remember those 3 faces (and his too) as seen for the first time in the carriage on that first Sunday a.m. when the town realized that he had turned the road to church into a race course
>
> ---
>
> and nephew's and niece's faces had grown to be like the faces in an ogre tale between supper and bed, long before I was either old enough or big enough to ~~go out there to~~ be allowed to play with them—a child who was to remember those 3 faces (and his too) as seen for the first time in the carriage on that first Sunday a.m. when the town realized that he had turned the road to church into a race course. ~~I dont even remember ever seeing any of them before.~~—a child born 22 years too late yet who possessed that vouchsafed instinct of innocence which, when Ellen, dying, had only me to turn to and say 'Protect her at least. At least protect Judith' could answer what the mature wisdom of my elders apparently could not: 'Protect her? From whom and from what? He has already given them life: he does not need to harm them further. It is from themselves that they need protection'. "From themselves. ~~And~~ Not from him. And not by me. Because I had not been there. (Ms. 7/44–45 and 8/1–13)

A third attempt simply fleshes out the second. A comparison with the ogre's, or djinn's, stronghold is introduced, along with several vivid details in the account of the races:

15

. . . proportion to the actual years even of a child who had never been young. "Because I was born too late. I was born 22 years too late: a child to whom out of the overheard talk of grown people my own sister's and my nephew's and niece's faces had come to be like the faces in an ogretale heard between supper and bed long before I was old enough or big enough to be permitted to play with them—

---

a child who was to remember those 3 faces (and his too) as 'seen for the first time in the carriage on that first Sunday when the town [crossed-out illegible word] realized that he had turned the road to church into a race course, as tho the sister whom I had never seen and who had ~~removed~~ ⟨vanished⟩ before I was born into the stronghold of an ogre or djinn, was to return to the world on a one day's special(?) dispensation and I dressed for it (~~it~~ I was just 4 ⟨3⟩ then; doubtless I had seen them before but I cannot remember it, and doubtless this will be the picture of my first sight of them that I shall take to my grave) and then what I saw was a glimpse like the forefront of a tornado, of a carriage and Ellen's high white face [MARGIN: since she still had left doubtless what she meant by pride] and the two replicas of his face on either side of her and the face ~~of that wild negro driving who looked exactly like~~ the teeth of that wild negro who was driving and his face looking like the negro's save for the teeth, doubtless because of his beard, all in a thunder and a fury of ~~dust and~~ galloping and of dust;

---

and I ~~was~~[?] ⟨watching⟩ seeing for the first time to remember it the face of the ~~sister who was last to tu had only me to turn to when she lay~~ [MARGIN: yet to whom Ellen would have to turn when she lay] dying with one of the children vanished and doomed to be a murderer if not a fratricide and the other doomed to be a widow without having been a bride, let alone a wife— I, a child, yet who possessed that vouchsafed wisdom of innocence which, when Ellen said 'Protect her at least. At least protect Judith' could answer what the mature wisdom of my elders apparently could not: 'Protect her? From whom and what? He has already given them life: he does not need to harm them further. It is from themselves that they need protection.' (Ms. 8/14–32)

Still Faulkner was not satisfied. The narrative he was trying to continue in the reworked passage had already contained Ellen's dying words (see Ms. 7/23; cf. Book 21/18). To turn from that scene, as he was now doing, to the Sunday races and then back to Rosa's reply to Ellen seems an awkward arrangement. Thus in a fourth attempt (which, as far as it goes, is almost identical with the published text) he began by reversing the order of the third attempt:

. . . proportion to the actual years even of a child who had never been young. "Because I was born too late. I was born 22 years too late—a child to whom out of the overheard talk of grown people my own sister's and my sister's two children's faces had come to be like the faces in an ogre-tale between

16

supper and bed long before I was old enough or big enough to be permitted
to play with them, yet to whom that sister would have to turn at the last
when she lay dying, with one of the children vanished and doomed to be a
murderer and-the -other- a- already if not a fratricide and the other doomed
to be a widow without having been a bride, let alone a wife, and say, 'Protect
her, at least. At least protect Judith'—a child, yet whose child's vouchsafed
innocence could answer what the mature wisdom of her elders apparently
had not: 'Protect her? From whom and from what? He has already given
them life: he does not need to harm them further. It is from themselves
that they need protection'. (Ms. 8/33–42)

At this point Faulkner broke off again, as if uncertain how to make the
transition to the earlier time of the Sunday races. In a fifth attempt he
tried to solve his problem by dropping both of the troublesome episodes
and having Rosa turn to an account of Sutpen's first years in Jefferson:

. . . proportion- to-the actual years- even -of-a-child-who -had never-been -young.
Because ⟨Yes⟩ I was not there. I was -born -too- late I only heard about it.
I only heard how it was 5 years before any men or women in Jefferson
began to ⟨a⟩wake to him, tho even-from-the- very- first apparently it only took
him a matter of days to take the town's measure—that measure of crass
and-contemptible stupidity to which even the revelation of that first Spanish
coin ⟨gold piece⟩ would be only a matter of a two days agog✕/, as tho he
[MARGIN: who admitted and preferred to have neither] dared them not out of
recklessness but with actual contempt by paying for the recording[?] of the
land which no one knew yet how he had acquired, it with a coin found usually
in the possession of banks or pirates[?] and which, in the possession of the
man which he professed by acts to be, even conclusive evidence of that of
which even among men[?] would have been a symptom. No. I lived thru 5
years during which he held them spellbound with a- raree- show that[?] with
his -own-raree-show- until- even- they-could -no -longer- be- fooled.- -And-then- it
was- too-late. with that raree show which he conducted out there with his
wild negroes beasts[?] and that poor harried frightened little architect while
he built his house, sleeping on the bare floors and living on meat, during
which, so I have heard, those wild negroes would work down in the swamp
and then creep up and cut their throats with knives before the animal could
men wake and flee—a Punch and Judy booth[?] before which the men of the
town (oh there were others besides your grandfather and t my father) stood
entranced until even they could be fooled no more, until his contempt for
them became so crass that he returned from his final expedition bringing
his ⟨the⟩ actual itself [sic] with him in wagons. Then it was too late. He
did not need his own[?] raree show then, since the [illegible word] on ours[?]
and our father[?] was sufficient. Just exactly sufficient to permit them to
follow him to our gate that day without quite working themselves up to arrest
him—the sheriff and a dozen men and 50 a mob of 50 more and growing all
the time, following behind him as he walked up this very street here, with
that bouquet of flowers and turned into our gate, like so many dogs following
a hen and the hen not quite daring to run and none of the dogs quite daring to

17

chase yet, until he reached the gate out there and turned into it, and came into the house here. Walked into this house in that new hat and coat with that bouquet of flowers gathered out of ditches on the way ⟨road⟩ to town and plighted faith and honor, who did not possess either, to a fool young woman who did not possess judgment or discretion, either in herself or in the person[?] of the aunt who might have been expected to protect her. He knew that they were waiting for him out there at the gate. He knew what they were waiting for. But he did not think or did not bother to mention it to Ellen. He just turned and went back out and let them arrest him himself be arrested without a word and he paraded back to town at the head of his mob of blackguards and hooligans. Without the bouquet now. As tho he had brot the bouquet for that purpose: that he had known, realized that he would not have time to tell our neighbors what he was about to do [30–41 PASTED IN: and so he would have to use some symbol that they would recognize and understand before the sheriff overtook him. Or maybe he was just keeping the sheriff back with the bouquet, having realized that the pistols would not be enough now, until he could get into the house and get a foothold in security even tho knowing that he would have to return in a mom sooner or later and face the preliminaries of retribution at least. But apparently it was sufficient, since our father and your grandfather seem to have reached the courtroom even before he did and so that night he came back with papa to supper the I dont know how they got him out. But then I or Ellen nor any other woman in town ever knew just which of his crimes they had arrested him for in the first place. No. We, being women, were not to know that: we were only to furnish a wife for him. Besides, I was not there at the time. I was born 22 years too late. Maybe they were afraid. Perhaps the crime which they had learned of at last happened not to be minor[?] and so they een knew that they could not hold him prisoner[?] and perhaps they remembered how he the pistols and the way he was said to be able to use them which I dont doubt was true enough since it is a poor carpenter that cannot use his own tools.] Two months later he and Ellen were married. That p.m. he came back home with papa, to supper. And two months later he and Ellen were married. (Ms. 9/1–42)

Evidently Faulkner could find no way of getting back to Ellen's deathbed scene from the point he had reached here. Evidently, too, he felt he was getting ahead of his story. Having decided to save these episodes for the following chapter (see the reworking of them at pages 33–38 and 44–48), he returned to the point where he had broken off in his fourth attempt. In his sixth attempt he simply completed the fourth, without attempting yet to tie the two episodes together:

"No I was not there. I was born 22 years too late and hence a child to whom out of the overheard talk of grown people my own sister's and my nephew's and niece's faces had come to be like the faces of an ogre tale between supper and bed long before I was big enough or old enough to be permitted to go out there play with them//a child who was to remember those 3 faces "No. I was not there, born too late.—a child who was to remember those three faces (and his, too) as seen for the first time in the carriage on that first Sunday when the town finally realized that he had turned the road to church into a race course; ~~It was as tho as the~~ I was three then, and doubtless I had seen them before, but I cannot remember it, ever having seen Ellen before, even. It was as tho the sister whom I had never seen, ~~and~~ who had vanished before I was born, into the stronghold of an ogre or a djinn, was now to return for one day to the world thru a special dispensation and I, a child of three, waked early for the occasion, dressed and curled as tho for Xmas, for an occasion more serious than Xmas even, since now and at last this ogre or djinn who held my sister captive had agreed, for the sake of the wife and children, to come to church, to permit them at least to enter the realm of grace ~~to give at least~~ to at least give Ellen one chance to struggle with him for those children's souls on a battleground where she could be supported not only by Heaven but by her own family and people of her own kind, ~~tho he himself, for the moment chivalrous, was still (and would remain) unregenerate~~ and even for the moment submit himself to redemption, or lacking that, at least chivalrous even tho unregenerate. That's what I expected. This is what I saw [MARGIN: as I stood there before the church with my aunt holding my hand, waiting for the carriage to arrive from the 12 mile drive,] and tho I must have seen Ellen and the children driving[?] before this, this is the picture of my first sight of them which I shall carry to my grave: a glimpse like the forefront of a tornado of a carriage and Ellen's high white face since she still had left doubtless what she called pride and the two replicas of his face on either side of her and the teeth of the wild negro who was driving and his face on the front seat with the negro and looking exactly like the negro's except the teeth because of his beard doubtless—all in a thunder and a fury of wildeyed horses and of galloping and of dust. (Ms. 9/42–44 and 10/1–17)

Only in his final revision did Faulkner manage the transition which seems to have stymied him in trying to tie together the episodes of the Sunday races and Ellen's deathbed words. Instead of trying to tie them together he inserted between them a passage which brings us back to Quentin in Rosa's sitting room:

It should have been later than it was; it should have been late, yet the yellow slashes of mote-palpitant sunlight were latticed no higher up the impalpable wall of gloom which separated them; the sun seemed hardly to have moved. It (the talking, the telling) seemed (to him, to Quentin) to partake of that logic- and reason-flouting quality of a dream which the sleeper knows must have occurred, stillborn and complete, in a second, yet the very quality upon which it must depend to move the dreamer (versimilitude) to credulity—horror or pleasure or amazement—depends as completely upon a formal recognition of and acceptance of elapsed and yet-elapsing time as music or a printed tale. (Book 22/20–31)

Several other points are noteworthy in Chapter I. In connection with the portrayal of Sutpen it should be pointed out that in the manuscript Ellen called him "Charles" (Ms. 12/35, 38, 39). Later, in Chapter V, Faulkner was to try "John" before settling on "Thomas," which by comparison seems somehow the one correct name for Sutpen.

A striking group of revisions consists of reversals in word order. These occur so regularly throughout the book that they might at first seem to be no more than an arbitrary sort of tinkering.[9] On closer inspection one is struck by Faulkner's close attention to such aspects of sentence construction as emphasis, tightness, and logical sequence of items. Changes in emphasis are obvious in the following examples:

> "rank with female old flesh in virginity long embattled" (Ms. 1/20) versus "the rank smell of female old flesh long embattled in virginity" (Book 8/10–11)
>
> "practically threw[?] his sister's murdered fiance's corpse" (Ms. 6/11) versus "practically fling the bloody corpse of his sister's sweetheart" (Book 18/27–28)
>
> "like he was a caged snake and the shirt was a stick" (Ms. 12/35) versus "as though the coat were a stick and he a caged snake" (Book 30/11–12)

Sentence elements are noticeably tightened in reversals like the following:

> "trying to throw the cotton and slaves both away" (Ms. 5/12) versus "bent on throwing away their cotton and slaves" (Book 17/17)
>
> "looked at his face once" (Ms. 5/18) versus "looked once at his face" (Book 17/29)
>
> "return for one day to the world thru a special dispensation" (Ms. 10/6) versus "return through a dispensation of one day only, to the world" (Book 23/8–9)

Finally, the sequence of items is made more logical in a number of reversals:

> "quality almost of permanence, solidity" (Ms. 3/40) versus "quality almost of solidity, permanence" (Book 13/20)
>
> "thorns and briers in a thicket" (Ms. 4/45) versus "briers and thorns in a thicket" (Book 16/21)
>
> "note of hand on peace and contentment and pride" (Ms. 6/5) versus "notes of hand on pride and contentment and peace" (Book 18/20–21)

---

[9]A more or less complete list of such reversals throughout the novel is as follows: Book 8/10–11, 13; 10/17; 11/7; 12/8–9; 13/2, 15–16, 20; 16/4, 21–22; 17/9, 17–18, 19, 26–27, 28; 18/20, 28–29; 19/6–7; 24/2, 8; 28/23; 29/13–14; 30/11–12; 37/17; 58/1; 64/21; 65/10, 20–21; 72/16, 17; 73/16; 74/10; 76/31; 77/7, 23; 82/33; 85/6, 11; 86/5; 92/14; 93/30; 94/19; 96/11; 97/31–32; 99/12; 100/31; 105/8; 107/17; 110/27–28; 112/7–8; 113/30–31; 115/10, 15–16, 18; 117/17; 120/18, 23; 121/29; 123/4, 22; 124/16; 125/26; 127/30; 129/18; 132/12, 33; 133/6; 137/16, 23, 29; 138/28; 140/27; 142/29; 143/24; 144/10; 147/1; 148/5, 23, 29; 149/28; 150/1, 6, 19; 151/15, 19; 161/13; 162/16, 28; 166/21; 168/32; 169/3, 30; 176/27; 177/12–13; 179/2–3; 182/6, 9; 184/15; 185/7, 24; 186/9; 187/20; 190/13; 191/13–14; 193/21; 194/19–20; 196/16; 197/2; 199/21–22, 32; 206/24; 209/10, 21; 214/12; 216/5; 217/23; 218/2, 7–8, 18; 219/19; 221/16; 223/7; 225/1–2; 228/33; 230/22; 231/12; 232/28; 233/1; 235/5; 236/6, 11; 237/25; 239/13; 241/6; 243/23; 244/31; 245/19; 246/5; 247/32; 248/21; 251/12–13; 252/13–14; 255/24;

CHAPTER II

There are fewer significant changes in Chapter II than in the opening chapter. Perhaps the most notable is the first of a number of changes Faulkner made in the viewpoint of narration.[10] In the book the omniscient author's account of Sutpen's arrival and establishment in Jefferson ends when Sutpen leaves to fetch the furnishings for his house (Book 43/21), from which point Mr. Compson narrates the rest of the chapter. In the manuscript, however, Mr. Compson picked up the story only with the account of Sutpen's wedding (Ms. 20/22. See Book 48/27). The most interesting thing about the change is that Faulkner simply introduces quotation marks five pages earlier in the book than he had done in the manuscript. In turning a passage of omniscient narration into oral discourse he made no changes to give the telling a colloquial tone. Indeed, no matter which narrator is speaking, the style throughout the book remains uniformly poetic and intricately structured. This is not versimilitude, of course, but a stylistic device used to dramatize the extent to which each of the four narrators (five including the omniscient author) is caught up in the process whereby each generation must try to reach the truth about the past, not merely by assembling all available facts but by tying loose ends and supplying motivations in an act of imaginative re-creation. As Shreve later remarks to Quentin, "Dont say it's just me that sounds like your old man," in reply to which Quentin thinks, "Yes. *Maybe we are both Father. . . . Or maybe Father and I are both Shreve, maybe it took Father and me both to make Shreve or Shreve and me both to make Father or maybe Thomas Sutpen to make all of us*" (Book 261/23 ff.).

The effect of changing the viewpoint in the present instance is to bring us closer to the man Sutpen at one of the crucial points in his life, for Mr. Compson has heard various eyewitnesses tell about the vigilance committee's arrest of Sutpen. To point up this fact, Faulkner added several statements in revision: "All I ever heard is how the town, the men on the gallery of the Holston House saw Sutpen and the committee . . ." (Book 45/16–18); ". . . according to your grandfather . . ." (Book 48/21–22); and in particular the enlivening comparison of Sutpen's social graces with John L. Sullivan's self-taught schottische (Book 46/2 ff.).

Throughout the chapter Faulkner sharpened his imagery in revision. In the following examples the passages not found in the manuscript are italicized:

256/29; 260/2, 23; 270/13–14; 276/5; 278/30–31; 279/4; 280/20; 281/4–5; 283/2; 286/17; 287/22–23; 289/31; 291/27; 294/4; 303/6; 319/1; 321/23; 322/7–8; 323/10, 29; 325/21; 327/24–25; 329/6; 332/21; 333/21; 334/19; 336/7, 21; 339/9; 341/2; 342/27; 347/27; 351/18; 352/16–17; 356/9; 363/33; 364/14; 366/18; 367/11; 378/27.

[10]Also see Book 181/15; 187/12; 207/13; 210/10; 261/23; 277/7; 346/28.

Not like a man who had been peacefully ill in bed and had recovered *to move with a sort of diffident and tentative amazement in a world which he had believed himself on the point of surrendering,* but like a man who had been through some solitary furnace experience . . . (Book 32/19–24)

. . . when, *about three months after he departed, four wagons left Jefferson to go to the River and meet him, it was known that Mr Coldfield was the man who hired and dispatched them. They were big wagons, drawn by oxen, and when they returned the town looked at them and knew, no matter what they might have contained,* that Mr Coldfield could not have mortgaged everything that he owned for enough to fill them; . . . (Book 44/6–13)

I have seen her begin to raise her hand (*perhaps with the thimble on one finger*) *as though to protect herself* and the same look come into her face . . . (Book 55/4–6)

Equally striking is an addition which sharply focuses Ellen's character in some twenty words: "He did not forget that night, *even though Ellen, I think, did, since she washed it out of her remembering with tears. Yes, she was weeping again now;* it did, indeed, rain on that marriage." (Book 58/4)

The omissions are as noteworthy as the additions. One example will illustrate the effectiveness of suggestive understatement: ". . . Akers claimed to have walked one of them out of the absolute mud like a sleeping alligator and screamed just in time" (Book 36/19–21). The manuscript adds: "for Sutpen to hear him" (Ms. 15/9).

In another passage Faulkner eliminated from Mr. Compson's detached account a jarring reminder of Rosa's febrile judgment of Sutpen:

"Yes," Miss Coldfield said. "Arrested him as soon as he stepped off papa's property. He knew they were there waiting; he knew what they were waiting for. Yet he walked into that house with that bouquet of flowers wrapped in a piece of newspaper and plighted faith and honor which he did not possess to a fool young (Ms. 19/42)

Needless elaboration of a point is avoided by the omission of a comment on Sutpen's attitude toward a showy wedding:

He [Mr. Coldfield] had not only public opinion but his own disinclination for the big wedding to support it without incongruity or paradox. [The manuscript adds:] *as Ellen had her aunt as well as her own desire for the big wedding to support it without incongruity or paradox. While Sutpen wanted the big wedding actually more than Ellen did, yet his judgment forewarned him of how the town would take it even more than Mr Coldfield did. So that while Ellen was weeping her tears not only to ~~persuade~~ ⟨coerce⟩ her father but to persuade Sutpen to put his weight into the balance, he had one enemy. But when he refused, ~~to~~ when he remained neutral, he had 3, counting the aunt.* (Ms. 23/4–9)

Begun Oxford, 1935
Continued, Columbia, 1936
Finished, Oxford, 1936

William Faulkner
Oxford, Miss

First page of the original manuscript.

Page 3 of the original manuscript.

Page 7 of the original manuscript.

Absalom, Absalom!

William Faulkner

Mississippi, 1935
California, 1936
Mississippi, 1936

Rowanoak,
31 June 1936

Last page of the original manuscript.

CHAPTER III

In the manuscript Mr. Compson's narration (Chapters II, III, IV) was enclosed in quotation marks. The first change in revising Chapter III was to eliminate the quotation marks in favor of italicized speech tags (only three in number: *"Quentin said"* Book 59/2; *"Mr. Compson said again"* Book 59/3; *"Quentin said"* Book 61/20). The change serves no apparent purpose beyond simplification of a practically unbroken monologue. In writing the chapter Faulkner at one point forgot, however, that it is oral discourse. Instead of the revised wording "as your grandfather said," the manuscript reads: "as Quentin's grandfather once said" and "as General Compson said" (Ms. 35/32, 35). It is true that both these phrases occur in one of the pasted-in passages, indicating there must have been an earlier, omniscient version of at least part of the chapter. Even so, Faulkner's inclusion of the passage, with which he had to be minutely familiar to dovetail it into the manuscript as smoothly as he did, suggests that he was not jarred by the violation of viewpoint. As in the previous chapter and for the same reason, there is no attempt here to make the recital sound like the actual talk of a man telling his son a story.

In addition to the changes of date already noted (Book 59/5 and 61/13), Faulkner made several others in this chapter. When Rosa was born, Ellen had been married six years in the manuscript (25/4), seven years in the book (59/10). When Rosa was asked by Ellen to protect Judith, she was eighteen years old in the manuscript (37/2), seventeen in the book (86/3). At one time Rosa looked as if she might have been forty in the manuscript (31/36), fifty in the book (73/13). And instead of 1859 in the manuscript (32/1), the year of Mr. Coldfield's admission that war was unavoidable becomes 1860 in the book (73/32). This change, like that of the year Sutpen returned home, is in line with Faulkner's updating of Civil War episodes throughout the book (see notably 345/20; 346/28; 347/16).

More significantly, Faulkner was to decide at the end of Chapter IV that the story had got ahead of itself at the end of Chapter III. Wash Jones's disclosure that Henry had killed Bon is not adequately prepared for in the present chapter, where the spotlight is kept on Rosa. But the relationship of Henry, Bon, and Judith is the exclusive subject of the following chapter, so that Henry's shooting of Bon is a logical climax there instead of here. Moreover, to end Chapter III as Faulkner does in the book, withholding Jones's disclosure (Book 87/33), is dramatically effective. We know only that Jones came to relay some information about Henry, whose whereabouts had been unknown to Rosa for four years. To report Bon's death at this point would diminish suspense in the next chapter.

Particularly interesting is another of the reworked passages showing the stages of Faulkner's revision. Of the four drafts of the paragraph dealing with Rosa's volte-face in agreeing to marry Sutpen (Book 67/21), the first does not include the speculation about her probable conduct if Bon had lived (Book 67/26), and it ends with an analysis of her feelings about Sutpen, which Faulkner was to discard:

"But-she-now- saw more-of-her-sister-and niece-than-she-ever- had. "Now the period began which ended in the catastrophe, the happening, which caused the complete volteface in her actions tho not her character. It had not changed. Despite the 4 years which she spent feeding her father secretly at night while he hid from both Confederate provost marshals and at the same time writing her heroic poetry about the war and the actual men who would have shot or hung her father if they had ever found him, (and of whom the ogre of her childhood now made one and—he brot home with him ⟨a⟩ his citation him a personal citation in Lee's own hand—a good one). The face which she carried out to Sutpen's Hundred when she went out to live with Judith and fulfill the promise which she had given Ellen, was the same face which had watched his across the dinner table the first time she had seen him—the face which he probably likewise could not have said how many times he had seen it nor when and which when he did see it he could not have described it later, and from behind which the woman herself watched him with that cold[?] hushed intensity. And not with fear. Apparently she had never been afraid of him, tho Ellen was. It was not even personal disapproval. It was just a profound and unshakable conviction of dissimilarity: she accepted the fact and-reality[?] of his reactions and his capability and even willingness[?] for harm as she would that of a tornado; if you had told her at any time prior to the day he left with the regiment or the day he returned or maybe even the day she agreed to marry him that she would someday do this, she would have looked at you with the same cold and curious speculation as if you had told her that she would be betrothed to the tornado. (Ms. 28/18–33)

In the second draft Faulkner introduced the speculation about what would have happened if Bon had lived, and also introduced two elaborations of Rosa's attitude toward Sutpen, which were to be discarded:

"Now the period began which ended with the happening which caused the complete volte-face, not in her character but in her actions. Her character had ⟨did⟩ not change. If Charles Bon had not died, she still might would have gone out to live with Judith after her father's death and she might have even passed the rest of her life there, as she doubtless believed she would when she went out. But with Judith and Charles married and Henry also in the house, it would have been as the aunt which she actually was: she would never have agreed to marry him. Because Despite the 4 years which she had spent feeding her father secretly at night while he hid from Confederate provost marshals in the attic, and at the same time writing her heroic poetry about the very men who would have shot or hung him if they had discovered him (and of whom the ogre of her childhood made one, and—he brot home a personal citation in Lee's own hand—a good one), the face which she carried out there when she went to live with Judith and fulfill the promise she made Ellen, was the same one which had watched him across the dinner table and which he likewise could not have said later how many times he had seen it or

24

when and could not have described it probably 10 minutes after he ceased looking at it, and from behind which the child herself[?] had watched him with that curious ~~hushed~~ and cold intensity.

"Not fear: apparently she had never been afraid of him, tho Ellen was.— neither during her childhood nor during the time when she waited for him to come home, apparently having no doubt that he would return and unscathed, nor[?] even at the very moment when she ~~must-have-realized-with-a-sort-of awed- unbelief- that -she -was- irrevocably- promised -to- marry-him-in-order-to fulfill- Ellen's -dying -request -to -marry -him- -reached -that-point- which- she must- have- believed -she -had,- when -she -must-choose-between-saving- Judith or-saving -herself,- must-have-believed,- with -a -kind -of- amazed -incredulity, that- she -was- irrevocably- promised -to- marry-him.~~ reached whatever point it was that she evidently believed she had, when she must choose between saving Judith, (the last of her own blood, ~~or-herself~~ let alone her promise to Ellen) or herself and chose and then realized, with a kind of amazed incredulity probably, that she was actually and irrevocably promised to him. It was not even personal disapproval: it was just an unshakable conviction of dissimilarity: she accepted the fact of his existence and his capability and even willingness for harm as she would that of a tornado; if you had told her at any time prior to the day he left or the day he returned or perhaps the day she agreed to marry him even, that she would someday do it, she would have looked at you with the same cold and curious speculation as if you had told her that someday she would be betrothed to the tornado. Exclusive of the fact that he was Judith's and Henry's father and her sister's husband and still alien[?] and hence still a source of unpredictable threat and danger, she ~~simply~~ was absolutely indifferent to him. She simply did not like him—how he ~~looked~~ lived and what he did, whether for pleasure or profit, or how he looked or what he wore or what he seemed to stand for, represent, and what goal seemed to control his ambition. (Ms. 28/34–46 and 29/1–17)

The third draft, a reworking of the second, breaks off prematurely because, it would seem, Faulkner felt caught in a circular motion that brought him back to his starting point instead of enabling him to move forward:

"~~She-had-never-been-afraid- of-him,- not -even as- a -child, the -Ellen- was//~~
~~not even- as a child~~

"~~Now -she -did- not- see-her- anymore//she-heard.~~ "Now the period began which ended with the happening which caused the complete volte-face, ~~in~~ not in her character but in her actions. Her character did not change. If Charles Bon had not died, she still in all probability would have moved out to ~~live- with- Judith~~ Sutpen's Hundred after her father's death and would without doubt have passed the rest of her life there, as she doubtless believed she would when she did go out. But if Bon had lived and he and Judith had married, ~~she~~ and Henry remained in the known world, she would have moved (if she had moved) out there only when she was ready to and she would have lived ~~in -the- house -(if -she)~~ (if she had lived) in the house as the aunt which she actually was. It was only the happening which sent her out there and only it that caused or brot her to agree to marry him . . . (Ms. 29/18–26)

The fourth draft is the final one except for minor changes:

‘~~Now-the -period- began- which- ended- with-the happening-which caused the complete- volte-face-that- complete- volte-face~~ "Now the period began which ended with the happening that caused a reversal so complete in her as to enable her to agree to marry the man whom she had grown up to look upon as a demon. It was not a volte-face of character: that did not change. Even her behavior did not change appreciably. Even if Charles Bon had not died, she would in all probability have gone out to Sutpen's Hundred to live after her father's death sooner or later, and once she had done so, would have probably passed the rest of her life there, as she doubtless expected to when she did go. But if Bon had lived and he and Judith married, and Henry remained in the known world, she would have moved (if she had moved) out there only when she was ready to, and she would have lived (if she had lived) in her dead sister's family only as the aunt which she actually was. It was not her character: despite the probably 6 years since she had actually seen him and certainly ~~the~~ 4 years fil[?] ~~during~~ which she had spent ~~secretly~~ feeding her father secretly at night while he hid from Confederate provost marshals in the attic and at the same time writing heroic poetry about the very men from whom he was hiding and who would have shot him or hung him if they had found him—(and incidentally of whom the ogre of her childhood made one, and—he brot home with him a personal citation in Lee's own hand—a good one)—the face which she carried out there when she moved out to live with Judith and fulfill the promise she made ~~to -Ellen~~ the dying mother, was the same one which had watched him across the dinner table and which he likewise probably could not have said how many times he had seen it nor where, not for the reason that he was unable to forget it but because he could probably not have remembered it enough to have described it ten minutes after looking away, from behind which the same woman who had been that child now watched him with that same ~~curious~~ ⟨grim⟩ and cold intensity. (Ms. 29/27–46)

Throughout this chapter one is struck less by what Faulkner added in revision than by what he omitted. He was particularly concerned with economy of detail and of phrasing: for example, see Ms. 25/25–28; 27/25–27; 30/39–43; 33/15, 21, 27; 34/36–37; 35/11–15; 36/6–12; 37/17–22, 28–30. Noteworthy also is the tightening of sentences: see Book 63/12; 64/25; 65/32; 66/14; 70/28; 71/17; 80/20; 82/4.

CHAPTER IV

Except for church services, Rosa had not left her home after dark in forty-five years in the manuscript (38/14), a figure changed to forty-three in the book. Judith saw Bon for an elapsed time of seventeen days in the manuscript (44/39; 45/29; 53/26), twelve days in the book. Henry broke with his father on December 23 in the manuscript (47/18), December 24 in the book. After supposedly rescuing the wounded Bon, Henry watched him for three more years in the manuscript (55/11), two more years in the book.

Bon wrote to Judith in 1864 in the manuscript (57/9), 1865 in the book. And Bon had three years in which to renounce his octoroon mistress in the manuscript (58/6), four years in the book.

Several false starts are of interest in this chapter. When Mr. Compson resumed his narration after bringing out Bon's letter for Quentin to read (Ms. 38/33), he began by elaborating on the speculations in which he had indulged at the end of the previous chapter. Faulkner rejected this passage (reserving the comments on Henry and Judith for later development: see Book 91/18, 29), and substituted a discussion of Henry's love for Bon (Ms. 39/1–5), which he also discarded. In the final version (Ms. 39/5 ff.) he played down the speculative element.

In the account of Henry's break with his father and the imposition on Bon and Judith of a four-year probation, Faulkner marked out a first version (Ms. 39/22–43); and in writing the expanded version (substantially that of the book) he reworked one section (Ms. 40/14–23) to add the elaboration on the relationship of Henry and Judith (see Book 91/27 ff.). The manuscript records a third account of Henry's break with his father (Ms. 41/1–17), which was cancelled in the shifting of pages back and forth (the page in question carries two earlier numbers, successively crossed out); this version would have telescoped the narrative to include none of the elaboration found in the book between the quarrel and the trip to New Orleans (Book 90/23 to 106/12).

In writing the account of the noncourtship of Bon and Judith, Faulkner cancelled a first version when he again shifted the order of his pages (see Ms. 44/1–20). Both this and the previous reordering of pages occurred in the process of elaborating Mr. Compson's analysis of the relationship of Henry, Judith, and Bon. Comparable cancellations were caused by the reordering of three other pages in this section of the chapter: Ms. 45/1–3; 49/1–17; 51/5–18.

A final reworked passage is interesting in a different way. Faulkner originally wrote the account of Bon's death as an uninterrupted part of Mr. Compson's narrative:

> . . . the ~~ultimatum accomplished and discharged beside the gate~~ beyond the ultimatum discharged beside the gate to which the two of them may have, must have, ridden side by side; ~~the one implacable, calm and undeviating, perhaps, unresisting, the fatalist to the last; the other implacable~~ the one calm and undeviating, perhaps unresisting even, the fatalist to the last; ~~the other implacable, remorseless with implacable and unalt~~[?] ⟨unalterable⟩ ~~grief and despair, the~~ ⟨two⟩ ~~faces worn and calm, the voices not~~ even raised: 'Dont ride past the shadow of that limb, Charles,' and 'I shall ride past it, Henry': and then Wash Jones on the Sutpen mule before Miss Rosa's gate shouting her name into the empty and peaceful p.m., at the empty[?] house, saying 'Air you Miss Coldfield? Then you better come on out yon. Henry has done shot that durn French feller. Killed him dead as a beef.' " (Ms. 58/9–15)

This passage was followed by a revised version which included a shift to Quentin's point of view:

(It seemed to Quentin that he could actually see them, facing one another at the gate. Inside the gate what was once a park now spread, unkempt, in shaggy desolation, with an air dreamy remote and aghast ~~the~~ like the unshaven face of a man just rousing[?] from ether, up to a huge house [MARGIN: where a woman waited in a wedding gown and veil made from stolen scraps,] partaking too of that air of scaling desolation, not having suffered from invasion but a shell marooned and forgotten in a backwater of catastrophe—a skeleton giving of itself in slow driblets of curtain[?] and carpet, linen and silver and furniture, to help to die ~~men~~ torn and anguished men who knew, even while dying, that for years now the sacrifice and the anguish was in vain. They faced one another on the two gaunt horses, two men, young, not yet in the world, not yet breathed over and felt[?] sure long enough, to be old but with old eyes, with long unkempt hair and faces gaunt and weathered as tho cast by some spartan and even niggard hand from bronze, in worn and patched gray weathered now to the color of dead leaves, the one with the tarnished braid of an officer, the other plain of cuff, the pistol lying yet over the saddle bow and not aimed, the two worn faces even calm, the voices not even raised: *Dont you pass the shadow of that limb, Charles,* and *I am going to pass it, Henry*) . . . (Ms. 58/16–27)

The enlivening details imagined by Quentin could, of course, have been imagined by Mr. Compson. Presumably Faulkner chose to introduce Quentin here as a transition to the following chapter, where Rosa is again talking to him.

Several other added passages are notable. In one instance the characterizations of Mr. Compson and of Bon are sharpened by an addition to Bon's imagined reply to Henry's shocked reaction, " 'But a bought woman. A whore.' ":

Though He must have been young once, surely He was young once, and surely someone who has existed as long as He has, who has looked at as much crude and promiscuous sinning without grace or restraint or decorum as He has had to, to contemplate at last, even though the instances are not one in a thousand thousand, the principles of honor, decorum and gentleness applied to perfectly normal human instinct which you Anglo-Saxons insist upon calling lust and in whose service you revert in sabbaticals to the primordial caverns, the fall from what you call grace fogged and clouded by Heaven-defying words of extenuation and explanation, the return to grace heralded by Heaven-placating cries of satiated abasement and flagellation, in neither of which—the defiance or the placation—can Heaven find interest or even, after the first two or three times, diversion. So perhaps, now that God is an old man, he is not interested in the way we serve what you call lust either, . . . (Book 115/29–33 and 116/1–12)

The characterization of Bon is again amplified in a passage added to the letter he wrote Judith:

INTRODUCTION

(There. They have started firing again. Which—to mention it—is redundancy too, like the breathing or the need of ammunition. Because sometimes I think it has never stopped. It hasn't stopped of course; I dont mean that. I mean, there has never been any more of it, that there was that one fusillade four years ago which sounded once and then was arrested, mesmerized raised muzzle by raised muzzle, in the frozen attitude of its own aghast amazement and never repeated and it now only the loud aghast echo jarred by the dropped musket of a weary sentry or by the fall of the spent body itself, out of the air which lies over the land where that fusillade first sounded and where it must remain yet because no other space under Heaven will receive it. So that means that it is dawn again and that I must stop. Stop what? you will say. Why, thinking, remembering—remark that I do not say, hoping—; to become once more for a period without boundaries or location in time, mindless and irrational companion and inmate of a body which, even after four years, with a sort of dismal and incorruptible fidelity which is incredibly admirable to me, is still immersed and obliviously bemused in recollections of old peace and contentment the very names of whose scents and sounds I do not know that I remember, which ignores even the presence and threat of a torn arm or leg as though through some secretly incurred and infallible promise and conviction of immortality. But to finish.) I cannot say when to expect me. (Book 131/8–37)

CHAPTER V

Now that there was occasion to use Sutpen's Christian name for the first time since the end of Chapter I, Faulkner reconsidered. Instead of "Charles," he called Sutpen "John" throughout the manuscript version of the present chapter (59/12; 66/8; 70/15, 31; 71/16; 72/8; 74/22). There is also a change in Sutpen's age: in the manuscript he was fifty-five at the end of the war (73/36); in the book he is fifty-nine.

Another of the reworked passages preserved in the manuscript records four stages of revision. In writing the first draft of Rosa's account of being blocked by Clytie from going up to Judith on the day of Bon's death, Faulkner hardly began before he broke off:

'Rosa?' I cried. 'To me? To my face?' Then she touched me. Possibly, even then, my body did not stop; possibly the second voice broke and parted us before it (my body) had . . . (Ms. 61/28–30)

The repeated word *possibly* seems to have qualified the action too much to suit Faulkner. In a second draft he dealt with that problem but promptly ran into another problem:

'Rosa?' I cried. 'To me? To my face?' Then she touched me. But even then, I did not stop at once. Possibly my body never did stop, that the second voice broke and parted us before it (my body) had ever actually stopped, because I can still remember how, ~~the~~ in the actual shocked ~~amazement~~ too soon and quick to be amazement and outrage yet, ~~my blind~~

29

~~body-still-thrust-against-hand-voice-and-all//all-that-solid-yet-imponderable~~
~~weight-(she-not-owner:-instrument;-I-still-say-that~~) . . . (Ms. 61/30–33)

Lost in wordy abstraction, Faulkner again broke off and started over.
This time he emphasized concrete detail:

'Rosa?' I cried. 'To me? To my face?' Then she touched me—the hand
pale limp and (yes) cold. I knew it would be cold, even tho I had never
touched her flesh before. As a child I had more than once seen her and
Judith and even Henry scuffling in the ~~games~~ rough games which they
(possibly all children: I do not know) played, and (so I heard) she and
Judith even slept together. They had always used the same bedroom, but
Judith in the bed and she on a pallet on the floor ostensibly. But I have
heard how on more than one occasion Ellen had found them both together
on the pallet, and (once) in the bed together. But not I. Even as a child I
would not even play with the same objects . . . (Ms. 61/34–42) There is
something in the touch of flesh with flesh which abrogates, cuts sharp and
straight across the devious intricate channels of decorous ordering, which
enemies as well as lovers know because it makes them both—touch and
touch of that which is the citadel of the central I-Am's private own: not
spirit, soul; the liquorish and ungirdled mind is anyone's to take in any
casual doorway of this earthly tenement. But let flesh touch with flesh,
and see the fall of all the eggshell shibboleths of caste and color too.
~~Possibly-even-then-my-body-did-not-stop,-since-I-seemed-to-be-aware-of-it,~~
~~even-despite-the-hand,-still-thrusting-blindly-against-that-solid-yet-imponder-~~
~~able~~ . . . (Ms. 62/1–8)

Apparently feeling that the final detail came too late in the narrative,
Faulkner reworked the entire passage once more, supplying still more
detail:

'Rosa?' I cried. 'To me? To my face?' Then she touched me, and then
I did stop dead. Possibly even then my body did not stop, since I seemed
to be aware of it, ~~even-despite~~ thrusting blindly against ~~that~~ the solid yet
imponderable weight (she not owner: instrument; I still say that) of that
will to bar me from the stair; possibly the sound of the other voice, the
single word spoken from the stairhead above us, had already broken and
parted us before it (my body) had even paused. I do not know. I know only
that my entire being seemed to run at blind and full tilt into something
monstrous and immobile with a shocking impact too soon and too quick
to be mere ⟨simple⟩ amazement or outrage at that black arresting and
untimorous hand on my white woman's flesh, because there is something
in the touch of flesh with flesh which abrogates, cuts sharp and straight
across the devious intricate channels of decorous ordering, which enemies
as well as lovers know because it makes them both—touch and touch of that
which is the citadel of the central I-Am's private own: not spirit, soul; the
liquorish and ungirdled mind is anyone's to take in any darkened doorway
of this earthly tenement. But let flesh touch flesh, and see the fall of all
the eggshell shibboleth of caste and color too. Yes, I stopped dead—no
woman's hand, no negro's hand, but bitted bridle-curb to check and guide

the furious and unbending will—I crying not to her: to it; speaking to it through the negro only because of the shock not yet the outrage because it would be terror soon: 'Take your hand off me, nigger!'—expecting and receiving no answer because we both knew that it was not to her that I spoke.

I got none. We just stood there—I motionless in the attitude and action of running; she furious in that complete immobility, joined by that hand and arm which held us like a fierce rigid umbilical cord twin sistered ~~to~~ *victims to the same fell and haunted darkness. The hand was cold. I knew it would be, even tho I had never touched her flesh before. As a child I had more than once seen her and Judith and even Henry scuffling in the rough games which they (possibly all children; I do not know) played, and (so I* ~~had~~ ⟨have⟩ *heard) she and Judith even slept together, in the same room but with Judith in the bed and she on a pallet on the floor ostensibly. But I have heard how on more than one occasion Ellen had found them both* ~~in the same bed and~~ *on the pallet, and (once) in the bed together. But not I. Even as a child, I would not even play with the same objects which she and Judith played with, as though that warped and spartan solitude which I called my childhood, which had taught me (and little else) to listen before I could comprehend and to understand before I even heard, had also taught me not only to instinctively fear her and what she was, but to shun the very objects which she had touched.* (Ms. 62/8–37)

In this fourth draft, almost identical with the corresponding passage in the book, Faulkner increased the impact of Clytie's touch, not only by adding several details but also by reversing the order of the passages *"As a child I had more than once seen her and Judith and even Henry scuffling . . ."* and *"There is something in the touch of flesh with flesh . . ."*

A number of discarded passages are notable as further examples of the false starts found in the previous chapter. In Rosa's comment on her meeting with Judith after Bon's death (Ms. 64/3–26), the climactic effect of the first version was weaker than that of the second, which ended instead of began with the statement about "that might-have-been which is more true than truth . . ." (Book 143/12–13).

Before completing a first draft of Rosa's explanation of her feelings toward Bon (Ms. 65/34–41 and 66/1–5), Faulkner cancelled it and reworked what he had written, filling in background in one added passage (see Book 145/27–33 and 146/1–5) and elaborating on Rosa's infatuation in another addition (Book 146/10–22).

In reworking a first account of Bon's death (Ms. 68/19–38), he elaborated on Rosa's reaction to the event by adding a number of details (see Book 150/29–33 and 151/1).

In Rosa's explanation for staying on at Sutpen's Hundred (Ms. 69/38–43 and 70/1–12), characterization was heightened in a second draft by the addition of a passage enumerating the reasons she might have given to justify herself (see Book 153/16–33 and 154/1–3).

A first draft of the account of Sutpen's return from the was (Ms. 72/21–40

31

and 73/1–21) did not include the vividly detailed scene of his greeting the three women in the vegetable garden (see Book 158/29–33 and 159/1–31).

In the last of the reworked passages—Rosa's comment on her engagement to Sutpen (Ms. 75/37–41 and 76/1–6)—the first version would apparently have summarized the following twelve months in a sentence instead of developing Sutpen's character as was done in the second draft of the passage, which was almost identical with the published text (see Book 165/22–29).

In addition to supplying detail in several other passages (for example, see Book 154/8–10; 156/19–21; 158/8–10; 161/4–9; 169/22–28) and eliminating needless explanation (for example, see Ms. 62/26–28; 62/41 and 63/1–3; 70/8–9; 73/2–4; 74/36–37; 75/24–25; 77/35 [MARGIN]; 78/23–27), Faulkner made three other noteworthy changes. In the published version of Rosa's account of what the townspeople said about her when she moved out to Sutpen's Hundred, Rosa begins speaking of herself in the third person half a page earlier than she did in the manuscript (see Book 169/20–33 to 170/1–7). The simplest explanation is that the new arrangement accords with the beginning of a sentence in the book where no sentence began in the manuscript.

Less problematical is the change from *he* to *you* in Rosa's reply to news of Sutpen's death (Book 172/4–5), a revision which dramatizes her obsession with a still-present past.

Finally, there is a reversal in the use of italic and roman type in the two conversations at the end of the chapter (Book 172/23–29, 30–34). Since Rosa's chapter-long narrative about the past is set in italics, which end where the point of view changes to that of Quentin (Book 172/5), it seems consistent to use italics for the speeches of Henry and Judith—summoned as they are by Quentin from the past—and to keep all of the present action in roman type.

CHAPTER VI

It was in Chapter VI that Faulkner found the Christian name he wanted for Sutpen. Jones addressed him as "Mister John" in the scuppernong-arbor scene (Ms. 86/27), but in the inscriptions on the tombstones at Sutpen's Hundred the name became "Thomas" (Ms. 88/22, 23). Another change of name is interesting because it suggests (like the change of time setting in Chapter I from 1910 to 1909) that before his final revision Faulkner had occasion to think back over *The Sound and the Fury*. In the manuscript he gave the name "Dan" to the ghost-fearing Negro groom (Ms. 88/3); for the book he changed it to "Luster," although the hunting episode in *Absalom, Absalom!* occurred before 1909, while in the earlier book Luster is a fourteen-year-old boy in 1928.

There are several changes of dates. Ellen died in 1862 in the manuscript (88/23), in 1863 in the book. Both the Chronology and the Genealogy, however, retain the date 1862 and also list Ellen's year of birth as 1818 instead of 1817 as it is given in both the manuscript and the book (see Book 188/20). Sutpen died on June 29, 1869, in the manuscript (88/24), on August 12, 1869, in the book. Bon died on April 19, 1864, aged 29 years and 5 months in the manuscript (88/19), on May 3, 1865, aged 33 years and 5 months in the book. Neither manuscript nor book is in accord with the Chronology, which lists Bon's year of birth as 1829 instead of 1836 or perhaps 1835 as it would be in the manuscript, or 1832 or perhaps 1831 as it would be in the book. Bon's son was born in 1858 in the manuscript (89/23), in 1859 in the book. The Chronology gives the date as 1859, and spells the name "Velery" instead of "Valery," as Faulkner also did several times in the manuscript. Judith sold her father's store in 1871 in the manuscript (89/24), in 1870 in the book. And Judith sent Clytie to fetch Bon's son from New Orleans in 1873 in the manuscript (91/7), in 1871 in the book.

The most significant revisions in this chapter are changes in the viewpoint of narration. As has been pointed out above, in both versions Shreve takes over the story early in the chapter (see Book 176/10), and in the manuscript his recital continued for the rest of the chapter. In the book, however, most of Shreve's narration is eliminated in favor of two long shifts to Quentin's visualization of the events. The first of these shifts (Book 181/15 to 187/6) is emphasized by the addition of a passage which includes a description of Shreve, moved here from an earlier point in the manuscript (84/18):

> *He sounds just like father* he thought, glancing (his face quiet, reposed, curiously almost sullen) for a moment at Shreve leaning forward into the lamp, his naked torso pink-gleaming and baby-smooth, cherubic, almost hairless, the twin moons of his spectacles glinting against his moonlike rubicund face, smelling (Quentin) the cigar and the wistaria, seeing the fireflies blowing and winking in the September dusk. *Just exactly like father if father had known as much about it the night before I went out there as he did the day after I came back* thinking *Mad impotent old man* . . . (Book 181/15–24)

To avoid confusion about the change in point of view, the whole of Quentin's first reverie is printed in italics except for one line in which Quentin replies to Shreve, who, we gather, is still reciting the portion of the story Quentin is no longer hearing but now remembering for himself. The effect of this shift is twofold. The final episode in Sutpen's life is highlighted, and Quentin's obsessive involvement in the past is dramatized. It is noteworthy that in turning Shreve's recital into Quentin's reverie Faulkner did not modify the phrasing except for such changes as from *you* to *he*.

In the book Faulkner hardly allows Shreve to resume his narration (187/7–12) before having Quentin slip again into reverie. Here (though Shreve is still talking, as before) the remembered voice is that of Mr. Compson (187/12 to 210/9), and matters become complicated indeed.

Toward the end of the remembered narrative Quentin retreats still deeper into a reverie within a reverie (207/13 to 208/32). At one point he becomes fleetingly aware of Shreve (". . . thinking *Yes, Shreve sounds almost exactly like father* . . ."). Later Quentin again interrupts the remembered narrative to visualize for himself the scene of the graves (210/10 to 211/5). Twice more he is briefly aware of Shreve: "*Yes* he thought *Too much, too long*" (210/10) and "thinking *Yes, too much, too long. I didn't need to listen then but I had to hear it and now I am having to hear it all over again because he sounds just like father*" (211/6–8). The story of Judge Benbow he apparently remembers for himself (211/9 to 212/30), but here the viewpoint of narration becomes ambiguous. In the manuscript this account of Judge Benbow was enclosed in single quotation marks within double quotation marks, for Shreve was quoting Mr. Compson verbatim (Ms. 97/6 to 98/1); in the account of the haunted Sutpen house, which follows, the manuscript returned to double quotation marks only, indicating a return to Shreve's own wording. In the book both of these sections are italicized, presumably to indicate that Quentin is remembering instead of hearing, but beginning with the account of the haunted house (212/31) there is a shift to second-person narration, which corresponds to the usage in the manuscript: ". . . *what your father was saying did not tell you anything so much as it struck, word by word, the resonant strings of remembering*" (213/1–3). Is it actually Shreve's narration which we are now hearing in the book, as in the manuscript, and if so why are the italics dropped and quotation marks introduced when Shreve unmistakably resumes the narration (215/4)? Presumably the ambiguity is deliberate, not a careless lapse, the point being that Shreve's voice is interchangeable for Quentin with that of his father, which itself becomes interchangeable with his own visualization of the scene.

Throughout this chapter Faulkner's revisions are more numerous than in the earlier chapters, as is indicated by the length of the collation. There are three false starts in which brief passages were reworked (Ms. 84/25 to 85/41; 97/31 to 98/26; 99/15–29); and two other cancellations are the result of the renumbering of pages (80/20 and 81/31). Among the various passages added in revision, one seems of questionable effectiveness: Quentin's imagined scene of Sutpen and Jones in the next world (Book 186/22) could be said to reflect his yearning for tranquillity as the aftermath of Sutpen's fevered struggle, but to suggest that Sutpen's lifelong inhumanity and Jones's righteous indignation are not of lasting significance seems to contradict the basic point of the tragic story Quentin is reconstructing. Two other additions fill out the characterization of Judith by supplying information about the tombstones she financed (Book 191/16–25 and 193/5–7). Particularly notable is the account of the travelers from Arkansas, which was not included in a first, cancelled account of the haunted house; Faulkner added the incident in a reworked passage (see Ms. 97/31–45 and 98/1–12) and amplified it slightly in the book, where it heightens Luster's sense of the threatening presence of Sutpen even after his death. Finally, one is struck by the number of periods Faulkner introduced in revising a chapter which in the manuscript had few sentence divisions. For example, the section of Mr. Compson's narrative extending in the book from 198/30 to 206/29 consisted in the manuscript of two sentences.

CHAPTER VII

Again Faulkner made changes which emphasize Quentin's involvement in the Sutpen story. In the manuscript Shreve's comparison of the South to a stage melodrama elicited from Quentin a perfunctory agreement (100/10); in the book, however, "Quentin did not answer" (217/18). The change points up Quentin's preoccupation with the past, his detachment from the present, as does another added statement later in the chapter: when Shreve again resorts to levity, "Quentin paid no attention whatever" (Book 275/10).

Sutpen's talk with General Compson about his design is interrupted in the book by a passage added to emphasize the effect of the story on Quentin:

> "Dont say it's just me that sounds like your old man," Shreve said. "But go on. Sutpen's children. Go on."
> "Yes," Quentin said. "The two children" thinking *Yes. Maybe we are both Father. Maybe nothing ever happens once and is finished. Maybe happen is never once but like ripples maybe on water after the pebble sinks, the ripples moving on, spreading, the pool attached by a narrow umbilical water-cord to the next pool which the first pool feeds, has fed, did feed, let this second pool contain a different temperature of water, a different molecularity of having seen, felt, remembered, reflect in a different tone the infinite unchanging sky, it doesn't matter: that pebble's watery echo whose fall it did not even see moves across its surface too at the original ripple-space, to the old ineradicable rhythm* thinking *Yes, we are both Father. Or maybe Father and I are both Shreve, maybe it took Father and me both to make Shreve or Shreve and me both to make Father or maybe Thomas Sutpen to make all of us.* (Book 261/21 to 262/3)

Two other passages added in revision have already been discussed in connection with Cleanth Brooks's discussion of Quentin's discovery of Bon's Negro blood: "Your father," Shreve said. "He seems to have got an awful lot of delayed information awful quick, . . ." (Book 266/14–15) and "Your old man," Shreve said. "When your grandfather was telling this to him, he didn't know any more what your grandfather was talking about than your grandfather knew what the demon was talking about . . ." (Book 274/22–25).

In another addition, which echoes again Quentin's obsession with the story, Faulkner has Shreve interrupt:

> "So he got his choice made, after all," Shreve said. "He played that trump after all. And so he came home and found——"
> "Wait," Quentin said.

"——what he must have wanted to find or anyway what he was going to find——"

"Wait, I tell you!" Quentin said, though still he did not move nor even raise his voice—that voice with its tense suffused restrained quality: "I am telling" *Am I going to have to have* [sic] *to hear it all again* he thought *I am going to have to hear it all over again I am already hearing it all over again I am listening to it all over again I shall have to never listen to anything else but this again forever so apparently not only a man never outlives his father but not even his friends and acquaintances do*—(Book 277/1-14)

Not content with calling attention to Quentin in this passage, Faulkner continued to dramatize Quentin's own involvement in the story by changing the viewpoint of narration in the ensuing account of Sutpen's return from the war. In the book we have, instead of Quentin's uninterrupted narration as in the manuscript (124/9 ff.), his visualization of the scene of the return (277/14 to 278/6); then we have Quentin listening in memory to his father's account of the outrageous proposal to Rosa (278/6 to 280/4).

In revising this chapter Faulkner was particularly concerned with the presentation of Sutpen's early life, as can be seen in several reworked passages. Instead of the sharply focused, revealing analysis of the backwoods boy as we have it in the book (220–222), the first draft was thin and pedestrian:

"It was in West Virginia, in the mountains; he was born there—("Not in West Virginia," Shreve said. "——What?" Quentin said. "Because ~~there wasn't any West~~ if he was ~~in Mississippi in 1833 and~~ 25 years old in Mississippi in 1833, he must have been born in 1808. And there wasn't any West Virginia in 1808 because——" "All right," Quentin said. "——West Virginia wasn't admitted——" "All right, all right," Quentin said. "——into the United States until——" "All right all right all right," Quentin said) "——in a cabin; there wasn't anything there but a few other cabins where hunters and squatters lived and the only colored folks were Indians and you only looked down at them over a gun barrel and so nobody looked down on you because nobody had any more than you had ~~and he didn't know that there were people who had~~ because everybody had just what they could take and no sane man would go to the trouble to take more than he could eat or buy powder and whiskey with. And so he didn't even know that there was more than that to have or that there were people that had it, had other people, niggers, to do what no man wanted to do, like handing him a bottle[?] of drink or pulling off his ~~boots~~ . . . (Ms. 101/12–23)

Again, the account of the family's move from the West Virginia mountains to Tidewater Virginia, as first written, was equally undeveloped (cf. Book 224–225). It contained little detail and it was almost a one-dimensional narrative, with the presence of the later Sutpen telling General Compson about himself hardly to be felt:

. . . somebody else threw water on the fire and shut the door and they walked down the mountain: and after a while they had two mules and a cart and he (he was 10 then, the two older boys had left home some years before and had not been heard of since) driving the cart, since as soon as they acquired it his father ~~began-to~~ formed the habit of ~~performing-that-portion~~ accomplishing that portion of the translation devoted to movement flat on his back in the cart and snoring with alcohol. That was how he told it to Grandfather; he didn't remember if it was weeks they travelled or months or a year, whether it was ~~some season's-completed cycle-which overtook-and passed-them-on-the road~~ that winter and spring and then summer overtook them in turn and passed them or whether they overtook and passed winter and then spring into the summer as they descended; a period alternating between a kind of furious inertia and hopeless immobility [MARGIN: while his father drank himself insensible] and phases[?] of dreamy and pointless[?] ~~pregress~~[?] ⟨loco⟩ motion [MARGIN: after they got his unconscious form[?] into the ~~cart again~~ cart again] ~~upon~~[?] ~~the~~ [two crossed-out illegible words] ~~cart~~ behind the plodding mules, during which they did not progress at all themselves but hung suspended while the earth changed, broadened and flattened out of the mountain gorge[?] where he had been born, mounting, rising about them and flowing past, separating[?] like a [illegible word] and bringing into the ~~gran~~[?] ~~and-astonished~~ sober and astonished country . . . (Ms. 103/1–13)

Finally, the account of Sutpen's brief schooling gave Faulkner trouble (cf. Book 241–242). He made two false starts before he was able to visualize the scene sharply and bring the teacher alive:

He didn't recall how he came to be sent, just what might have entered his father's mind, what nebulous shape not of ambition for him but perhaps the same revolt against his lot which the son had and which in the father was perchance merely ~~en~~[?] vindictive envy [MARGIN: toward one or two men] while with the son it was for vindication and revenge upon an entire system. He just remembered that he went, an adolescent boy with a good deal of the mental and moral equipment of a grown man, in a class of children 3 or 4 years younger than he and 3 or 4 years more advanced. He must have been almost as big as and probably a good deal stronger of will than the teacher, who must have brot into the cramped single room which contained the entire school his countryman's[?] grim and alert reserve and a certain ~~intracti-bility~~ ⟨latent⟩, ~~possibly~~ a ⟨an⟩ insubordination which he was not even aware of nor that the teacher himself never dared take issue with it, because it ~~was~~ not intractibility but ~~mountain-man's/pride~~ pride inherited from those mountain solitudes where some of his blood at least had come from.—an [crossed-out illegible word] [MARGIN: a quality] which forbade him to condescend to the memorizing of dry lines and sums but which listened to the reading of history and tales of esoteric events with profound attention

He didn't remember how he came to go to school. That is, why his father decided to send him, what notion might have entered his old man's mind, what nebulous shape that wasn't ambition probably nor any desire to see the boy better himself for his own sake; it was probably some instant of blind revolt against . . . (Ms. 109/37 to 110/10)

37

In addition to several added touches which sharpen the characterization of Sutpen (see Book 250/12–21; 278/11–18, 26–28), and three other false starts (Ms. 101/11–24; 103/1–13; 114/23–35), one more change is noteworthy. In the manuscript version of the last episode in Jones's life (as in the story, "Wash," published a year before the novel was begun), Jones had five gallons of kerosene which he used to ignite his shack before charging at the waiting men with lifted scythe (see Ms. 129/28 to 130/5). One might surmise that Faulkner omitted the fire in his revision mainly for fear the climactic burning of the Sutpen house would seem repetitious.

It should be recalled at this point that in the story "Wash," which was presumably the original conception of the Sutpen chronicle, Sutpen's unnamed son "had been killed in action the same winter in which his wife had died."[11] The story contains no hint that Sutpen had had another son by a first wife. In other words, the callous unconcern for Jones's granddaughter by an old man frustrated and embittered by the loss of everything to which he had devoted his life is the only basis for presenting him as one of the "bragging and evil shadows" the truth about whom is such a revelation to Jones that "he now saw for the first time, after five years, how it was that Yankees or any other living armies had managed to whip them" (Book 547). In developing the story into the novel, Faulkner probed into the conditions which had made Sutpen what he was. The result was a drama of doom—the doom set in motion when Sutpen repudiated a first wife and son because they turned out to have a trace of Negro blood and thus had to be dealt with, in Sutpen's world, not as human beings to whom he was obligated but simply as instruments no longer serviceable for accomplishing his purpose.

CHAPTER VIII

In the manuscript Bon went to the University of Mississippi at an age that seems to have been first written as 23 and marked over as 26 (137/19); farther on it is changed to 28 (139/31). In the book Bon's age is twenty-eight. In the Chronology, however, his meeting with Henry is dated 1859 (which seems correct), and his year of birth is given as 1829, so that either he should have been born in 1831 or he should have been thirty when he went to the University. According to the Sutpen data assembled by the hypothetical lawyer, the year of a possible incest threat was 1858 in the manuscript (138/22), but is changed to 1859 in the book. The Confederate retreat across Alabama into Georgia and Carolina was dated '63 and '64 in the manuscript (157/7; 158/1, 15, 32), but is dated 1864 and 1865 in the book.

Faulkner first wrote in the manuscript that "Bon found Henry where he lay on the ground" (156/31). Presumably at some later time (since the entry is in a different shade of ink) he noted in the margin: "Henry saves Bon.

[11]*Collected Stories of William Faulkner* (New York: Random House, 1950), p. 538.

H says 'I wish it was me here. That would settle it.' Bon suggests that Henry leave him to die to settle it.'' This marginal note alongside the uncancelled earlier statement suggests that Faulkner was unsure whether he wanted Shreve's account to differ from Mr. Compson's earlier account (Book 124/21). In his final revision he confirmed and emphasized his original intention with an added passage:

"... And listen," Shreve cried; "wait, now; wait!" (glaring at Quentin, painting himself, as if he had had to supply his shade not only with a cue but with breath to obey it in): "Because your old man was wrong here, too! He said it was Bon who was wounded, but it wasn't. Because who told him? Who told Sutpen, or your grandfather either, which of them it was who was hit? Sutpen didn't know because he wasn't there, and your grandfather wasn't there either because that was where he was hit too, where he lost his arm. So who told them? Not Henry, because his father never saw Henry but that one time and maybe they never had time to talk about wounds and besides to talk about wounds in the Confederate army in 1865 would be like coal miners talking about soot; and not Bon, because Sutpen never saw him at all because he was dead—it was not Bon, it was Henry, . . . (Book 344/17)

The pointed contradiction of Mr. Compson may well have been added to accord with the earlier changes in which he is made ignorant even of the fact that Bon was Sutpen's son until Quentin told him.

In this chapter Faulkner made a final change in the viewpoint of narration. In the manuscript the account of the Confederate retreat was part of Shreve's narration (157/33 to 160/2). In the book this passage—an italicized interruption of Shreve's recital—is presented as a shared visualization of the action instead of an oral account of it (346/28). The change is in line with the downgrading of Shreve's role in Chapter VI.

Other noteworthy revisions include several added passages that sharpen the characterization of Bon. In surmising about his relationship with his mother, Shreve says that Bon probably realized his mother had been conditioning him to serve some purpose of her own but did not care about that,

because probably by that time he had learned that there were three things and no more: breathing, pleasure, darkness; and without money there could be no pleasure, and without pleasure it would not even be breathing but mere protoplasmic inhale and collapse of blind unorganism in a darkness where light never began. And he had the money because he knew that she knew that the money was the only thing she could coerce and smooth him into the barrier with when Derby Day came, so she didn't dare pinch him there and she knew he knew it: so that maybe he even blackmailed her . . . (Book 300/1–11)

Again, in imagining how Bon must have felt toward Sutpen in the beginning when Sutpen failed to acknowledge him as his son, Shreve has him think that he would never make any claim *upon any part of what he now possesses, gained at the price of what sacrifice and endurance and scorn (so they told me; not he: they) only he knows; knows that so well that it would never have occurred to him just as he knows it would never occur to me that this might be his reason, who is not only generous but ruthless, who must have surrendered everything he and mother owned to her and to me as the price of repudiating her . . .* (Book 330/33 to 331/6)

Such additions, in emphasizing the qualities of perceptiveness and a youthful highmindedness as the other side of his worldliness, help to make Bon the sympathetic character he is. A comparable addition is a passage in which Bon is endowed with intuitive sensitivity:

. . . (because he knew that Sutpen had returned, was now in the house; it would be like a wind, something, dark and chill, breathing upon him and he stopping, grave, quiet, alert, thinking *What? What is it?* Then he would know; he could feel the other entering the house, and he would let his held breath go quiet and easy, a profound exhalation, his heart quiet too) . . . (Book 333/4–10)

Three false starts are of interest: Ms. 146/31–39; 149/1–7; 151/18–30. (Another cancellation resulted from the reordering of pages: 142/1–16.) And the vividness of several episodes is strikingly increased by the addition of details, for example, Book 305/4–11; 313/19–33; 317/6–13; 324/1–6; 326/4–14; 344/16–32; 357/1–15.

CHAPTER IX

The most significant revision in Chapter IX is the added emphasis given to Jim Bond in the closing pages of the book. The manuscript version did not include the italicized portions of the following passages:

. . . she believed *it was that same black wagon for which she probably had had that nigger boy watching for three months now,* coming to carry Henry into town for the white folks to hang him for shooting Charles Bon. And I guess *it had been him who had kept that closet under the stairs full of tinder and trash all that time too, like she told him to, maybe he not getting it then either but keeping it full just like she told him,* the kerosene and all, for three months now, *until the hour when he could begin to howl——"* . . . (Book 374/10–19)

. . . the monstrous tinder-dry rotten shell seeping smoke through the warped cracks in the weather-boarding as if it were made of gauze wire and filled with roaring *and beyond which somewhere something lurked which bellowed, something human since the bellowing was in human speech, even though the reason for it would not have seemed to be.* (Book 375/6–12)

. . . —the tragic gnome's face . . . possibly even serene above the melting clapboards *before the smoke swirled across it again—and he, Jim Bond, the scion, the last of his race, seeing it too now and howling with human reason now since now even he could have known what he was howling about.* But they couldn't catch him. They could hear him; he didn't seem to ever get any further away but they couldn't get any nearer and maybe in time they could not even locate the direction any more of the howling. They—the driver and the deputy—held Miss Coldfield . . . as the house collapsed and roared away, *and there was only the sound of the idiot negro left.* (Book 376/3–22)

. . . there was nothing left now, *nothing out there now but that idiot boy to lurk around those ashes and those four gutted chimneys and howl until someone came and drove him away. They couldn't catch him and nobody ever seemed to make him go very far away, he just stopped howling for a little while. Then after awhile they would begin to hear him again.* And so she died." (Book 376/28–34)

"You've got one nigger left. *One nigger Sutpen left. Of course you can't catch him and you don't even always see him and you never will be able to use him. But you've got him there still. You still hear him at night some-times. Don't you?*" (Book 378/10–14)

Except when Quentin and Rosa invade the house (Ms. 171/28–35) and when Rosa returns to the buggy (172/2–10), the only references to Jim Bond in the manuscript were two sentences in Shreve's final speech (175/19, 27). The highly dramatic effect of the idiot Negro heir who haunts the ruins at Sutpen's Hundred was thus added in revision.

A final change was the reversal Faulkner made in the use of italics. In the manuscript all of Quentin's thoughts were underlined (164/14; 169/23, 24; 170/2, 33; 171/13, 18, 33, 36, 38; 172/3, 21, 33, 35; 173/20), and Quentin's conversation with Henry Sutpen was set off with quotation marks (173/3–15). In the book the opposite arrangement gives emphasis to the climactic scene of Quentin's confrontation with Henry.

* * *

Along with the revisions that have been discussed, the reader in going through the collation will be struck by many other examples of the skill with which Faulkner reworked his first version so as to regulate the tempo of his narrative, to build suspense where the flow has slackened, to highlight his characters so that we glimpse the flicker or twitch of live flesh, and finally to get a firm hold on the theme toward which he had felt his way in the manuscript. One will wish to study particularly the revisions by means of which structure comes to reveal meaning. Attention has already been called to the changes whereby Quentin becomes the one who unlocks the old mystery and who is still obsessively involved in the story of a guilt which he, as a Southerner, must share. His involvement is not explicitly stated but is implicit in the pattern of his repeated usurpations from Shreve of sections of the narrative not dominated by him in the first version. As a result of this alteration of Quentin's role, the chronicle of the Sutpen family becomes

41

more nearly a kind of detective story in which a missing piece of information finally makes a coherent whole out of a bewildering collection of facts. The structure of the story thus forces the reader to join in the conjecturing and himself to participate in the undertaking which is the basic subject of the book—man's attempt to comprehend and deal with the past. Again, as a result of revision at the end of the book, the heritage of man's long inhumanity to man suddenly stands before us in the blighted figure of Jim Bond. Once more the story does not *mean* something; it *becomes* the thing.

In studying the collation one might be struck, most of all, by the extent to which Faulkner—unlike writers who make relatively few changes in their first drafts—went through a second stage of creative effort. The sheer number of changes testifies to the meticulousness of his reworking. As soon becomes evident, however, it was not an external sort of meticulousness concerned with polishing a work that was already wrought. Rather, Faulkner actually relived the story, feeling out again the nuances of each scene, each character, each sensory impression. One final quotation will serve to illustrate the point. In revising Mr. Compson's account of the day Sutpen went to propose to Ellen Coldfield, Faulkner added a passage that could have been written only by an author who was living the story even more sensitively the second time than he had done the first time. (The passage also furnishes another example of structure determined by meaning, for the book deals not so much with Sutpen himself as with his effect on others.) The manuscript reads: ". . . he turned [MARGIN: carrying his portmanteau and the woven basket] and entered the hotel, saluting the watching men on the gallery with that arrogant and slightly florid gesture to the hat which they knew, and commanded a chamber" (19/18–19). The book reads:

> . . . he turned, and he looked at the other men sitting with their feet on the railing and watching him too, men who used to come out to his place and sleep on the floor and hunt with him, and he saluted them with that florid, swaggering gesture to the hat (yes, he was underbred. It showed like this always, your grandfather said, in all his formal contacts with people. He was like John L. Sullivan having taught himself painfully and tediously to do the schottische, having drilled himself and drilled himself in secret until he now believed it no longer necessary to count the music's beat, say. He may have believed that your grandfather or Judge Benbow might have done it a little more effortlessly than he, but he would not have believed that anyone could have beat him in knowing when to do it and how. And besides, it was in his face; that was where his power lay, your grandfather said: that anyone could look at him and say, *Given the occasion and the need, this man can and will do anything*). Then he went on into the house and commanded a chamber. (45/31 to 46/16)

Textual Collation

of the Manuscript and the Published Book

CHAPTER I

MANUSCRIPT

Page 1 [1]

[Top of page] March 30, 1935

Begun Oxford, 1935
Continued, California, 1936
Finished, Oxford, 1936

William Faulkner
Oxford, Miss

BOOK

Page 7

	MANUSCRIPT		BOOK
3	for 45 summers	5	for forty-three summers
6	of motes that Quentin ~~always~~ thot	9-10	of dust motes which Quentin thought
7	blinds by sunrays like wind might.	11-12	blinds as wind might have blown them.
8	vine [MARGIN: blooming for the second time that summer] on	12-13	vine blooming for the second time that summer on
10	for 45 years	17	for forty-three years
11-12	the ~~chair~~ straight hard chair that was too tall for her so that	19-20	the straight hard chair that was so tall for her that
14	amazed outraged voice	23	amazed voice
15	and then the dead man himself would appear [MARGIN: as tho by outraged recapitulation evoked,] quiet	24-25	and the long-dead object of her impotent yet indomitable frustration would ap-

Page 8

	MANUSCRIPT		BOOK
		1	pear, as though by outraged recapitulation evoked, quiet
19-20	hyperdistilled and now and then the sparrows with a loud cloudy flutter like a flat limber ~~switch~~ stick	8-9	hyperdistilled, into which came now and then the loud cloudy flutter of the sparrows like a flat limber stick
20-21	boy and rank with female old flesh in virginity long embattled and the wan ~~dim~~ haggard	10-11	boy, and the rank smell of female old flesh long embattled in virginity while the wan haggard
21-22	the chair too tall for her so that she resembled a crucified child, and	13-14	the too tall chair in which she resembled a crucified child; and
23	intervals of self-confounding unsurprise like a stream a	15	intervals like a stream, a

NOTE: Angle brackets are used in the collation to indicate interlinear insertions.

CHAPTER I

MANUSCRIPT		BOOK	
25	sand ~~until the~~ as the ghost appeared with shadowy docility as tho it	16-17	sand, and the ghost mused with shadowy docility as if it
31-32	bearded, hand palmlifted like a racing[?] banner, the horseman would sit;	25-26	bearded and hand palm-lifted the horseman sat;
32	wild niggers and	26-27	wild blacks and
35	to ~~watch~~ ⟨see⟩ them	29-30	to watch them
36-45	uppalm ~~pontific~~ immobile and pon-tific, the Be Sutpen's Hundred like the oldentime Be Light. Then hearing would re-	33	up-palm immobile and pon-
		Page 9	
		1-3	tific, creating the Sutpen's Hundred, the *Be Sutpen's Hundred* like the oldentime *Be Light*. Then hearing would reconcile and he

concile and he would seem to listen to two Quentins now talk to one another in the long silence of notpeople in notlanguage: It seems that this demon—his name was Sutpen—(Colonel Sutpen)—Colonel Sutpen. Who came out of nowhere and without warning upon the land with a band of strange niggers and build a planta-tion—(Tore violently a plantation, Miss Rosa Coldfield says)—tore violently. And married her sister Ellen and begot a son and a daughter—(without gentleness begot, Miss Rosa Coldfield says)—without gentleness. Which should have been the jewels of his pride and the shield and comfort of his old age, only—(Only they de-stroyed him or something or he de-stroyed them

Page 2 [2]

1	[1-24 PASTED IN: and he		
2	outraged ghosts,	6	outraged baffled ghosts,
4-5	ghost yet having	10	ghost, but nevertheless having
6	was—talking to one another	11-12	was—the two separate Quentins now talking to one another
6	notlanguage [MARGIN: , like this:] *It*	13	notlanguage, like this: *It*
11	*gentleness begot.*	20	*gentleness.*
13	*something, and died)—Without*	22-23	*something. And died)—and died. Without*
		Page 10	
22-23	indoors listening to her talk about	6	indoors and listening while she talked about

44

MANUSCRIPT		BOOK	
24	be outdoors with young friends of your own age.'']	8	be out among young friends of your own age.''
25	thot. [MARGIN: *It's because she wants it told*] It	11	thought. *It's because she wants it told.* It
27-28	call on her, come and see her—	14	call and see her—
29	neat ~~small~~ cramped faded script	17	neat faded cramped script
31-32	after dinner, walking	23	after the noon meal, walking
32-33	and into the house ~~which~~ (it	25	and so into the house. It
35-36	itself) where in the dim gloom of the shuttered hall where the air	30-31	itself. There in the gloom of the shuttered hallway whose air
36-37	the ⟨~~recurrent~~⟩ suspiration of [MARGIN: slow] heatladen ⟨~~slow~~⟩ time	32-33	the suspiration of slow heat-laden time
37	the 45 years—the	33	the forty-
		Page 11	
		1	five [*sic*] years, the
38-41	urgent, and intent as she invited him in. ~~Only she dont~~ ~~Only she dont mean that, he told himself.~~ *It's because she wants it told,* he thot. *So*	4-5	urgent and intent, waited to invite him in. *It's because she wants it told,* he thought, *so*
42	*never seen her face nor heard her name will*	7	*never heard her name nor seen her face will*
Page 3 [3]			
1	[1-11 PASTED IN: she had merely wanted it told, written and even printed, she would not have needed to call in anyone—	13-14	she had merely wanted it told, written and even printed, she would not have needed to call in anybody—
2	his father's youth had already established (even if not affirmed) herself	15-16	his (Quentin's) father's youth had already established herself
4-12	undefeat; and these from a woman whose family's martial[?] background as both town and county knew consisted of the father who, a conscientious objector on religious grounds, had starved himself to death ~~hidden~~ (some said, walled up) in the attic of his house, hidden there from Confederate provost marshals ~~while the same daughter~~ and fed secretly at night by the same daughter who now celebrated the lost cause's unregenerate[?] vanquished in verse, and the nephew who, ~~missing from home for 3 years, returned~~ served	19-20	undefeat. It would

3 years in the same company with
his sister's fiance and then shot the
fiance to death before the gate to the
house where his sister waited in her
wedding gown on the eve of the wedding and then fled, ~~none~~ vanished,
none knew where.]
     It would

	MANUSCRIPT		BOOK
15	this ~~Sunday~~ September p.m. in 1910 and	26	this September afternoon in 1909 and
16-17	his house apparently	29	his house, his mansion, apparently
18	[18-37 PASTED IN: the daughter who had not yet been a bride—and so accomplished his allotted course to its violent end.	31-33	the daughter who had not yet been a bride—and so accomplished his allotted course to its violent (Miss Coldfield at least would have said, just) end.

Page 12

19	that. He	1-4	that; the mere names were inter-changeable and almost myriad. His childhood was full of them; his very body was an empty hall echoing with sonorous defeated names; he
19-22	entity, a sentience: he was a com-monwealth.⟨—⟩ ~~He was~~ a barracks full of stubborn backlooking ghosts recovering from the fever which had cured them of a disease, waking from the fever without even being aware that they had fought against the fever which cured them and not against the sickness.⟨—⟩ ~~His youth had been filled with the~~ of ~~old wraiths~~ ⟨people⟩ look-ing	4-10	entity, he was a commonwealth. He was a barracks filled with stubborn back-looking ghosts still recovering, even forty-three years afterward, from the fever which had cured the disease, waking from the fever with-out even knowing that it had been the fever itself which they had fought against and not the sickness, looking
22	disease, weak from the fever and free	11	disease with actual regret, weak from the fever yet free
23-24	impotence. "But why tell me?" he said to his father that p.m; "why must she tell	13-17	impotence. ("But why tell me about it?" he said to his father that evening, when he returned home, after she had dis-missed him at last with his promise to return for her in the buggy; "why tell
26	name is Sutpen or not."	21	name happens to be Sutpen or Cold-field or not."
28-30	said, "You want the real reason	25-31	said, "Do you want to know the real

MANUSCRIPT   BOOK

why she chose you? It's because she   reason why she chose you?'' They
would need someone, a man and a   were sitting on the gallery after sup-
gentleman, yet one still young enough   per, waiting for the time Miss Cold-
to do what she asked. And   field had set for Quentin to call her.
                                              ''It's because she will need someone
                                              to go with her—a man, a gentleman,
                                              yet one still young enough to do what
                                              she wants, do it the way she wants it
                                              done. And

30-31   friend which Sutpen ever had here in   32-33   friend Sutpen ever had in this county,
        Jefferson and she believes that Sutpen   and she probably believes
        might have   *Page 13*
                                                  1   that Sutpen may have

31-32   about her and him. Might even have   2-5   about himself and her, about that
        told your grandfather what happened   engagement which did not engage,
        the reason why she did not marry   that troth which failed to plight.
                                                         Might even have told your grand-
                                                         father the reason why at the last she
                                                         refused to marry

33-34   so in a sense the matter, no matter   6-8   so, in a sense, the affair, no matter
        what happens out there, would still   what happens out there tonight, will
        be in the family, the   still be in the family; the

34-35   closet. Or more than that, even.   8-9   closet. She may believe
        She may believe

36   responsible for what   12-13   responsible through heredity for what

37-43   him.'']   14-28   him.'')
        Whatever the reason was, Quentin   Whatever her reason for choosing
        thot, whether that was it or not, the   him, whether it was that or not, the
        getting to it took a long while time.   getting to it, Quentin thought, was
        Meanwhile, as time passed and as tho   taking a long time. Meanwhile, as
        in inverse ratio to the vanishing of   though in inverse ratio to the van-
        the voice, the invoked ghost of the   ishing voice, the invoked ghost of the
        brother-in-law with whom at one   man whom she could neither forgive
        time she herself[?] had been engaged   nor revenge herself upon began to
        to marry began to assume a quality   assume a quality almost of solidity,
        almost of permanence, solidity. It-   permanence. Itself circumambient
        self circumambient and in turn en-   and enclosed by its effluvium of hell,
        closed by the effluvium of hell, the   its aura of unregeneration, it mused
        aura of unregeneration, it mused with   (mused, thought, seemed to possess
        that quality peaceful and now harm-   sentience, as if, though dispossessed
        less even inattentive—the ogre shape   of the peace—who was impervious
        which, as the voice went on, began to   anyhow to fatigue—which she declined
        resolve out of itself the two   to give it, it was still irrevocably
                                                         outside the scope of her hurt or
                                                         harm) with that quality peaceful and
                                                         now harmless and not even very
                                                         attentive—the ogre-shape which, as

MANUSCRIPT   BOOK

Miss Coldfield's voice went on, re-
solved out of itself before Quentin's
eyes the two

43-44 the 4th, the wraith[?] of the mother,   30-31 the fourth one. This was the mother,
the dead sister Ellen: a Niobe   the dead sister Ellen: this Niobe

45   without tears and ⟨who⟩ now, at this   33   without
distance shadowy[?] too, had an air   *Page 14*
Page 4 [4] [Lines 1-14 are crossed out but, 1   weeping, who now had an air of tran-
with the following changes, are re-   quil
tained in the book.]

1   [1-30 PASTED IN: of ~~quiet and~~ tranquil

2   all—the 4 of them arranged ~~like t~~ into 3-4   all. Quentin seemed to see them, the
the family group of the time, with   four of them arranged into the conventional family group of the period,
with

3   photograph enlarged   6-7   photograph itself would have been
seen enlarged

6-7   last known member of which had been 13-14 last member of which had been dead
dead 20 years   twenty-five years

9   *for 45 years*   19   *for forty-three years*

10   *after 45 years*   20-21 *after forty-three years*

11   it was even a cry aloud once, he thot, 22-24 it (the voice, the talking, the incredulous and unbearable amaze-
ment) had even been a cry aloud once,
Quentin thought,

13   the old lonely thwarted flesh em-   27-28 the lonely thwarted old female flesh
battled for 45 years by the   embattled for forty-three years in
the

14-20 was his death: 30-33 was Sutpen's death:
"He came here with a horse and   "He wasn't a gentleman. He wasn't
two pistols and nothing else, ~~and~~   even a gentleman. He came here with
~~Jefferson gave him shelter~~ looking   a horse and two pistols and a name
for shelter; ~~and concealment~~ and   which nobody ever heard before, knew
Yoknapatawpha County gave it to him.   for certain was his own
He wanted the guarantee of older[?]   *Page 15*
men to make his presence secure;   1-12 any more than the horse was his own
and Jefferson gave him that. Then   or even the pistols, seeking some
he wanted respectability to make his   place to hide himself, and Yoknapa-
position impregnable; and our father   tawpha County supplied him with it.
gave him that. ~~Because I dont hold~~   He sought the guarantee of reputable
~~any brief for Ellen, any more than I~~   men to barricade him from the other
~~do for myself, even tho we were born~~   and later strangers who might come
~~women and hence fools. Nor do I for~~   seeking him in turn, and Jefferson
~~father, tho there were others besides~~   gave him that. Then he needed
~~him, more than him. Not that~~ I hold   respectability, the shield of a virtuous

MANUSCRIPT		BOOK	

any brief for Ellen, ~~any more than I do for myself:~~ blind

woman, to make his position impregnable even against the men who had given him protection on that inevitable day and hour when even they must rise against him in scorn and horror and outrage; and it was mine and Ellen's father who gave him that. Oh, I hold no brief for Ellen: blind

21   fool just as later

13   fool, then later

21-27   she no longer had even youth and inexperience to guide her and she lay dying there in that house which she had exchanged pride and peace both for and nobody there but Judith who was already a ~~grim~~[?] ~~widow~~ the same as a widow ~~and with the years~~[?] ~~was~~ without ever having been a bride and within the year was going to be a widow sure enough without ever having been anything at all, and Henry who had repudiated the very roof he was born under and would return to it just once more before disappearing for good and that ~~just long enough to kill the man his sister was waiting~~ already a murderer and almost a fratricide; and he in Virginia too where

14-24   she no longer had either youth or inexperience to excuse her, when she lay dying in that house for which she had exchanged pride and peace both and nobody there but the daughter who was already the same as a widow without ever having been a bride and was, three years later, to be a widow sure enough without having been anything at all, and the son who had repudiated the very roof under which he had been born and to which he would return but once more before disappearing for good, and that as a murderer and almost a fratricide; and he, fiend blackguard and devil, in Virginia fighting, where

28   that every man

26-27   that he would return, that every man

29   ball touched him;

28   ball found him;

29-30   child mind you, 2 years younger than the very niece I was being asked to protect and save,

28-30   child, mind you, four years younger than the very niece I was asked to save,

30-31   least.']
      "Blind

31   least.' Yes, blind

Page 16

33-35   a man so far as anyone (including the father who was to give his daughter to him in marriage) knew had no past at all or at least none that he dared to reveal—

3-5   a man who so far as anyone (including the father who was to give him a daughter in marriage) knew either had no past at all or did not dare reveal it—

36   of half-tamed wild

7   of wild

36-37   than they were in whatever heathen place he had come from,

8-9   than even they were in whatever heathen place he had fled from,

38-39   negroes. ~~He was not even a gentleman. Marrying Ellen or marrying~~

11   negroes—a man

MANUSCRIPT   BOOK

10,000 thousand Ellens could not have
made him one.—a man

39   behind ⟨respectability, behind⟩ that   12-13   behind respectability, behind that
        100 miles   hundred miles

41-42   [41-45 PASTED IN: ignorant Indians,   14-17   ignorant Indians, nobody knows how,
        nobody knows how, and a house the   and a house the size of a courthouse
        size of a courthouse where he lived   where he lived for three years with-
        for three years in it without a window   out a window or door or bedstead in
        or door in it and still called it   it and still called it Sutpen's Hundred
        Sutpen's Hundred as tho it were a   as if it had been a king's
        king's

44-45   rest of it as he would have accepted   20-31   rest of respectability as he would
        the necessary discomfort of the   have accepted the necessary dis-
        thorns and briers in a thicket if it   comfort and even pain of the briers
        could have given him protection.   and thorns in a thicket if the thicket
        a man]   could have given him the protection

Page 5 [5]   he sought.
1-2   He was not even a gentleman.   "No: not even a gentleman.
        Marrying Ellen or marrying 10,000   Marrying Ellen or marrying ten
        Ellens could not have made him one.   thousand Ellens could not have made
        He didn't even want to be or even to   him one. Not that he wanted to be
        be taken for one, since that was not   one, or even be taken for one. No.
        necessary, [MARGIN: since all he   That was not necessary, since all he
        would need would be Ellen's and our   would need would be Ellen's and our
        father's names on a wedding license   father's names on a wedding license
        (or any other patent of respectability)   (or on any other patent of respect-
        for people to look at and read just as   ability) that people could look at and
        he would might have wanted our   read just as he would have wanted
        father's (or any other reputable   our father's (or any other reputable
        man's) signature on a note of hand]   man's) signature on a note of hand
        since our father   because our father

                                                       Page 17
7-8   choose respectability to hide behind   7-9   choose respectability to hide behind
        respectability was proof enough (if   was proof enough (if anyone needed
        anyone still needed proof) that he   further proof) that what he fled from
        must have fled from some opposite   must have been some opposite

10-13   [10-31 PASTED IN: privations of   12-19   privation of clearing virgin land and
        clearing virgin land and establishing   establishing a plantation in a new
        a plantation in a new country just for   country just for money; not a young
        money; not a young man without any   man without any past that he appar-
        past that he apparently cared to dis-   ently cared to discuss, in Missis-
        cuss, in Mississippi in 1833, with a   sippi in 1833, with a river full of
        river full of steamboats loaded with   steamboats loaded with drunken fools
        drunken fools covered with diamonds   covered with diamonds and bent on
        and trying to throw the cotton and   throwing away their cotton and slaves
        slaves both away before the boat   before the boat reached New
        reached New Orleans just one hard   Orleans—not with all this just one
        night's ride   night's hard ride

CHAPTER I

13   handicap or ~~detriment~~ ⟨obstacle⟩ the other   20   handicap or obstacle being the other

16-18   negroes and tell that they might have ~~eeme~~ (and probably did) come from a much older country than Carolina or Virginia but that it wasn't quiet: and anyone could have looked at his face once and known that he would choose the steamboats and   25-29   negroes of his and tell that they may have come (and probably did) from a much older country than Virginia or Carolina but it wasn't a quiet one. And anyone could have looked once at his face and known that he would have chosen the river and

19   waiting in the actual earth which   31   waiting for him in the very land which

20   myself, and I was engaged to marry him too. I hold   ?3   myself.
                                                    Page 18
                                                  1   I hold

21   had 22 years in which to watch him, see him, where Ellen had only 5.   1-2   had twenty years in which to watch him, where Ellen had had but five.

22-23   those to see him but only to hear about what he was doing, and not even that because apparently half of what he did during those 5 years nobody knew about and   3-6   those five to see him but only to hear at second hand what he was doing, and not even to hear more than half of that, since apparently half of what he actually did during those five years nobody at all knew about, and

24-31   to a woman, a wife, let alone a young girl. He came here and put on a raree show that lasted 5 years and Jefferson paid him for the privilege by at least shielding him in it by not telling their womenfolk about it if by no more; doubtless the reason that your grandfather was the only one who admitted to having offered him money on his own signature was because your grandfather was at least that rare type of man whose life was too open and unable to even conceal his mistakes. I had had all my life to watch him in, since apparently and for what reasons Heaven has not seen fit to divulge to me, my life was destined to cease there, since even anyone who has had as little in his life as I have had would not call my life since I came back to the house living. So I had 20 years to watch him in, or rather the 16 years until he went away with the regiment.]   7-32   to a wife, let alone a young girl; he came here and set up a raree show which lasted five years and Jefferson paid him for the entertainment by at least shielding him to the extent of not telling their womenfolks what he was doing. But I had had all my life to watch him in, since apparently and for what reason Heaven has not seen fit to divulge, my life was destined to end on an afternoon in April forty-three years ago, since anyone who even had as little to call living as I had had up to that time would not call what I have had since living. I saw what had happened to Ellen, my sister. I saw her almost a recluse, watching those two doomed children growing up whom she was helpless to save. I saw the price which she had paid for that house and that pride; I saw the notes of hand on pride and content-ment and peace and all to which she had put her signature when she walked into the church that night, begin to fall

MANUSCRIPT   BOOK

Page 6 [5 6]

1-14   I saw what had happened to Ellen, my sister. I saw her almost a recluse, watching those two doomed children growing up—my own nephew and niece whom I was not permitted to play with save when our aunt or Ellen was, and not because they were older than I: wasn't it to me that Ellen was to turn when she lay dying and say 'Protect her. Protect Judith'? I saw the price which Ellen had paid for that house—or for which our father had been fooled[?] or tricked or maybe forced, into selling her for. I saw the note of hand on peace and contentment and pride and all which she had put her name to when she went thru that ceremony fall due in its successive steps (I dont speak of our childhood and the shadow on our father's life of regret ~~or remorse~~[?] ~~if not remorse~~[?] at least even if not remorse for his mistake)—the one when he forbade the marriage of his daughter which he himself at one time had sanctioned and following which Henry renounced his birthright and the roof under which he had been born; I witnessed that one when Ellen, dying, had none but me to turn to and ask to protect and save the child which she had left; I saw that one when Henry returned and practically threw[?] his sister's murdered fiance's corpse at the hem of her wedding gown; I saw the man return who had caused all this, who had created two children not only to destroy one another and his own line but to ~~destroy~~ put an end to ours also. ~~I saw this man return~~ Yet I agreed to marry him.

due in succession. I saw Judith's marriage forbidden without rhyme or reason or shadow of excuse; I saw Ellen die with only me, a child, to turn to and ask to protect her remaining child; I saw Henry repudiate his home and birthright and then return and practically fling the bloody corpse of his sister's sweetheart at the hem of her wedding gown; I saw that man return—the evil's source and head which had outlasted all its victims—who had created two children not only to destroy one another and his own line, but my line as well, yet I agreed to marry him.

16-17   [16-24 PASTED IN: dont plead youth, since what creature in the South since 1861, man woman nigger or mule had time or opportunity [MARGIN: not only to have] to have ever been young but

33   don't [*sic*] plead youth, since

Page 19

1-3   what creature in the South since 1861, man woman nigger or mule, had had time or opportunity not only to have been young, but

52

CHAPTER I

MANUSCRIPT		BOOK	
23-24	her position but to vindicate the honor of a family the good name of whose women has never been impugned, by accepting the]	13-15	her situation but to vindicate the honor of a family the good name of whose women has never been impugned, by accepting the
28	but the names and stature of	21-22	but with the names and statures of
31-35	she was born, and ~~so in her eyes, even if he had villain dyed tho he~~ the man who had done that, villain dyed tho he be, would have possessed in her eyes the stature and proportions of a hero too—and now he too emerging from the same holocaust with nothing to face what the future held for a bled and vanquished land save his bare hands and the sword which he at least had never surrendered and the citation for bravery from the hand of his	26-31	she had been born. And the man who had done that, villain dyed though he be, would have possessed in her eyes, even if only from association with them, the stature and shape of a hero too, and now he also emerging from the same holocaust in which she had suffered, with nothing to face what the future held for the South but his bare hands and the sword which he at least had never surrendered and the citation for valor from

Page 20

		BOOK	
		1	his
41	[41-43 PASTED IN: "~~Yet~~ ⟨But⟩ that	8	"But that
41-43	father, out of all of them that he knew of the ones who used to go out there to drink and gamble and watch him fight those negroes naked, whose daughters he might even have won at cards. That it should have been our father. How he could have]	9-13	father of all of them that he knew, out of all the ones who used to go out there and drink and gamble with him and watch him fight those wild negroes, whose daughters he might even have won at cards. That it should have been our father. How he could have

Page 7 [7]

		BOOK	
3	Methodist elder, merchant	18	Methodist steward, a merchant
5	[5-26 PASTED IN: who could have done nothing to advance his fortunes or prospects and who could have owned nothing that	18-21	who not only could have done nothing under the sun to advance his fortunes or prospects but could by no stretch of the imagination even have owned anything that
7	servants **and** whom he had already freed, who	23-24	servants whom he had freed as soon as he got them, bought them, who
8-11	between papa and a man who to my certain knowledge was never in a Jefferson church but twice before he and Ellen married—the once when he first saw her and the once when they rehearsed the ceremony—a man that anyone could look at once and see that, even if he apparently had no money now, he was accustomed to having had it and	26-31	between a man who to my certain knowledge was never in a Jefferson church but three times in his life— the once when he first saw Ellen, the once when they rehearsed the wedding, the once when they performed it—a man that anyone could look at and see that, even if he apparently had none now, he was accustomed to having money and

MANUSCRIPT	BOOK
	Page 21
12-13 man to apparently ~~find papa and~~ ⟨discover⟩ discover not only Ellen but papa too, in church.	1 man to discover Ellen inside a church.
14-15 dreg; fatality	4 dreg. Yes, fatality
20 own niece and nephew, that I was not to go out there except when papa went with me and I	13-14 own nephew and niece, I was not even to go out there save when papa or my aunt was with me and that I
21-22 Judith except inside the house (and not because I was 2 years younger than Judith and 4 years younger than Henry, mind: wasn't	15-17 Judith at all except in the house (and not because I was four years younger than Judith and six years younger than Henry: wasn't
22-23 turned when she died and said 'Protect her. Protect Judith'?)—	18 turned before she died and said 'Protect them'?)—
25-26 alone would be sufficient; what crime committed that would leave our family cursed to be instruments not only for that man's destruction, but for our own."]	21-23 alone be sufficient; what crime committed that would leave our family cursed to be instruments not only for that man's destruction, but for our own."
30-31 to ~~kurk~~ stand,	29 to stand,
	Page 22
34-45 pro	3 proportion to

portion even to the actual years even
of a child who had never been young.
"Because I was born too late. I was
born a woman and hence a fool too,
but at least mine was that vouchsafed
instinct of innocence which, when
Ellen, dying, had only me to turn to
and say 'Protect her, at least. Protect Judith at least', could answer:
'Protect her? From whom and from
what? He has already given them
life: he does not need to harm them
any ~~more~~ further'. It is from themselves that they need protection'.
22 years too late: a child to whom
out of the overheard talk of grown
people my own sister's and my
nephew's and niece's and their father's faces had come to be like the
faces in an ogre tale between supper
and bed.—

a child who was to remember the 4

faces as seen for the first time in
her life on that first Sunday [MARGIN:
in the carriage] when the town realized that he had turned the road to
town into a race course.

---

portion to the actual years even of a
child who had never been young.
"Because I was not there. I was born
too late, 22 years too late; a child to
whom out of the overheard talk of
grown people my own sister's

Page 8 [8]

1-32   and nephew's and niece's faces had
grown to be like the faces in an ogre
tale between supper and bed [MARGIN:
long before ~~she~~ ⟨I⟩ was old enough or
big enough to go out there and play
with them]—a child who was to remember those 3 faces (and his too)
as seen for the first time in the
carriage on that first Sunday a.m.
when the town realized that he had
turned the road to church into a race
course

---

and nephew's and niece's faces had
grown to be like the faces in an ogre
tale between supper and bed, long
before I was either old enough or big
enough to ~~go out there to~~ be allowed
to play with them—a child who was to
remember those 3 faces (and his too)
as seen for the first time in the
carriage on that first Sunday a.m.
when the town realized that he had
turned the road to church into a race
course. ~~I dont even remember ever
seeing any of them before:~~—a child
born 22 years too late yet who
possessed that vouchsafed instinct of
innocence which, when Ellen, dying,
had only me to turn to and say 'Protect her at least. At least protect
Judith' could answer what the mature
wisdom of my elders apparently
could not: 'Protect her? From whom
and from what? He has already given
them life: he does not need to harm
them further. It is from themselves

that they need protection'. "From
themselves. ~~And~~ Not from him. And
not by me. Because I had not been
there.

---

portion to the actual years even of a
child who had never been young.
"Because I was born too late. I was
born 22 years too late: a child to
whom out of the overheard talk of
grown people my own sister's and
my nephew's and niece's faces had
come to be like the faces in an
ogretale heard between supper and
bed long before I was old enough or
big enough to be permitted to play
with them—

---

a child who was to remember those 3
faces (and his too) as seen for the
first time in the carriage on that first
Sunday when the town [crossed-out
illegible word] realized that he had
turned the road to church into a race
course, as tho the sister whom I had
never seen and who had ~~removed~~
⟨vanished⟩ before I was born into the
stronghold of an ogre or djinn, was
to return to the world on a one day's
special[?] dispensation and I dressed
for it (~~it~~ I was just 4 ⟨3⟩ then; doubtless I had seen them before but I
cannot remember it, and doubtless
this will be the picture of my first
sight of them that I shall take to my
grave) and then what I saw was a
glimpse like the forefront of a tornado, of a carriage and Ellen's high
white face [MARGIN: since she still
had left doubtless what she meant by
pride] and the two replicas of his
face on either side of her and the
face ~~of that wild negro driving who
looked exactly like~~ the teeth of that
wild negro who was driving and his
face looking like the negro's save for
the teeth, doubtless because of his
beard, all in a thunder and a fury of
~~dust and~~ galloping and of dust;

MANUSCRIPT   BOOK

and I was[?] ⟨watching⟩, seeing for
the first time to remember it the face
of the sister-who-was-last-to tu-had
only me-to-turn to-when she lay
[MARGIN: yet to whom Ellen would
have to turn when she lay] dying with
one of the children vanished and
doomed to be a murderer if not a
fratricide and the other doomed to be
a widow without having been a bride,
let along a wife—I, a child, yet who
possessed that vouchsafed wisdom of
innocence which, when Ellen said
'Protect her at least. At least protect
Judith' could answer what the mature
wisdom of my elders apparently could
not: 'Protect her? From whom and
what? He has already given them
life: he does not need to harm them
further. It is from themselves that
they need protection.'

33	portion to		
34	of grown people my	6	of adults my
37-38	murderer and-the-other a-already if not a fratricide and the other	12	murderer and the other
38	widow without having been a bride, let alone a wife, and	13	widow before she had even been a bride, and
39-40	vouchsafed innocence could answer what the	15	vouchsafed instinct could make that reply which the
42	protection'.	19-32	protection.' "

Page 9 [8 9]

1-44   portion-to the-actual-years even-of a
child-who-had-never-been-young.
"Because ⟨Yes⟩ I was not there. I
was-born-too-late I only heard about
it. I only heard how it was 5 years
before any men or women in Jefferson began to ⟨a⟩wake to him, tho
even-from-the-very-first apparently it
only took him a matter of days to
take the town's measure—that measure of crass and-contemptible
stupidity to which even the revelation
of that first Spanish coin ⟨gold piece⟩
would be only a matter of a two days
agog #, as tho he [MARGIN: who
admitted and preferred to have

It should have been later than it
was; it should have been late, yet the
yellow slashes of mote-palpitant
sunlight were latticed no higher up
the impalpable wall of gloom which
separated them; the sun seemed
hardly to have moved. It (the talking,
the telling) seemed (to him, to
Quentin) to partake of that logic- and
reason-flouting quality of a dream
which the sleeper knows must have
occurred, stillborn and complete, in
a second, yet the very quality upon
which it must depend to move the
dreamer (verisimilitude) to credulity—
horror or pleasure or amazement—
depends as completely upon a formal

neither] dared them not out of
recklessness but with actual contempt by paying for the recording[?]
of the land which no one knew yet
how he had acquired, ~~it~~ with a coin
found usually in the possession of
banks or pirates[?] and which, in the
possession of the man which he professed by acts to be, ~~even~~ conclusive
evidence of that of which even among
men[?] would have been a symptom.
No. I lived thru 5 years during which
he held them spellbound ~~with a raree
show that~~[?] ~~with his own raree
show until even they could no longer
be fooled. And then it was too late.~~
with that raree show which he conducted out there with his wild ~~negroes~~
beasts[?] and that poor harried
frightened little architect while he
built his house, sleeping on the bare
floors and living on meat, during
which, so I have heard, those ~~wild~~
negroes would work down in the
swamp and then creep up and cut
their throats with knives before the
animal could ~~mon~~ wake and flee—a
Punch and Judy booth[?] before
which the men of the town (oh there
were others besides your grandfather
and ~~t~~ my father) stood entranced until
even they could be fooled no more,
until his contempt for them became
so crass that he returned from his
final expedition bringing ~~his~~ ⟨the⟩
actual itself [*sic*] with him in wagons.
Then it was too late. He did not need
his own[?] raree show then, since the
[illegible word] on ours[?] and our
father[?] was sufficient. Just exactly sufficient to permit them to
follow him to our gate that day without quite working themselves up to
arrest him—the sheriff and a dozen
men and ~~50~~ a mob of 50 more and
growing all the time, following behind
him as he walked up this very street
here, with that bouquet of flowers ~~and~~
turned into our gate, like so many

recognition of and acceptance of
elapsed and yet-elapsing time as
music or a printed tale. "Yes. I
was born too late. I was a child who
was to remember

dogs following a hen and the hen not
quite daring to run and none of the
dogs quite daring to chase yet, until
he reached the gate out there and
turned into it, and came into the
house here. Walked into this house
~~in that new hat and coat and~~ with that
bouquet of flowers gathered out of
ditches on the ~~way~~ ⟨road⟩ to town and
plighted faith and honor, who did not
possess either, to a fool young
woman who did not possess judgment
or discretion, either in herself or in
the person[?] of the aunt who might
have been expected to protect her.
He knew that they were waiting for
him out there at the gate. He knew
what they were waiting for. But he
did not think or did not bother to
mention it to Ellen. He just turned
and went back out and let ~~them arrest
him~~ himself be arrested without a
word and he paraded back to town at
the head of his mob of blackguards
and hooligans. Without the bouquet
now. As tho he had brot the bouquet
for that purpose: that he had known,
realized that he would not have time
to tell our neighbors what he was
about to do [30-41 PASTED IN: and so
he would have to use some symbol
that they would recognize and understand before the sheriff overtook
him. Or maybe he was just keeping
the sheriff back with the bouquet,
having realized that the pistols would
not be enough now, until he could get
into the house and get a foothold in
security even tho knowing that he
would have to return ~~in a mom~~ sooner
or later and face the preliminaries
of retribution at least. But apparently
it was sufficient, since our father and
your grandfather seem to have
reached the courtroom even before
he did ~~and so that night he came back
with papa to supper tho~~ I dont know
how they got him out. But then I or
Ellen nor any other woman in town

ever knew just which of his crimes
they had arrested him for in the first
place. No. We, being women, were
not to know that: we were only to
furnish a wife for him. ~~Besides, I
was not there at the time. I was born
22 years too late.~~ Maybe they were
afraid. Perhaps the crime which they
had learned of at last happened not to
be minor[?] and so they ~~een~~ knew
that they could not hold him prisoner[?] and perhaps they remembered
~~how he~~ the pistols and the way he was
said to be able to use them which I
dont doubt was true enough since it is
a poor carpenter that cannot use his
own tools.] ~~Two months later he and
Ellen were married.~~ That p.m. he
came back home with papa, to supper.
And two months later he and Ellen
were married.

"No I was not there. I was born
22 years too late and hence a child to
whom out of the overheard talk of
grown people my own sister's and my
nephew's and niece's faces had come
to be like the faces of an ogre tale
between supper and bed long before I
was big enough or old enough to be
permitted to ~~go out there~~ play with

Page 10 [9-10]

1-2   ~~them // a child who was to remember
those 3 faces~~ "No. I ~~was not there.~~
born too late.—a child who was to
remember

                              Page 23

3-4   turned the road to church into a race   2-3   turned that road from Sutpen's Hundred
       course; ~~It was as tho as tho~~ I   in to the church into a race track. I

4-5   before, but I cannot remember it,   4-6   before; I must have. But I do not
       ever having seen Ellen before, even.   remember it. I do not even remember
       It   ever having seen Ellen before that
                                                         Sunday. It

5-6   never seen, ~~and~~ who had vanished   7-10   never laid eyes on, who before I was
       before I was born, into the strong-   born had vanished into the stronghold
       hold of an ogre or a djinn, was now   of an ogre or djinn, was now to re-
       to return for one day to the world   turn through a dispensation of one
       thru a special dispensation and I,   day only, to the world which she had
                                                         quitted, and I

MANUSCRIPT	BOOK
8-9	djinn who held my sister captive had agreed, for the sake of the wife and children, to come	13-14	djinn had agreed for the sake of the wife and the children to come

8-9   djinn who held my sister captive had agreed, for the sake of the wife and children, to come

13-14   djinn had agreed for the sake of the wife and the children to come

9   to enter the realm of grace ~~to give at least~~ to at least

14-15   to approach the vicinity of salvation, to at least

11-12   kind, ~~tho he himself, for the moment chivalrous, was still (and would remain) unregenerate~~ and even for the moment submit himself

18-19   kind; yes, even for the moment submitting himself

12-13   chivalrous even tho unregenerate. That's what

20-21   chivalrous for the instant even though still unregenerate. That is what

13-14   saw [MARGIN: as I stood there before the church with my aunt holding my hand, waiting for the carriage to arrive from the 12 mile drive,] and tho I must have seen Ellen and the children driving[?] before this, this is the picture of

21-25   saw as I stood there before the church between papa and our aunt and waited for the carriage to arrive from the twelve-mile drive. And though I must have seen Ellen and the children before this, this is the vision of

14-17   tornado of a carriage and Ellen's high white face since she still had left doubtless what she called pride and the two replicas of his face on either side of her and the teeth of the wild negro who was driving and his face on the front seat with the negro and looking exactly like the negro's except the teeth because of his beard doubtless—

27-31   tornado, of the carriage and Ellen's high white face within it and the two replicas of his face in miniature flanking her, and on the front seat the face and teeth of the wild negro who was driving, and he, his face exactly like the negro's save for the teeth (this because of his beard, doubtless)—

19-21   plenty to abet him, to assist him yet; there were maybe 10 with the sheriff that day, the others being mere black- guards curious[?]; there were plenty of them: at 10 o'clock on those Sunday a. ms and the carriage on two wheels up to the very church door itself and that wild negro looking in his Chris- tian clothes exactly

33   penty [sic] of them to abet him, assist him,

Page 24

1-3   make a race of it; ten oclock on Sunday morning, the carriage racing on two wheels up to the very door to the church with that wild negro in his Christian clothes looking exactly

22-26   hat and Ellen with ~~her face~~ her face calm and no drop of blood in it and holding those two children [MARGIN: who were not crying and who did not need to be held in either] ~~in~~ who sat there perfectly still too, with in their faces that infantile enormity in their faces which we did not yet quite realize[?]; oh, there were plenty to

4-19   hat, and Ellen with no drop of blood in her face, holding those two children who were not crying and who did not need to be held, who sat on either side of her, perfectly still too, with in their faces that infantile enormity which we did not then quite compre- hend. Oh, yes, there were plenty to aid and abet him; even he could not

MANUSCRIPT		BOOK	
	abet him. [MARGIN: ;even he could not have held a horserace without some-one to race against] It was not even public opinion: it was the minister speaking in the name of the women of the town and so he quit coming to church. He did not come again. It was just Ellen and the children and at least we knew there was no betting now because now we could not tell if		have held a horse race without some-one to race against. Because it was not even public opinion that stopped him, not even the men who might have had wives and children in carriages to be ridden down and into ditches: it was the minister himself, speaking in the name of the women of Jefferson and Yoknapatawpha County. So he quit coming to church himself; now it would be just Ellen and the children in the carriage on Sunday morning, so we knew now that at least there would be no betting now, since no one could say if
26-29	not since now, with his own absent, it was only the wild negro's perfectly inscrutable and with the teeth glinting a little; and if there was any triumph it must have been on that absent face 12 miles back which did not even re-quire to see or even to be present. No, it was that negro	19-25	not, since now, with his face absent, it was only the wild negro's perfectly inscrutable one with the teeth glinting a little, so that now we could never know if it were a race or a runaway, and if there was triumph, it was on the face twelve miles back there at Sutpen's Hundred, which did not even require to see or be present. It was the negro
29-30	team as well as to his own something without words, not ~~words~~[?] ⟨needing⟩ words	26-27	team too as well as to his own—some-thing without words, not needing words
31-34	in to bring them there ⫝̸;—up to the church door and women and children scattering and screaming and men catching at the bridles of ~~those~~ the other maddened team while the wild negro let Ellen and the children out at the door and took the carriage on around behind the church and beat	30-33	in and brought them here—the dust, the thunder, the carriage whirling up to the church door while women and children scattered and screamed before it and men caught at the bridles of the other team. And the negro
		Page 25	
		1-2	would let Ellen and the children out at the door and take the carriage on around to the hitching grove and beat
34-35	fool once who tried to interfere and the negro turned on him	3-4	fool who tried to interfere once, whereupon the negro turned upon him
37	[MARGIN: "Yes. From them, from themselves. And] "This	7	"Yes. From them; from them-selves. And this
37	minister; it	8	minister. It
40	of the house, it was not	15	of the front door, it was not
42-43	and ~~they carried her kicking~~ began	19	and began

CHAPTER I

44	present; I claim no triumphant	21-22	present. Nor do I claim a lurking triumphant
44-45	curtain; probably he would have been amazed as we were since we could all realize now that we had more than a child's hysteria:	22-25	curtain. Probably he would have been as amazed as we were since we would all realize now that we were faced by more than a child's tantrum or even hysteria:

Page 11 [11]

4-5	quiet the screams of that child (the niece, the bloodkin whom I hardly knew, whom ~~I~~ as far as my memory went, I had not yet seen a halfdozen times) still	33	quiet and peace the screams of that child still
6-7	I didn't ask then; I	2	I did not ask at once. I
8-9	had come to see my sister and nephew and niece for the first time, ~~saying 'What room is Ju~~ looking at the house (I ~~could~~ had been in it	5-7	had been dressed to come and see my sister and my nephew and niece for the first time, looking at the house. I had been inside it
11	I was to remember	11	I always remember
11-12	first) and saying	12-13	first. No, not asking even then, but just looking at that huge quiet house, saying
12	papa?' ~~and merely wondering with~~ ⟨with that ~~hushed~~ quiet⟩ that aptitude	13-14	papa?' with that quiet aptitude
13	inexplicable, [MARGIN: ~~as I now know, comprehend~~ ⟨realize⟩ tho I now know that even then I was ~~imagining~~[?] wondering] what	14-16	inexplicable, though I now know that even then I was wondering what
19-20	conviction ~~that~~ (that same instinctive knowledge which ~~had~~ enabled me to tell Ellen that it was not from him that Judith would need protection) that	27	conviction, knowing that
21-22	trivial affair even beneath our notice— that quiet darkened bedroom	29-30	trivial business even beneath our notice too. Yes, that quiet darkened room
22-23	the white pillow ~~with a~~ beneath a folded cloth,	32-33	the pillow beneath a camphor cloth,

Page 27

27	with ~~that~~ triumph while papa and Ellen talked.	7	with triumph.
33	that blank door, afraid, standing	16-17	that door because I was afraid to be there but more afraid to leave it, standing

CHAPTER I

34   living ~~presence being~~ ⟨spirit⟩, presence,

38-41   others. And after a while a servant came and said that our buggy was ready. ~~He was thru then~~
"Then he showed us why even this triumph was beneath our notice. Or rather we found out, Ellen found out: not I. Because ~~I had scarcely~~ it was six years now, during which time I

43   and ~~the children would~~ Henry and Judith would spend the day with us. Not him; that know [*sic*]

Page 12 [12]

1   him, tho I

2-3   because the only way under the sun in which papa could have served him was by giving him respectability—an unimpeachable position by the gift of his daughter—and papa had already done that and so not even gratitude,

4-5   of spending a family day at the home of his wife's father. So

6-7   learn even if I had had the time. So it was 6 years. Tho ~~even~~ it ~~Ellen did not know since the ones that did know it had not dared to tell tho why should they~~ ⟨was no secret to Ellen⟩ and it

8-10   house [MARGIN: , the only difference being that they would hitch their ~~horses~~ saddle horses and teams in] the grove behind the stable ~~full of saddled mares and buggies and mules~~ so they could come up across the pasture without being seen from the house since there was a woman in it now. Yes, plenty

11   witnesses for ~~our expiation~~ the discharge of our curse not only[?] from among people, gentlefolks, of our own

20   living spirit, presence,

28-33   others. Then a servant came and said our buggy was ready.
"Yes. From themselves. Not from him, not from anybody, just as nobody could have saved them, even himself. Because he now showed us why that triumph had been beneath his notice. He showed Ellen, that is: not me. I was not

Page 28

1   there; it was six years now, during which I

4-6   and the children would come in and spend the day with us. Not he; that I know

9   him. But I

10-12   because since papa had given him respectability through a wife there was nothing else he could want from papa and so not even sheer gratitude,

14-15   of taking a family meal with his wife's people. So

17-20   learn now even if I had had the time.
"So it was six years now, though it was actually no secret to Ellen since it

21-25   house, the only difference between now and the time of his bachelorhood being that now they would hitch the teams and saddle horses and mules in the grove beyond the stable and so come up across the pasture unseen from the house. Because there were plenty

26-27   witnesses to the discharge of our curse not only from among gentlefolks, our

CHAPTER I

MANUSCRIPT	BOOK
12-13 itself now even from the rear; Ellen	30-31 itself under any other circumstances, not even from the rear. Yes, Ellen
13-15 stable, a row with lanterns nailed to the posts, a row of white faces on 3 sides and negro faces on the 4th and in the center of it him and [MARGIN: these two wild negroes it, the two of them] fighting not like white men fight by rules and bare hands ⟨and weapons⟩ but like negroes fight, with bare hands to hurt	33 stable a hollow square of faces in the lantern light, the white *Page 29* 1-4 faces on three sides, the black ones on the fourth, and in the center two of his wild negroes fighting, naked, fighting not as white men fight, with rules and weapons, but as negroes fight to hurt
16 bad. No. Ellen	4 bad, Ellen
16-17 did until that night, as tho there is a kind of breathing point in outrage where you can even accept it by thinking *Thank God this*	5-8 did; that was not it. She accepted that—not reconciled: accepted—as though there is a breathing-point in outrage where you can accept it almost with gratitude since you can say to yourself, *thank God, this*
18-19 clinging to that doubtless even when she ran into the very stable itself and behind that crowd of saw, instead of the two black men ⟨beasts⟩ which she had expected to see, a black one and a white one, naked	9-14 clinging still to that when she ran into the stable that night while the very men who had stolen into it from the rear fell back away from her with at least some grain of decency, and Ellen seeing not the two black beasts she had expected to see but instead a white one and a black one, both naked
21-22 spectacle and perhaps as a matter of sheer deadly policy to retain fore-thought toward the retention of domi-nation,	18-20 spectacle, as a grand finale or per-haps as a matter of sheer deadly forethought toward the retention of supremacy, domination,
23-35 of them himself. Yes. Naked to the waist and the negro screaming lying on the ground on his back and another negro too looking with the blood and sweat like he had been painted with axel grease and another negro throwing water on him he standing there with his teeth shining[?] and another negro wiping the blood off of him with a towsack and Ellen already running down the hill from the house bareheaded, when the sound began. Apparently it came from among the negroes, on the 4th side and apparently he and the spectators all turned and looked and one of them somebody	20-33 of the negroes himself. Yes. That's what Ellen saw: her husband and the father of her children standing there naked and panting and bloody to the waist and the negro just fallen evi-dently, lying at his feet and bloody too, save that on the negro it merely looked like grease or sweat—Ellen running down the hill from the house, bareheaded, in time to hear the sound, the screaming, hearing it while she still ran in the darkness and before the spectators knew that she was there, hearing it even before it oc-curred to one spectator to say, 'It's a horse' then 'It's a woman' then 'My

65

said 'It's a horse' and then 'It's a woman' and then he said 'My God it's a child'. Yes. And Ellen ran in and the men fell back and then Henry came plunging out from among the negroes who had been trying[?] to hold him, screaming and vomiting, and Ellen not even looking at the faces, not even stopping, kneeling down in the dirt and stable filth beside Henry and looking up at that man with his face like it used to be in the carriage on Sunday. 'I know you will excuse us gentlemen,' she said. But they were already going, nigger and white, until at last it was only Ellen, and Henry in the dirt holding[?] to her and crying, and he standing there bloody to the waist and the third nigger prodded his shirt at him like he was a caged snake and the shirt was a stick. 'Where is Judith, Charles?'

God, it's a child'—ran in, and the spectators falling back to permit her to see Henry plunge out from among the negroes who had been holding him, screaming and vomiting—not pausing, not

Page 30

1-12 even looking at the faces which shrank back away from her as she knelt in the stable filth to raise Henry and not looking at Henry either but up at *him* as he stood there with even his teeth showing beneath his beard now and another negro wiping the blood from his body with a towsack. 'I know you will excuse us, gentlemen,' Ellen said. But they were already departing, nigger and white, slinking out again as they had slunk in, and Ellen not watching them now either but kneeling in the dirt while Henry clung to her, crying, and *he* standing there yet while a third nigger prodded his shirt or coat at him as though the coat were a stick and he a caged snake. 'Where is Judith, Thomas?'

36-37 his triumph had outrun even him; he had builded better in evil than even he had counted on.

13-15 his own triumph had outrun him; he had builded even better in evil than even he could have hoped.

38 to me, Charles,'

16 to me, Thomas,'

38 your wanting Henry to see this;

17-18 your bringing Henry here to see this, wanting Henry to see this;

39 Judith, Charles. Not my baby girl, Charles.'

19-20 Judith, Thomas. Not my baby girl, Thomas.'

40-41 But I have never brot Judith down here.

22-24 But I didn't bring Judith down here. I would not bring her down here.

42-43 she ~~said~~ [MARGIN: called in a voice calm and sweet and full of despair]

26-27 she called in a voice calm and sweet and filled with despair:

CHAPTER II

Page 13 [~~12~~ 5][Lines 1-8 are crossed out but, with the following changes, are retained in the book.]

Page 31

2	supper [MARGIN: until it would be time for Quentin to start] while
2	below fireflies blew
4	in 1910 even yet mostly that
6	on the June ⟨Sunday⟩ a.m. in 1833 (and,
8	sky)—a Sunday
9-10	[9-47 PASTED IN: with the bells ringing peaceful and peremptory and a little cacophonous—the denominations in concord though not in tune—and ladies
13	House veranda looked

3-4   supper until it would be time for Quentin to start, while

4-5   below the veranda the fireflies blew

9-10   in 1909 mostly about that

12   on that Sunday morning in 1833 and,

16   sky. That Sunday

17-19   with the bells ringing peaceful and peremptory and a little cacophonous— the denominations in concord though not in tune—and the ladies

24-25   House gallery looked

Page 32

19	stable, ~~3 churches~~ a saloon ~~and maybe~~ frequented
26	recovered but
28	the natural hardships of
30	to ~~suffer~~[?] ⟨endure⟩ and ~~endure~~ ⟨survive⟩ but
31	prize ⟨for⟩ which he first accepted the gambit.

9-10   stable, a saloon frequented

20-23   recovered to move with a sort of diffident and tentative amazement in a world which he had believed himself on the point of surrendering, but

25-26   the normal hardship of

29-30   to endure and survive but

31   prize for which he accepted the original gambit.

Page 33

33	once [MARGIN: visionary and alert, ruthless and reposed] ~~ruthless alert and reposed~~ in
34-35	appearance of having come recently out of some terrific oven of fever either of soul or of environment which had given it the dead impervious surface of pottery. That

1-2   once visionary and alert, ruthless and reposed in

2-5   appearance of pottery, of having been colored by that oven's fever either of soul or environment, deeper than sun alone beneath a dead impervious surface as of glazed clay. That

MANUSCRIPT		BOOK	
36	was months and even years before	6	was years before
38	the clean shirt and razor, and	9-10	the spare linen and the razors, and
39	he handled with	11-12	he used with
40	a trot around	13	a canter around
46	to traverse to	23	to cross to
47	that w should and would]	25-26	that would or should have
Page 14 [~~13-5 13~~ 6]			
1	have		
		Page 34	
6-7	Compson ~~alone~~ who first ~~discovered~~ knew that	2	Compson who first realized that
10	for hurry, of	8	for haste, of
17	deed to	21	deed, patent, to
19-20	gone, ~~paid his bill and~~ where to they still did	25-26	gone, where to again they did
21	that that Spanish coin with which he paid to have his land recorded	28-29	that the Spanish coin with which he had paid to have his patent recorded
22	last one which	29-30	last one of any kind which
23-24	anticipated [MARGIN: in believing (and even in saying aloud, now that he was not present,] what Sutpen's future ~~(and t~~ (and then unborn) sister-in-law	31-33	anticipated in believing (and even in saying aloud, now that he was not present) what Sutpen's future and then unborn sis-
		Page 35	
		1	ter-in-law
25-26	he was either returning to the cache to replenish his pockets ~~or perhaps had~~ even	3-4	he had returned to the cache to re-plenish his pockets, even
30-31	have gone unnoticed ⟨only⟩ on a Paris boulevard #.	12	have created no furore on a Paris boulevard,
31-33	years—the expression of fatalistic and amazed determination and the somberly theatric clothing—while his white employer or client	14-16	years—the somberly theatric clothing and the expression of fatalistic and amazed determination—while his white client
		Page 36	
44	Sutpen's tribe of wild	1	Sutpen's wild
Page 15 [~~14-6 14~~ 7]			
1	by mere association	4	by sheer association
1	of spare and	5	of gaunt and
3	the night before and	8-9	the previous night and

MANUSCRIPT		BOOK	
3-4	reach his property in order to try	9-10	reach Sutpen's Hundred and the river bottom to try
9-10	have ~~blundered upon one of them asleep in the mud and barely escaped with his life.~~ [MARGIN: walked one of them out of the absolute mud like a ⟨sleeping⟩ alligator and screamed just in time for Sutpen to hear him] The	20-21	have walked one of them out of the absolute mud like a sleeping alligator and screamed just in time. The
17-18	planer which was in the wagon too when it came through town—a ~~windlass~~ ⟨capstan⟩ with	32	planer which he had brought in the wagon—a capstan with
18-19	the roan horse and the negroes in	33	the
		Page 37	
		1	negroes in
19-20	slowed—as tho the	2	slowed, hitched to it—as if the
23-24	with so much as a nod, ~~did not even~~ apparently	8-9	with as much as a nod, apparently
24-25	a ~~clump and~~ kind of curious ~~and watchful~~[?] ~~alert clump~~ quiet	10	a curious quiet
26-27	brick up out of that swamp where the clay and the timber	12-13	brick out of the swamp where the clay and timber
29	had been wearing when he rode first into	16-17	had worn when he first rode into
29-31	ones which they had ever seen him in, and few of the women in the town and the county had even laid eyes on him at all yet.	17-19	ones in which they had ever seen him, and few of the women in the county had seen him at all.
32-33	would ~~have to~~ be the ~~one weapon~~ only	22	would be the only
33-39	could ~~overcome the final~~ conduct the final assault upon the ultimate capstone of ~~res the respectability which he seemed to want~~//whatever his secret and undeviating plan was ~~and~~ which Miss Coldfield and perhaps others believed to be respectability, and which General Compson, who claimed to know more, considered as being ⟨far⟩ more important than the mere gaining of a ~~wife~~ chatelaine for the house: that it was to be the final stone on the [illegible word] which Sutpen had built out of nothing with his bare hands and through which now the deliberately[?] coursed current	23-27	could conduct the last assault upon what Miss Coldfield and perhaps others believed to be respectability— that respectability which, according to General Compson, consisted in Sutpen's secret mind of a great deal more than the mere acquisition of a chatelaine for his house. So

CHAPTER II

MANUSCRIPT   BOOK

of his destiny and dream would run
undammed and undamnable. So

42-43   a kind of ~~grim~~ invincible   33   a sort of invincible

Page 38

43-44   the windows and hardware ~~and the~~   1-2   the windowglass and the ironware
    which   which

45   winter with ~~cold~~ ⟨quiet⟩ and   4   winter, with quiet and

Page 16 [~~15-7 15~~ 8]

1-2   years. He baked his own brick and   5-6   years, he and his crew of imported
    made his own timber with his crew   slaves which his adopted fellow citi-
    of imported slaves which his adopted   zens
    citizens

3-4   while ~~the onlookers sat their horses~~   9   while parties
    ~~and watched~~ parties

9-12   house, ~~15 years after it was finished,~~   18-21   house, twelve miles from Jefferson,
    ~~and not only an architect as Quentin's~~   in its grove of cedar and oak, seventy-
    ~~grandfather~~ 12 miles from Jefferson,   five years after it was finished. And
    in its grove of cedars and oaks, 75   not only an architect, as General
    years after the day it was finished;   Compson said, but
    and not only an architect as Quentin's
    grandfather said but

15   and haste and curbed the dream   26-27   and hurry and still manage to curb
                                                           the dream

18-19   overweening ~~desire for~~ vanity   32   overweening vanity

19-20   was (at the time even General Comp-   33   was (even General Compson
    son did not know which) and

Page 39

1   did not know yet) and

20   the [MARGIN: architectural] victory   1-2   the victory

24-25   more backed and enclosed by   8-9   more surrounded by

25-26   smokehouses and cribs;   10   smokehouses;

27   left hoofprints   12   left delicate prints

27-34   formal brick beds where there would   12-16   formal beds where there would be no
    be   flowers for four years yet. Now there
                                                           began a period, a phase, during which
-----
    no flowers for 4 years yet. And now   the town and the county watched him
    there began a period during which the   with more puzzlement yet. Perhaps
    town and the county watched him with   it was because the next step toward
    more puzzlement ~~than~~ still, perhaps   that secret end which
    because the next step ~~of~~ [?] ~~whatever~~
    ~~purpose~~ [?] toward whatever secret
    end he was working toward appeared
    to require time instead of action; now
    it was that some of the ladies began

CHAPTER II

MANUSCRIPT

BOOK

to suspect what this next step would
be.

---

no flowers for 4 years yet. Now there
began a period, a phase during which
the town and the county watched him
with more puzzlement yet. Perhaps
it was because the next step toward
that secret end toward which he was
working and which

MANUSCRIPT		BOOK	
35-36	required passive time instead of action that driving fury with which he had built his house; now	18-20	required patience or passive time instead of that driving fury to which he had accustomed them; now
38	that his aim was now to get a wife.	23	that he wanted a wife.
39	husbands as well as bachelors,	24-25	husbands and bachelors both,
40-41	been for some of them, husbands and bachelors both, a perfect	27-28	been to them a perfect
41	there, 6 miles	28	there, eight miles
43	the biggest edifice	31	the largest edifice

Page 17 [16-8 16 9]

Page 40

3	was said (or believed) that	6-7	was believed (or said) that
3-4	a sleeping buck and cut its throat before it could stir. It	7-9	a bedded buck and cut its throat before it could move. It
4-11	invite ⟨the⟩ parties of men out to hunt, to camp in blankets in the naked rooms [MARGIN: as Miss Coldfield told Quentin,] on the barren floors of embryonic formal opulence; they hunted and at night played cards and drank. Then it was that there began to filter back to Jefferson accounts of the other doings[?] at which Miss Coldfield just hinted to Quentin and which, according to her, Henry was to see without being able to bear the sight while his sister and her negro companion looked on unmoved. But at this time it was just a rumor which some of the guests took back to town with them and which back in Jefferson took the form of a war[?] of horrified female outrage 70 years before Miss Coldfield was to hint at it to Quentin and then tell him. Sutpen	9-17	invite the parties of men of which Miss Coldfield told Quentin, out to Sutpen's Hundred to camp in blankets in the naked rooms of his embryonic formal opulence; they hunted, and at night played cards and drank, and on occasion he doubtless pitted his negroes against one another and perhaps even at this time participated now and then himself—that spectacle which, according to Miss Coldfield, his son was unable to bear the sight of while his daughter looked on unmoved. Sutpen

71

MANUSCRIPT		BOOK	
12-13	he had managed to supply the whiskey himself.	20	he himself had managed to supply some of the liquor.
17-18	of ~~nothing~~ ⟨virgin swamp⟩ and plowed and planted with seed cotton which General Compson loaned him, then	26-29	of virgin swamp, and plowed and planted his land with seed cotton which General Compson loaned him. Then
20	or desire anything	32-33	or want anything
		Page 41	
22-23	lend (or perhaps to be requested to lend) him	3	lend him
24-26	past, tho of course the town and county did not know this. It was General Compson who knew that the Spanish coin with which Sutpen paid to have[?] his land was the last cent which he possessed at the time, as	5-7	past. It was General Compson who knew first about the Spanish coin being his last one, as
29	borrow to ~~finish the house~~ supply what the house lacked because	11-12	borrow money with which to complete the house, supply what it yet lacked, because
31-32	husbands ~~too~~ and brothers as well	16	husbands as well
35	the ladies had	21	the women had
38	expiration of the 3 years and again on Sunday and	26-28	expiration of this second phase, three years after the house was finished and the architect departed, and again on Sunday morning and
39	same clothes in	29-30	same garments in
		Page 42	
42	The ladies merely	1	The women merely
44	they realized whom	6	they comprehended whom
Page 18 [~~17-9 17~~ 10]			
3-6	shell of house and plantation, then for 3 years it had watched him settled down and static as tho he were run by electricity and the switch had been cut, in that brush[?] crayon sketch of bachelor magnificence while the town's womenfolk gradually convinced it that he was merely waiting to find a wife with a dowry to finish it. So	12-16	shell of a house and laid out his fields, then for three years he had remained completely static, as if he were run by electricity and someone had come along and removed, dismantled the wiring or the dynamo. So
8	him until they realized that	20	him, until they became aware that
10	laid siege	24	laid deliberate siege
13	Methodist elder,	29	Methodist steward,

MANUSCRIPT		BOOK	

MANUSCRIPT

15 own as well as a mother and sister to

16-17 absolute and unimpeachable and

17-19 opportunity, and who neither drank nor gambled nor hunted. They did not even ~~remember at the time that he had a daughter~~ consider his daughter ~~at~~ as a factor at

19-20 They would have thot (and did) of

21 in speculation

21-22 whatever ~~en~~ secret

22 Rosa did not. From

28-30 [28-41 PASTED IN: Then one day he quitted Jefferson for the second time. He ~~now~~ took with him 4 hired wagons besides his own; it was no secret where he was going; he was going to the river to meet a steamboat. When he returned he had the furniture and the windows. The town knew that Mr Coldfield could not even have mortgaged all that

BOOK

31-32 own, let alone a dependent mother and sister, to

Page 43

1-2 absolute and undeviating and

3-6 opportunity, who neither drank nor gambled nor even hunted. In their surprise they forgot that Mr Coldfield had a marriageable daughter. They did not consider the daughter at

7 They thought of

9 in amazed speculation

11 whatever secret

12 Rosa Coldfield did not. Because from

21-33 "Then one day he quitted Jefferson for the second time," Mr Compson told Quentin. "The town should have been accustomed to that by now. Nevertheless, his position had subtly changed, as you will see by the town's reaction to this second return. Because when he came back this time, he was in a sense a public enemy. Perhaps this was because of what he brought back with him this time: the material he brought back this time, as compared to the simple wagon-load of wild niggers which he had brought back before. But I dont think so. That is, I think it was a little more involved than the sheer value of his chandeliers and mahogany and rugs. I think that the affront was born of the town's realization that he was getting it involved with himself; that whatever the felony which

Page 44

1-12 produced the mahogany and crystal, he was forcing the town to compound it. Heretofore, until that Sunday when he came to church, if he had misused or injured anybody, it was only old Ikkemotubbe, from whom he got his land—a matter between his conscience and Uncle Sam and God. But now his position had changed, because when, about three months after he departed, four wagons left Jefferson to go to the River and meet him, it was known that Mr Coldfield was the man who hired and dispatched them. They were big wagons, drawn by oxen, and when they returned the town looked at them and knew, no matter what they might have contained, that Mr Coldfield could not have mortgaged everything that

31	enough to pay for them;	13	enough to fill them;

31-32   were men as well as women who pictured him in that absence with a silk handkerchief over his face perhaps and

14-15   were more men than women even who pictured him during this absence with a handkerchief over his face and

34   dark [MARGIN: of a muddy landing] and

18   dark of a muddy landing and

34-36   behind, which ⟨probably⟩ explains what happened next. They saw him come back with his 5 wagonloads of furniture and material; it seems that even the ones who used to eat his food and shoot his game and touch glasses with him and call him

18-21   behind. They saw him pass, on the roan horse beside his four wagons; it seems that even the ones who had eaten his food and shot his game and even called him

38-45   somewhat civilized negroes installed the windows and hung the doors of that home whose threshold no woman had yet crossed, until he was done, until even in town they knew that it was finished, with a stove-in proper spits and pans and pots in the kitchen and ⟨crystal chandeliers in the parlors and⟩ curtains at the windows and beds suave[?] with linen in the bedrooms:] it was the same ⟨luckless⟩ Akers who had stumbled on the mudcouched negro 5 years ago who came ⟨rushed⟩, a little wildeyed and considerably slackmouthed, into the Holston House bar one evening and cried, "Men, this time he stole the whole durn steamboat!" They waited; that is, it came to waiting. Doubtless they discussed it, probably [MARGIN: the town was becoming] intrigued now by the new turn[?] of homogeneity, civic virtue; anyway[?], one day and

24-33   somewhat tamed negroes had installed the windows and doors and the spits and pots in the kitchen and the crystal chandeliers in the parlors and the furniture and the curtains and the rugs; it was that same Akers who had blundered onto the mudcouched negro five years ago who came, a little wild-eyed and considerably slack-mouthed, into the Holston House bar one evening and said, 'Boys, this time he stole the whole durn steamboat!'

"So at last civic virtue came to a boil. One day and with the sheriff of the county among them, a party of eight or ten

Page 45
took

74

MANUSCRIPT   BOOK

Page 19 [~~18-10 18~~ 11]

1   with the sheriff of the county among
          them, leading them, a part of 8 took

3-9   [3-42 PASTED IN : horse, in the hat
          which they knew; he had a portman-
          teau on his saddle and he was carry-
          ing something in a woven basket on
          his arm. He stopped the roan in the
          road ~~and looked at them with his~~ hard
          ~~china/colored eyes above his short~~
          ~~strong reddish beard~~ (it was April
          then, tho the road was still a quag-
          mire; they noticed that he sat in his
          saddle on a section of tarpaulin
          turned back and fastened about his
          feet and legs) and looked at them
          [MARGIN: from one face to the next]
          with his hard chinacolored eyes
          above the short strong reddish beard.
          "Good

3-12   horse, in the frock coat and the beaver
         hat which they knew and with his legs
         wrapped in a piece of tarpaulin; he
         had a portmanteau on his pommel
         and he was carrying a small woven
         basket on his arm. He stopped the
         roan (it was April then, and the road
         was still a quagmire) and sat there
         in his splashed tarpaulin and looked
         from one face to the next; your grand-
         father said that his eyes looked like
         pieces of a broken plate and that his
         beard was strong as a curry-comb.
         That was how be put it: strong as a
         curry-comb. 'Good

10   Doubtless

14   "Doubtless

11-13 the parties involved told of it, and so
          all that the town people knew was
          what they saw when Sutpen and the
          vigilance committee all rode into
          town together, with Sutpen a little in
          front, erect, his legs

15-19 the vigilance committee ever told it
         that I know of. All I ever heard is
         how the town, the men on the gallery
         of the Holston House saw Sutpen and
         the committee ride onto the square
         together, Sutpen a little in front and
         the others bunched behind him—
         Sutpen with his legs

14   the neat worn

21   the worn

15-45 beaver hat cocked a little, doubtless
          talking to them steadily and pleas-
          antly over his shoulder, with his pale
          eyes hard and reckless and possibly
          even quizzical if not contemptuous.
          They stopped before the Holston
          House and the negro hostler ducked
          out and took the roan's head and
          Sutpen threw the reins to him and
          unfastened the tarpaulin and the
          portmanteau and got down; it was
          told how he turned and looked at them
          again where they huddled indeter-
          minately on their horses, with ~~doub~~
          probably something unpleasant about
          his mouth too that the beard hid, be-
          fore he turned [MARGIN: carrying his

22-33 beaver cocked a little, talking to them
         over his shoulder and those eyes hard
         and pale and reckless and probably
         quizzical and maybe contemptuous
         even then. He pulled up at the door
         and the negro hostler ducked out and
         took the roan's head and Sutpen got
         down, with his portmanteau and the
         basket and mounted the steps, and I
         heard how he turned there and looked
         at them again where they huddled on
         their horses, not knowing what to do
         exactly. And it might have been a
         good thing that he had that beard and
         they could not see his mouth. Then he
         turned, and he looked at the other men
         sitting with their feet on the railing

portmanteau and the woven basket]
and entered the hotel, saluting the
watching men on the gallery with that
arrogant and slightly florid gesture to
the hat which they knew, and commanded a chamber. This would have
been the committee's chance to tell
the onlookers what had transpired in
the road but it seems that they did
not. They just sat there while 4 or 5
others on horses came up and joined
them and even the men with their
comfortable feet on the gallery railing
began to catch the infection, and saw
Sutpen emerge again. He wore a new
hat now and a new broadcloth coat,
and they saw now what the basket had
contained tho at the moment it merely
puzzled them more than ever. Doubtless he paused again, doubtless and
looked at them face by face; doubtless
his hard bleak gaze combed the new
faces which had gathered in his absence. But he seems to have said
nothing at all this time. He just
turned and walked on across the
square and into the street where his
destination lay, without looking back
again, erect, with the new hat cocked
too and carrying in his hand that
which probably seemed to them the
final gratuitous bafflement and even
insult. They followed him, tho even
they did not quite have the face to
dismount and follow on foot. They
just rode along the parallel street a
little behind him; it was those who
had joined the committee at the
Holston House and who had no mounts
who followed him on foot. But even
these followed a hundred feet behind,
augmenting[?], while ladies and children and women slaves came to the
doors of the residences as they went
on and saw Sutpen, still without once
looking back, enter Mr Coldfield's
gate and stride on to the house, in his
new hat and coat and carrying his
newspaper cornucopia of flowers.
They waited for him again, and now

and watching him too, men who used
to come out to his place and sleep on
the

Page 46

1-33 floor and hunt with him, and he sa-
luted them with that florid, swaggering gesture to the hat (yes, he was
underbred. It showed like this always, your grandfather said, in all
his formal contacts with people. He
was like John L. Sullivan having
taught himself painfully and tediously
to do the schottische, having drilled
himself and drilled himself in secret
until he now believed it no longer
necessary to count the music's beat,
say. He may have believed that your
grandfather or Judge Benbow might
have done it a little more effortlessly
than he, but he would not have believed
that anyone could have beat him in
knowing when to do it and how. And
besides, it was in his face; that was
where his power lay, your grandfather said: that anyone could look
at him and say, *Given the occasion
and the need, this man can and will
do anything*). Then he went on into
the house and commanded a chamber.

"So they sat on their horses and
waited for him. I suppose they knew
that he would have to come out some
time: I suppose they sat there and
thought about those two pistols. Because there was still no warrant for
him, you see: it was just public
opinion in an acute state of indiges-
tion; and now other horsemen rode
into the square and became aware of
the situation, so that there was quite
a posse waiting when he walked out
onto the gallery. He wore a new hat
now, and a new broadcloth coat, so
they knew what the portmanteau had
contained. They even knew now what
the basket had contained because he
did not have that with him now either.
Doubtless at the time it merely
puzzled them more than ever, because, you see, they had been too

CHAPTER II

MANUSCRIPT

BOOK

the crowd drew[?] to itself—men, and
even negroes from the adjacent
homes, clotting about the 8 horsemen
who sat watching ~~the door~~ Mr Coldfield's door with that air of huddled
determination, until Sutpen emerged
again. It was a long time and now he
no longer carried the cornucopia of
flowers, and when he came out of the
house he was engaged to be married.
But they did not know that, because
as soon as he reached the gate again
they arrested him. They took him
back to town ~~and to the courthouse~~
with the women and]

"Yes," Miss Coldfield said. "Arrested him as soon as he stepped off
papa's property. He knew they were
there waiting; he knew what they
were waiting for. Yet he walked into
that house with that bouquet of flowers
wrapped in a piece of newspaper and
plighted faith and honor which he did
not possess to a fool young

Page 20 [~~19~~ 12]

1-15   [1-20 PASTED IN: and the children and
the house servants watching him from
behind the curtains in the windows
and the flowering shrubs on the lawns
and the corners[?] of the kitchens
where doubtless food was already
beginning to scorch, and back to the
square where the rest of the men
quitted offices and stores to follow,
so that when he reached the courthouse, Sutpen was enclosed by a mob
of men and youths and boys like a
runaway slave. They arraigned him
before the justice, tho by that time
General Compson and Mr Coldfield
had arrived. They signed his bond
and ~~that night~~ he late that p.m. he
went home with Mr Coldfield, walking
along the same street which he had
first traversed as a prisoner and
doubtless watched from behind the
same window curtains by the same
~~worn~~ faces, to the betrothal supper

busy speculating on just how he was
planning to use Mr Coldfield and,
since his return, too completely outraged by the belief that they now saw
the results even if the means were
still an enigma, to remember about
Miss Ellen at all.

Page 47

1-33   "So he stopped again doubtless
and looked from face to face again,
doubtless memorizing the new faces,
without any haste, with still the beard
to hide whatever his mouth might
have shown. But he seems to have
said nothing at all this time. He just
descended the steps and walked on
across the square, the committee
(your grandfather said it had grown
to almost fifty by now) moving too,
following him across the square.
They say he did not even look back.
He just walked on, erect, with the
new hat cocked and carrying in his
hand now that which must have
seemed to them the final gratuitous
insult, with the committee riding
along in the street beside him and
not quite parallel, and others who
did not happen to have horses at the
moment joining in and following the
committee in the road, and ladies
and children and women slaves coming to the doors and windows of the
homes as they passed to watch as
they went on in grim tableau, and
Sutpen, still without once looking
back, entered Mr Coldfields's gate
and strode on up the brick walk to the
door, carrying his newspaper cornucopia of flowers.

"They waited for him again. The
crowd was growing fast now—other
men and a few boys and even some
negroes from the adjacent houses,
clotting behind the eight original
members of the committee who sat
watching Mr Coldfield's door until
he emerged. It was a good while and
he no longer carried the flowers, and
when he returned to the gate, he was

77

without wine or any whiskey before
or after; ~~Two months later he and~~
~~Ellen Coldfield were married.~~ it
was said that during none of the
three passages thru that street
did his air and bearing alter—the
same unhurried stride to which the
new broadcloth coat swung, the same
angle to the new hat above the ~~alert~~
~~and hard alert eyes~~ hard alert eyes.
Something of that faience appearance which the flesh of his face above
the beard had when he first came to
town had gone now and now his flesh
had an honest sunburn tho the beard
and the eyes had not changed. And
he was not fleshier either; the flesh
on his bones had merely become
quiet, as tho

engaged to be married. But they did
not know this, and as soon as he
reached the gate, they arrested him.
They took him back to town, with the
ladies and children and house niggers
watching from behind curtains and
behind the shrubbery in the yards
and the corners of the houses, the
kitchens where doubtless food was
already beginning to scorch, and so
back to the square where the rest of
the able-bodied men left their offices
and stores to follow, so that when he
reached

Page 48

1-18   the courthouse, Sutpen had a larger
following than if he actually had been
the runaway slave. They arraigned
him before a justice, but by that time
your grandfather and Mr Coldfield
had got there. They signed his bond
and late that afternoon he returned
home with Mr Coldfield, walking
along the same street as of the fore-
noon, with doubtless the same faces
watching him from behind the window
curtains, to the betrothal supper with
no wine at the table and no whiskey
before or after. During none of his
three passages that day through that
street did his bearing alter—the
same unhurried stride to which that
new frock coat swung, the same angle
to the new hat above the eyes and the
beard. Your grandfather said that
some of the faience appearance which
the flesh of his face had had when he
came to town five years ago was gone
now and that his face had an honest
sunburn. And he was not fleshier
either; your grandfather said that
was not it: it was just that the flesh
on his bones had become quieter, as
though

16-18 now with a quality still swaggering a   20-23 now, with that quality still swaggering
little but now without braggadocio or   but without braggadocio or belliger-
~~belligerence. Two months later he~~   ence, though according to your grand-
~~and Ellen were married Not bellig-~~   father the quality had never been
~~erence, but alertness~~ not belligerence,   belligerence, only watchfulness. And

78

MANUSCRIPT   BOOK

so much as alertness tho the quality
had never been belligerence so much
as alertness. And

19-20   could not trust his eyes alone to   24-25   could trust his eyes alone to do the
        watch without the flesh on his bones   watching, without the flesh on his
        also standing sentry.   bones standing sentry also.

20-22   later, he and Ellen Coldfield were   26-27   later, he and Miss Ellen were mar-
        married as Miss Coldfield] told   ried.
        Quentin, he and Ellen were married.   ''It was in June of 1838, almost
            ''It was in June, in 1838,'' Mr   five years to the day from
        Compson said. ''Five years to the
        day almost from

24-25   where Miss Rosa says that he saw   30-31   where he saw Ellen for the first
        Ellen first. The aunt had even forced   time, according to Miss Rosa. The
        or cajoled nagged Mr nagged   aunt had even forced or nagged

26   face. This was   33   face for the occasion. The powder
                                                         was

                                                 Page 49
26-27   streaked again and caked and chan-   2   streaked, caked and channelled. Ellen
        nelled. She seems   seems

29   it for   7   it (the rain) for

33   be; of the two men (I dont mean Ellen,   12   be. You [Opening parenthesis omitted
        of course: in fact you   by error. See closing parenthesis at
                                                         l. 26 below.]

35   waked at night, with   14   waked after midnight, with

37-38   betrayal; that regardless of children   19   betrayal? that regardless of the
        the

42-43   train) it was Sutpen who desired (or
        hoped; I have this from something
        your grandfather let drop one day and
        which he doubtless had from Sutpen
        himself in the same
Page 21 [20 13]
1-6   accidental fashion, since Sutpen never   26-33   train). Of the two men, it was Sutpen
        even told Ellen that he wanted it,   who desired the big wedding, the full
        which (the fact that at the last minute   church and all the ritual. I have this
        he refused to support her in her de-   from something your grandfather let
        sire and insistence upon it) accounts   drop one day and which he doubtless
        partly for the tears out of which she   had from Sutpen himself in the same
        emerged for a moment to be married   accidental fashion, since Sutpen never
        and then returned) a big wedding, the   even told Ellen that he wanted it, and
        full church and all the ritual and   the fact that at the last minute he re-
        trappings. Mr Coldfield apparently   fused to support her in her desire and
        intended merely to employ the   insistence upon it accounts partly for
        church, apart from its spiritual   the tears. Mr Coldfield apparently

CHAPTER II

MANUSCRIPT   BOOK

significance, merely as he would have   *Page 50*
any other object, concrete or ab-   1   intended
stract, to which he had given a cer-
tain amount of his time. He seems
to have intended

7   labor for   3   labor and money for

10   raised [MARGIN: —that, and no more] 8-9 raised—that, and no more. Perhaps
       Perhaps this was due   his wanting a small wedding was due

12   which had fitted into one spring wagon 12-13 which ten years ago had fitted into a
       ten years before, or   single wagon; or

14-15 whom two months before he had been   16-19 whom just two months ago he had
       actively[?] instrumental in getting out   been instrumental in getting out of
       of jail. Not any lack of courage. Re-   jail. But it was not due to any lack
       gardless   of courage regarding the son-in-law's
                                                       still anomalous position in the town.
                                                       Regardless

16-17 at that time of any crime (and remem- 21   at the time of any crime, he would
       ber that his standards of probity were
       almost puritan) Mr Coldfield would

20-21 own reputation if the affair had been 27-31 own good name even though the arrest
       a repercussion of that business which   had been a direct result of the busi-
       Sutpen had involved him in beyond his   ness between himself and Sutpen—
       depth, even tho when it reached the   that affair which, when it reached a
       point where his conscience refused   point where his conscience refused
       to sanction it he had withdrawn and   to sanction it, he had withdrawn from
                                                      and

23-24 he suffered, tho he let his daughter 33   he had suffered, though he did permit
       marry Sutpen. Which was   his
                                            Page 51
                                            1-2   daughter to marry this man of whose
                                                  actions his conscience did not ap-
                                                  prove. This was

25-26 party, [MARGIN: of the hundred who   5-7   party, of the hundred who had been
       had been invited] tho when they came   invited; though when they emerged
       out (it was a [*sic*] night: from the church (it was at night:

26-27 with ~~light~~ and burning pine knots) 8-10 with burning pine knots) the rest of
       ~~there were about a hundred//⟨the rest~~   the hundred were there in the per-
       ~~of the hundred were there in⟩~~ [MARGIN: sons of boys and youths and men
       the rest of the hundred were there in
       the persons of] boys and youths, ~~and~~
       ⟨but⟩ mostly men

30-31 wedding. Sutpen had not expressed   14-15 wedding. But Sutpen wanted it. He
       himself. But he wanted it too. In   wanted, not
       fact, Miss Rosa was righter than she
       knew: he did want, not

80

CHAPTER II

MANUSCRIPT		BOOK	
33	patent—yes, the patent,	17	patent. Yes, patent,
37-39	the disapproval of communities of mankind toward any ~~ev~~ situation which it does not understand, built it. And pride: she admitted to you that he was brave; perhaps she will even allow him pride. Certainly it was pride:	24-27	the disapprobation of all communities of men toward any situation which they do not understand. And pride: Miss Rosa had admitted that he was brave; perhaps she even allowed him pride:
40	cost and then lived	29	cost. And then he lived
41	it like he wanted it—	30-31	it as it should be furnished—

Page 52

43	But he never told Ellen, or anyone: in fact, when	1	But when

Page 22 [~~21~~ 14]

3-4	which sometime during the 5 years before that day had swallowed him even ~~if it had not~~ tho he had not lain	6-8	which at some moment during the five preceding years had swallowed him even though he never had quite ever lain
5	him, and	10	him. And
6-7	the jaw served instead as two propped sticks holding the maw open and harmless while he walked out of it unscathed.	12-14	the outraged jaw served instead as props to hold the jaw open and impotent while he walked out of it unharmed.
9-10	for his refusal to have any past and	18-19	for not having any past, and
11-12	chance to thrust him back into the ~~maw~~ ⟨gullet⟩ of public opinion which had tried at first to refuse him, not only to ~~justi~~ secure	21	chance not only to secure
13-15	having sanctioned ~~the mar~~ and permitted the wedding which in reality she could not have prevented. ~~//this, as Miss Rosa told you, for the sake Or maybe~~ —this, as Miss Rosa told you, for	23-26	having apparently sanctioned and permitted the wedding which in reality she could not have prevented. It may have been for
17	even simpler than this and	28-29	even less complex than that and
18	villain to be preferred to	30-31	villain preferable to
19	tears, and Sutpen who knew probably about	32-33	tears; and Sutpen, who probably knew about

Page 53

20	time neared more and more thoughtful, speculative.	1	time drew near graver and graver.
20	just alert, like	2	just watchful, like

MANUSCRIPT		BOOK	
21	day and hour when	2	day when
22-25	grandfather. Just the same age that Henry was that night in the stable which ~~he~~ Miss Rosa told you about, which Henry could not quite stand up to) set out ~~to acquire his fortune mansion and state estate~~ into a world which even in theory ~~he k geograph~~ the average geographical scheme[?] of the normal boy of 14, he	4-5	grandfather) set out into a world which even in theory he
26-29	which ~~men of 30 often do not~~ most men do not set up until ~~after 30~~ the blood begins to slow at 30 or more, and then only because the image to them represents peace and indolence or at least a crowning of ~~ambi~~ vanity instead of the vindication of a past affront in the person of a son ~~not yet even begotten the~~ [MARGIN: whose] seed ~~of whose~~ was not yet, and would not be for years yet, planned. —that	6-10	which most men do not set up until the blood begins to slow at thirty or more and then only because the image represents peace and indolence or at least a crowning of vanity. Even then he had that
30	aside, (like the clothing which without doubt and for a time at least he had to sleep in as well as live in) and	11-12	aside, like the clothing which he had to sleep in as well as live in, and
32-34	learn and where because of this he was to make that mistake which if he had acquiesced to it would not have been even an error and which, since he refused to be stopped by it, became his doom—that ~~alertness unsleeping~~ unsleeping	14	learn—that unsleeping
39-40	cannot. ~~// with which he~~ "His	22-24	cannot, that actually it is the stronger. "His
40	the ~~lone~~[?] ~~one.~~ lonely one.	24-25	the solitary one.

Page 23 [~~22~~ 15]

| 4-9 | paradox as Ellen had her aunt as well as her own desire for the big wedding to support it without incongruity or paradox. While Sutpen wanted the big wedding actually more than Ellen did, yet his judgment forewarned him of how the town would take it even more than Mr Coldfield did. So that while Ellen was weeping her tears not only to ~~persuade~~ ⟨coerce⟩ her father but to persuade Sutpen to put his weight into | 32 | paradox. Then |

MANUSCRIPT	BOOK

the balance, he had one enemy. But
when he refused, ~~to~~ when he remained
neutral, he had 3, counting the aunt.
Then

9-10	invitations ~~and sent them around~~ —Sutpen	33	invitations—Sutpen

Page 54

11-12	the rehearsal) when they reached the church on the night before the cere-mony, to rehearse it, and found the church itself empty, ~~and the tears came down again.~~ and	2-5	the dress rehearsal) when they reached the church for the rehearsal on the night before the wedding and found the church itself empty and
13	two [MARGIN: two of old Ikkemotubbe's, Sutpen's neighbor, ⟨and the man who had sold him his land⟩ Chickasaws] ~~Chickasaw Indians who were Sutpen's neighbors⟩~~ standing guard[?] in	6	two of old Ikkemotubbe's Chickasaws) standing in
14	Ellen held up thru the rehearsal, but after it the	8	Ellen went through the rehearsal, but afterward the
16-17	I think I know who vetoed it. ~~The~~ It	13	I know who vetoed it. It
18-19	house, in a house dress and a shawl over her head and	16-18	house, the invitation list in her hand, in a house dress and a shawl and
22	wedding: ~~doubtless~~ the aunt ~~knew~~ must	22-23	wedding: the aunt must
23-24	was doubtless past all ratiocination by that time; she came to our house too. Father	24-25	was probably past all ratiocination by then. Father
24-25	and ~~your grand~~ mother was a stranger in Jefferson [MARGIN: and ~~I dont believe~~ she had yet met the aunt and ~~was probably~~[?] ~~nritt~~[?] did not even know who ~~she was~~ the aunt was] and	26-27	and mother was a stranger in Jeffer-son and

Page 55

29	happened [MARGIN: ; there was nothing comic in it to her]	1-2	happened. There was nothing comic in it to her.
30	begin to put her hand up and the same	4-6	begin to raise her hand (perhaps with the thimble on one finger) as though to protect herself and the same
33	the wedding had	10	the situation had
33-36	spread ~~beyond the town itself~~ not only beyond the town but beneath it, penetrated into the livery stable backroom and the drovers' tavern on the edge of town which was to furnish	10-14	spread not only beyond the town but beneath it, penetrating the livery stable and the drovers' tavern which was to supply the guests who did at-tend it. Ellen of course was not

most of the guests who did attend it, not only as notification but as a blanket threat. Ellen of course did not know this, anymore than the aunt did or

aware of this, anymore than the aunt herself was, or

36-38 had had clairvoyance, ~~to actually foresee the p.m.~~ could have actually foreseen what was to happen before time produced it. Sutpen I suppose could have told them, but doubtless he knew that the aunt would not have believed him. Not

15-16 had been clairvoyant and could actually have seen the rehearsal of events before time produced them. Not

38 herself incapable of being thus further affronted, but that she

17-18 herself insulated against being thus affronted, she

40-41 have ~~this result~~ any result other than the end for which she had [MARGIN: ~~performed at the price of all not only~~ ⟨surrendered for the time not only all⟩ of Coldfield dignity but ⟨all⟩ female modesty as well] ~~acted.~~ Probably

19-23 have any result other than the one for which she had surrendered for the time not only all Coldfield dignity but all female modesty as well. Sutpen I suppose could have told her, but doubtless he knew that the aunt would not have believed him. Probably

42 depend, and arm them with the ~~pine knots~~ lighted

26-28 depend, the only men on whom he could depend, and arm them with the lighted

Page 24 [~~23~~ 16]

1 and Mr Coldfield noticed that

32-33 and possibly Mr Coldfield remarked that

1-6 up at the church door they were halted in the shadows across the street, and probably only Sutpen saw that the occupants ~~were still in them~~ had not dismounted ~~but instead~~ and that now the banquette before the church door was the center of an arena lighted by the smoking pine torches which Sutpen's negroes held aloft, but unsteady light of which wavered upon the crowd of still quiet faces of the men, the drovers and traders and such from the tavern, who stood just where light and darkness met above the door. There

33 up before the door and
Page 56
1-6 empty, they were halted across the street and still occupied, and that now the banquette before the church door was a sort of arena lighted by the smoking torches which the negroes held above their heads, the light of which wavered and gleamed upon the two lines of faces between which the party would have to pass to enter the church. There

6-8 aunt saw or suspected anything wrong yet. Because by the time Ellen walked out of the weeping and so into the church, empty yet [MARGIN: save for

7-16 aunt suspected that anything was wrong.
    ''For a time Ellen walked out of the weeping, the tears, and so into

	MANUSCRIPT		BOOK
	your grandfather and grandmother and perhaps a half dozen more who might have come for the same reason of loyalty to a friend—to him[?] or to the Coldfields—or who probably came in order to be close and so miss nothing of what the town seemed to have anticipated as well as Sutpen did] and to be still empty even after the ceremony started and progressed and concluded. Because Ellen		the church. It was empty yet save for your grandfather and grandmother and perhaps a half dozen more who might have come out of loyalty to the Cold-fields or perhaps to be close and so miss nothing of what the town, as represented by the waiting carriages, seemed to have anticipated as well as Sutpen did. It was still empty even after the ceremony started and concluded. Ellen
9-10	fortitude; she made her responses firmly enough, because the men out-side were quiet yet, ~~possibly out of respect~~ doubtless out	18-20	fortitude; besides, nothing had hap-pened yet. The crowd outside was quiet yet, perhaps out
10-11	aptitude of the Anglo-Saxon for ~~mystical and~~ [illegible word] ~~immola-tion of~~ complete mystical acceptance of conventionally immolated	20-22	aptitude and eagerness of the Anglo-Saxon for complete mystical accep-tance of immolated
13	moving under that pride which would not let those in the church see her weep again. she	24-25	moving beneath that pride which would not allow the people inside the church to see her weep. She
15-16	was—~~passing her as she turned~~ passing her or maybe the changing light itself as ~~the one of the negroes, the torch-bearers,~~ she	29-30	was—passing her, or perhaps the changing light itself as she
17	negroes, the torch-bearers, his	31	negroes, his
17	springing into the crowd when	32	springing toward the crowd, the faces, when
			Page 57
19-20	the carriages across the street, in the torchlit arena of the church ban-quette—the bride shrinking around behind him in startled terror and	2-4	the halted carriages across the street—the bride shrinking into the shelter of his arm as he drew her behind him and
21-22	almost like smiling on his face, holding	9-10	almost of smiling where his teeth showed through the beard, holding
24	would have been killed) ~~to~~ while	12	would not have lived ten seconds if he had sprung) while
24-25	the ~~faces~~ circle of faces, with open mouths and torch reflecting eyes, seemed to advance and waver and ~~vanish~~ shift	13-15	the circle of faces with open mouths and torch-reflecting eyes seemed to advance and waver and shift
26	retreated tho where [sic] his carriage waited, holding[?] the two women somehow behind the shield of his	16	retreated to the carriage, shielding the two women with his

C H A P T E R   I I

MANUSCRIPT		BOOK	
27	word, still facing the crowd. But	17-18	word. But
28	come prepared with the missiles. In	19-20	come armed and prepared with the ones they did throw. In
28-29	the crisis of the entire	21	the entire
29-30	the sheriff followed him down the street to Mr Coldfield's gate that day.	22-23	the vigilance committee followed him to Mr Coldfield's gate that day two months before.
30-31	drovers, ~~returned to the stables and work~~[?] returned, vanished back into, the the [*sic*] region	24-25	drovers and teamsters, returned, vanished back into the region
34	the surreys and	31	the carriages and
35-37	hunt ~~and eat~~ his game and eat his food and on occasion ~~watch him match~~ gathering in the stable at night while he matched 2 of ~~the~~ his	33	hunt his game and eat his food again and on oc-
		Page 58	
		1-2	casion gathering at night in his stable while he matched two of his
37	against each other or	2-3	against one another as men match game cocks or
38	He ~~was not~~ did not forget ~~it~~ that night, as did Ellen. It	4-7	He did not forget that night, even though Ellen, I think, did, since she washed it out of her remembering with tears. Yes, she was weeping again now; it

CHAPTER III

Page 25 [5 24]

[Above line 1] "If he threw her over, I
    wouldn't think she would want to tell
    anybody about it," Quentin said.

1   "Ah" Mr Compson said again.
    "When her father died in '64, she
    moved

1-3   Judith. Mr Coldfield was a con-
    scientious objector to the war. He
    had never been an irascible[?] man
    and until war was actually declared
    and She was 20 then, 2 years younger
    than the niece

4   from the niece's father apparently

4   already 6 years

6   Rosa apparently never forgave her
    father)

9   it, and raised

15-17 it (he was an steward in the Metho-
    dist Church, a curious[?] man silent
    man—that queer silent man [MARGIN:
    not only] whose only companion and
    friend seems to have been his but the
    only thing in the world which he
    cared about, was his seems

19-20 revenge upon for the fiasco of the
    marriage Ellen's

21-22 snake, who ⟨had⟩ taught her (Miss
    Rosa) to

24   the world which she had quitted, held

25-28 a man (his face the same which her
    father now saw and had seen ever
    since that day when, with the future
    son-in-law for ostensible yoke mate
    but actually whip, Mr Coldfield's
    conscience had set the mark[?] and,

Page 59

1-2   If he threw Miss Rosa over, I
    wouldn't think she would want to tell
    anybody about it *Quentin said.*

3-4   *Ah Mr Compson said again* After
    Mr Coldfield died in '64, Miss Rosa
    moved

5-6   Judith. She was twenty then, four
    years younger than her niece

7-8   from the family's doom which Sutpen
    seemed bent on accomplishing, ap-
    parently

10   already seven years

13   Rosa never forgave her father for it)

19   it. She was raised

Page 60

4-6   it—that queer silent man whose only
    companion and friend seems

11-12 revenge for the fiasco of Ellen's

15   snake. The aunt had taught Miss
    Rosa to

19-20 the irrevocable world, held

21   a man who

MANUSCRIPT		BOOK	
	surrendering even his share of the cargo, he and the son-in-law had parted) who		
29	on–a grim	23	on. In a grim
33-36	and afflicted her to overtake the [illegible word] of convinced disapprobation which regarding any and everything which could have penetrated her family thru the agency of a man, particularly her father, which the aunt seems to have put on her at birth along with the swaddling clothes) to was passed.　Perhaps [quotation marks omitted through oversight]	30-33	and betrayed her to overtake the disapprobation regarding any and every thing which could penetrate the walls of that house through the agency of any man, particularly her father,
			Page 61
		1-3	which the aunt seems to have invested her with at birth along with the swaddling clothes.　Perhaps
36	as not only an orphan but a pauper to	4	as an orphan and a pauper, to
37	her kin for food and protection, and this kin to be the niece	4-6	her next of kin for food and shelter and protection–and this kin the niece
37-38	–perhaps she saw in this fate	6-7	–perhaps in this she saw fate
38-39	request.　Doubtless up to the very last she saw herself Perhaps	8	request.　Perhaps
39-40	retribution, if not as an active instrument strong enough in herself to	9-10	retribution: if not in herself an active instrument strong enough to
40	symbol of ⟨inescapable⟩ reminding to rise from	11-12	symbol of inescapable reminding to rise bloodless and without dimension from
41	in '65 and	13	in '66 and
43	get of what Miss Rosa called his	16-17	get of his
44-45	them.　She didn't tell you that two of them were women?"　("No, sir," Quentin said.	17-21	them.　Miss Rosa didn't tell you that two of the niggers in the wagon that day were women?　No, sir, *Quentin said.*
Page 26 [25]			
4	of months or even weeks.	27-28	of weeks or perhaps even days.
7	any woman, white or black, in	33	any white woman in
		Page 62	
9	before Judith and Henry and Clytie even,	3-4	before Clytie and Henry and Judith even,
10-11	naming himself the his own ironic fecundity of dragon's teeth which, with the two exceptions, were girls.	5-6	naming with his own mouth his own ironic fecundity of dragon's teeth.

MANUSCRIPT		BOOK	
14	in '65, she had	12	in '66, Miss Rosa had
16	count or remember,	15	count nor recall,
24-25	would come in with the children to	31-32	would bring the children in to
			Page 63
27	visits too that	3	visits also that
29	of unresistance: and	7-8	of his passive rectitude: and
32	been some delicacy for his father-in-law, the	12-13	been because of some delicacy for his father-in-law. The
32-33	between whom and himself neither the aunt or Ellen or	13-14	between Mr Coldfield and himself neither aunt, Ellen, or
33	knew, which Sutpen never divulged to but the one	15	knew, and Sutpen was to divulge to but one
34	of secrecy as	16	of confidence as
34	Coldfield's [illegible word] security maybe; certainly[?] for his carefully	17	Coldfield's carefully
36-39	was that one which Miss Rosa told you and which the aunt gave her: that now that he had got out of ~~Mr Coldfield all that~~ his father-in-law all which Mr Coldfield possessed which Sutpen could have used or wanted, he (Sutpen) ~~did not~~ had	20-21	was that now since he had got out of his father-in-law all that Mr Coldfield possessed that Sutpen could have used or wanted, he had
39	the common decency	23-24	the grace and decency
40	believe for that very reason:	26-27	believe because of that very fact:
43	That [quotes omitted] was the face which, when she saw	30	That was the face which, when Miss Rosa saw
44-46	dereliction (she now kept house for her father as the aunt had done until the night when she climbed out of the window) ~~and~~ there was not only any[?] one to [illegible word crossed out] ~~her to~~ make her try to play with her nephew and niece, ~~there w~~ on those days, occasions formal	33	dereliction (Miss Rosa now kept her fa-
			Page 64
		1-4	ther's house as the aunt had done, until the night the aunt climbed out the window and vanished) there was not only no one to make her try to play with her nephew and niece on those days formal
Page 27 [26]			
1	even go out there to breathe	4-5	even have to go out there and breathe
2	still ~~lurked~~ remained,	6	still remained,
2-3	what she called sardonic and watchful triumph, save once a year now when,	7-8	what seemed to her sardonic and watchful triumph. She went out to Sutpen's Hundred just once a year now when,

MANUSCRIPT		BOOK	
4-5	who instigated the visits—[5-13 PASTED IN: ~~It was Mr Coldfield who instigated this,~~ perhaps	11-13	who insisted on the visits, who had never gone out with them while the aunt was there, perhaps
6	perhaps for the reason that it	15	perhaps because it
8	in steadily augmenting unease	18-19	in a steadily increasing unease
9-10	between father and grandfather which Mr Coldfield was not sure yet that	20-21	between them which Mr Coldfield was not yet sure that
12	that it was at war because	25	that he was at war. Because
13-14	facing across the] dinner table and without support now even	28-29	facing him across the dinner table, without support even
14-15	metamorphosis, perhaps into ~~that next lustrum of the ancient~~ her next lustrum with the complete[?] finality	30-31	metamorphosis, emerging into her next lustrum with the finality

Page 65

17	as compared with, weighed	2	as weighed
19-20	chairs, the ones which she would inherit or the ones—the objects—she would accumulate as complement to individual chairs, as people do; as	4-5	chairs—as
20-21	small-boned too,	5	small-boned also,
22	her life had	8	her days had
23	eyes even still young,	10	eyes still even young,
24	dewlaps now and not cheeks,	11-12	dewlaps and not cheeks any longer,
25-27	candelabra which he had fetched to town in wagons almost 20 years ago, to the astonished and affronted outrage of his fellow citizens), and	14	candelabra) and
28-29	father;—~~the eyes that still looked, like as you put it, like pieces of coal pushed into soft dough//the creature~~ this creature, this face that hardly ever spoke	17	father; this face which rarely spoke
30-31	prim ~~mousecolored~~ hair of that peculiar ~~shade of~~ mouselike shade of hair on which the sun does not shine often,	19-21	prim hair of that peculiar mouse-like shade of hair on which the sun does not often shine,
34	last minute and	26	last moment and
37	escape from it	32	escape it
37-38	schoolgirl's heroic poetry about the also-dead—the face, the smallest face in company,	32-33	schoolgirl's poetry about the also-dead. The face, the smallest face in the company,

90

CHAPTER III

MANUSCRIPT

BOOK

Page 66

38	with hushed and	1	with still and
42	them correct, of	8-9	them right, and of
43	marry its owner.	11	marry the late owner of it.
45	set: one	14	set for the visit. One
46-47	year until Ellen married and then 53 times each year since ~~and which he would be buried in~~ until	17-18	year since until Ellen married, and then fifty-three times a year after the aunt deserted them, until

Page 28 [27]

1	him and so died in it; whereupon Miss	20-21	him and threw the hammer out the window and so died in it. Then after breakfast Miss
2	wear even	24	wear on Sundays and occasions even
3	until her	25	until the day when her
4	and drive away,	28	and depart,
5	two free negroes for the meal	29-30	two negroes for the noon meal
6	the one which	31-32	the crude one of leftovers which

Page 67

8	discharged, since Henry was away	3-4	discharged what with Henry away
9-10	and maturity where	6	and womanhood where
17-46	thigh.	20-23	thigh.

~~"But she now saw more of her sister and niece than she ever had.~~ "Now the period began which ended in the catastrophe, the happening, which caused the complete volteface in her actions tho not her character. It had not changed. Despite the 4 years which she spent feeding her father secretly at night while he hid from ~~both~~ Confederate provost marshals and at the same time writing her heroic poetry about the war and the actual men who would have shot or hung her father if they had ever found him, (and of whom the ogre of her childhood now made one and—he brot home with ~~him~~ ⟨a⟩ ~~his citation~~ him a personal citation in Lee's own hand—a good one). The face which she carried out to Sutpen's Hundred when she went out to live with Judith and fulfill the promise which she had

Now the period began which ended in the catastrophe which caused a reversal so complete in Miss Rosa as to permit her

91

MANUSCRIPT   BOOK

given Ellen, was the same face which
had watched his across the dinner
table the first time she had seen
him—the face which he probably likewise could not have said how many
times he had seen it nor when and
which when he did see it he could not
have described it later, and from
behind which the woman herself
watched him with that cold[?] hushed
intensity. And not with fear. Apparently she had never been afraid of
him, tho Ellen was. It was not even
personal disapproval. It was just a
profound and unshakable conviction
of dissimilarity: she accepted the
fact and reality[?] of his reactions
and his capability and even willingness[?] for harm as she would that
of a tornado; if you had told her at
any time prior to the day he left with
the regiment or the day he returned
or maybe even the day she agreed to
marry him that she would someday
do this, she would have looked at you
with the same cold and curious speculation as if you had told her that she
would be betrothed to the tornado.

"Now the period began which
ended with the happening which caused
the complete volte-face, not in her
character but in her actions. Her
character had ⟨did⟩ not change. If
Charles Bon had not died, she still
might would have gone out to live
with Judith after her father's death
and she might have even passed the
rest of her life there, as she doubtless believed she would when she
went out. But with Judith and Charles
married and Henry also in the house,
it would have been as the aunt which
she actually was: she would never
have agreed to marry him. Because
Despite the 4 years which she had
spent feeding her father secretly at
night while he hid from Confederate
provost marshals in the attic, and at

the same time writing her heroic
poetry about the very men who would
have shot or hung him if they had discovered him (and of whom the ogre of
her childhood made one, and—he brot
home a personal citation in Lee's
own hand—a good one), the face which
she carried out there when she went
to live with Judith and fulfill the
promise she made Ellen, was the
same one which had watched him
across the dinner table and which he
likewise could not have said later
how many times he had seen it or
when and could not have described it
probably 10 minutes after he ceased
looking at it, and from behind which
the child herself[?] had watched him
with that curious hushed and cold
intensity.

Page 29 [28]

1-29   'Not fear: apparently she had
never been afraid of him, tho Ellen
was.—neither during her childhood
nor during the time when she waited
for him to come home, apparently
having no doubt that he would return
and unscathed, nor[?] even at the very
moment when she ~~must have realized
with a sort of awed unbelief that she
was irrevocably promised to marry
him in order to fulfill Ellen's dying
request to marry him reached that
point which she must have believed
she had, when she must choose between saving Judith or saving herself,
must have believed, with a kind of
amazed incredulity, that she was
irrevocably promised to marry him.~~
reached whatever point it was that
she evidently believed she had, when
she must choose between saving
Judith, (the last of her own blood, ~~or
herself~~ let alone her promise to
Ellen) or herself and chose and then
realized, with a kind of amazed incredulity probably, that she was
actually and irrevocably promised to
him. It was not even personal dis-

approval; it was just an unshakable
conviction of dissimilarity: she
accepted the fact of his existence
and his capability and even willingness for harm as she would that of
a tornado; if you had told her at any
time prior to the day he left or the
day he returned or perhaps the day
she agreed to marry him even, that
she would someday do it, she would
have looked at you with the same
cold and curious speculation as if
you had told her that someday she
would be betrothed to the tornado.
Exclusive of the fact that he was
Judith's and Henry's father and her
sister's husband and still alien[?]
and hence still a source of unpredictable threat and danger, she simply
was absolutely indifferent to him.
She simply did not like him—how he
looked lived and what he did, whether
for pleasure or profit, or how he
looked or what he wore or what he
seemed to stand for, represent, and
what goal seemed to control his
ambition.

"She had never been afraid of him,
not even as a child, tho Ellen was//
not even as a child
    "Now she did not see her any-
more//she heard. "Now the period
began which ended with the happening
which caused the complete volte-face,
in not in her character but in her
actions. Her character did not change.
If Charles Bon had not died, she still
in all probability would have moved
out to live with Judith Sutpen's Hundred after her father's death and
would without doubt have passed the
rest of her life there, as she doubtless believed she would when she did
go out. But if Bon had lived and he
and Judith had married, she and
Henry remained in the known world,
she would have moved ⟨⟨if she had
moved⟩⟩ out there only when she was

ready to and she would have lived
in the house (if she) (if she had
lived) in the house as the aunt which
she actually was. It was only the
happening which sent her out there
and only it that caused or brot her
to agree to marry him

'Now the period began which
ended with the happening which caused
the complete volte/face that complete
volte/face 'Now the period began
which ended with the happening that
caused a reversal so complete in her
as to enable her

	MANUSCRIPT		BOOK
29	as a demon.	24	as an ogre.
30	change appreciably	25-26	change to any extent.
32-33	the rest of her life there, as she doubtless expected to when she did go out. But	29-30	the remainder of her life there. But

Page 68

36	character: despite the probably 6 years since	1-2	character that changed: despite the six years or so since
36-37	certainly the 4 years fil[?] during which she had spent secretly feeding	3	certainly the four years which she had spent feeding
38	attic and at	5	attic. At
39	him if	7-8	him without trial if
39-42	—(and incidentally of whom the ogre of her childhood made one, and—he brot home with him a personal citation in Lee's own hand—a good one)—the face which she carried out there when she moved out to live with Judith and fulfill the promise she made to Ellen the dying mother, was the same one which	8-12	—and incidentally the ogre of her childhood was one of them and (he brought home with him a citation for valor in Lee's own hand) a good one. The face which Miss Rosa carried out there to live for the rest of her life was the same face which
43	likewise probably could	13	likewise could
46	same curious ⟨grim⟩ and	19	same grim and

Page 30 [29]

1	"Tho she was not to see him again, she	20	Although she was not to see Sutpen again for years, she
5	which his wife, Nature, had signed her name. She was	29-30	which Fate's wife, Nature, had signed his name. Ellen was

6-8   marks ~~living had left on her~~ face
       being in the world had left on her
       face up to ⟨a⟩ the time the aunt had
       left them, had been removed, erad-
       icated at least, from between

9   annealing flesh.

11   meager limits which

16   nonsense, voluble, speaking

17   duchess moving with

18   and ~~unencumbered~~ uncompelled

19   stardom, might have even taken the
       role of the matriarch arbitrating

22   "Often

23   the ~~actual~~ world, [MARGIN: the woman
       who had ~~departed~~ quitted home and
       kin on a flood of tears and in a sha-
       dowy miasmic region something like
       the bitter purlieus of styx had pro-
       duced two children and then risen
       like the swamp-hatched ~~moth~~ butter-
       fly, unimpeded by weight of stomach,
       ~~into the perennial bright vacuum of~~
       ~~sun//the woman~~ and all the heavy
       organs of suffering and experience,
       into the perennial bright vacuum of
       sun—~~the~~] and the young

22-23 living, ~~with that~~ in that complete de-
       tachment from [MARGIN: and imper-
       viousness to] actuality

25   object of the aunt's

26   and not even the factual aunt.

27   the 2 of them was the most unreal
       to her in

30-31 time—in the summer when Judith was
       17—on their way overland to ⟨Mem-
       phis to⟩ buy Judith some clothes.
       That was the summer after Henry's
       first year in the

31-33 marks being in the world had left
       upon it up to the time the aunt
       vanished had been removed from
       between

Page 69

2-3   annealing and untroubled flesh.

7-8   meager possibilities which

18   nonsense, speaking

20   duchess peripatetic with

21   and uncompelled

23-24 stardom in the role of the matriarch,
       arbitrating

27   Often

29-33 the world—the woman who had
       quitted home and kin on a flood of
       tears and in a shadowy miasmic
       region something like the bitter
       purlieus of Styx had produced two
       children and then rose like the
       swamp-hatched butterfly, unimpeded

Page 70

1-3   by weight of stomach and all the
       heavy organs of suffering and exper-
       ience, into a perennial bright vacuum
       of arrested sun—and Judith, the young

3-4   living, in her complete detachment
       and imperviousness to actuality

7   object and victim of the vanished
       aunt's

9-10   and certainly not the factual aunt
       herself.

11-12 the two, sister or niece, was the most
       unreal to Miss Rosa in

17-20 time, in the summer when Judith was
       seventeen, stopping in on their way
       overland to Memphis to buy Judith
       clothes; yes: a trousseau.
            That was the summer following
       Henry's first year at the

MANUSCRIPT	BOOK
33-36 Orleans. It was the summer when Sutpen himself went away (on business, Ellen said, told; doubtless unaware—such was her existence then—that she did not know where her husband had gone and not even conscious that she was not curious, and no one but your grandfather ever to know (or perhaps Clytie) ever to know that he had gone to New Orleans too). They would enter the ⟨that⟩ dim grim tight house where even yet, after 4 years, the aunt still seemed to be just outside any door and with	24-33 Orleans; the summer in which Sutpen himself went away, on business, Ellen said, doubtless unaware, such was her existence then, that she did not know where her husband had gone and not even conscious that she was not curious. No one but your grandfather and perhaps Clytie was ever to know that Sutpen had gone to New Orleans too. They would enter Miss Rosa's house, that dim grim tight little house where even yet, four years after she had left the aunt still seemed to be just beyond any door with

Page 71

39-40 sister and who in actual experience and hope and opportunity should herself have been the niece, ignoring the mother and to	5 sister ignoring the mother to
41 yearning, projecting	7 yearning and not one whit of jealousy, projecting
42 and abortive youth,	9 and frustrated youth,
42-43 gift (and it of necessity offered to the bride's equipment and not to the bride:—it was Ellen who told this, with shrieks of merriment[?], more than once)	9-11 gift (it was Ellen who told this, with shrieks of amusement, more than once)
44 laundry, and received for	12 laundry, receiving for

Page 31 [30]

2 impenetrable bemusement; when	16-17 impenetrable dreaming. When
4 "That	20 That
4-5 home at Xmas, with his	21-22 home Christmas with Charles Bon, his
5-6 heard of the balls and parties out at Sutpen's Hundred but	23-24 heard about the balls and parties at Sutpen's Hundred during the holidays, but
10 as Sutpen now and	33 as his father and

Page 72

| 12 to bear the actual pomposity. | 3 to support the pomposity. |
| 14 [14-28 PASTED IN: in the county now, which state he had attained in the by | 5-6 in the county now, attained by |

CHAPTER III

MANUSCRIPT   BOOK

16   the indicated ones which they   9-10   the ones which the town could not
      naturally[?] could not, must seem   see must appear to it. There
      to them. That is, there

18   actual violent and dark   13   actual dark

19   and somehow get more for his   15-16 and so get more per bale for his
      cotton per bale than   cotton than

20   who apparently believed that   16-17 who believed apparently that

23   He did that—   24   He accomplished this—

25   within the first 10 years after his   27   within ten years of the wedding,
      wedding,

26-27 put a little flesh   29   put flesh

28   his was a forced peak too and that   31-33 his flowering was a forced blooming
      while he was still playing the scene   too and that while he was still playing
      to the audience, behind]   the scene to the audience, behind

                                             Page 73

31   seen him, standing   5   seen Henry. She was standing

32   hardly coming to mother's shoulder,   6-7   hardly reaching your grandmother's
                                                    shoulder,

33   which she [MARGIN: she had cut down   8-9   which Miss Rosa had cut down to fit
      to fit herself,] who   herself, who

33-34 she assumed the housekeeping who   9-10   she had assumed the housekeeping
      had never been taught to cook and   and

34-35 cook; nor taught to do anything out of 11-12 cook nor taught to do anything save
      save hide behind doors listen thru   listen through closed doors,
      closed doors—

36   been 40 years old instead   13-14 been fifty instead

39   seeing even Ellen: that   16   seeing Ellen even. That

Page 32 [31]
1   furniture, and the food and how pre-   31-32 furniture and how the food was pre-
      pared and even the hours at which   pared and even the hours at which
      eaten.   it was eaten.

1-2   now came (it was 1859; even Mr   32-33 now approached (it was 1860, even
      Coldfield probably admitted that there   Mr Coldfield probably ad-
      would be war)   *Page 74*
                                             1   mitted that war was unavoidable)

4   rising, almost indescribably ⟨imper-   4   rising almost imperceptibly
      ceptibly⟩ and

5-6   and that the 4 peaceful swimmers had   7-8   and the four peaceful swimmers
      turned suddenly around to face   turning suddenly to face

98

C H A P T E R I I I

MANUSCRIPT	BOOK
6-7 set; none of them at that point yet where	9-10 set, none of them yet at that point where
9-10 see) Charles Bon at all. ~~It was only thru Ellen alone~~—Charles Bon, of	15-16 see alive) Charles Bon at all; Charles Bon of
12 that ~~cosmo~~⟨metro⟩politan and	20-21 that worldly and
13 a certain worldly	22 a worldly
13-14 assurance, [MARGIN: handsome,] apparently	22-23 assurance beyond his years, handsome, apparently
14 than parents—a man	24-28 than any parents—a personage who in the remote Mississippi of that time must have appeared almost phoenix-like, fullsprung from no childhood, born of no woman and impervious to time and, vanished, leaving no bones nor dust anywhere—a man
16 was a little crude, and Henry actually a hobble-de-hoy. This was the picture, the image.	30-32 was clumsy bluff and Henry actually a hobble-de-hoy. Miss Rosa never saw him; this was a picture, an image.

Page 75

MANUSCRIPT	BOOK
19 which women who	4 which mothers who
22-23 it. It was just a finished and perfectly closed subject	11-12 it. Love, with reference to them was just a finished and perfectly dead subject
23 be ~~to your~~ a child [*sic*] was born.	13 be after the birth of the first grandchild.
24-25 one or perhaps one inanimate object for which she and her family would find 3 concordant uses for—a	14-16 one, or perhaps one inanimate object for which she and her family would find three concordant uses: a
26 and make complete the household; and	18-19 and complete the furnishing of her house and position, and
28 postulated 10 elapsed	22 postulated the elapsed
29 looked now with a kind of	24 looked with a sort of
30 and sense, the	26-27 and experience, the
32 postured.—This,	29-30 postured and laughed and wept. This,
33 at 16; sat beneath	32-33 at sixteen, sitting beneath

Page 76

MANUSCRIPT	BOOK
36-40 Judith. Ellen told this, too. 'Rosa always was a sentimental fool,' she said, told your grandmother. No. She was not jealous. It was not self-	4-12 Judith. It was not selfpity either, sitting there blinking steadily at her sister, while Ellen talked, in one of those botched-over house dresses

99

	MANUSCRIPT		BOOK
	pity, either, sitting there in one of those botched-over house dresses (the clothes which Ellen gave her were always silk, of course) which the aunt had abandoned when she eloped with the horse-trader, perhaps in the hope or even intention of never wearing such again, blinking steadily at her sister while Ellen talked. It		(the clothes, castoff sometimes but usually new, which Ellen gave her from time to time were always silk, of course) which the aunt had abandoned when she eloped with the horse-and-mule-trader, perhaps in the hope or even the firm intention of never wearing anything like them again. It
41-43	It ~~sounded like a fairy tale even when Ellen told it to your~~ sounded like a fairy tale when Ellen told it to your grandmother, but like a	15-16	It sounded like a fairy tale when Ellen told it later to your grandmother, only it was a
43	fashionable women's club.	17	fashionable ladies' club.
45-46	amused tho fretted astonishment. 'We deserve him,' Miss Rosa said. 'Deserve? Him?' Ellen said, probably shrieked too. 'Of	20-22	amused and fretted astonishment. "We deserve him," Miss Rosa said. "Deserve? Him?" Ellen said, probably shrieked too. "Of

Page 33 [32]

3	this; at	27	this. At
4-5	She had two now, another one bequeathed likewise to	30-31	She possessed two now, this one likewise bequeathed to
5	her to keep house by climbing out a window ~~at~~ ⟨one⟩ night,	32-33	her both to keep house and how to fit clothes by climbing out a window one night,

Page 77

7	the clothes even by cutting them down.	3-4	the discarded clothing even by cutting the garments down.
9	[9-27 PASTED IN: clothes from her father's store, she	5	cloth from her father's store. She
9	else; your	6	else. Your
10	Rosa could actually not count change, money;	7-8	Rosa actually could not count money,
12-13	shop from store to store for the things which Mr. Coldfield did not carry in his store, with no coin or mention[?] of	11-13	shop at certain stores which Mr Coldfield had already designated, with no coin nor sum of
15-21	him. And as he had brot his entire business to Jefferson in one wagon, and that at a time when he had a mother, sister, wife and child to support out of it, ~~and~~ as against now	17-19	him, though his stock which had begun as a collection of the crudest necessities and which apparently could not even feed himself and his daughter from its own shelves, had

when he had only one child to support
out of it, and weighed along with this
that profound disinterest in material
accumulation which had permitted
conscience to cause him to withdraw
from that old affair in which his
future son-in-law had involved him
not only at the cost of his just profits
but at the sacrifice of his original
investment, his stock had~not~and
business~had~not~increased.~which
had started out as a collection of
the crudest necessities (a stock
which apparently could not even feed
him and his daughter unassisted from
its own shelves) had

23	make the a young girl's intimate garments which were for	21-22	make those intimate young girl garments which were to be for
24-27	unassisted. Nor does anyone know how she got it from her father. By that time the matter was no secret; Ellen had covered[?] the town well. But Mr Coldfield knew Ellen too. And even if the wedding had been settled, I am not so sure that he would	25-27	unassisted. Nobody knows how she managed to get the material from her father's store. He didn't give it to her. He would
27-28	to furnish his granddaughter with clothes, unless she was ragged or cold] or (more likely) indecently clad. So	28-30	to supply his granddaughter with clothes if she were indecently clad or if she were ragged or cold, but not to marry in. So
29-31	store; he was owner[?] clerk porter[?] and all; from any point in it, your grandfather said, he could oversee every other) perhaps with amoral boldness, that instinctive affinity for brigandage, of women, but more likely (or so I like to think) by	32-33	store and he was his own clerk and from any point in it he could see any other point) with that amoral

		Page 78	
		1-2	boldness, that affinity for brigandage in women, but more likely, or so I would like to think, by
31-33	bald and~transparent~innocence ⟨and desperate⟩ transparence concocted by innocence desperation that its very simplicity fooled him. "She	3-5	bald and desperate transparence concocted by innocence that its very simplicity fooled him. So she
33	see them anymore, not even Ellen. Apparently Ellen too had served	5-6	see Ellen anymore. Apparently Ellen had now served

MANUSCRIPT		BOOK	
35	but that one time more [MARGIN: dying in bed in] in bed in	9	but the one time more dying in bed in
35-36	in a house which fateful mischance had already laid its hand on to	10-11	in the house on which fateful mischance had already laid its hand to
36-37	been built and removing the husband into the risk and chance of war and removing the son its	12-13	been erected and removing its
37-38	the danger of	13-14	the risk and danger of
38-39	heard that too when[?] she spent her days (and nights) in the grim little house, sewing	15-17	heard of that too while she was spending her days (and nights; she would have to wait until her father was asleep) sewing
41	raveled string and sewing	21-22	raveled and hoarded string and thread and sewing
41-43	garments while the nation was one half of the nation flung a gauntlet in the face of the other half by the election of a president and the other half flung it back by firing cannon at a United States flag. Henry	22-27	garments while news came of Lincoln's election and of the fall of Sumpter, [sic] and she scarce listening, hearing and losing the knell and doom of her native land between two tedious and clumsy stitches on a garment which she would never wear and never remove for a man whom she was not even to see alive. Henry
44	and the friend came again to pass the holidays, the wealthy handsome	29-30	and Bon came home again to spend the holidays, the handsome
45-46	now; they	32	now. They
Page 34 [33]		*Page 79*	
3-4	to leave until	7	to quit until
7-8	roof he had been born under and that he and the friend had	14-15	roof under which he had been born and that he and Bon had
9	life—and then[?] this was the	18	life: this the

10-12	the throat is slit, though Ellen of course did not know that either. But we (Jefferson) just took Henry's behavior to be the fiery nature of youth
	    "That's
		18-20	the beast's throat is cut.
			    That's

13	Judith's attitude toward	23-24	Judith's behavior toward
14-17	this, since they would be seen in the carriage together in town now and then, when from their behavior nothing had occurred between them,	25-32	this. They would be seen together in the carriage in town now and then as though nothing had occurred between them at least, which certainly would

	MANUSCRIPT		BOOK
	anyway, which certainly would not have been the case if the fiance had been involved and probably not if it were only Henry, since the town knew that between Judith and her brother there had been a relation- ship closer even than the habitual loyalty of brother and sister—a		not have been the case if the quarrel had been between Bon and the father, and probably not the case if the trouble had been between Henry and his father because the town knew that between Henry and Judith there had been a relationship closer than the traditional loyalty of brother and sister even; a

Page 80

	MANUSCRIPT		BOOK
19	eat the same food and	1-2	eat from the same dish and
21-23	all she knew about it, too. She would not have known any more than the town knew, because the ones who knew (Sutpen or Judith: Ellen would not have known either, been told probably or remembered, assimilated it, if she had—Ellen, the	5-10	all Miss Rosa knew. She could have known no more about it than the town knew because the ones who did know (Sutpen or Judith: not Ellen, who would have been told nothing in the first place and would have forgot, failed to assimilate, it if she had been told—Ellen the
25	but just filled	14	but merely filled
27-28	more, and doubtless she did not ask, not even Judith, perhaps knowing that she would not be told, or perhaps because she was just waiting. And she	17-18	more. And she
29	to make the garments of Judith's trousseau; she	20-21	to sew on the garments for Judith's wedding. She
31-36	raising a regiment; she did not see the uniforms, because her father forbade her; she did not even see the regiment when it departed. Sutpen (he was second in command) riding at Colonel Sartoris' left hand, on the black stallion named out of Scott, be- neath the regimental colors which he and Sartoris had designed and which Sartoris' wife and womenfolk had sewn together from their silk dresses. she was still waiting[?] apparently[?] and sewing on the garments when the regiment departed in '61 [MARGIN: the regiment departed in '61, with Sutpen (he was second in command) riding at Colonel Sartoris' right hand, on the black stallion named out of Scott,	23-28	raising the regiment which departed in '61, with Sutpen, second in com- mand, riding at Colonel Sartoris' left hand, on the black stallion named out of Scott, beneath the regimental colors which he and Sartoris had designed and which Sartoris' women- folks had sewed together out of silk dresses.

CHAPTER III

MANUSCRIPT   BOOK

beneath the regimental colors which
he and Sartoris had designed and
Sartoris' womenfolks had sewed
together out of silk dresses.] ~~with
no word yet from Henry (Sutpen with
Sutpen (he was second in command
of it.~~ He had

37-38 [37-45 PASTED IN: physically from   29-31 physically from what he had been
      what he had been not only when he   not only when he first rode into
      first rode into Jefferson that Sunday   Jefferson that Sunday in '33, but
      in '33, but from what he had been   from what he had been when he and
      when he and Ellen Coldfield married   Ellen married. He was not portly
      (of which time even the kilncolored[?]
      look was gone from his face). He was
      not ~~portly yet~~ portly

                                      Page 81

45   and, earthward bound,   11   and, earthbound,

45-46 lifeless,] ~~by the envelope which it~~   12-14 lifeless, by the envelope which it
      ~~had betrayed) riding at Colonel~~   had betrayed.
      ~~Sartoris' left hand, on the black~~   She
      ~~stallion named out~~
Page 35 [3~~5~~ 34] [At top of page: ~~IV~~]
      by the envelope which it had betrayed.
        "She

3   of send-off, tho not   17   of its departure, though not

5-7   [5-25 PASTED IN: an irascible man   19-22 an irascible man and before war was
      and before war was actually declared   actually declared and Mississippi
      and Mississippi seceded, his acts and   seceded, his acts and speeches of
      speeches of protest had been not only   protest had been not only calm but
      calm but logical and quite sensible.   logical and quite sensible. But after
      But after the die was cast he seemed   the die was cast he seemed to change
      to change his character overnight   overnight, just
      just

7-8   to be mobilized in Jefferson, he   24   to appear in Jefferson he closed his
      closed his store. and   store and

8-9   period while troops were being   25-27 period that soldiers were being
      organized and drilled, and even when   mobilized and drilled, and later,
      casual passing troops would bivouac   after the regiment was gone, when-
      for the night nearby, refusing   ever casual troops would bivouac for
                                        the night in passing, refusing

10   price not only to military commis-   28-29 price to the military and, so
      sariats but, so

11-13 Not only did he refuse to permit his   31   He refused to permit his sister to
      sister (the aunt: 4 or 5 years before   come

104

CHAPTER III

MANUSCRIPT		BOOK	
	she had eloped with an itinerant ~~mule~~ stocktrader) to come		
13	her husband was in the army, but he	32-33	her horse-trader husband was in the army, he
		Page 82	
14	passing troops.	1	passing soldiers.
14-15	store and was at home ~~most of the~~ all the time now, tho he was not yet to shut himself into the attic. ~~where~~ He	1-2	store permanently and was at home all day now. He
16-17	front blinds closed and fastened, where, so the neighbors said, he spent the day ~~armed~~ behind	4-5	front shutters closed and fastened. He spent the day, the neighbors said, behind
17-18	a ~~sentry and~~ ⟨picket⟩ armed ~~like~~ not	6	a picquet on post, armed not
18-20	bible in which ~~his birth and marriage and Ellen's birth and marriage and the b~~ and his sister's birth and his marriage and Ellen's birth and marriage and the birth of her two children and of Miss Rosa, and Mrs Coldfield's death	7-9	Bible in which his and his sister's birth and his marriage and Ellen's birth and marriage and the birth of his two grandchildren and of Miss Rosa, and his wife's death
22	Coldfield's and Charles Bon's tho there had been no marriage, and	12	Coldfield's own, and Charles Bon's and
25-26	as he would have placed a row of cartridges] on the	17-19	as the actual picquet would have ranged his row of cartridges along the
31-32	[31-47 PASTED IN: with a small stock of goods and supporting five people out of it in comfort and security at least. He did it by close trading to	27-29	with a small stock of goods and supporting five people out of it in comfort and security at least. He did it by close trading, to
32	it except by	29-30	it save by
32-33	as Quentin's grandfather once said, of him, a man	30-31	as your grandfather said, a man
34	and thimbles would already have been locked	33	and salt meat would have been already locked
		Page 83	
35-36	as General Compson said,	2-3	as your grandfather said,
38-39	night of the looting of the store, they had lived out of it.	8-9	night when it was looted, they had lived out of the store.
43-44	became poorer and poorer in quality and harder and harder to get, and	16-17	became harder and harder to come by and poorer and poorer in quality, and

105

MANUSCRIPT		BOOK	
44	rope fastened to	18-19	rope attached to
45	scarcely enough for	21	scarcely sufficient for
46	And ~~the~~ she may not have known before ~~th~~ that	21-22	And she may not have known before that
47	odes celebrating Southern	24	odes to Southern
47-48	which ~~by~~ ⟨in⟩ 1885] when your grand-father saw it contained	24-25	which when your grandfather saw it in 1885 contained
48	year and at 2:00 a.m.	26-27	year of her father's voluntary in-carceration and dated at two oclock in the morning.

Page 36 [~~36~~ 35]

1	[1-5 PASTED IN: Then he died; one [Opening quotes omitted]	28	Then he died. One
1	draw the rope, the basket, into the window.	29	draw up the basket.
3	cause, with 3 days' uneaten food beside ~~him~~ his	32-33	cause, even if he had repudiated it and them, with three days' uneaten food beside his
4-5	as tho he had spent the three days in a mental balancing of his terrestrial accounts, found the result and proved it and then turned upon his contem-porary scene of folly and outrage and injustice the dead and consistent]	33 *Page 84* 1-4	as if he had spent the three days in a mental balancing of his terrestrial accounts, found the result and proved it and then turned upon his contem-porary scene of folly and outrage and injustice the dead and consistent
6-12	disapproval. [7-26 PASTED IN: She was not only an orphan, but a pauper too. The father had kept the store closed almost con-stantly for 5 months before he mounted to his mausoleum as it were, ⟨and⟩ with the hammer and the hand-ful of nails ~~and~~ nailed the door behind him and threw the hammer out the window. And since he had refused to sell to soldiers or ~~even~~ the fami-lies of any[?] sympathizers, he had lost what business he had had, which to begin with he had built up from a single wagonload of goods and out of which he had supported not only his own family but his mother and sister too. So he had not renewed his stock	5-11	disapproval. Now Miss Rosa was not only an orphan, but a pauper too. The store was just a shell, the deserted building vacated even by rats and containing nothing, not even goodwill since he had irrevocably estranged himself from neighbors, town, and embattled land, all three by his behavior. Even the two negresses were gone now—whom he had freed

MANUSCRIPT		BOOK	

in a long time, and since then he and
his daughter had eaten that up. Even
the two negresses ~~which he had come
to own~~ he had freed

15-16	full until the current market value at which he had assumed them should be discharged—	14-15	full against the discharge of their current market value—
17	the Federal troops away. So ~~now he had~~ when he died he ~~not only~~ had	17	the Yankee troops. So when he died, he had
19-20	son-in-law; ~~but in the moral~~ [illegible word] ~~the money's moral quality as a the money's moral representation sav~~—not	21	son-in-law—not
22-23	business was not ~~the fact of what use~~[?] ~~and pleasure~~ loss	25	business with Sutpen was not the loss
24	and self denial, to	27	and abnegation, to
25	already gained and	28-29	already established and
25-26	as tho he had had to pay the same note twice because of some trifling oversight of date or signature.]	29-30	as if he had had to pay the same note twice because of some trifling oversight of date or signature.
27	"Both orphan and pauper, with	32	So Miss Rosa was both pauper and orphan, with
27	dust save Judith,	33	dust but Judith

Page 85

31-32	[31-46 PASTED IN: a gale and blown against a wall and clinging there feebly beating, not with life or any particular stubborn clinging ⟨to⟩ to it, not in pa particular pain [MARGIN: since it was too light to have struck hard] nor	5-8	a gale and blown against a wall and clinging there beating feebly, not with any particular stubborn clinging to life, not in particular pain since it was too light to have struck hard, nor
33-35	even to any great extent changed despite the year of bad (or even no) food, since all of Sutpen's negroes deserted with the first Yankee troops to pass thru Jefferson. (The wild blood Mr Compson said, which	11-14	even changed to any great extent despite the year of bad food, since all of Sutpen's negroes had deserted also to follow the Yankee troops away; the wild blood which
37	own, and	17	own. And
39	acquired not from the people who breathe or have breathed in them so much but rather inherent	20-22	acquired, not so much from the people who breathe or have breathed in them inherent

CHAPTER III

MANUSCRIPT   BOOK

41   them—an incontrovertible affirmation   24-25   them—in this house an incontrovert-
     of emptiness even if not actual   ible affirmation for emptiness,
     desertion: an   desertion; an

42-43   strong)—~~but a pauper. The father had~~   27   strong. Ellen had
     ~~kept his store closed almost con-~~
     ~~stantly~~ She had

46   her hair), the same almost plump   33-34   her hair evidently for years), the
     soft (tho]   same almost plump soft (though

Page 37 [34 36]
1   [1-5 PASTED IN: now unringed) hands   34   now unringed) hands on the coverlet,
     on the coverlet, and only the baffle-   and only the
     ment of the   *Page 86*
                                           1   bafflement in the

2   the 18 year old sister (Henry   3-4   the seventeen-year-old sister to
                                            protect the remaining child. (Henry

3-4   not returned yet to kill Charles Bon   5-7   not yet returned to play his final
     on the doorstep—this, Mr Compson   part in his family's doom—and this,
     said, spared Ellen, not   your grandfather said, spared Ellen
                                                  too, not

5-7   alive, could not have felt any more of   9-11   alive, would have been incapable now
     wind or violence)] and ask to protect   of feeling anymore of wind or vio-
     the remaining child.   lence.) So
        ~~"But she didn't go out to live with~~
     ~~Judith then~~ "So

17-22   from that old blood which battled   30-34   from the old blood that crossed
     whatever uncharted seas of wilder-   uncharted seas and continents and
     ness hardships and lurking circum-   battled wilderness hardships and
     stances and fatalities with tranquil   lurking circumstances and fatalities.
     disregard of whatever onerous[?]   That's what she would have
     costs ~~and~~ to leisure and even peace
     which the precursor[?] of it incurs
     upon what might be called the con-
     temporary[?] transmutable fountain
     head who contrives to keep the now[?]
     foodheavy corpuscles sufficiently
     numerous and ~~active~~ healthy in the
     stream.
        "That's what she should have

                                           Page 87
22-23   did not. Tho Judith was an orphan   1   didn't. Yet Judith still had those
     too, yet Judith at least had those

23-24   and let alone Wash Jones, who still   2-4   and Wash Jones to feed her as Wash
     fed Judith as he had fed Ellen before   had fed Ellen before she died. But
     she died. But she didn't go there to   Miss Rosa didn't go out there at
     live.   once.

CHAPTER III

MANUSCRIPT

BOOK

	MANUSCRIPT		BOOK
25	have; tho Ellen	5	have gone. Although Ellen
26-27	even vicarious[?] love had supplied her with (that of Judith and Bon, the one whom she hardly knew and the other whom she had not even seen) could	7	even deferred love could
27-28	with will to exist, endure, this long, then the actual love must have made Bon impervious even to death. So, tho she must	8-13	with the will to exist, endure for this long, then that same love, even though deferred, must and would preserve Bon until the folly of men would stalemate from sheer exhaustion and he would return from wherever he was and bring Henry with him—Henry, victim too of the same folly and mischance. She must
28-30	and perhaps ev[?] Judith even suggested that she come out there and live, perhaps[?] this is the reason why she never mentioned Bon and so Henry, and why Judith never told her. Because [MARGIN: Because Judith knew. She may have known for sometime; even Ellen may have known, only probably ⟨to⟩ Ellen at that time absence was not a qualitative state, that absence into ignominy and or into oblivion were the same thing and so it it[sic] may not have occurred to her to tell her sister; that to another the uncertainty of days and the certainty of oblivion might be two things. Or perhaps Judith had not told Ellen either. Perhaps Clytie did not know herself until after Ellen died, that Henry and Bon were now privates in the company which their classmates in the University had organized. But Miss Rosa didn't know it at all.][1] The first word she had in 4 long[?] years	14-23	and Judith probably urged her to come out to Sutpen's Hundred to live, but I believe that this is the reason she did not go, even though she did not know where Bon and Henry were and Judith apparently never thought to tell her. Because Judith knew. She may have known for some time; even Ellen may have known. Or perhaps Judith never told her mother either. Perhaps Ellen did not know before she died that Henry and Bon were now privates in the company which their classmates at the University had organized. The first intimation Miss Rosa had had in four years
31	Jones stopped	24-25	Jones, riding Sutpen's remaining mule, stopped
31	shout.	26	shout her name.
32	man with	27-28	man malaria-ridden with

[1] Faulkner inserted a question mark beside this addition.

CHAPTER III

MANUSCRIPT

BOOK

33-34 and 65 (he was actually several years younger than Sutpen, even tho he was a grandfather), sitting on a saddle-less

29-30 and sixty, sitting on the saddleless

35-36 door. 'You Rosie Coldfield?' he said. Yes, she told him. 'Then you better come on out yon. Henry has done shot that durn French fellow. Kilt him dead as a beef.'

31-33 door; whereupon he lowered his voice somewhat, though not much. "Air you Rosie Coldfield?" he said.

110

CHAPTER IV

Page 38 [37]	*Page 88*
7-8 would ~~have~~ [MARGIN: be wearing already] a black	13-14 would be wearing already the black
9-10 keys, door closet and cupboard, ~~which~~ ⟨that⟩ the	17 keys, entrance closet and cupboard, that the
11 weather since	20-21 weather and season since
13-14 meeting in the entire 45 years	24-25 meeting, in the entire forty-three years
	Page 89
16-19 fireflies [MARGIN:—a fuller and more prolonged random in the twilight following 60 days without rain and 42 without even dew—] below the veranda where he ~~and Mr Compson~~ sat. ⟨stood up⟩ [MARGIN: rose from his chair] as Mr Compson ⟨carrying the letter,⟩ emerged from the house, snapped on the porch light, ~~the single globe stained and bugfouled from the long summer and which even when clean gave off but little light.~~ "You	4-7 fireflies below the gallery, where he rose from his chair as Mr Compson, carrying the letter, emerged from the house, snapping on the porch light as he passed. "You
21 "Perhaps even	10 "Maybe even
23-24 light—"which man ~~invented~~ had to invent to his need since, relieved of the onus[?] of sweating[?] to live, he is apparently reverting (or evolving) back into a nocturnal animal, would	13 light—"would
27 once or murdering[?] once or dying	20 once or dying
29 and divorces.	23 and divorcements.
33-44 linen clad leg. "Yes, Judith knew where they were. She probably knew as soon as they knew themselves where they were going to be. She knew from Bon certainly and maybe even from Henry. Or maybe it was the other way around and it was Henry who wrote her, sent her word that they were all right; Henry holding all 3 of them in that durance, that probation, ~~since~~ ⟨that	31-32 linen leg. "Because Henry loved Bon. He repudiated

111

tho) it was he who had repudiated his
father and cast his lot with Bon, ~~even
tho he~~ he may have (even must have)
believed what his father told him
even tho he told Sutpen to his face
that he lied. Yes, it was Henry's
probation, the 4 years of it. And
Judith acquiesced, for a time. That
must have been understood between
them, between her and Henry, perhaps between the 3 of them, Judith
and Henry and Bon himself, because
Judith would not have obeyed a mere
injunction of her father's and Sutpen
probably knew this. But she would
(and did) obey Henry up to that certain
point, not because he was the man of
the two, the male relation, more than
just brother, but because as I told
you there was more between them
than just the squabbling and mutually
impatient and even contemptuous
antagonistic loyalty of brother and
sister; and they both knew that she

Page 39 [38]

1-5   "Because Henry loved Bon, ~~enough
to repudiate blood-birthright and
material security for Bon, for the
sake of the man who, according to
Henry's father, was a blackguard, a
bigamist if Henry's father was correct, was a scoundrel. He loved him
enough to sacrifice blood birthright
and material security for him. He
loved him enough to sacrifice repudiate blood birthright and material
security for him. If you cannot believe that, then the whole thing~~ He
repudiated

                                   Page 90

5-6   man ~~whom Henry's father considered~~   1   man who was at least an intending
who, according to Sutpen, was at   bigamist
least a practicing bigamist

7   was actually to   3   was to

9   have known that   5-6   have realized that

9-11   it, ~~severed voluntarily severed him-
self voluntarily from~~ himself, struck   7-9   it, Henry himself striking the blow
the blow with his own hand. Yet he   with his own hand, even though he
                                              must have known that what

CHAPTER IV

MANUSCRIPT   BOOK

must have known that it was true
what

11-12 child and the man whom he had come   10   child was true. He must
       to love was true. It is as tho h Henry
       must

13   time that Xmas eve and repeated   11-12 time behind himself that Christmas
                                                    eve and must have repeated

18-22 truth, not what his father had told   21   truth? But who
       him, what he had denied and refused
           "Because to believe that Sutpen did
       not tell him that night is simply in-
       credible. Even granting that that is
       not reason enough for Henry to have
       repudiated his father, even granted
       that that is drawing[?] things[?] a
       little too what else [sic] could Sutpen
       have told him, what other reason for
       his refusal to permit the marriage.
       to accept even tho, despite himself,
       he must actually have believed? But
       who

22-43 clings to and nurses[?] above all   22-23 clings, above all the other well
       other well members, the arm ⟨or leg⟩   members, to the arm or leg which he
       which he knows must come off?   knows must come off? Because
           "Because he loved Bon: that was
       why the probation, the 4 years. I can
       imagine him and Sutpen in the library
       that Xmas eve, father and brother,
       percussion and repercussion like a
       thunderclap and its echo, the state-
       ment and the giving of the lie, the
       decision instantaneous between father
       and friend even tho at the instant of
       giving the lie he knew that it was the
       truth. and that someday he would have
       to admit it: Yes, the probation was at
       Henry's instigation and the other two—
       Judith and Bon—accepting it. There
       could have been no explanation among
       them, even if there had been time
       that night, which there was not, since
       I believe that Miss Rosa was correct
       and Judith never saw them again until
       that p.m. 4 years later when they
       carried Bon into the house and she
       found the photograph in his pocket
       that was not her face nor her child.
       And he would no more have told Bon

113

what Sutpen had said than he would
have asked Bon to deny it, maybe
because, he knew that it was true and
so no matter what Bon answered even
if it had been false, he could not now
go back to his father and tell him that
he knew that, if Bon denied it, it would
be a lie. So there could have been no
explanation among them and apparently
none was necessary, since even Judith
apparently acquiesced for a time, as
tho it were mutually understood without words between Henry and Judith
that there must be an armistice
probably must be. It must have been
like that. I know that she never knew
about the other woman until she found
the picture and Bon was already dead,
and besides, she would have refused
to obey a mere injunction of her
father's as Henry was to deny him.
Yet she did obey Henry up to that
point—not the male relation, the
brother, but because of that curious
relationship which was so much more
than the squabbling and mutually impatient antagonistic loyalty and even
contemptuous loyalty of brother and
sister and they both knew that she
would obey him, give him the benefit
of the interval, only up to that mutually
recognized tho unstated point and both
knew doubtless that when that point
was reached
            "Because

Page 40 [39]

3	instantaneous between	27-28	instantaneous and irrevocable between
5	vain, from that very Xmas eve,	33	vain, even then, on that Christmas eve,

Page 91

6-7	then; he must have known that Bon, who had not changed up until then, would not change later, and	2-4	then, who had not changed until then and so would in all probability not change later; and
9	youth hardly 20,	6-7	youth scarcely twenty,
10	away from the house that	9	away that

MANUSCRIPT

BOOK

11   was the truth ~~that someday he would have to~~ ⟨that he was doomed to⟩ kill.

10-11   was true, that he was doomed and destined to kill.

14-23   the ~~injured~~ ⟨dear suffering⟩ arm or leg is ~~well~~ ⟨strong⟩ and sound and only the well ~~ones are~~ ⟨ones⟩ sick.

16-18   the dear suffering arm or leg is strong and sound and only the well ones sick.

"It

"It was Henry's probation. He established it and then—the 3 of them—accepted it. There could have been no explanation, even if there had been time, that Xmas eve; I believe Miss Rosa was right and Judith never saw either of them again until that p.m. 4 years later when they carried Bon dead into the house and she found the photograph in his pocket that was not her face and not her child. And he would no more have told Bon what his father had told him than he would have ~~asked Bon to deny it because he knew even then that, if Bon denied it, it would be a lie~~ returned to his father and told him that Bon denied it, since to do the one he would have to do the other and he knew that Bon's denial would be a lie, and tho he could have borne Bon's lie himself he could not have borne to have ⟨either⟩ his father ~~bear it~~ or Judith bear it.

"~~It was Henry's probation, Henry holding the 3 of them in that durance~~
"It

24   happened.

20-21   happened in the library that night.

25   ever did, not until that p.m. ⟨4 years later⟩ when

21-22   ever suspected, until that afternoon four years later when

27   note, left, the

26   note, remaining, the

27-28   to let Bon write—

27   to allow Bon to write—

31   them ~~closer than~~—that personality

33   them—that single personality

Page 92

32   would obey him, give him the

3-4   would observe the probation, give him (Henry) the

33   tho unspoken point

5-6   though unstated and undefined point

35   requiring or needing or even

9-10   requiring or even

36   Bon came there to support

10   Bon be present to support

115

CHAPTER IV

BOOK

37   man ~~would~~ first before consenting to   12-13   man first, before consenting to revert
          ~~beeome~~ revert to the woman, the   to the woman, the loved, the bride.
          bride.

37-38   Bon: ~~Henry would have needed to~~   14   Bon: Henry would have no more told
          ~~tell him~~ Henry would no more have
          told

39   him (than   15   him than

41-42   borne to have either Judith or Sutpen   19-21   borne for either Judith or his father
          hear it): Henry would not have needed   to hear it. Besides, Henry would not
          to tell him what his father said. Bon   need to tell Bon what had happened.
          must have ~~known~~, learned   "Bon must have learned

Page 41 [~~38-39/a~~ 40]

1-17   \ So Henry gave his father the lie,
          repudiated blood birthright and ma-
          terial security for the sake of the man
          who, according to his father, was a
          blackguard. Because he loved Bon, \
          so much so that he could give his
          father the lie on a statement which \
          he must have known that Sutpen could
          not and would not have made without
          foundation and proof. It's as tho
          Henry said to him, must have said \
          when he closed the library door be- \
          hind him that Xmas eve and repeated
          while he and Bon rode side by side \
          thru the iron darkness of that Xmas \
          a.m. away from the house where
          Henry had been born and would never \
          see but one time again, and that with
          the fresh blood of the man who now \
          rode beside him on his hands: *I will*
          believe; I will. I will. Even if it is \
          so, even if what father says is true
          and what, in spite of myself I cannot
          keep from knowing is true, I will still
          believe. Because what could he have
          hoped to find in New Orleans, if not \
          the truth, not what Sutpen had found
          out and what he himself had denied \
          and refused to accept? But who knows
          why a man, tho suffering, clings to \
          and nurses[?] the arm or the leg \
          which he knows must come off? \

          "Because they went straight there,
          to New Orleans; they reached the \
          River the next day and got the steam-

116

CHAPTER IV

MANUSCRIPT   BOOK

boat. Henry didn't have to go. 'Tho
he was now homeless, granted that
his pride would not let him return to
the house which he had just repudiated, he could have gone to his grandfather's. Henry's life would have
been almost unbearable there, but he
could have gone: and that more concomitant with pride than the [illegible
word] and ever changing[?] of a man
whose equal he had been and until 24
hours ago, who was no kin to him.
Instead of that, he went to New
Orleans

[17-22 PASTED IN: if Bon ever looked   23-24   if Bon, until he saw
on the matter as cause for secrecy
until he saw

19   were also involved   27-28   were likewise involved

21   organization to which he belonged had   30-31   organization which he had

22   his future bride's family reacted to   32-33   his intended bride's family reacted to
      the discovery of it was doubtless the   the discovery of it was doubtless the
      first and]   first and

                                          Page 93
24   complete and fullblown,   3-4   complete,

25   years, enclosed by a kind of   5-6   years and enclosed and surrounded
                                                  by a sort of

28-29 [28-44 PASTED IN: realized that   9-12   realized that Sutpen was going to
      Sutpen was going to prevent the   prevent the marriage if he could, he
      marriage if he could, he (Bon) seems   (Bon) seems to have withdrawn into a
      to have withdrawn into a mere spec-   mere spectator, passive, a little
      tator, passive, a little quizzical and   sardonic, and

32   a young Roman   17   a youthful Roman

35-37 about his mistress and he now   23-26   about the mistress and child and he
      contemplated ⟨found⟩ Sutpen's action   now found Sutpen's action and Henry's
      and Henry's reaction to it the ⟨a⟩   reaction a fetish-ridden moral blun-
      fetish-ridden and mental blundering   dering which did not deserve to be
      which did not even deserve the word   called thinking, and
      'thinking', to be contemplated and

38-39 sophistication beside which Sutpen 29-30 sophistication in comparison with
      and Henry both were almost trog-   which Henry and Sutpen were trog-
      lodytes.   lodytes.

                                          Page 94
41   that same sardonic and   1   that fatalistic and

117

C H A P T E R   I V

MANUSCRIPT		BOOK	
42-43	waited as if he knew even then that he had only to wait, that he had seduced Henry and Judith both to have [*sic*] any reason to fear	3-8	waited for them to do whatever it would be that they would do, as if he had known all the while that the occasion would arise when he would have to wait and that all he would need to do would be to wait; had known that he had seduced Henry and Judith both too thoroughly to have any fear
44	stupid original[?] shrewdness half instinct and ~~half sheer belief~~ belief]	9-10	stupid shrewdness part instinct and part belief in luck, and part muscular
Page 42 [~~40~~ 41]			
1	in luck and half muscular		
2	pessimism, ~~a mentality~~ stripped long ~~ago~~ generations ago	12-13	pessimism stripped long generations ago
6	would doubtless have added 'after	19-20	would have added doubtless 'after
6	his prospective father in law was to learn, this	20-21	his intended father-in-law soon learned, this
8-9	distinction he might between this with a white woman and the other, possibly because he was a Catholic of sorts. Because	24-26	distinction (he was a Catholic of sorts) he might between this one with a white woman and that other. Because
10	[10-19 PASTED IN: you will see the letter. ~~It is~~ not the only one he ever wrote her but at least the only	26-27	you will see the letter, not the first one he ever wrote to her but at least the first, the only
Page 95			
14-16	her provided it was Judith who destroyed them, which would have been when she ~~had Bon brot into the house~~ found in Bon's pocket the	2-4	her (provided of course it was she herself who destroyed them) which would have been when she found in Bon's coat the
18-21	appeared more splendid—to the girl or to the youth, the one with the old unfailing difference in sex to sharpen the image, the other with the irrevocable ~~difference~~ similarity of] sex to sharpen the image for the same identical reason [21-36 PASTED IN: reason merely observed—the one with the hope,	8	appeared the more splendid—to the one with hope,
21-22	possession; the other with the knowledge, even the subconscious[?] to the desire, of the insurmountable	9-11	possession; to the other with the knowledge of the insurmountable
22-23	which that similarity of gender ~~set intervened~~ hopelessly intervened:	11-12	which the similarity of gender hopelessly intervened—
24-25	campus in	14-15	campus on foot in

118

MANUSCRIPT		BOOK	
26	reclining perhaps on a window seat in his room, in a brocaded robe—	17-18	reclining in a flowered, almost feminized gown, in a sunny window in his chambers—
31-32	accident, ~~no better than yourself~~ in no way superior to yourself and	26-27	accident, in no way superior to yourself; and

Page 96

36	forbade Judith to marry Bon; yes, he loved Bon,]	2	forbade the marriage. Yes, he loved Bon,
37-38	Judith. ~~{I dont mean that vulgar~~[?] [illegible word] ~~of capitulation which was never~~[?] ~~taught or~~ [illegible word] ~~not only to expect but to demand:~~ ~~apparently Bon paid Judith the dubious compliment~~—the country	3	Judith—the country
40	[40-45 PASTED IN: planters' sons whom Bon permitted to become intimate with him, who **aped** presently aped	5-6	planters' sons whom Bon permitted to become intimate with him, who aped
41	they could) his very manner of life,	7-8	they were able) his very manner of living,
42-43	upon (or rather, had thrust upon him) a talisman or touchstone not to ~~pow~~[?] invest him with wisdom or wealth or power but	10-11	upon a talisman or touchstone not to invest him with wisdom or power or wealth, but
45	satiety; and the very fact that lounging before them in the outlandish and almost feminine garments of his]	14-15	satiety. And the very fact that, lounging before them in the outlandish and almost feminine garments of his

Page 43 [~~41~~ 42]

1-4	satiety but increased not only the amazement but the bitter and hopeless outrage;—Henry, the provincial, the clown almost, given to instinctive and violent action rather than to thinking, ratiocination, who may have been subconsciously aware that his fierce provincial's pride in his ~~kinsman's~~ ⟨sister's⟩ virginity was a false quantity which could not endure in order	16-22	satiety only increased the amazement and the bitter and hopeless outrage. Henry was the provincial, the clown almost, given to instinctive and violent action rather than to thinking who may have been conscious that his fierce provincial's pride in his sister's virginity was a false quantity which must incorporate in itself an inability to endure in order
7	would ~~have been~~ ⟨wish to be⟩ if	27	would be if
7	husband, ~~which~~ by whom he would be despoiled if	28-29	husband; by whom he would be despoiled, choose for despoiler, if

MANUSCRIPT		BOOK	

11-15   other agreement, knowing that it the[?] [MARGIN: 4 years, the hope, the waiting,] would be in vain.//Henry it was, not Bon: witness the entire queerly placid course of his relationship with Judith, who paid her the dubious compliment of not only not attempting to ruin her but of not even proposing[?] the marriage after Henry had sided before Sutpen objected to it//an engagement 4 years of hope and waiting would be in vain/. Yes, Henry; not Bon: as

4-6   other marriage, knowing that the four years of hoping and waiting would be in vain.

"Yes, it was Henry who seduced Judith: not Bon, as

17   [17-26 PASTED IN: lasting for a whole year yet comprising two holiday visits as her brother's guest and which primarily[?] Bon

8-10   lasting for a whole year yet comprising two holiday visits as her brother's guest which Bon

21   in his days in the house when
16   in the crowded days when

22   the closest you
18   the nearest you

23   people were separated and
19-20   people were doubtless separate and

26-27   ceased; No, not Bon: Henry, and the others,] the 5 or 6 classmates of Henry's age and kind, who—Henry
26   ceased—Henry

28   had scarcely[?] even been away
27-28   had never been away

28   he took up residence at the
28-29   he went to the

28-29   his country clothes
29   his countrified clothes

29-34   groom and only in the surface matter of the clothes and his food and how he filled his time different from the groom and the other negroes who supported him—the same sweat which [31-41 PASTED IN: upon[?] him; Because they were country boys too Henry who up to that time had never even been to Memphis, who had scarcely been away from home before that September when he took up residence in the University with his country clothes and his saddle horse and negro groom—the 6 or 7 of them only
30-31   groom; the six or seven of them, of an age and background, only

36   them who did not have to sweat in fields:
3-4   them because they did not have to sweat in the fields:

CHAPTER IV

MANUSCRIPT

BOOK

37   pleasures, on the one hand the gam-
ling

5   pleasures: the one, gambling

39   and the young man's jewelry for the
same reason—the

9   and watches, and for the same reason; the

41   champagne, and now in dirt-floored
cabins with smoking pine knots and
calico]

12-13   champagne, now in dirt-floored
cabins with smoking pine knots and
calico

45   good

21   good enough to cause

Page 44 [4~~2~~ 43]

1-20   ~~had not yet seen either, thru that cunning telepathy, rapport between them~~ and water sweetened with molasses. Because at that time Bon had not seen Judith either. He had probably not paid enough attention to Henry's inarticulate recounting of his brief and conventional background and history to have remembered that Henry ~~had a sister~~ good enough to cause him to endure it and apparently too serious or private to be divulged to what acquaintances he now pos-sessed [7-12 PASTED IN: ~~to his companions~~—the man who later showed the same indolence, almost uninter-est, the same detachment when the uproar about that engagement which, so far as Jefferson knew, never formally existed, which he himself never affirmed nor denied, arose and he in the background, impartial and passive, as tho it were not only not himself involved or he acting on behalf of some absent friend, but as tho the person involved and interdict were someone whom he had never seen ~~before~~ nor heard of before and cared nothing about; ~~It was Henry who seduced himself as he seduced Judith also, from that distance be-tween Sutpen's Hundred and Oxford and the man whom she had not yet even seen~~ [MARGIN: ~~They saw one another 3 times in 2 years, for a total of about 17 days; this not counting the time which Ellen consumed~~] You see? There was not even any court-ship. There was no time for it. It's

121

MANUSCRIPT   BOOK

> as tho Henry seduced Judith along
> with himself, from that distance be-
> tween Sutpen's Hundred and Oxford
> and the man whom she had not yet
> even seen, as tho by means of that
> telepathy, rapport ~~which~~ with which
> they seemed at times to anticipate
> one another's actions as children as
> two birds leaving a limb simultane-
> ously—that rapport not like the
> illusory one between twins but rather
> like that ⟨h⟩ which could exist be-
> tween two people who, regardless of
> sex or color[?] or heritage of tongue,
> ~~might possess~~ who had been marooned
> at birth on a desert island.
> You see? There was not even any
> courtship

good enough to cause

	MANUSCRIPT		BOOK
24	person actually involved	30	person involved
25-26	someone he had never seen and cared nothing about. You see? There was not even a courtship; apparently	31-33	someone whom he had never heard of and cared nothing about. There does not even seem to have been any courtship. Apparently

Page 99

27-28	this in a man with a reputation already established for some prowess among women, even tho neither Sutpen nor Henry knew about it yet. ~~He and Judith saw one another 3 times~~ No engagement,	2-5	this, mind you, in a man who had already acquired a name for prowess among women while at the University, long before Sutpen was to find actual proof. No engagement,
31-32	between ~~Ox~~ Sutpen's Hundred and Oxford and the man whom she had never even seen,	12-13	between Oxford and Sutpen's Hundred, between herself and the man whom she had not even seen yet,
33	limb simultaneously;—	16	limb at the same instant;
34	like the illusory one between twins but rather like that which might	17-18	like the conventional delusion of that between twins but rather such as might
35	of age sex or color or heritage or tongue,	19	of sex or age or heritage of race or tongue,
35-36	island in this case Sutpen's Hundred, the solitude ~~that~~ ⟨the⟩ shadow of that father with ~~whom the town and~~ whom	20-21	island here Sutpen's Hundred; the solitude, the shadow of that father with whom
38	are; look at them—a girl, a young	25	are: this girl, this young
39	for 17 days	26-27	for twelve days

MANUSCRIPT		BOOK	
40	of defying her brother to commit homicide if not murder to prevent it and	28-30	of forcing her brother to the last resort of homicide, even if not murder, to prevent it, and
40-41	years since she last saw him; a father who should see that man one time, yet have reason	30-33	years during which she could not have been always certain that he was still alive; this father who had seen that man once, yet had reason

Page 100

| 43 | reason to forbid the marriage [MARGIN: granted that the existence of the 8th part negro mistress and the 16 part negro son, granted that to a family[?] [illegible word] man such as Sutpen must have been, even the formal morganatic ceremony which—a situation which was as much a part of a wealthy young New Orleansian's fashionable equipment as his dancing slippers, was reason enough to authorize[?] this step] the brother | 3-4 | reason for forbidding the marriage; this brother |
| 44 | happiness, ~~based upon the granted~~ based upon the evidence of the curious and unusual relationship which existed between them, | 5-7 | happiness, granted that curious and unusual relationship which existed between them, should have been more jealous and precious than to the father even, yet |

Page 45 [44 42 44]

| 1-3 | ~~"They didn't go back to school. Even Sutpen knew that, and the next year being 1861, doubtless Sutpen and Judith both knew that Henry at least would never return to school. They went to New Orleans. And now Henry found out what his father already knew.~~ | | |

should have been more delicate and precious than to the father even yet

4-5	rejected lover; ~~and the lover~~ for 4 years	9-10	rejected suitor for four years
5-6	the very reason that 4 years ago he quitted his own roof to champion;	11-12	the very identical reason which four years ago he quitted home to champion;
6	volition became	13	volition or desire became
7	same static and almost sardonic spirit—	15	same passive and sardonic spirit,
7-8	upon consummating the marriage	16	upon the marriage

CHAPTER IV

MANUSCRIPT		BOOK	
9	Henry [MARGIN: let alone to the obviously more travelled father,] the	19-20	Henry, let alone the more travelled father, the
13-14	explain. to ⟨now.⟩ [14-20 PASTED IN: Or perhaps that's it. Perhaps They	28-29	explain. Or perhaps that's it: they
14-15	few ancient mouth-to-mouth tales, we	30-31	few old mouth-to-mouth tales; we
15	trunks and drawers and boxes letters without signatures[?] and memos[?] in	31-32	trunks and boxes and drawers letters without salutation or signature, in
		Page 101	
20	letters from that]	9-10	letters from that
21-22	carefully the	10	carefully, the
22	[22-26 PASTED IN: the letters faded,	11	the writing faded,
24-25	re-read, make sure that you have neglected nor forgotten nothing that the paper calls for; you	15-16	re-read, tedious and intent, poring, making sure that you have forgotten nothing, made no miscalculation; you
25-26	again and nothing happens: just the words, the symbols, the shapes themselves, shadowy inscrutable and serene, against that turgid background of a horrible and bloody mischancing of human]	17-20	again and again nothing happens: just the words, the symbols, the shapes themselves, shadowy inscrutable and serene, against that turgid background of a horrible and bloody mischancing of human
28	"They rode home from	21	"Bon and Henry came from
29-30	of 17 days in one and a half years, yet to remember so that, 4 years from the time when she last saw him (he	24-25	of twelve days, yet to remember so that four years later (he
30	time; Henry	25	time. Henry
32	wedding gown and	28-29	wedding dress and
33-34	childlike and undeviating[?] voracity she was bent on including in the household furnishings and decorations;	31-32	childlike voracity she essayed to include in the furnishing and decoration of her house;
34	after one sight and	32-33	after seeing once and
		Page 102	
34-35	wife's female and illogical mind, he saw at once as a potential threat to the ⟨now⟩ peaceful coronation	1-2	wife's mind, he saw as a potential threat to the (now and at last) triumphant coronation
36-37	enough (and if not of clairvoyance, then what?) to warrant a 600 mile journey to find what he seems to have known he would find—this	3-4	enough to warrant a six hundred mile journey to prove it—this
38	a 100 mile	6-7	a ten mile
39	see? You have to catch yourself. You almost	7-8	see? You would almost

124

CHAPTER IV

MANUSCRIPT		BOOK	
39	Sutpen's journey to	8	Sutpen's trip to
41	to hold matches to in preference to ⟨any⟩ another,	12-13	to pour boiling water into in preference to any other,
43	vacation riding together and reading together (Bon	16-17	vacation talking together and riding and reading (Bon

Page 46 [45]

1	him from home for staying there;— this, the perfect outlet for	20	him for remaining—this, the perfect setting for
2	still countable in	22-23	still numbered in
3-4	besides Henry—yes, he corrupted Henry to the law too ~~and himself~~; Henry changed in midterm—and himself) while	24-25	beside Henry and himself—yes, he corrupted Henry to the law also; Henry changed in midterm) while
4	perhaps; and	26-27	perhaps. And
5	man and it ~~was likely~~ Henry who had foisted upon him now	28-29	man on whom Henry foisted now
7-8	Memphis, ~~to buy some clothes~~ with	33	Memphis, with

Page 103

12-13	day, for in order to go to New Orleans and so find	9-10	day, to go to New Orleans and find
13	known he	10	known all the while that he
15	at that first glance	15	at a glance
16-17	which ~~success brings.~~ success brings to ~~the man~~ ⟨him⟩ ~~who started with from~~[?] ~~nothing, and nowhere.~~ him	18	which success brings to him

| 18-24 | of fortunate, lucky. | 19-24 | of merely lucky. |

18-24 "~~They came home.~~ Henry ~~brot~~ ⟨and⟩ Bon ⟨came⟩ home ~~with him~~ at the end of school, Bon to spend two days before riding on to the River to take the steamboat home, to New Orleans. ⟨where⟩ Sutpen ~~was~~ ⟨had⟩ ~~gone then, on to New Orleans too tho none knew it, least of all Ellen~~ where Sutpen had already gone tho none knew it, least of all Ellen. ~~I say brot deliberately.—Bon may~~

"Then June came and the end of the school year, and Henry and Bon returned to Sutpen's Hundred, Bon to spend a day or two before riding on

19-24 "Then June came and the end of the school year and Henry and Bon returned to Sutpen's Hundred, Bon to spend a day or two before riding on to the River to take the steamboat home, to New Orleans where Sutpen had already gone. He stayed but two

CHAPTER IV

MANUSCRIPT   BOOK

	MANUSCRIPT		BOOK
	to the River, to take the steamboat home, to New Orleans where Sutpen had already gone tho none knew it, least of all Ellen. He stayed only two		
26-27	known this, since Sutpen (granted that the following Xmas, the moment when Sutpen was to absolutely forbid the marriage was in the cards) tho but	27-28	known it, since Sutpen, though but
31-32	[31-39 PASTED IN: Bon with opportunities for trysts and pledges with a coy and unflagging ubiquity which they must have tried to evade	33	Bon with
		Page 104	
		1-2	opportunities for trysts and pledges with a coy and unflagging ubiquity which they must have tried in vain to evade
33	with fretted yet	3	with annoyed yet
34-36	been one of the familiar transient outer[?] ~~manif~~ traits of that impenetrable and shadowy ~~man~~: ~~And then, the fact that even an unspoken engagement survived speaking well of the~~ [illegible word] ~~the postulation that they did love one another, since~~ man—yes,	5-6	been the ordinary manifestation of the impenetrable and shadowy character. Yes,
37-38	mother, which you have seen.—And this,	11	mother. And this:
38	an unspoken engagement survived speaking	12-13	an undefined and never-spoken engagement survived, speaking
39	perished dead of sheer]	15	perished, died of sheer
41-42	instead, Bon would not have had to die as he did; if Henry had gone to New Orleans then and seen, found out about the woman and the child; Henry who, ~~might~~ before	18-21	instead of waiting until the next, Bon would not have had to die as he did; if Henry had only gone then to New Orleans and found out then about the mistress and the child; Henry who, before
Page 47 [46]			
4	Sutpen came back, from	32-33	Sutpen returned home too, from
		Page 105	
8	but now was already	8	but was now already
10-11	nothing of what he had learned—Henry, even Judith suspected nothing—but just waiting, for what nobody knows; perhaps	13-15	nothing yet about what he had learned in New Orleans but just waiting, unsuspected even by Henry and Judith, waiting for what nobody knows, perhaps
12	he must learn, that	16	he would be obliged to, that

MANUSCRIPT		BOOK	
12	would not return	17-18	would realize that the game was up and not even return
14	both—made weekly trips now, ~~in~~ ⟨by⟩	20-21	both now—making weekly journeys by
16	out and found his trouble, he ~~sometimes~~ ⟨even⟩ went out and manufactured it. This	25-26	out to meet his troubles, he sometimes went out and manufactured them. But this
18	that 23 of December 1860, and ~~then on the night of~~ the negro children,	29-30	that twenty-fourth of December, 1860, and the nigger children,
19	already appearing about	31	already lurking about
19-21	''Xmas gif'!' in thin treble voices to the white people, the brother and ⟨the lover,⟩ the rich city sharper come courting and Sutpen saying nothing yet,	32-33	'Christmas gift' at the white people, the rich city man come to court Judith, and Sutpen saying nothing even
		Page 106	
		1	yet,
21	unless maybe it was Henry, maybe Henry who	1	unless possibly by Henry who
23	the dark room	5	the shuttered room
26	away from Sutpen's Hundred in	10	away in
28-29	steamboat, it still Henry doing the bringing. He didn't	14-17	steamboat, Henry still doing the leading, the bringing, as he always did until the very last, when for the first time during their entire relationship Bon led and Henry followed. Henry didn't
29-34	pauper, but he could have gone to his grandfather, since altho he probably was better mounted than any other undergraduate at the University, not excepting Bon himself, he probably had very little of money beyond what he could raise hurriedly[?] on his horse and what jewels he happened to be wearing when he and Bon rode away. No, he didn't have to go, and he doing the bringing this time too, and Bon riding beside him while the dawn made[?], trying to find out from him what his father had said. Bon	17-20	pauper but he could have gone to his grandfather. No, he didn't have to go. Bon was riding beside him, trying to find out from him what had happened. Bon
34-35	Sutpen ~~knew~~ had found out in New Orleans, but he wanted to know	21-22	Sutpen had discovered in New Orleans, but he would need to know
35-36	him, doubtless with the new mare going fast	23-26	him. Doubtless Henry was riding the new mare which he probably knew he

MANUSCRIPT		BOOK	
			would have to surrender, sacrifice too, along with all the rest of his life, inheritance, going fast
37	scenes of	28	scene of [*sic*]
38-39	whom, tho he had resigned birthright and heritage and all for his sake, for the sake of the love and loyalty which he had surrendered to the friend, he still	29-30	whom, despite the sacrifice which he had just made out of love and loyalty, he still
39-40	that Sutpen had told him the truth.	31-32	that what Sutpen had told him was true.

Page 107

| 41-42 | poverty and disinheritance and all. But he could not have faced that lie from Bon. | 1-3 | poverty, disinheritance, but he could not have borne that lie from Bon. Yet |

Page 48 [47]

1	"Yet		
3	him [MARGIN: , trying to find out what Sutpen had told him—Bon] who	8-9	him, trying to find out what Sutpen had told him—Bon who
3-4	half he had watched aping his (Bon's) clothing and speech and ideas, who had projected upon him (Bon) that complete	9-11	half now had been watching Henry ape his clothing and speech, who for a year and a half now had seen himself as the object of that complete
5	youth, ~~gi~~ never a woman, gives to ~~a man~~ another	12	youth, never a woman, gives to an-other
6-7	had succumbed to and with	14-15	had already succumbed to, and this with
7	on his part, with hardly the lifting of a hand on his part, as tho it were actually the brother	15-17	on the seducer's part, without so much as the lifting of a finger, as though it actually were the brother
8-10	which ~~lived in Bon's body~~ walked and breathed ~~in~~ with Bon's body and not himself;—yes, not Bon, who had lifted no hand. And yet there is the letter, this letter here, written	18-20	which walked and breathed with Bon's body. Yet here is the letter, sent four years afterward, written
10	in Virginia,	21	in Carolina,
11-13	stores, as the letter itself tells. You see? There was the letter, sent 4 years afterwards, after she had had any word from him save the messages thru Henry that he was still alive; there was the letter. So	22-24	stores; four years after she had had any message from him save the messages from Henry that he (Bon) was still alive. So
17-18	believe that it was just in order to	31-33	believe it was just to preserve Henry

MANUSCRIPT		BOOK	
	preserve Henry at least as an ally in order to someday marry Judith. It was because he not		as an ally, for the crisis of some future need. It was because Bon not

Page 108

MANUSCRIPT		BOOK	
19	his ascetic fatalism	2	his fatalism
21	youth;—Or m perhaps even // this celibate Don Juan this cerebral	5-6	youth—this cerebral
22-23	love that which he had injured; perhaps even more than the youth and the girl: perhaps	7-8	love what he had injured; perhaps it was even more than Judith or Henry either: perhaps
23-24	peace and sanctity he	9-10	peace he
27	told him, showed him.	14	told Henry, broke it to him.
28-29	been to Memphis [29-43 PASTED IN: Memphis;	16	been in Memphis,
29	experience, scattered and diffuse tho it might have been, yet consisted	16	experience consisted
30	at houses other houses, plantations, exactly like his own, where	17-18	at other houses, plantations, almost interchangeable with his own, where
30-31	routine pursuits which	18-19	routine which
33	of a gig or trap or even a surrey;	23	of a trap or perhaps even a carriage;
37-38	heritage [MARGIN: , that heritage peculiarly Anglo-Saxon] of fierce mystical pride proud mysticism and the ability	31-32	heritage—that heritage peculiarly Anglo-Saxon—of fierce proud mysticism and that ability
38-39	city esoteric and	33	city foreign and

Page 109

MANUSCRIPT		BOOK	
39	its air at	1	its atmosphere at
40	a puritan ⟨granite⟩ heritage	2-3	a granite heritage
39	houses, ⟨let alone the clothing and conduct,⟩ are built in the image of a grim and jealous	3-4	houses, let alone clothing and conduct, are built in the image of a jealous
42-43	and angels handsome angels in the image of their houses and clothing ornaments personal ornaments and godless lives voluptuous lives. Yes, Bon now did the bringing: I]	8	and personal ornaments and voluptuous lives. Yes, I

Page 49 [48 (written over an illegible number) 48]

1-17   "They didn't go back to school. Even Sutpen knew that at once, and the next year being 1861, doubtless Sutpen and Judith both knew that Henry at least would never return to

school. They went to New Orleans,
and so Henry learned what his father
had already discovered. He discovered the thing which had already
set Sutpen against the marriage and
hence [MARGIN: Bon must have believed,] was bound to have somewhat
the same effect on Henry, even
granted Bon's influence on him. Yet
they went to New Orleans. As far as
Henry was concerned, that's even
enough to understand. There was
nowhere else for Henry to go save
where Bon would take him since his
only other kin was Miss Rosa and his
fat grandfather, in the same county
where he had already repudiated one
household, even if granted that his
life there with that grandfather would
have been bearable, and since tho he
may have been well mounted and perhaps was better mounted than any
undergraduate in the University, not
excepting Bon himself, he probably
had very little of cash beyond what he
could raise hurriedly[?] on his horse
and what jewelry he happened to be
wearing that night when he and Bon
rode away. Yet Bon loved him then.
You see? The whole thing just becomes the more inexplicable and con-
fusing? Because if, finding out about
the octoroon mistress and the child
was sufficient grounds for Henry to
kill Bon 4 years later, he could not
have known about them that night
when he repudiated his father and
home. Then what could Sutpen have
told him that would have caused him
to repudiate the other and east[?]
make himself a pauper in order to
side with Bon? And then, why the 4
years?--Why, when Henry found out
about the octoroon and so discovered
his father's reason for forbidding the
marriage; why, if he and then, why

Yes, I

	MANUSCRIPT		BOOK
	raised the crop which he wanted. It would be the fact of the ceremony, regardless of what kind, that Henry would find hard to pass: Bon knew that.		he wanted. It would be the fact of the ceremony, regardless of what kind, that Henry would balk at: Bon knew this.
20-21	mistress and child, not even the negro mistress and child, even less the child in that case because of the negro blood, since	14-16	mistress or even the child, not even the negro mistress and even less the child because of that fact, since
23	where ~~women~~ the other sex is ~~divided~~ ⟨separated⟩ into	20	where the other sex is separated into
24-25	chasm which proved but a one way crossing—ladies and women and females—	21-23	chasm which could be crossed but one time and in but one direction—ladies, women, females—
25-26	courtesans with whom they consorted in the cities, the slave girls and women possibly[?] to whom, or upon whom, the very virginity of that first caste was built upon—	24-27	courtesans to whom they went while on sabbaticals to the cities, the slave girls and women upon whom that first caste rested and to whom in certain cases it doubtless owed the very fact of its virginity—
27	hunting [MARGIN: to heat and make importunate the young man's blood] to which	28-30	hunting to heat and make importunate the blood of a young man, to which
28	and ~~women-of-the~~ forever inaccessible	31	and inaccessible
29	and so only the slave women,	33	and hence only the slave girls,
		Page 110	
30	girls who worked[?] in the fields	1-2	girls with sweating bodies out of the fields
31-32	say, 'Send me Juno' or Missylena or Chlory' and then ride on into the bush[?] and dismount and wait.	3-5	says Send me Juno or Missylena or Chlory and then rides on into the trees and dismounts and waits.
35	retain or accept.	12	retain, accept.
36	Henry slowly into	12-13	Henry gradually into
37-38	therefore, to Henry's mind, opulent; the commerce, the inference	16-17	therefore to Henry opulent, sensuous, sinful; the inference
38-39	of tediously gradual[?] inching of human sweating figures	18-19	of a tedious inching of sweating human figures
39-40	of myriad carriage wheels in which women seemed to lead the fleshless life of pictures, portraits, paintings, beside men in linen a little finer and diamonds a little brighter and]	20-23	of a [sic] myriad carriage wheels, in which women, enthroned and immobile and passing rapidly across the vision, appeared like painted portraits beside men in linen a little finer and diamonds a little brighter and

CHAPTER IV

MANUSCRIPT

BOOK

43-44 food and clothing and shelter too, whose dressing gowns and walk and speech and his attitude toward women and his notions of honor and pride too Henry had tried to ape, watching

27-30 food and shelter and clothing too, whose clothing and walk and speech he had tried to ape, along with his attitude toward women and his ideas of honor and pride too, watching

Page 50 [49]

1 the bottom ⟨which holds it up.⟩' — 'You mean this is not it? ~~the world itself~~ That

33 the foundation. It can belong to
Page 111
1 anyone': and Henry, 'You mean, this is not it? That

2 this?' — 'Yes.

2-3 this, more select than this?': and Bon, 'Yes.

2 the base, the bottom'—a dialogue

3-4 the foundation. This belongs to anybody.': a dialogue

5-6 it that same one which said, *I*

9-10 it saying *I*

6 the next image which

11 the next picture which

7 next image,

12 next picture,

8 the grave and

14 the sober and

10-11 it.' ⫽ ~~'You~~ and receiving the reply: 'You mean, it is still above this, still higher than this?'

19-20 it': and Henry, 'You mean, it is still higher than this, still above this?'

14-20 the final picture would show; tiny[?], scarce seen yet refreshed, relaxed, ineradicable:—~~a trap, a riding horse at a deserted and not quite fashionable door in some neighborhood orfec[?] and~~, and a ~~little~~ deeadent, ~~even a little sinister and Bon naming the horse's owner~~ a trap, a riding horse standing before a closed and curiously monastic doorway in a neighborhood a little decadent, a little sinister even, and Bon mentioning the owner's name in a tone casual, cryptic too, corrupting Henry subtly anew by putting into Henry's mind the belief that ~~Bon think that Henry knew~~ here one man of the world speaking to another man of the world, that Bon knew that Henry knew what he was talking about; and Henry

25-32 the complete picture would show, scarce-seen yet ineradicable—a trap, a riding horse standing before a closed and curiously monastic doorway in a neighborhood a little decadent, even a little sinister, and Bon mentioning the owner's name casually—this, corruption subtly anew by putting into Henry's mind the notion of one man of the world speaking to another, that Henry knew that Bon believed that Henry would know even from a disjointed word what Bon was talking about, and Henry

20-21 nothing rather than surprise;—a ~~facade~~ blank, [illegible word] drowsing[?] facade in steamy

34 nothing at all rather than sur-
Page 112
1-2 prise or incomprehension—a façade shuttered and blank, drowsing in steamy

MANUSCRIPT		BOOK	
21-22	with a quality of barbaric[?], of a secret nest[?] of curious and un- imaginable delights; without	3-4	with something of secret and curious and unimaginable delights. Without
22-23	he sees it as tho to Henry the blank and scaling ~~wall~~ barrier, in dis- solving produces and reveals not comprehension of the	4-6	he saw it was as though to Henry the blank and scaling barrier in dis- solving produced and revealed not comprehension to the
24	discards but instead striking straight	7-8	discards, but striking instead straight
24-25	primary and ancient blind	8	primary blind
25-26	of the young man's blood and desire— a row of faces or a wall of music like ~~flowers in a garden,~~ ⟨a bazaar of flowers,⟩ as mindless as flowers ⟨and doomed,⟩ the supreme	9-10	of all young male living dream and hope—a row of faces like a bazaar of flowers, the supreme
26-27	of human flesh ⟨~~the two races~~⟩ bred ⟨of the two races⟩ for that sale as carefully as horse flesh is bred for racing—	11-12	of human flesh bred of the two races for that sale—
27	flowerlike faces	12	flower faces
28	the ~~trim~~ ⟨youthful⟩ ~~neat shape of men~~ elegant	13	the elegant
30-31	something with which they are both familiar, counting upon, depending upon still the	18-19	something they both understand, depending upon, counting upon still, the
31-32	ignorance, or more[?] perhaps, who	20	ignorance, who
32-33	him: suppressing that first deep smothered cry	21-22	him, and Henry not showing either, suppressing still that first cry
34	seen, heard. But now slowing, now would be the	24-25	seen, but now slowing: now would come the
34-35	Bon ~~would~~ will have builded—the closed unscalable wall, the grave and	25-26	Bon had builded—a wall, unscalable, a gate ponderously locked, the sober and
35	why nor what;	27	why? or what?
36-37	of ~~lacelike grill~~ lacelike grill and Bon knocking at an adjacent smaller doorway and a swarthy man resem- bling probably a movie[?] character actor[?] out of some French Revolu- tion scene erupting,	28-31	of the lacelike iron grilling and they passing on, Bon knocking at a small adjacent doorway from which a swarthy man resembling a creature out of an old woodcut of the French Revolution erupts,
38	at ~~Henry~~ ⟨the daylight⟩ and then at ~~the daylight~~ ⟨Henry⟩ and	32-33	at the daylight and then at Henry and

MANUSCRIPT	BOOK
	Page 113
39 him, an	2 him? An
41 sight beyond the	6 sight or evidence above the
43 walling again even the broad strip of earth covered[?] with powdered shell fresh raked	8-10 walling yet again the strip of bare earth combed and curried with powdered shell, raked
44-45 voice,—the mentor, the guide— ~~casually and pleasantly anecdotal~~ standing aside to watch the provincial	11-12 voice—the mentor, the guide standing aside now to watch the grave provincial

Page 51 [46 50]

2 [1-7 PASTED IN: and when the cloak tightens you turn and fire, tho there ~~have~~ are	16-17 and when you feel the cloak tauten you turn and fire. Though there are
5-18 question, ~~until it came: 'What would you // they be fighting for?'~~ who knew himself already now without the asking: 'What would ~~you // they be fighting for?~~]¹ toward anything which is a matter of sense instead of logic, fact, for the next image which the mentor, the corruptor, intended for it; the next step, the next image following[?] the acceptance and fixation of which the mentor would say again, perhaps with words now: still watching the other's now grave and now thoughtful face tho still serene in the knowledge of that puritan heritage which must show disapproval but never surprise, which must even show nothing at all rather than have the disapprobation construed as absolvement: 'But even this is not it.'—~~'You mean, there is one~~ ~~which~~ the world itself is still higher than this?' ~~But no words?—spoken:~~ ~~Henry would not speak it, he would~~ ~~just listen and Bon answer the words~~	22-25 question, who knew already now before he asked it: 'What would you—they be fighting for?' "Yes,

¹This pasted-in slip covers the following passage written on the page as it originally stood:

in broadcloth a little trimmer and with hats raked a little more darkly swaggering than any Henry had ever seen before; and the mentor, the man for whose sake he had repudiated blood and kin and (yes) [illegible word] clothing and food and shelter as well, whose dressing gowns and manner of walking and breathing [?] and his attitude toward women and his very [?] notions [?] of honor and pride Henry had tried to ape, watching him with that cold and cat-like inscrutable calculation, watching the picture resolve and become fixed and then telling Henry: 'But that's not it. That's just the base, the bottom.'—'You mean the world itself is above this, higher than this?'—'Yes.' This is only the base, the bottom'—a dialogue without speech, you see, which would fix and then remove without obliterating it [illegible word] this background, leaving [?] the plate prepared and innocent again—the plate docile with the puritan's humility

~~which had never been said: 'This is the way we hunt: What we do while you—~~'Yes. This is just the way we ride and hunt. We do this while you rush foxes and shoot hares. Because it's too hot here' but not saying, adding aloud, this since he could put thoughts into Henry's mind without the need for speech: *Because we are more civilized than you: we have learned ~~to live at night~~ how to stay awake at night.*

you—they be fighting for?' Yes,

19	blows, touch,	28	blow, stroke, touch,
21	the crude and ~~the unimportant~~ the random.	30-31	the random and crude.
22	resist, would find hard to stomach, assimilate.	32-33	resist, find hard to stomach and retain.
22-23	for ~~2 years now~~ some weeks	33	for weeks

Page 114

24-27 the ultimate visit, seeing, finicking over the fit of a coat; {he would have had Henry fitted with a new coat, he would have done that; ~~half his aim would be accomplished~~ by means of that coat the entire atmosphere of the visit would be established before Henry ever saw the woman, half the purpose of the visit accomplished before Henry ~~left the house~~ started out}; and Henry,

3-8 the visit, finicking almost like a woman over the fit of the new coat which he would have ordered for Henry, forced Henry to accept for this occasion, by means of which the entire impression which Henry was to receive from the visit would be established before they even left the house, before Henry ever saw the woman: and Henry,

31-33 those secret and inscrutable doorways like that before which he had seen the other trap, and so into a place which to his puritan country mind ~~would have been no har~~[?] must have appeared a sacrificial room in which all of morality and godliness both had perished—

15-19 those inscrutable and curiously lifeless doorways like that before which he had seen the horse or the trap, and so into a place which to his puritan's provincial mind all of morality was upside down and all of honor perished—

34 senses, ~~an a~~ [MARGIN: where the country boy with his simple and erstwhile untroubled code in which women were whores or ladies or white women or negresses, looked upon this] the ultimate apotheosis

20-23 senses, and the country boy with his simple and erstwhile untroubled code in which females were ladies or whores or slaves looked at the apotheosis

MANUSCRIPT   BOOK

34–35   victim: a woman with ~~the tragic f~~ a   24   victim—a woman with a face
        face

35   the ~~one-who-suffers~~ eternal   25   the eternal

36–38   him to sell if he wished like a horse   27–29   him body and soul to sell (if he chose)
        or dog or sheep~~/-and-the-country-boy~~   like a calf or puppy or sheep; and the
        ~~with his simple, heretofore untroubled~~   mentor watching again,
        ~~code in which women were whores or~~
        ~~ladies, or white women or negresses;~~
        and the mentor watching him again,

39–40   counting on and depending on that   32   counting upon that

40   show nothing rather than grief or   33   show neither surprise nor despair,
        surprise, but having   having

                                          Page 115

41   What about it?'   2   What do you say about it?'

42   unpredictable ~~actions~~ of future acts   3–4   unpredictable actions of
        of

42   instinct and action and not   4   instinct and not

43   woman,' ~~Henry~~ A whore'; and Bon,   5–6   woman. A whore': and Bon, even
        ⟨gently now, even:⟩ 'Not   gently now, 'Not

43–45   In fact never ~~say that aloud~~ refer to   6–9   In fact, never refer to one of them
        one of them aloud that way in New   by that name in New Orleans: other-
        Orleans, if you value your life. Be-   wise you may be forced to purchase
        cause there are a thousand men there   that privilege with some of your
        who would wish[?] for the honor of   blood from probably a thousand men',
        letting your blood over that word',   and perhaps
        and perhaps

45   gently now   10   gently, perhaps now even
Page 52 [51]
1   perhaps even

2   us. We—the white men—made   13–14   us, the thousand. We—the thousand,
                                                              the white men—made

3   which establish that one eighth of   15–16   which declare that one eighth of a
        blood of a ~~certain~~ ⟨specified⟩ kind   specified kind of blood shall
        shall

4–6   have also made them slaves, laborers;   17–21   have made them slaves too, laborers,
        cooks and maids and even field hands,   cooks, maybe even field hands, if it
        if ~~he~~ it ~~had~~ ⟨were⟩ not for a few men   were not for this thousand, these few
        ~~in New Orleans~~ like myself, without   men like myself without principles or
        principles and honor too, you may   honor either, perhaps you will say.
        consider it. We   We

6–7   not want to, save them all; perhaps   21–23   not even want to, save all of them;
        the ones we do save are not one in   perhaps the thousand we save are
        10,000.   not one in a thousand.

MANUSCRIPT

8-12 And quite possibly ~~if~~ ⟨when⟩ your God looks into such an establishment as you saw tonight, He would not want any one of us to be God either. So perhaps He does not require quite that of us, anymore than we save that one sparrow which we do save for any commendation from Him. But we save that one, who without us would have been sold to any man—trader[?], gambler, river tough, thief—who had the price,

BOOK

26-33 And perhaps when God looks into one of these establishments like you saw tonight, He would not choose one of us to be God either, now that He is old. Though He must have been young once, surely He was young once, and surely someone who has existed as long as He has, who has looked at as much crude and promiscuous sinning without grace or restraint or decorum as He has had to, to contemplate at last, even though the instances are not

Page 116

1-16 one in a thousand thousand, the principles of honor, decorum and gentleness applied to perfectly normal human instinct which you Anglo-Saxons insist upon calling lust and in whose service you revert in sabbaticals to the primordial caverns, the fall from what you call grace fogged and clouded by Heaven-defying words of extenuation and explanation, the return to grace heralded by Heaven-placating cries of satiated abasement and flagellation, in neither of which—the defiance or the placation—can Heaven find interest or even, after the first two or three times, diversion. So perhaps, now that God is an old man, he is not interested in the way we serve what you call lust either, perhaps He does not even require of us that we save this one sparrow, anymore than we save the one sparrow which we do save for any commendation from Him. But we do save that one, who but for us would have been sold to any brute who had the price,

12 white whore but

17 white prostitute, but

13-14 with impunity and he discarded or sold or even murdered her when she became worn out, with impunity.; yes:

18-21 with more impunity than he would dare to use an animal, heifer or mare, and then discarded or sold or even murdered when worn out or when her keep and her price no longer balanced. Yes:

CHAPTER IV

MANUSCRIPT   BOOK

14-15   to raise. Because tho ~~the~~ men,   22   to mark. Because though men,

16-18   principle other than our cold ~~north one~~ bleached one, more apt and docile to be taught pleasures which her white sister still flees from. But not whores.

26-33   principle which existed, queenly and complete, in the hot equatorial groin of the world long before that white one of ours came down from trees and lost its hair and bleached out—a principle apt docile and instinct with strange and ancient curious pleasures of the flesh (which is all: there is nothing else) which her white sisters of a mushroom yesterday flee from in moral and outraged horror—a principle which, where her white sister must needs try to

Page 117

1-5   make an economic matter of it like someone who insists upon installing a counter or a scales or a safe in a store or business for a certain percentage of the profits, reigns, wise supine and all-powerful, from the sunless and silken bed which is her throne. No: not whores.

18   chosen one from a possible 1,000, and raised

6   chosen and raised

19-20   nun, and by a person who gives them the ~~care and~~ unsleeping attention which no mother ever yet gave—for

7-9   nun, than any blooded mare even, by a person who gives them the unsleeping care and attention which no mother ever gives. For

20-22   but offered for that trade thru a system and plan more formal and rigid than any that white girls are sold thru; ~~Yes. Not whores. raised never to see a man's face hardly until they are brot to the ball or reo~~[?] ~~to be offered~~ raised

10-13   but a price offered and accepted or declined through a system more formal than any that white girls are sold under since they are more valuable as commodities than white girls, raised

24-25   by a man who in return for it not can ~~not~~ and not will but *must* supply her with the proper surroundings in which

15-17   by some man who in return, not can and not will but *must*, supply her with the surroundings proper in which

26   true virgins in

20-21   true chaste women, not to say virgins, in

27   to him ⟨not merely⟩ until he dies ~~or discards them~~ or frees them, ~~and then after~~ but

22   to that man not merely until he dies or frees them, but

138

CHAPTER IV

BOOK

30   patient; but it would be the iron, the   27   patient, though still the iron, the
          steel/ *H* /.   steel—

31   then: a   29   then. A

31-32   game; no preacher nor ordained   30   game, performed by someone created
          minister; if ordination there was in
          the person of one created

32   mumbling ⟨in a⟩ [MARGIN: in an air-   31-32   mumbling in a dungeon lighted by a
          less cave lighted by a handful of   handful of burning hair, something
          burning hair.] something

33-36   girls understand anymore, based[?]   33   girls themselves understand any-
          no more in any economics of the   more,
          slave or of the child which might   *Page 118*
          ensue, vesting no new rights in any-   1-7   maybe not even the crone herself,
          one, denying no one of old rights—a   rooted in nothing of economics for
          ritual as meaningless as that of   her or for any possible progeny since
          wearing a dark coat after 6 oclock;   the very fact that we acquiesced,
          as meaningless as that of the society   suffered the farce, was her proof and
          formed by college boys in the dark-   assurance of that which the ceremony
          ness of shuttered and secret rooms,   itself could never enforce; vesting no
          even   new rights in no [*sic*] one, denying to
                                                           none the old—a ritual as meaningless
                                                           as that of college boys in secret
                                                           rooms at night, even

37-38   a paid prostitute means the same   9-12   a hired prostitute consists of the
          removing of the same clothes in the   same suzerainty over a (temporarily)
          same order and later[?], the same   private room, the same order of re-
          conjunction of two breed horses in   moving the same clothes, the same
          the same bed?   conjunction in a single bed?

44   last deep bitter   24   last bitter

45   right, not   26   right. Not

Page 53 [52]
2-3   by ~~that stupid~~ the War, by   30-31   by the War by [*sic*]

3   the [MARGIN: high (and impossible)]   31-32   the high (and impossible) destiny
          destiny

                                                  Page 119
5   to employing human   2-3   to using human

7   not do.   8   not renounce.

8   fact, [MARGIN: as time went on and   9-10   fact, as time passed and Henry be-
          Henry became accustomed to the   came accustomed to the idea of that
          idea of a ceremony that still was no   ceremony which was still no marriage,
          ceremony,] that   that

9   bigamy but was merely to make of   13-14   bigamy but that it was apparently to
          his sister   make his (Henry's) sister

139

MANUSCRIPT	BOOK
12 do; enlisted	19-20 do. They enlisted
14 Judith if he did, but	23-24 Judith with Henry not there to stop it, but
14-15 Judith and the loss[?] would lie in the fact that Henry would betray himself by being glad, reconciled, surrendered; the	24-28 Judith and then he (Henry) would have to live for the rest of his life with the knowledge that he was glad that he had been so betrayed, with the coward's joy of surrendering without having been vanquished; the
16-17 who did not want Judith without Henry (Bon must have never had any doubt that he could marry Judith when he wished, let who object that would) since, as	28-31 who could not have wanted Judith without Henry since he must never have doubted but what he could marry Judith when he wished, in spite of brother and father both, because as
17-19 object either of Bon's love nor of Henry's solicitude: she was just a blank shape, an empty vessel into which each of those men—the man and the youth, /who had known con seducer and seduced—who	32-33 object of Bon's love or of Henry's solicitude. She was just the blank shape, the empty *Page 120* 1-4 vessel in which each of them strove to preserve, not the illusion of himself nor his illusion of the other but what each conceived the other to believe him to be—the man and the youth, seducer and seduced, who
22 the war would settle the question,	11 the War would settle the matter,
25-26 her except this way? You cannot, surely, believe that Bon had corrupted her to fatalism in that ~~17~~ 17 days, who had not only not	16-18 her but this way? Surely Bon could not have corrupted her to fatalism in twelve days, who not only had not
26-27 father, who (Judith) was anything	19 father. No: anything
27 Sutpen [MARGIN: with the Sutpens' simple code of taking what you wanted if you were strong enough] of	20-21 Sutpen with the ruthless Sutpen code of taking what it wanted provided it were strong enough, of
27 Coldfield [MARGIN: with the Coldfield's cluttering of morality, of right and w[?] ⟨wrong⟩ by rules]; who, while Henry ~~cried~~ screamed	22-24 Coldfield with the Coldfield cluttering of morality and rules of right and wrong; who while Henry screamed
28 loft on the spectacle of her father fighting	24-25 loft that night on the spectacle of Sutpen fighting
28 halfnaked wild niggers	26 halfnaked niggers
31 father: because if she	31 father. Because, even if she

CHAPTER IV

MANUSCRIPT   BOOK

32   acted: she would have taken Bon   33   acted with anyone who tried to cross
      anyway; I   *Page 121*
                                              1   him: she would have taken Bon any-
                                                    way. I

35   alive, because Henry would not let   6-7   alive. It
      Bon write himself, nor did Bon try
      to. It

36   any word, promise, between   8   any promise between

38-39 belief ~~or at~~ that   14   belief, the only possible belief, that

40-41 pity? as in Judith's case: trust,   16-19 pity? Judith, giving implicit trust
      where she had given love, love where   where she had given love, giving
      she had derived breath, but mainly   implicit love where she had derived
      pride, true   breath and pride: that true

44   *I shall never hear from him again;*   24-25 *I will never see him again, if wrong*
      if wrong, he will come himself or   *he will come or*

45   *be, I will; if suffer I must, I can*   25-26 *be I will, if suffer I must I can.*
      Because   Because

Page 54 [53]
1-2   jot—the same two [illegible word] and   27-30 jot; to see them together, Bon might
      serene and impenetrable faces seen   never have even existed—the same
      together in town in the carriage,   two calm impenetrable faces seen to-
      during   gether in the carriage in town during

                                              Page 122
4-5   were like two   3   were as two

5-6   power, the necessity to   5   power, the need, to

7   not learn until   9   not discover it until

11   sisters of   17   sisters and kin and sweethearts of

12   families, with super[?] wagons of   19   families with food and bedding and
      food and negro servants, to   servants, to

12-13 the households, of Oxford itself, ~~poor~~ 20-21 the houses, of Oxford itself, to watch
      ~~and rich, aristocrat and hillman~~
      ~~redneck,~~ to watch

15   more moving than that of   24-25 more so than the spectacle of

15-16 to Priapus—the spectacle of   26   to some heathen Principle, some
                                                    Priapus—the sight of

17   to a war. ~~There would be music~~ And 29   to a battle. And

18   the ~~candles~~ blazing candles,   30   the blazing candles,

18-20 blowing curtains in the tall windows   31-33 blowing of curtains in tall windows on
      on April nights, the swing of crinoline   the April darkness, the swing of crino-
      ~~and~~ indiscriminate within ~~the gold~~   line indiscriminate within the circle of
      ~~banded sleeve of a commis or~~   plain gray cuff of the soldier or the
      the plain gray cuff of ~~rank~~ of soldier   banded gold of rank, of

MANUSCRIPT   BOOK

MANUSCRIPT		BOOK	
	or the ~~gold~~ banded gold of rank of an army, even if not a war, of gentlemen; where	*Page 123* 1	an army even if not a war of gentle-men, where
21-22	counter covered[?] with cheese or calico or strap	4	counter in a store laden with calico and cheese and strap
22-23	above [illegible word] poems[?], above the suave powdered shoulders of women, or above two raised glasses of ~~wine, claret or champagne~~ scuppernong	5-6	above the suave powdered shoulders of women, above the two raised glasses of scuppernong
25-26	romantic and Bon the fatalist, not there, hidden	11-12	romantic not there and Bon the fatalist, hidden
27	June [MARGIN: in which bugles blew] entering a ~~thousand~~ hundred	14-15	June filled with bugles, entering a hundred
27-28	widows slept in virgin dream un-meditant	16	widows dreamed virgin unmeditant
28-29	five of them, 5 youths, the company, ~~and Henry and Bon not of these~~—a file of 5, mounted with grooms and servants	17-18	five of the company, mounted, with grooms and body servants
30	wagon, made	19	wagon, in their new and unstained gray made
31	house so that each man of the com-pany's sweetheart could take a few	22-23	house until the sweetheart of each man in the company had taken a few
32	departed, who must	24-25	departed. They must
32-42	from wherever it was that ~~they lay hidden~~ they lay hidden, emerging as tho unnoticed from some brake or thicket on the roadside and falling in,	25-33	from whatever place it was that they lurked in, emerging as though unno-ticed from the roadside brake or thicket, to fall in as the marching company passed; the two of them—the youth and the man, the youth deprived twice now of his birthright, who should have made one among the candles and fiddles, the kisses and the desperate tears, who should have made one of the color guard it-self which toured the State with the unsewn flag; and the man who should not have been there at all, who was too old
	unremarked, while the company marched, the two of them, the youth and the man—the youth deprived twice of his birthright now, who should have made one at the nightly dancing, who should have made one of the file who carried the unsewn flag around the state; ~~the man~~ and the man who should not have been there at all, who was too old to be there, both in years and in experience, ~~yet whose curious fate it was to be~~ that mental and spiritual orphan whose fate it was to thrive[?] always among people too young for him and to be	*Page 124* 1-9	to be there at all, both in years and experience: that mental and spiritual orphan whose fate it apparently was to exist in some limbo halfway between

orphaned by the very situation by
which and into which he was doomed—
at the University, by the sheer accumulation of years behind him, into
a law extra academic, into a law
class of 5 or 6; by ⟨in⟩ the war, and
by the same force force, into com-
missioned rank. He received a
lieutenant's commission before the
company went into it's first engagement. I dont think he wanted it; I
imagine him trying to decline it. But
there it was.

where his corporeality was and his
mentality and moral equipment desired to be—an undergraduate at the
University, yet by the sheer accumulation of too full years behind him
forced into the extra-academic of a
law class containing six members;
in the War, by that same force removed into the isolation of commis-
sioned rank. He received a
lieutenancy before

Yes, the 2 of them, the youth and the
man—the youth who deprived twice
now of his birthright, who should have
been one of that file which toured the
state with the unsewn flag; and the
man who should not have been there
at all, who was too old to be there at
all, both in years and in experience:
that mental and spiritual orphan
whose fate it was apparently to exist
in some limbo

Page 55 [5̶3̶ 54]

1-4 halfway between where he should
     have been and where he apparently
     was equipped to be, perhaps even
     wanted to be—an undergraduate at the
     University, yet by the sheer accumu-
     lation of years behind him forced into
     extra-academic, into a law class of
     5 or 6; in war, by the same force re-
     moved into the isolation of commis-
     sioned rank. He received a
     commission before

5   can imagine him even trying

10-11 can even imagine him trying

7   what Arbiter or Judge between

16   what Judge or Arbiter between

7   less, nothing halfway, would

17-18 less would do, nothing halfway or
       reversible would

8   advantage [MARGIN: of being able to
     say *You* go there,] of

19-20 advantage of being able to say *You*
       go there, of

10   Yankee artillery at

23   Yankee guns at

11   for 3 years

25   for two years

14-15 troops who passed through Jefferson
       with the proclamation of freedom, she

32-33 troops to pass through Jefferson, she

MANUSCRIPT		BOOK	
		Page 125	
16	a baby while	2	a child while
17	and ~~keeping a kitchen garden of sorts to keep them alive. And~~ keeping	4	and keeping
18-19	and decaying fishing camp in the ~~bottom~~ river bottom	6	and rotting fishing camp in the river bottom
19	and where	8	and the last deer and bear hunter went out of it, where
20	Wash [MARGIN: and Wash's infant granddaughter] to live, supplying them with fish	9-11	Wash and his daughter and infant granddaughter to live, performing the heavy garden work and supplying Ellen and Judith and then Judith with fish
20-21	now who had never approached nearer to it before than	12-13	now, who until Sutpen went away, had never approached nearer than
23	guffawing;—not	19	guffawing. It was not
25-26	vanished, ~~and~~ none knew why nor where and none asked, just as now none asked when	24	vanished. When
27	drawn by a mule now, a plow mule, and	26-27	drawn now by a mule, a plow mule, soon the plow mule, and
28	to have put the mule into it or waiting to take the mule out,	28	to put the mule in the harness and take it out,
28-29	women where (there were wounded in Jefferson during that first and second summers) in	29-30	women—there were wounded in Jefferson then—in
30	of injured	32	of strange injured
31	and bedding of the houses where they lived;—none	33	and sheets and linen of the
		Page 126	
		1	houses in which they had been born; there were none
32	husbands and sweethearts, with	3	husbands with
33-34	knowledge; she waiting too and not even knowing for what and why. (Henry and Bon not having known for what either, but at least they knew why) Then	4-6	knowledge. Judith waiting too, like Henry and Bon, not knowing for what, but unlike Henry and Bon, not even knowing for why [*sic?*]. Then
35	the shadow impervious	8	the shade impervious
35-36	very intrinsic weightlessness; no body to be buried—just the shape, the remembrance, translated on some quiet and peaceful	9-11	very weightlessness: no body to be buried: just the shape, the recollection, translated on some peaceful

MANUSCRIPT		BOOK	
38	powderlight	12	powder—light [*sic*]
38	the ~~1000 lbs~~ 1000 lbs. of stone monument	13	the thousand pounds of marble monument
39	annual officers' election)	15-16	annual election of regimental officers the year before)
40	set over the faint ~~sunken-in~~ grassy	17	set above the faint grassy
41	was her grave; and	18	was Ellen's grave. And
41	death in	19	death nailed up in
41	doubtless asking Miss	20	doubtless inviting Miss
41-42	Rosa refusing, waiting too apparently, upon the letter, the first from Bom, the first word from him in	21-23	Rosa declining, waiting, too, apparently upon this letter, this first direct word from Bon in
42	him too beside her mother's monument, she brot in herself,	23-24	him, too, beside her mother's tombstone, she brought to town herself,

Page 56 [~~56~~ 55]

1	[1-22 PASTED IN: no more why she chose your grandmother than your grandmother knew—	29-30	no more why she chose your grandmother to give the letter to than your grandmother knew;
2	which, tho older, had	32	which had
2-3	young, and yet impenetrable, absolutely serene—	33	young and yet absolutely impenetrable,

		Page 127	
6	born with	7	born at the same time with
8	loom and it	13-14	loom only each one wants to weave his own pattern into the rug; and it
10	keep on having	16-17	keep on trying or having
10-11	a chunk of marble with rows of scratches	18	a block of stone with scratches
11	someone who thot about or had time to have	19	someone to remember to have
12	up and	20	up or had time to, and
14-16	paper, a stick—something, anything, not to mean anything and them not even trying to read it nor keep it, but at least it would be a scratch, something else, something that might—" and your grandmother looking[?] at the impenetrable, the absolutely	25-33	paper—something, anything, it not to mean anything in itself and them not even to read it or keep it, not even bother to throw it away or destroy it, at least it would be something just because it would have happened, be remembered even if only from passing from one hand to another, one mind to another, and it would be at least a scratch, some-

MANUSCRIPT   BOOK

			thing, something that might make a mark on something that *was* once for the reason that it can die someday, while the block of stone cant be *is* because it never can become *was*
			Page 128
		1-2	because it cant ever die or perish...' and your grandmother watching her, the impenetrable, the calm, the absolutely
18	"Oh. I? ~~Die?--For love?--Women dent do that~~. No,	6	" 'Oh. I? No,
21-22	now, wherever it is, if it is. ~~Like a the~~ It would be full already. Glutted. Like a theater, an opera house, if what you expect to find is forgetting, diversion, entertainment; like a bed already too full if what]	12-16	now, for them to go to, wherever it is, if it is. It would be full already. Glutted. Like a theater, an opera house, if what you expect to find is forgetting, diversion, entertainment; like a bed already too full if what
25	the sheet [MARGIN: the dry[?] dessicated square,] were	20	the sheet, the dessicated square, were
25	of it: and	22-23	of its former shape and substance: and
25-26	voice not ceasing, speaking still while	23-24	voice speaking on while
27	them: gallant, flowery, indolent, frequent and insincere: sent	25-26	them, gallant flowery indolent frequent and insincere, sent
28	that 30 country miles	26	that forty miles
29	flattering ~~gesture to~~ and (doubtless to him) meaningless gesture	28-29	flattering (and doubtless to him, meaningless) gesture
			Page 129
32-33	their neatly and tediously contrived turns, until	1-2	their elegant and gallant and tediously contrived turns of form and metaphor, until
35	that mark on the oblivion	7-8	that undying mark on the blank face of the oblivion
37	impressed onto the paper by a living hand	10-11	impressed upon the paper by a once-living hand
38-39	any moment while he still did:	13-14	any instant while he still read:
39-40	after ⟨4 years and then after⟩ about 50 years; gentle, ~~even whimsical, incurably pessimistic and sardonic quizzical~~ ⟨sardonic⟩ yet ~~sincere;~~ whimsical	14-16	after the four years and then after almost fifty more, gentle sardonic whimsical

CHAPTER IV

41	I will neither insult you by saying that this is a voice from the dead, nor myself ⬧[?] that it is merely from	18-20	*You will notice how I insult neither of us by claiming this to be a voice from the defeated even, let alone from the dead. In fact, if I were a philosopher I should deduce*

Page 57 [56]

1-2	the forgotten; and certainly not the two of us by saying that it is not dead because not forgotten. In fact, ~~if~~ even tho I am no philosopher, I can deduce		
2-3	commentary and even augur of the times from this paper, this letter	21	*commentary on the times and augur of the future from this letter*
5	a gutted aristocrat, written	24-25	*a ruined aristocrat; and written*
9	1864,	30	*1865,*
9	could be but sheer	30	*would be sheer*

Page 130

15	the foot and	6	*the sole of the foot and*
15-16	from that of a beast. So let it go that we	7	*from the foot of a beast. So say we*
18-19	find ~~place~~ ⟨room⟩ ~~to pause~~ room either to pause to breathe	12	*find space either to pause or* [sic] *breathe*
21	plump ~~wagons~~ defenseless wagons	15	*defenseless sutlers' wagons,*
24-25	Crown, the scarecrows clawing at the boxes with bare hands and with bayonets and opening them and find- ing—	20-22	*Crown, and the scarecrows clawing at the boxes with stones and bayonets and even with bare hands and opening them at last and finding—*
29-30	that you laugh best also when hungry or when frightened. But	28-31	*that only when you are hungry or frightened do you extract some ultimate essence out of laughing just as the empty stomach extracts the ultimate essence out of alcohol. But*

Page 131

31	see: and	1	*see. And*
33-34	enough. (You see again[?], I do not insult you by saying I have waited long enough.) And	3-4	*enough. You will notice how I do not insult you either by saying I have waited long enough. And*
36	what *is*, is	8-32	*what IS— (There. They have started firing again. Which—to mention it— is redundancy too, like the breathing or the need of ammunition. Because sometimes I think it has never stopped. It hasn't stopped of course; I dont mean that. I mean, there has never been any more of it, that there was that one fusillade four years ago*

CHAPTER IV

*which sounded once and then was
arrested, mesmerized raised muzzle
by raised muzzle, in the frozen attitude of its own aghast amazement
and never repeated and it now only
the loud aghast echo jarred by the
dropped musket of a weary sentry or
by the fall of the spent body itself,
out of the air which lies over the
land where that fusillade first
sounded and where it must remain
yet because no other space under
Heaven will receive it. So that means
that it is dawn again and that I must
stop. Stop what? you will say. Why,
thinking, remembering—remark that
I do not say, hoping——; to become
once more for a period without
boundaries or location in time, mindless and irrational companion and
inmate of a body which, even after
four years, with a sort of dismal and
incorruptible fidelity which is incredibly admirable to me, is still
immersed and obliviously bemused in
recollections of old peace and contentment the very names of whose
scents and sounds I do not know that
I remember, which ignores even the
presence and threat of a torn arm or
leg as though through some secretly
incurred and infallible promise and
conviction of immortality. But to
finish.) I cannot say when to expect
me. Because what IS is*

Page 132

39   and will survive,

3-4   *and which therefore, whether it likes
it or not, will have to survive,*

40-41   live. So I cannot say, when[?]; and I
do not ~~have~~ need to say, wait. I just
say, look for me.

5-6   *live.*
      "And

Page 58 [57]

1   "And

4-5   Henry, *I have waited long enough;* ~~I
gave myself a good chance to die and
it seems that I am doomed to live~~
and Henry saying *Do you renounce,
then?*

13-14   Henry *I have waited long enough* and
Henry saying to the other *Do you
renounce then?*

CHAPTER IV

MANUSCRIPT		BOOK	

MANUSCRIPT   **BOOK**

6   *For 3 years*   15   *For four years now*

8-9   fire, ~~the ultimatum accomplished and discharged beside the gate beyond~~ the ultimatum discharged beside the   18-19   fire, the ultimatum discharged before the

9-15   them may have, must have, ridden side by side; ~~the one implacable, ⟨calm and undeviating, perhaps,⟩ unresisting, the fatalist to the last; the other implacable~~ the one calm and undeviating, perhaps unresisting even, the fatalist to the last; ~~the other implacable, remorseless with~~ implacable and unal[?] ⟨unalterable⟩ ~~grief and despair, the~~ ⟨two⟩ ~~faces worn and calm, the voices not~~ even raised: 'Dont ride past the shadow of that limb, Charles,' and 'I shall ride past it, Henry': and then Wash Jones on the Sutpen mule before Miss Rosa's gate shouting her name into the empty and peaceful p.m., at the empty[?] house, saying, 'Air you Miss Coldfield? Then you better come on out yon. Henry has done shot that durn French feller. Killed him dead as a beef.' "   20-22   them must have ridden side by side almost: the one calm and undeviating, perhaps unresisting even, the fatalist to the last; the other

the other

19   house [MARGIN: where a woman waited in a wedding gown and veil made from stolen scraps,] partaking   28-29   house where a young girl waited in a wedding dress made from stolen scraps, the house partaking

20-21   driblets of curtain[?] and carpet, linen and silver and furniture, to help to die ~~men~~ torn   32   driblets of furniture and
Page 133
1   carpet, linen and silver, to help to die torn

21   for years now   2   for months now

23   with long unkempt   6   with unkempt

23-24   as tho cast   7   as if east [*sic*]

25-26   yet over the saddle bow and not aimed, the two worn faces even calm,   10-11   yet across the saddle bow unaimed, the two faces calm,

26-27   *of that limb, Charles,* and   12-13   *of this post, this branch, Charles;* and

27   saddleless Sutpen mule   14   saddleless mule

27   Rosa's house,   14-15   Rosa's gate,

CHAPTER V

MANUSCRIPT

BOOK

Page 59 [58]
[Top of page] October 15, 1935

Page 134

9   *me, whose granddaughter was not only to supersede Ellen but was to supplant me, if*

15   *me, if*

11   *who* [MARGIN: (brute instrument of that justice which presides over human events which, incept in the individual, runs smooth, less claw than velvet: but which, by man or woman flouted, drives on like fiery steel and over-rides both weakly just and unjust strong, both vanquished and innocent victimized, ruthless for appointed right and truth)] *was*

16-22   *who (brute instrument of that justice which presides over human events which, incept in the individual, runs smooth, less claw than velvet: but which, by man or woman flouted, drives on like fiery steel and over-rides both weakly just and unjust strong, both vanquisher and innocent victimized, ruthless for appointed right and truth) brute who was*

12   *shapes of John Sutpen's*

22-23   *shapes and avatars of Thomas Sutpen's*

Page 135

18   *I ~~rode~~ traversed those ~~12 miles,~~ ~~those~~ same*

7   *I traversed those same*

19   *the 1̶8̶〈9〉 since I saw light and breathed̶/ ?)*

9   *the nineteen years since I saw light and breathed?)*

28   *upraised and empty dress.*

22-23   *up-raised and unfinished wedding dress.*

Page 136

37-39   *shell, ~~the (so I thot) cocoon casket marriage-bed-of-love-and-grief, and found that I had come, not too late as I had thot, but come too soon.~~ the, (so I thot) cocoon-casket*

3-4   *shell, the (so I thought) cocoon-casket*

Page 60 [59]
13   *at 80,*

31   *at seventy-four,*

14   *miles and*

33   *miles behind that*
Page 137
1   *walking mile and*

15   *enter at last*

1-2   *enter the door at last*

17   *flesh) I should—the*

4   *flesh) that I would enter—The*

150

MANUSCRIPT		BOOK	
20-21	*rising upward into the dim upper cavern where*	10	*rising into the dim upper hallway where*
24	*take: 'Judith! Judith!' I said.*	16	*take. 'Judith!' I said. 'Judith!'*
27	*it really knows*	19-20	*it actually knows*
28-29	*that power, ~~that dark and inexplicable fierce yet absolutely immobile~~ furious yet absolutely immobile and rocklike antagonism*	22-23	*that force, that furious yet absolutely rocklike and immobile antagonism*
33	*was looking not at*	29	*was not looking at*
35-36	*profound and aural[?] attentive and distracted listening to something*	32-33	*profoundly attentive and distracted listening to or for something*

42-43	*kneeling by it~~//while the inscrutable face still watched me familiar coffee/colored face still watched me//while still the inscrutable familiar~~*	9-10	*kneeling beside it—and I*

Page 61 [60]

1	*—and I*		
1-2	*that); but ~~carrying me I running on toward that face inscrutable familiar coffee/colored face~~—I,*	11	*that)—I,*
4	*inscrutable familiar coffee-colored*	13-14	*inscrutable coffee-colored*
8	*'Dont go*	20	*'Dont you go*
10-11	*were, our voices not raised,*	24	*were, neither of our voices raised,*
14-15	*and it again as tho she had not said it herself but as tho the house spoke it—*	28-29	*and again it was as though it had not been she who spoke but the house itself that said the words—*
16	*have created, produced*	31	*have produced*
17-18	*shell ~~and~~ in which Ellen ~~would be forever~~ [?] ~~a stranger and Henry and Judith not residents but either~~ had had to live and die a stranger and Henry*	32-33	*shell in which Ellen had had to live and die a stranger, in which Henry*

22-23	*name. ~~But it was not that, not her, since she too was but half Sulpen, even tho the wild blood made a better half Sulpen than Goldfield blood did~~. And*	5	*name. And*
24-25	*child. ~~But it was not that.—It Because it was not that.—That~~ But*	7	*child. But*

151

28-42   *child.* ~~'Rosa?' I cried. 'To me?~~   12   *child. 'Rosa?'*
~~To my face?' Then she touched me.~~
~~Possibly, even then, my body did not~~
~~stop; possibly the second voice broke~~
~~and parted us before it (my body)~~
~~had~~

~~Then sh~~ *'Rosa?' I cried. 'To me?
To my face?' Then she touched me.
But even then, I did not stop at once.
Possibly my body never did stop,
that the second voice broke and
parted us before it (my body) had
ever actually stopped, because I can
still remember how,* ~~the~~ *in the actual
shocked* ~~amazement~~ *too soon and
quick to be amazement and outrage
yet,* ~~my blind body still thrust against
hand voice and all (all that solid yet
imponderable weight (she not owner:
instrument; I still say that)~~ *'Rosa?'
I cried. 'To me? To my face?'
Then she touched me—the hand pale
limp and (yes) cold. I knew it would
be cold, even tho I had never touched
her flesh before. As a child I had
more than once seen her and Judith
and even Henry scuffling in the* ~~games~~
*rough games which they (possibly all
children: I do not know) played, and
(so I had heard) she and Judith even
slept together. They had always used
the same bedroom, but Judith in the
bed and she on a pallet on the floor
ostensibly. But I have heard how on
more than one occasion Ellen had
found them both together on the pallet,
and (once) in the bed together. But
not I. Even as a child I would not
even play with the same objects*

Page 62 [61]

1-8   *There is something in the touch of
flesh with flesh which abrogates,
cuts sharp and straight across the
devious intricate channels of decorous ordering, which enemies as well
as lovers know because it makes
them both—touch and touch of that
which is the citadel of the central*

MANUSCRIPT	BOOK

I-Am's private own: not spirit, soul;
the liquorish and ungirdled mind is
anyone's to take in any casual door-
way of this earthly tenement. But let
flesh touch with flesh, and see the fall
of all the eggshell shibboleths of
caste and color too. Possibly even
then my body did not stop, since I
seemed to be aware of it, even
despite the hand, still thrusting
blindly against that solid-yet-impon-
derable

'Rosa?'

	MANUSCRIPT		BOOK
13	*blind and full*	20	*blind full*
14	*mere* ⟨simple⟩ *amazement or outrage*	22	*mere amazement and outrage*
15	*flesh, because*	23	*flesh. Because*
19	*darkened doorway of*	29	*darkened hallway of*
20	*touch flesh, and see the*	30	*touch with flesh, and watch the*

Page 140

	MANUSCRIPT		BOOK
23-24	*soon: 'Take your hand off me, nigger!'—expecting and receiving no answer because we both knew that it was not to her that I spoke.*	2-4	*soon, expecting and receiving no answer because we both knew it was not to her I spoke: 'Take your hand off me, nigger!'*
25-26	*running; she furious in that complete immobility, joined*	6-7	*running, she rigid in that furious immobility, the two of us joined*
26-28	*cord twin sistered to victims to the same fell and haunted darkness. The hand was cold. I knew it would be, even tho I had never touched her flesh before. As*	8-9	*cord, twin sistered to the fell darkness which had produced her. As*
28	*once seen her*	9	*once watched her*
30	*I had ⟨have⟩ heard)*	11	*I have heard)*
32	*than one occasion Ellen had found them both in the same bed and on*	14	*than once [sic] occasion Ellen has [sic] found them both on*
37	*touched. I touched it now. We stood there so: and now it was not outrage, it was and then*	21-22	*touched. We stood there so. And then*
38	*outrage upon which I waited,*	22	*outrage that I waited for,*
39	*itself; I*	24	*itself. I*
41	*words, since I still am not certain of just what was said between us from the moment I entered*	26-27	*words (and not*

153

CHAPTER V

Page 63 [62]

1-3   *the door until Judith called her name*
       from ~~above~~ beyond the stairs we
       said in words and what we did not
       say in words, not because we did
       not have time to, not because we did
       not need to, but because we did not
       dare—(not

3   *perhaps already I knew,*   27   *perhaps I knew already,*

4   *was both more and less than Sutpen,*   28-29 *was at once both more and less than*
       knew what   *Sutpen, perhaps I knew even then*
                                                      what

6-7   *which* [7-17 PASTED IN: ~~perhaps,~~   33   *which knew*
       ~~to emerge from some door which~~
       knew

                                                Page 141
10   *would know if*   4-5   *would recognize if*

15-17 *altered to the actual dream ~~in~~ which,* 12-16 *altered to fit the dream which, con-*
       conjunctive with the dreamer, be-   *junctive with the dreamer, becomes*
       comes immolated and apotheosized: *immolated and apotheosized:*
       'Mother and Judith are in the nursery   *'Mother and Judith are in the nur-*
       with the children, and Father and   *sery with the children, and Father*
       Charles are walking in the garden.   *and Charles are walking in the gar-*
       Wake up, Aunt Rosa;]   *den. Wake up, Aunt Rosa;*

20   [20-28 PASTED IN: *(Ay, wake up,*   19-20 *(Ay, wake up, Rosa; wake up—not*
       Rosa; wake up—not from what was,   *from what was, what used to be,*
       what ~~might have been,~~ ⟨used to be,⟩   *but*
       but

28   *and 18 years*   32   *and nineteen years*

28-29 *instead ~~yourself)//and she the~~ your-* 33   *instead yourself) I* [sic]
       self.) I

                                                Page 142
34   *again, but Judith's*   8   *again, though it was Judith's*

35-36 *I knew that*   11   *I realized that*

38   *standing in the hall before*   14   *standing before*

41   *unfinished dress.*   19   *unfinished wedding dress.*

42   *in ~~midstride~~ running's midstride*   20   *in running's midstride*

Page 64 [63]
2-10   *book.*   25-26 *book.*
       That's what I found. Perhaps it's   *That's*
       what I sought—that is, knew (even
       at 19) that I should find. ~~Even~~ Even

154

at 19, which even more than female 16 does, clings to that might-have-been which is more true than truth, from which the dreamer, wakening, says, not 'Did I but dream?' but rather says, indicts high heaven's very self with, 'Why did I wake, since waking I shall never sleep again?' Perhaps I couldn't have wanted more than that, could not have accepted less, since ~~there are con-stant and per~~ living is one constant and perpetual instant when the arras veil between mind and what will be hangs docile and even willing to ~~the~~ ⟨the⟩ ~~lightest thrust~~ [MARGIN: the lightest naked thrust] if we but dared, were brave (not wise, not wisdom needed) enough to make the rending ~~gash~~ That's

11	*couldn't have even wanted*	29	*couldn't even have wanted*
13	*even ~~willing~~ glad*	32	*even glad*
14	*naked ~~touch~~ thrust*	32	*naked thrust*
14-15	*brave ~~enough to make the rending gash.~~ (not wise enough: no wisdom needed here) enough to make*	33	*brave enough (not wise enough: no wisdom needed*

Page 143

		1	*here) to make*
22	*all these years has*	9-10	*all the years of time has*
29-30	*from one to one of the obscurity's*	19-20	*from mote to mote of obscurity's*
33	*and only worthy of*	24-25	*and worthy only of*
37	*experience.—Once there was—they*	31-32	*experience. Ay, grief goes, fades; we know that—but ask the tear ducts if they have forgotten how to weep.— Once there was (they*

Page 144

37-39	*cap* [38-43 PASTED IN: *itulate condensed into one spring, one summer: the ~~summertime~~ spring*	2-3	*capitulate condensed into one spring, one summer: the spring*
42	*urge and ~~sun and weather~~ ⟨time⟩ year and weather;*	7	*urge and hour and weather;*
43-44	*not ~~as woman~~ more child than woman but as even as less than any female]* ~~flesh. Nor do I say even leaf, warped bitter~~	9-10	*not more child than woman but even as less than any female flesh.*

155

MANUSCRIPT	BOOK

Page 65 [64]

1	[1-15 PASTED IN: *flesh.*		
1-2	*green that might have drawn the tender*	12	*green which might have drawn to it the tender*
4	*the* |ɟ*Eves* |*unsistered*| *since*	15-16	*the unsistered Eves since*
4	*chrysalis and canister of*	16	*chrysalis of*
8	*the* ~~summer when I was 14, the~~ *miscast*	21	*the miscast*
9	*of a woman's heart)*	22-23	*of the female heart)*
9-10	*but as* ~~a man~~ *the man which perhaps I should*	23-24	*but rather as the man which I perhaps should*
11	*years, while in that* ~~lightless and~~ *unpaced*	25-26	*years while in that unpaced*
12	*but* ⟨~~which~~⟩ *was some projection of the* ~~womb~~ *lightless womb itself, and I*	26-27	*but rather some projection of the lightless womb itself; I*
14	*free, waiting not*	30	*free, I waited not*
15	*endure;* ~~not growing and~~] *and I*	32	*endure; I*
17	[17-27 PASTED IN: *insulated spark whose origin the fish no longer remembers, which beats at* ~~the~~ ⟨*its*⟩ *crepuscular and lethargic* ~~w~~ *tenement*	33	*insulated spark whose origin the fish*
		Page 145	
		1-2	*no longer remembers, which pulses and beats at its crepuscular and lethargic tenement*
20	*love;* ~~not growing and developing, beloved and loving light, but~~ ~~equipped~~—*yes,*	5	*love—yes,*
23-24	*the normal time I lurked,* ~~from one blank forbidden closed door to the next~~ *unapprehended as tho shod with the damp*	10-11	*the childhood's time I lurked, unapprehended as though, shod with the very damp*
27	*gained my idea of*	15	*gained conception of*
27-28	*it only* ~~thru a piece of smoke~~ *warped and filtered by] a piece*	15-16	*it through a piece*
30	*nightly ravishing by the inescapable* ~~dead~~ *and*	20	*nightly violation by the inescapable and*
32	*breathes.* ~~ǂyes 14 and a girl~~ ꝑ*But*	22	*breathes. But*
34-41	*panoplied like a man instead of hollow woman/:* ~~because I was a man~~ *then. Not* ~~mistress,~~ ⟨*Judith*⟩ ~~not beloved;~~ *I was* ~~the absent lover:~~ ⟨*Charles Bon*⟩ ~~I was all polymath love's androgynous advocate.~~	26-27	*panoplied as a man instead of hollow woman.* *It was*

CHAPTER V

MANUSCRIPT   BOOK

I had never seen him. I never saw him. I never even saw him dead. I heard a name, I saw a photograph, I saw a grave.—That was all.—I helped to make a grave:—and that was all. I saw a shape, a shadow with a name, emerging from the vain and foolish garrulity of my sister, I saw something which yet even had no face reflected by the secret bemused face of a gaze of a young girl; once, on the way back to school that New Year's Henry brot him by the house to see me, but I was not there

Page 66 [66 65]

1-5   [1-11 PASTED IN: *because I went on to out to Sutpen's Hundred and lived two months and (who had learned nothing of love, not even parents' love: that fond dear constant violation of privacy, that stultification of the burgeoning I-Am which is the meed and due of all mammalian meat) assumed became not mistress, not beloved, but more than either: became all polymath love's androgynous advocate.*

―――――――――――――

It was

MANUSCRIPT		BOOK	
5	*first Xmas when Henry brot him home, after the two*	27-28	*first Christmas that Henry brought him home, the summer following the two*
5-6	*vacation before*	29	*vacation which he spent at Sutpen's Hundred before*
8	*John Sutpen*	33	*Thomas Sutpen*

Page 146

MANUSCRIPT		BOOK	
9-11	*his (twice) (now twice) widowed hands competent enough to reach a kitchen shelf, count spoons and hem a sheet and measure milk into a churn yet good for nothing else, yet still too valuable to be left]*[1]	2-5	*his (now twice) widowed hands, I competent enough to reach a kitchen shelf, count spoons and hem a sheet and measure milk into a churn yet good for nothing else, yet still too valuable to be left*

[1] This pasted-in slip covers the following passage written on the page as it originally stood:

who [illegible word] to watch, touch [?] [illegible word] that maiden revery [?] of solitude which is the first thing [?] that [illegible word] in our virginity [several illegible crossed-out words] not to [crossed-out illegible words] such a part of our victory but to [illegible passage of 4 lines]

157

MANUSCRIPT		BOOK	
16	*stay, it*	12	*stay that summer, it*
17	*love* ~~perhaps but just for~~ ⟨perhaps⟩ *(I*	14	*love perhaps (I*
18-19	*person)* ~~yet quick for something~~ *and quick*	16	*person) and quick*
23-24	*incorrigible I-Am which*	24	*incorrigible I which*
26	*to make a child's vacant living fairy-tale* ~~exist~~ *live in*	28-29	*to cause a child's vacant fairy-tale to come alive in*
28	*him (how*	32	*him. (How*
		Page 147	
29	*(and still I say,*	1	*(and I still say,*
31	*has recently whipped*	3-4	*has just whipped*
32	*penny: it was not*	6	*penny. But not*
33-34	*loving.* ~~And it was not man's jealousy, the jealousy of the lover~~ *(Why,*	8	*loving. Why,*
35	*seen no more of his face than that photograph, that picture*	9-10	*seen nothing of his face but that photograph, that shadow, that picture*
37	*roses—I could*	13	*roses, because even before I saw the photograph I could*
43	*make-be-*	24-25	*make-believe.—A*
Page 67 [66]			
1	[1-25 PASTED IN: *lieve—a*		
3	*I lived in*	28	*I dwelt in*
5	*voice.) And it was not man's*	31	*voice. And if jealousy, not man's*
5-6	*lover;* ~~but the lover's self who~~ *it was not the lover's*	32	*lover; not even the lover's*
		Page 148	
8-9	*the* ~~sleepy~~ *flushy sleep* ~~altho the~~ *shame*	4	*the flushy sleep though shame*
13	*secluded bush or*	11	*secluded vine or*
13-14	*what* ~~promise~~ *vow,*	12	*what vow,*
17	*held the imprint*	17	*held invisible imprint*
21	*enough to not need*	23	*enough not to need*
24	*her and been received*	25	*her entitled to be received*
24	*that* ~~secret~~ ⟨maiden⟩ *shameless*	26	*that maiden shameless*
25-26	*what is love' but did not do it because I should have had to say 'Dont*	29	*what love is,' yet who did not do it because I should have had to say*

MANUSCRIPT		BOOK	
	talk to me of love but let me tell you, who know al] ready		*'Dont talk to me of love but let me tell you, who know already*
27	*need.' And then my father came*	32	*need.' Then my father returned and came*
		Page 149	
30	*we use it*	4	*we mean it*
32	*that ~~modicum which~~ penny's*	6–7	*that penny's*
34–35	*he may not feel this giving's weight as he would never know*	11–12	*he will no more feel this giving's weight than he would ever know*
36–37	*cramped perennial unkempt[?] hidden*	14	*cramped small pallid hidden*
38–39	*answer, 'I dont know,' ~~because there is that might/have/been which must be true because it is the rock to which we cling above the maelstrom of unbearable unreality.~~ And*	15–16	*answer, "I dont know." ' And*
39–40	*stayed 4 years and heard*	16–17	*stayed five years, heard*
41	*door* [MARGIN: *and would not even let me pass it—*] *a woman*	20	*door which she would not allow me to enter—a woman*
43	*had started 4 years*	23	*had begun five years*
Page 68 [67]			
1	[1–16 PASTED IN: *had left in Ellen's where*	24–25	*had left in Ellen's, where*
3	*on Sutpen or Coldfield walls*	28	*on Coldfield or Sutpen walls*
6–7	*which must be true which is the single rock to which we cling above*	33	*which is the single rock we*
		Page 150	
		1	*cling to above*
8	*smoke till peace and joy and security*	3–4	*smoke until peace and security*
9	*hope and there was only left maimed*	4–5	*hope, and there was left only maimed*
10–11	*by husbands, brothers, fathers, sweethearts who carried the ~~honor's pride and hope of honor and~~ the pride ~~of hope~~ and hope*	6–7	*by fathers, husbands, sweethearts, brothers, who carried the pride and the hope*
12	*flags; else*	8	*flags; there must be these, else*
16–17	*salvage ~~something~~ at least from the humbled indicted dust something anyway of the old lost enchantment]*	15–17	*salvage at least from the humbled indicted dust something anyway of the old lost enchantment*
17	*heart. ~~And yet I found~~—and found*	17	*heart.—Yes, found*
18–27	*coffin up)*	20	*coffin up the stairs) with the photograph*

Yes. Standing there before that closed door which I was not to enter (and which to my knowledge she herself did not enter again until Jones and the other man carried the coffin in) the photograph hanging at her side and her face absolutely calm, looking at me who believed there must be a seemliness even to the semblance of grief, just raising her voice enough to carry down the stairs: 'Clytie, Miss Rosa will be here for dinner; you will have to get more meal.' ⟨Then: 'Shall we go down? I will have to speak to Mr Jones about a coffin.' That was all. Or rather, not all, since there is no all, no finish; it not the blow we suffer from but the tedious repercussive anti-climax of it, the rubbishy aftermath to clear away from off the very threshold of bereavement. ~~the food which Judith cooked and we ate within the very room which he lay over~~

---

with the photograph

28	*to carry down the stairs:*	22	*to be heard in the hall below:*
29-30	*you will have to get some more meal.' Then: 'Shall*	23-24	*you had better get out some more meal': then 'Shall*
30	*about a coffin.'*	25	*about some planks and nails.'*
33-34	*heard ~~that echoed shot. I saw that closed door~~ an echo but*	30	*heard an echo, but*
36	*boards ~~pulled~~ torn*	33	*boards torn*

Page 151

37-39	*stove —cooked within the very room which he lay over: and how in a ~~worn and shape~~ faded and shapeless sunbonnet which matched the gingham dress she stood and watched, directed them—how*	3-6	*stove—had cooked, ate it in the very room which he lay over, we could hear them hammering and sawing in the back yard, and how I saw Judith once, in a faded gingham sunbonnet to match the dress, giving them directions about making it; I remember how*
40	*sawed beneath that back parlor window; I remember the slow maddening*	7-8	*sawed right under the back parlor window—the slow, maddening*

CHAPTER V

MANUSCRIPT	BOOK

43	*and so screamed again until I*	12-13	*and then had to scream again: until at last I*
44	*a cloudy tide of chickens and then return*[?], *her*	14	*a cloud of chickens, her*

Page 69 [68]

1	[1-19 PASTED IN: *why it must be* ~~there~~ *just there?*	15	*why must it be just there?*
3	*some* ~~amazed~~ *fumbling and amazed ratiocination*	19	*some amazed and fumbling ratiocination*
5-6	*how when we carried him* ~~out and~~ *down*	22	*how as we carried him down*
6	*the* ~~weight~~ *full weight*	23	*the full weight*
6-7	*to some incredulous sense that*	24	*to myself that*
7-8	*tell, or could not, would not believe something I knew*	24-26	*tell. I was one of his pallbearers, yet I could not, would not believe something which I knew*
9-10	*the* ~~digestion might refuse~~ *stomach might refuse something which digestion could not compass—*	28-29	*the stomach sometimes refuses what the palate has accepted but which digestion cannot compass—*
11	*we strain and lean and watch*	31	*we watch*
11-12	*transpire in some soundless vacuum, diminishing, leaving us behind—That*	32-33	*transpire as though in a soundless vacuum, and fade, vanish; are gone, leaving us immobile, impotent, helpless; fixed, until we*

Page 152

		1	*can die. That*
12-13	*there. Something of me trod with the measured tread*	1-2	*there; something of me walked in measured cadence with the measured tread*
13	*and* ~~Isaac McCaslin who~~ *Theophilus*	3	*and Theophilus*
14-15	*unmanageable* ~~strong~~[?] *box* ~~down~~ *past the stair's close curve,* ~~and down~~ *where Judith, following, steadied it, cleared*[?] *it around the turn, and so down;*	4-6	*unmanageable box past the stair's close turning while Judith, following, steadied it from behind, and so down and out to the wagon;*
17	*stood by the gashy earth* ~~bene~~ *under the cedars' gloom*	9	*stood beside the gashy earth in the cedars' somber gloom*
18	*clods and*	10	*clods upon the wood and*
18-19	*said quietly*[?], *'He was a Catholic.* ~~Is anybody here~~ *Does anyone here know how the Catholics—'*	11-12	*said, 'He was a Catholic. Do any of you all know how Catholics—'*

161

CHAPTER V

19-20 *said,* ~~'Damn~~] *'Catholic be damned, he*

13 *said, 'Catholic be damned; he*

22 [22-27 PASTED IN: *something walked with Judith back*

16-17 *something walked with Judith and Clytie back*

25 *that calm unshaking hand*

22 *that firm untrembling hand*

27 *brief and final space*

25 *brief (and this time final) space*

27 *tears. One day he was not. Then*]

26 *tears. Yes. One day he was not. Then*

29 *on a bed,*

29 *on a mattress,*

30 *saw it. For all that I*

30 *saw him. For all I*

31 *murderer* [MARGIN: (we did not even speak of him that day, not one of us; I did not say—the aunt, the spinster— Did he look well or ill? I did not say one of the 1000 trivial things with which the indomitable womanblood ignores that man's world where the blood kinsman shows the courage or cowardice, the folly or lust or fear for which his fellows praise or crucify him)] *who*

31-33 *murderer (we did not even speak of Henry that day, not one of us; I did not say—the aunt, the spinster— 'Did he look well or ill?' I did not say*

Page 153

1-4 *one of the thousand trivial things with which the indomitable woman- blood ignores the man's world in which the blood kinsman shows the courage or cowardice, the folly or lust or fear, for which his fellows praise or crucify him) who*

36 *he* ~~came there of~~ *returned,*

12 *he returned,*

38-43 *Now you will ask me why I stayed there. I could say, I do not know, and be believed. But I do not say it. I stayed there waiting for John Sutpen to return home, to become engaged to marry him. I could say that I did not know at the time that that was why I stayed, and doubtless I would not be believed. Well, I did not know it then,* ~~tho I know now that was why I stayed~~ *what I was waiting for, tho I did know why I waited. I waited for what Judith and Clytie waited for, which was for him, because he was now all we had. Not that we needed him because we did not: we could not have blinded ourselves into that belief.*

14 *Now*

Page 70 [69]

1 *Now*

1 *give 1000 paltry*

15 *give ten thousand paltry*

CHAPTER V

MANUSCRIPT		BOOK	
3	*well in my own home as*	17-18	*well at my own home in town as*
3	*neighbors whose*	18	*neighbors, friends whose*
4	*conduct at least various*	20	*conduct various*
8-9	*kin, I did not and could not understand*	27	*kin to me, I did not understand*
9	*my own observation*	27-28	*my observation*
9-10	*not want to*	28	*not wish to*
11	*different ~~sexes~~ races*	30	*different races*
		Page 154	
13-14	*which ~~animals a bird~~ a beast and a bird would make to one another.*	2-3	*which a beast and a bird might make to each other.*
15	*for John Sutpen*	3-4	*for Thomas Sutpen*
16	*to marry him;*	5	*to him;*
16	*would say I*	6	*would believe I*
18	*for existing, continuing:*	8-9	*for continuing to exist, to eat food and sleep and wake and rise again:*
19	*would try at once*	10-11	*would begin at once*
19-21	*would need him* [MARGIN: I did not then think of marriage; you can believe me when I say so because I shall make no bones to say so when the moment comes to tell you when I did.] *No. We did not even need the first day of the life we were to lead together to blind ourselves into that belief—I who had kept my father's house and him alive for almost 4 years; Judith*	12-20	*would or did need him. (I had never for one instant thought of marriage, never for one instant imagined that he would look at me, see me, since he never had. You may believe me, because I shall make no bones to say so when the moment comes to tell you when I did think of it.) No. It did not even require the first day of the life we were to lead together to show us that we did not need him, had not the need for any man so long as Wash Jones lived or stayed there—I who had kept my father's house and he* [sic] *alive for almost four years, Judith*
21-22	*out there.—and*	20-22	*out here, and Clytie who could cut a cord of wood or run a furrow better (or at least quicker) than Jones himself.—And*
23	*need it is necessity.*	24-25	*need they (the spirit and the heart) are necessary.*
25	*he dismounted from his horse)*	28	*he even dismounted)*
25-26	*restore Sutpen's Hundred to what it*	28-30	*restore the place to what it had been*

MANUSCRIPT   BOOK

       was that he had sacrificed pity and   *that he had sacrificed pity and*
       gentleness and friendship and all   *gentleness and love and all*

26-27   *ever ~~had them~~ had them himself or*   30-31   *ever had them to sacrifice, felt their*
       wanted them   *lack, desired them*

                                       Page 155

31-33   *convent:* [32-35 PASTED IN: *vent:*   6-8   *convent: the walls we had were safe,*
       the walls we had were safe, imper-   *impervious enough, even if it did not*
       vious enough, even if it did not matter   *matter to the walls whether we ate*
       to the walls whether we ate or not.   *or not. And*
       ~~*We kept the house*~~ *And*

34-36   *but ~~with no~~ from no ~~weariness~~ joy in*   11-13   *but from no joy in weariness or re-*
       weariness nor regeneration and in   *generation, and in whom sex was*
       whom sex was some forgotten atrophy   *some forgotten atrophy like the rudi-*
       like the rudimen] *tary*   *mentary*

37   [37-39 PASTED IN: *part of it we lived*   14-15   *part of it we lived in, used;*
       in, used:

37   *which John Sutpen*   15   *which Thomas Sutpen*

39   *expense to get children and to house*   19   *expense of getting children and*
       them]   *housing them*

Page 71 [70]
1-2   *Henry's, as Judith and Clytie had*   21   *Henry's room, as Judith and Clytie*
       kept it, as tho he   *kept it that is, as if he*

2   *then run down*   22   *then ran* [sic] *down*

3-4   *cooked the food which came from it.*   24-25   *cooked and ate the food which came*
                                     out of it.

7   *the garments which we*   31   *the cloth we*

9-10   [9-28 PASTED IN: *ditch-side herbs to* 32-33   *ditch-side herbs to protect and guar-*
       protect and guarantee what spartan   *antee what spartan compromise we*
       compromise we dared or had the   *dared or had the time to make with*
       time to make with the natural ills of   *illness, harried*
       human flesh, harried

                                       Page 156

11   *winter's sustenance—*   2   *winter's warmth and sustenance—*

13   *cultivate flowers, which*   5-6   *cultivate a bed of flowers, let alone*
                                       a kitchen garden, which

14   *own inanimate agency in*   7-8   *own volition in*

16   *tradition into which John Sutpen's*   10-11   *tradition in which Thomas Sutpen's*
       ruthless force had   *ruthless will had*

17   *soft cocoon*   12   *soft insulated and unscathed cocoon*

17-18 *potent matriarch*   13   *potent and soft-handed matriarch*

MANUSCRIPT		BOOK	
20	save, who (~~abetted by Clytie~~ and	17-18	save for the sake of scrimping and saving, who (and
21-22	anyone who stopped and asked; and	19-21	anyone, any stranger in a land already beginning to fill with straggling soldiers who stopped and asked for it; and
22-23	yet could not be free who had never called herself a slave; holding	23-24	yet incapable of freedom who had never once called herself a slave, holding
23	none as the indolent wolf	24	none like the indolent and solitary wolf
24-26	wild, then 'Sutpen', some [illegible word] invincible viciousness like the tamer's whip) which the fates[?] blind hold docile to the fear's[?] hand but which is not, which if it be fidelity is faithful to	26-29	'wild,' then 'Sutpen' is the silent unsleeping viciousness of the tamer's lash) whose false seeming holds it docile to fear's hand but which is not, which if this be fidelity, fidelity only to
27	her skin represented	30	her flesh represented
28	(Clytie) what she declined to be just as she had declined to be that from]	32-33	(Clytie) that which she declined to be just as she had declined to be that from

		Page 157	
30	to [MARGIN: represent to] us the ~~portent of the other~~ threatful portent of the other. We	2-3	to represent to us the threatful portent of the old. We
31	cooked, the	4	cooked in unison, the
35	already ~~the~~ soldiers were beginning to ~~straggle home~~ come	10	already soldiers were beginning to come
38-39	who in his turn[?] abuses, from very despair and pity, the loved wife	16	who abuses from very despair and pity the beloved wife
41	wounds and despair if	19	wounds and left them whole again if

Page 72 [71]			
2	the very soul has	23-24	the attenuated and invincible spirit has
4	John Sutpen	28	Thomas Sutpen
6	would probably sweep us, ~~whether~~ with	31	would undoubtedly sweep us with

		Page 158	
8-9	of John Sutpen too, as tho they were both still in that period which that shot, those running mad feet, had obliterated, as if that	2-4	of his father, as if both they and we still lived in that time which that shot, those running mad feet, had put a period to and then obliterated, as though that

165

MANUSCRIPT

BOOK

10-12 *fall, after the ~~grass had~~ grass and weeds had died and the leaves had ceased to fall when ~~Judith~~ when Judith was absent, ~~I did not ask and I~~ to return at supper*

6 *fall when Judith was absent, returning at supper*

13 *had been to clear that grave—*

8-9 *had gone to clear that grave of dead leaves and the sere brown refuse of the cedars—*

16 *stream of things, a*

13-14 *stream of event: a*

16 *time planned by*

14-15 *time accomplished by*

17 *we refused,*

16 *we declined, refused,*

18 *for ~~37~~ months.*

18 *for seven months.*

18 *one p.m. John Sutpen*

18-19 *one afternoon in January Thomas Sutpen*

19 *looked ~~out a window~~ up from where we worked in the next year's garden and*

19-20 *looked up where we were preparing the garden for another year's food and*

20-29 *drive. And then we lived for ~~2~~ 4 ~~years~~ ⟨months⟩ more. And then one ~~a.m.~~ ⟨evening⟩ I became engaged to marry him.*

21-22 *drive. And then one evening I became engaged to marry him.*
    It took me just three months.

It took me just 4 months. Mind, I do not say he; I. Oh no. I hold no brief for myself: ~~4 months~~ just 4 months, who for ~~19~~ 20 years had looked on him—when I did—had to—look—as an ogre, some beast out of a tale to frighten children with, who had seen his own get upon my sister's body begin to destroy each other as they were doomed to do; just 4 months, until that noon when he who had been seeing me for almost 20 years, just raised his head and paused and looked at me. That was how it happened; that was all. He rode up that drive and into our lives again and ~~left no~~ made scarcely a ripple, because he was not there. The shell was there, using the room which we had kept for him and eating the food which we prepared as tho it could not feel the softness of the bed nor taste nor make distinction in the food by either quality or lack.

CHAPTER V

MANUSCRIPT

BOOK

It took me just 4 months.

	MANUSCRIPT		BOOK
29	*just 4 months,*	23	*just three months,*
32	*first moment,*	27	*first opportunity,*
34	*myself nor do I need them, who could (and would; ay, doubtless have) give*	30	*myself who could (and would; ay, doubtless have already) give*

Page 159

37	*have. No.*	1-2	*have, or for revenge. No.*
37	*not; perhaps*	3	*not. Perhaps*
38	*the ~~portico~~ rotting portico*	4	*the rotting portico*
39-40	*which the man himself did not seem to ride but rather to project*	5-6	*which he did not seem to sit but rather seemed to project*

Page 73 [72]

2-4	*braid/ ~~could not keep up~~ which contained the sentient tho nerveless shell, could not keep up with; ~~watched him dismount and approach Judith who had not moved and stoop and touch her forehead with his beard and heard him say, 'Well daughter~~ which seemed*	9-10	*braid containing the sentient though nerveless shell, which seemed*
4-5	*which he* [MARGIN: *and said, 'Well, daughter' and*] *leaned and*	11	*which he said 'Well, daughter' and stooped and*
7-8	*rapport of that same communal blood which I had felt in the hall that*	15-16	*rapport of communal blood which I had sensed that*
8	*stairs, like this: 'Henry. He's not—*	17	*stairs: 'Henry's not—?'*
9	*not cried yet,*	19	*not wept yet,*
10-11	*midrunning; yes,*	21	*midrunning at that closed door; yes,*
11	*of 4 months erupted instantaneously from every pore of it in*	22-23	*of seven months were erupting simultaneously from every pore in*
12	*then vanished as suddenly as if*	24	*then vanishing, disappearing as instantaneously as if*
13	*in had dried them up; and he still*	25-26	*in were drying the tears faster than they emerged: and still*
14	*Clytie?' and then at me ~~with no recognition in~~—the*	27-28	*Clytie' and then at me—the*
15	*eyes, only the hair ⟨and beard⟩ grizzled*	29	*eyes, the hair grizzled*
16-17	*in it at all until Judith said, 'That's Rosa. She lives here now.' and then he said, 'Ah, Rosa?' Yes, that was all: he*	30-32	*in the face at all until Judith said, 'It's Rosa. Aunt Rosa. She lives here now.' That was all. He*

167

MANUSCRIPT		BOOK	
18	*tears, because*	33	*tears. Because*

19-21	*we prepared as tho it could not feel the softness of the bed nor taste nor make distinction in the food by either quality or taste. Yes, he*	3-6	*we produced and prepared as if it could neither feel the softness of the bed nor make distinction between the viands either as to quality or taste. Yes. He*
28-29	*immobile haste, awareness of the need for haste, as tho he had just drawn his breath*	19-20	*immobile urgency and awareness of short time and the need for haste as if he had just drawn breath*
29	*old* [MARGIN: he was 60 ⟨55⟩ ⟨60⟩ then] *and*	21	*old (he was fifty-nine) and*
30	*age had left him impotent but*	22-23	*age might have left him impotent to do what he intended to do, but*
31	*time enough before he had to die.*	24	*time to do it in before he would have to die.*
32	*even stop for breath before he essayed*[?] *to restore his house and place. to* wh *as*	25-26	*even pause for breath before undertaking to restore his house and plantation as*
33	*nor did he. His*	28-30	*nor I believe did he. He could not have known, who came home with nothing, to nothing, to four years less than nothing. But it did not stop him, intimidate him. His*
34	*flagging immobility*[?] *he*	32	*flagging of the fierce constant will he*

36	*of 55 recuperate—*	3	*of fifty-nine recuperate—*
37	*had done, but of himself,*	5	*had been doing, but about himself,*
38	*years—the natural*	5-8	*years (for all he ever told us, there might not have been any war at all, or it on another planet and no stake of his risked on it, no flesh and blood of his to suffer by it)—that natural*
39	*the raged and incredulous recounting of that*	10-11	*the raging and incredulous recounting (which enables man to bear with living) of that*
39-40	*which, turning against him, declined to slay him who, alive still, yet*	12-13	*which makes that defeat unbearable which, turning against him, yet declined to slay him who, still alive, yet*

CHAPTER V

BOOK

41   *him, because he was gone*   15   *him. He would be gone*

42-43 *threat and even fear//Oh yes, I*   18-19 *threat, and at last force. That was*
       watched him, watched his old man's   *the winter when*
       fury fighting now not with the
       stubborn yet slowly

Page 74 [73]

1-5   *tractable earth as on that first house,*
      but now against the ponderable weight
      of all dead past as tho he tried to dam
      a river with his bare hands and a
      shingle, and for the same spurious
      reward which had already failed him
      once (failed? betrayed: and would
      this time destroy) him once, oh yes,
      I saw the analogy, saw the accelerat-
      ing circle's curve where his ruthless
      pride and lust for magnificence was
      leading him

      and even fear. That was the summer
      when

7-8   *gathered all day long about secret*   23-24 *gathered daily at secret*

9   *the first mud of autumn and*   26   *the mud of early March and*

9   *of yes or no, friend*   26-27 *of definite yes or no, with them or*
                                                    against them, friend

11-12 *wanted, saying that if every man*   29-31 *wanted, telling them that if every man*
       would see to the restoration of that   *in the South would do as he himself*
       which he had left to fight and then   *was doing, would see to the restora-*
       returned to, the general   *tion of his own land, the general*

12-13 *stood there in the door plain within* 33   *stood plain in the doorway holding*
       the lighted door and faced them,   *the*
       faced the ultimatum: Page 162
                                              1-2   *lamp above his head while their*
                                                    spokesman delivered his ultimatum:

19   *turned just 20 yet still a child 20*   11-12 *turned twenty true enough yet*
      true enough, yet

20   *as echo living echo*   13   *as living echo*

22   *women called—my father, Ellen, John* 16-17 *women—my father, my sister,*
      Sutpen, Henry, Judith, Bon—   *Thomas Sutpen, Judith, Henry,*
                                                    Charles Bon—

28   *there so, in the middle of the p.m.,* 26-27 *there in the path looking at me, in the*
      looking at me.   *middle of the afternoon.*

29   *been there, should have been absent,* 29-32 *been anywhere near the house at all*
      not at this point nor at that point, but   *but miles away and invisible some-*

169

MANUSCRIPT

BOOK

where among his hundred square
miles which they had not troubled to
begin to take away from him yet,
perhaps not even at this point or at
that point but

Page 163

30   *enlarged, encompassing*   1   *enlarged, magnified, encompassing*

31-33   *embracing) holding intact that ~~100~~*   2-7   *embracing and holding intact that*
       entire 10 mile square and facing from   *ten-mile square while he faced from*
       the brink of obscurity, implacable and   *the brink of disaster, invincible and*
       unafraid, ~~the destruction~~[?] ~~which~~   *unafraid, what he must have known*
       what he knew would be the final   *would be the final defeat) but instead*
       disaster) yet standing there quietly,   *of that standing there in the path*
       looking at me with something strange   *looking at me with something curious*
       about his face as if that garden barn   *and strange in his face as if the*
       had been   *barn-lot, the path at the instant when*
                                                   he came in sight of me had been

34   *without knowing he was about to*   8-10   *without having been forewarned that*
       [MARGIN: *, and then went on.*] *the*   *he was about to enter light, and then*
       same face,   *went on—the face,*

35-36   *had heard that his son had murdered*   11-12   *had been told that his son had done*
       and vanished and said, 'Ah.   *murder and vanished and said 'Ah.*

36-37   *Clytie. Well, Rosa.' Yes, he went*   13   *Clytie.' He went on to the house.*
       on; he must have, tho I do not re-   *But it was not love: I*
       member. But it was not love, I

37-39   *myself: ~~but as there is a metabolism~~*   14   *myself, I do*
       ~~of the spirit as well as of the entrails~~
       ~~in which the stored accumulations of~~
       ~~long time burn, generate, create and~~
       ~~make some break some maidenhead~~
       ~~of ravening meat //ay, in a second's~~
       ~~time~~. I do

41-42   *not. He was gone, on toward the*   18-19   *not know. He was gone; I did not*
       house, and I did not know that either,   *even know that either since there*
       because there

Page 75 [74]

1   [1-11 PASTED IN: *fierce obliteration.*   23-24   *fierce obliteration. This was my*
       This was mine, who   *instant, who*

1-3   *he was gone and knew not when he*   24-28   *he had gone on and did not remem-*
       walked on, who found my row of   *ber when he had walked away, who*
       mustard finished without remember-   *found my okra bed finished without*
       ing when I did the work, who sat at   *remembering the completing of it,*
       table with the familiar and dream-   *who sat at the supper table that night*
       clouded shell which we were used to   *with the familiar dream-cloudy shell*
                                                     which we had grown used to

MANUSCRIPT		BOOK	
4	*again) I*	29	*again during the meal; I*
4	*deluded filthy* [?] ⟨sewer-⟩ *rush of dreams does*	29-30	*deluded sewer-gush of dreaming does*
5	*Judith's room sat as he we always did, until he came in and*	31-32	*Judith's bedroom sat as we always did until he came in the door and*
6	*still coming in, then*	33	*still entering, then*
		Page 164	
7	*mind; you Rosa*	1	*mind. Rosa*
8	*have* [MARGIN: *of it,'*] *and came over and*	2	*have of it' and came and*
9	*at, save that by his*	4	*at while he spoke, save that by the sound of his*
10	*husband; you*	6	*husband. You*
11-12	*believe that I can promise you that I shall do no worse for you.'*] *So we became engaged; That was my courtship—that*	8-10	*believe I can promise that I shall do no worse at least for you.' That was my courtship. That*
13	*ukase, a serene*	12	*ukase, a decree, a serene*
15	*it, claim*	15	*it. I claim*
15-16	*not answer-yes* ⟨I wi⟩ *not because there was no answer*	16	*not answer*
21-22	*now and saw (analogy and paradox and madness too) Judith's extended palm before my face—that*	23-24	*now, heard Judith's feet, saw Judith's hand, not Judith—that*
23-24	*years of work, of heat and cold, harsh* [?] *work-and* [illegible word] *scoriating loom, of actual axe at times and all the tools*	26-27	*years of scoriating loom, of axe and hoe and all the other tools*
24-25	*use—and on it lying* [MARGIN: *in immobile paradox*] *the ring which he had given Ellen gave Ellen*	27-28	*use: and upon it lying the ring which he gave Ellen*
25-28	*and took that ring, felt him slip it on my finger in my turn and heard him* [MARGIN: *yes, listened to his voice and told myself, 'Why he is mad. He will decree this marriage for tonight, himself both groom and minister; pronounce his own wild benediction on it: and I mad to, [sic] for I will acquiesce, succumb, abet him and plunge down.'*] *as Ellen herself must have listened in her own vain halcyon*	29-33	*and felt, not watched, him slip the ring onto my finger in my turn (he was sitting now also, in the chair which we called Clytie's while she stood just beyond the firelight's range beside the chimney) and listened to his voice as Ellen must have listened in her own spirit's April thirty*
		Page 165	
		1	*years ago: he talking not about*

MANUSCRIPT		BOOK

spirit's vain April in her turn[?] *(he
was sitting now too, in the chair which
we—the 3 of us—called Clytie's while
she stood just beyond the firelight's
range beside the chimney⟩ talking
as Ellen had heard him, not about*

	MANUSCRIPT		BOOK
29-30	*no* ~~listener—mortal listener—but to the very dark forces of fate which he had evoked and dared~~ *sane*	2	*no sane*
31-32	*dream* ~~exactly as he must have told it to Ellen 30 years ago~~*, where an intact Sutpen's Hundred* ~~no more existed which no more rose~~ *existed which*	4-5	*dream where an intact Sutpen's Hundred which*
34-35	*it, freezing*[?] *it.*~~—sat there and listened to his~~*—yes, sat and*	8	*it, froze it. Yes. I sat there and*
35-36	*tonight, himself*	10	*tonight and perform his own ceremony, himself*
37-41	*his* ~~hand:—and I mad too, for I will acquiesce, succumb, abet him and plunge down.~~'	12	*his hand: and*

*No, I hold no brief, I ask no pity. If
I was saved that night, it was no fault,
no doing, of my own.* ~~but rather because, once he had restored the ring, he ceased to look at me except as he had done for 20 years. Perhaps it was some interval of sanity which he entered we lived another 12 months so.~~ *(Yes, I was saved; mine was to
be some later, colder sacrifice, when
we (I) should be free of all excuse of
the surprised and betraying flesh)*

Page 76 [75]

1	[1-20 PASTED IN: *hand: and*		
4-5	*me except as he had done for 20 years before that p.m. in the garden path, as tho he*	18-19	*me save as he had looked for the twenty years before that afternoon, as if he*
7	*that. For 6 months*	22	*that even. For three months*
9	*we furnished,*	25	*we supplied,*
9-10	*the unhampering of the mad*	26	*the mad*
10	*next ⟨4⟩ 2 months*	26	*next two months*

Page 166

17	*had not thot about*	4-5	*had never once thought about*

CHAPTER V

<table>
<tr><td>MANUSCRIPT</td><td></td><td>BOOK</td><td></td></tr>
<tr><td>18</td><td>*waited those 2 months) no more to him than the absence*</td><td>6-7</td><td>*waited two months or even two days to ask it)—my presence was to him only the absence*</td></tr>
<tr><td>20-21</td><td>*undefeat—and had at last and without] forewarning blundered out upon dry solid earth; light, sky and sun—if*</td><td>10-12</td><td>*undefeat—and blundered at last and without warning onto dry solid ground and sun and air—if*</td></tr>
<tr><td>27</td><td>*which (friends never, acquaintances once, but now enemies) discharged*</td><td>20-21</td><td>*which men who were once his acquaintances even if not his friends discharged*</td></tr>
<tr><td>28</td><td>*madman's ~~who~~ plan that gained him at the lowest price*</td><td>22-23</td><td>*madman's plan or tactics which gained him at the lowest possible price*</td></tr>
<tr><td>29</td><td>*point* [MARGIN: *; not madman, no: since surely there is something in madness, even the demoniac, which Satan flees aghast at his own handiwork and which God looks on in pity— some spark, some crumb to leaven and redeem that articulated flesh,* [illegible word] *sight hearing taste and being which we call human man*]— *But, no*</td><td>25-29</td><td>*point—not madman, no: since surely there is something in madness, even the demoniac, which Satan flees, aghast at his own handiwork, and which God looks on in pity—some spark, some crumb to leaven and redeem that articulated flesh, that speech sight hearing taste and being which we call human man. But no*</td></tr>
<tr><td>31-33</td><td>*told; I ~~could repeat to you the bold blank naked and outrageous words just as he spoke them; I could take that many sentences, and bequeath you~~ could*</td><td>33</td><td>*told; I could*</td></tr>
<tr><td></td><td></td><td colspan="2">*Page 167*</td></tr>
<tr><td>38</td><td>*see, I thot I was that sun, ~~who believed there was that crumb, that spark in madness~~ or thot I was, who*</td><td>7</td><td>*see, I was that sun, or thought I was who*</td></tr>
<tr><td colspan="2">*Page 77* [~~79~~ 76]</td><td></td><td></td></tr>
<tr><td>1</td><td>[1-25 PASTED IN: *associate with as tho my*</td><td>12-13</td><td>*associate with as if my*</td></tr>
<tr><td>2</td><td>*murder, parricide—*</td><td>15</td><td>*murder—*</td></tr>
<tr><td>3</td><td>*no) suffered—*</td><td>16-17</td><td>*no) courageously suffered—*</td></tr>
<tr><td>6</td><td>*memory and past, even*</td><td>21</td><td>*memory, even*</td></tr>
<tr><td>15</td><td>*love which would be sun*</td><td>3-4</td><td>*love that would be, might be sun*</td></tr>
<tr><td>16-17</td><td>*potently of no age ~~because of it~~ since*</td><td>6</td><td>*potently without measured and measurable age since*</td></tr>
<tr><td>18</td><td>*I will give you airy limitless space*</td><td>8</td><td>*I can give you airy space*</td></tr>
<tr><td>19-20</td><td>*of principle and belief, and*</td><td>11</td><td>*of pride and principle, and*</td></tr>
</table>

173

MANUSCRIPT		BOOK	
20	old ~~aghast~~ outraged	12	old outraged
20-21	lasted 45 years:⊢ he ~~rode~~ returned	13	lasted for forty-three years —he returned
21-24	you that he did not think of it until the moment—that moment which contained the distance to the house from where he was when he thot of it—when he said it. (aAnd that too coincident; it was the day, the very moment, when he saw that he had saved his land, when, no matter	15-21	you he had not thought of it until that moment, that prolonged moment which contained the distance between the house and wherever it was he had been standing when he thought of it: and this too coincident: it was the very day on which he knew definitely and at last exactly how much of his hundred square miles he would be able to save and keep and call his own on the day when he would have to die, that no matter
25	Hundred)—called,	22-23	Hundred even though a better name for it would now be Sutpen's One— called,
25-26	He did not even hitch the horse nor drop the] reins; he just stood so (and no hand on my head now even) and	24-26	He had not even waited to tether his horse; he stood with the reins over his arm (and no hand on my head now) and
27	words exactly as tho he were consulting with Jones about a cow	26-27	words exactly as if he were consulting with Jones or with some other man about a bitch dog or a cow
28-29	him; found a man but failed to keep	30-31	him; caught a man but couldn't keep
30	bitter country [MARGIN: orphaned] stick	32	bitter orphaned country stick
30-31	Coldfield ~~engaged-at-last~~ safely engaged at last; ~~Rosa-Coldfield-left an-orphan~~ they	33	Coldfield, safely engaged at last and so off the town,
		Page 169	
		1	the county; they
31-36	went to live (for the rest of my life they will tell you, doubtless that I saw in my nephew's murder an act of God to enable me to fulfill my sister's dying request to at least save one of the children which she had doomed when she conceived them) in that house which before I could walk I had been taught to look upon as inhabited by the sister who had been sold by her father to a demon [MARGIN: and in which, for some undivulged reason, the rest	1-6	went out there to live for the rest of my life, seeing in my nephew's murdering an act of God enabling me ostensibly to obey my dying sister's request that I save at least one of the two children which she had doomed by conceiving them but actually to be in the house when he returned who, being a demon, would

of my blood seemed doomed to run
out its tedious remaining span]:
but I not gone there to save that
child as I had promised, but because
it was the demon's house and he,
being a demon, ~~was~~ [illegible word]
would

	MANUSCRIPT		BOOK
37-38	*return: and I waiting for him to* *return because I was young still, at* *the age for marrying and in a house* *and place*	7-9	*return; I waiting for him because I* *was young still (who had buried no* *hopes to bugles, beneath a flag) and* *ripe for marrying in this time and* *place*
38-41	*the live ones (as happens in war)* *old or already married or too tired,* *too tired for love—this too at a time* *and in an environment where my* *chances at best (even lacking war)* *would have been slender enough,* *being as I was not only a Southern* *lady the very modest nature of whose* *background must needs be its own* *affirmation: that had I*	10-15	*the living ones either old or already* *married or tired, too tired for love;* *he my best, my only chance in this:* *an environment where at best and* *even lacking war my chances would* *have been slender enough since I* *was not only a Southern gentlewoman* *but the very modest character of* *whose background and circumstances* *must needs be their own affirmation* *since had I*

Page 78 [77]

1	*flowers ~~from~~ and notes* [?] *from* *almost no one* ⫽ ~~that~~ *and*	18	*flowers from almost no one and*
2-5	*business; that, young, I had buried* *no hopes to bugles, beneath a flag;* *and, daughter of an embusque, why* *should I have not turned to him—I* *who was already, even before then,* *doing my part toward embalming the* *war and its heritage of suffering* *and injustice by writing it into* *verse; and therefore I had been* *right in hating my father because* *if*	20-28	*business—Yes, they will have told* *you: who was young and had buried* *hopes only during that night which* *was four years long when beside a* *shuttered and unsleeping candle she* *embalmed the War and its heritage* *of suffering and injustice and sorrow* *on the backsides of the pages within* *an old account book, embalming* *blotting from the breathable* [sic] *air the poisonous secret effluvium* *of lusting and hating and killing—* *they will have told you: daughter of* *an embusque who had to turn to a* *demon, a villain: and therefore she* *had been right in hating her father* *since if*
5-6	*attic I would not have gone out there* *to ~~live~~ find food and shelter and* *protection: and if I had*	29-30	*attic she would not have had to go* *out there to find food and protection* *and shelter and if she had*

CHAPTER V

<table>
<tr><td colspan="2">MANUSCRIPT</td><td colspan="2">BOOK</td></tr>
<tr><td>6-8</td><td>food <s>to keep me alive</s> and clothing (even tho I helped to plant and weave it) to keep me alive and warm until simple justice (if nothing else) required that I make</td><td>30-32</td><td>food and clothing (even if she did help to grow and weave it) to keep her alive and warm, until simple justice demanded that she make</td></tr>
<tr><td>8-9</td><td>might desire of me commensurate with honor and pride, I would</td><td>33</td><td>might require of her commensurate with honor,</td></tr>
<tr><td></td><td></td><td colspan="2">Page 170</td></tr>
<tr><td></td><td></td><td>1</td><td>she would</td></tr>
<tr><td>10</td><td>night and ask myself Why</td><td>2-3</td><td>night asking herself Why</td></tr>
<tr><td>10-11</td><td>as I have done for 45 years—</td><td>3-4</td><td>as she has done for forty-three years:</td></tr>
<tr><td>11</td><td>hating my father—and that those 45 years of <s>outrage</s> impotent</td><td>4-5</td><td>hating her father and so these forty-three years of impotent</td></tr>
<tr><td>14-15</td><td>Coldfield, <s>weep</s> ⟨lose⟩ him, <s>lose</s> ⟨weep⟩ him; found a beau but</td><td>10-11</td><td>Coldfield, lose him, weep him; found a man but</td></tr>
<tr><td>16</td><td>women. They had</td><td>12</td><td>women, who had</td></tr>
<tr><td>16</td><td>that. They want</td><td>13</td><td>that; who want</td></tr>
<tr><td>18</td><td>belongings and come</td><td>17-18</td><td>belongings (that is, put on the shawl and hat again) and come</td></tr>
<tr><td>20-21</td><td>[20-44 PASTED IN: and gone and where Judith would come now and then and bring her some of what food they had out at Sutpen's Hundred: and</td><td>19-21</td><td>and gone and where Judith would come now and then and bring her some of what food they had out at Sutpen's Hundred and</td></tr>
<tr><td>21</td><td>necessity which [sic] brot her (Rosa Coldfield)</td><td>21-22</td><td>necessity, the brute inexplicable flesh's stubborn will to live, brought her (Miss Coldfield)</td></tr>
<tr><td>22</td><td>farmers, and negro</td><td>23</td><td>farmers passing, negro</td></tr>
<tr><td>23-27</td><td>plant in it and nobody to work it with herself even if she had known how, had learned more during her stay at Sutpen's Hundred than to do what Judith or Clytie told her to do, and doubtless would not have worked it if she had known, since she had never surrendered: and how she would reach thru the garden fence and gather <s>greens</s> vegetables, who would</td><td>26-30</td><td>plant one with, no tools to work it with herself, even if she had known completely how, who had had only the freshman year at gardening and doubtless would not have worked it if she had known; reaching through the garden fence and gathering vegetables though she would</td></tr>
<tr><td>27</td><td>would even have done</td><td>30-31</td><td>would have even done</td></tr>
<tr><td>28</td><td>who <s>used to</s> would</td><td>33</td><td>who would</td></tr>
</table>

176

MANUSCRIPT		BOOK	
29	*night: but*	34	*night. But*
		Page 171	
30	*could reach them,*	2	*could grasp them,*
31	*passed: and it not*	3-4	*passed. It was not*
33-34	*wrote her poems about*	7-8	*wrote verse about*
34-35	*him, found a beau but failed to keep him—(Oh*	9	*him; caught a beau but couldn't keep him; (oh*
36-37	*it; when she heard it realized like in a thunderclap that he might have been thinking it for*	12-13	*it about her so that when she heard it she realized like thunderclap that it must have been in his mind for*
37-38	*maybe—had been looking at her daily and thinking it and she did not know it—But I forgave him. Why*	14-16	*maybe, he looking at her daily with that in his mind and she not even knowing it. But I forgave him. They will tell you different, but I did. Why*
39	*him. Oh not*	17-20	*him: a certain segment of rotten mud walked into my life, spoke that to me which I had never heard before and never shall again, and then walked out; that was all. I never owned him; certainly not*
39-40	*and think (but you ~~I forgave~~ are wrong) that I mean.*	21	*and maybe think (but you are wrong) I mean.*
41	*owned, not articulated*	23-25	*owned by anyone or anything in this world, had never been, would never be, not even by Ellen, not even by Jones' granddaughter. Because he was not articulated*
41-42	*the* [MARGIN: light-blinded bat-like] *image of his own fierce*[?] *torment*	26-27	*the light-blinded bat-like image of his own torment*
42	*up thru the*	27-28	*up from beneath the*
43	*his ~~doomed~~*[?] ⟨descending⟩ [MARGIN: (ay, do you mark the gradation?)] *ellipsis,*	30	*his descending (do you mark the gradation?) ellipsis,*
44	*him, ~~the~~* [illegible word] *~~effigies~~*[?] *both*[?]]	32	*him, save him, arrest him—Ellen (do*
Page 79 [78]			
1	[1-13 PASTED IN: *—Ellen (ay, do*		
1-2	*that granddaughter slut of Jones's, to find rest and severance at last*	33-34	*that fatherless daughter of Wash Jones' only child who, so I heard once, died in a Memphis brothel—to find*

MANUSCRIPT BOOK

Page 172

1 severance (even if not rest and peace) at last

2 scythe. And I told that too tho not

2 scythe. I was told, informed of that too, though not

8-9 bed between them and then caught swiftly up and held before her by the white girl as

13-14 bed and then caught swiftly up by the white girl and held before her as

9-10 hair and his gaunt weathered worn face,

15-16 hair, his gaunt worn unshaven face,

13-20 turn, neither making any attempt to guard against]² the blows:
'Now you cant marry him.'
'Why cant I marry him?'
'He's dead.'
'Dead?'
'Yes. I killed him.'
He couldn't pass that; he

22-29 turn neither making any attempt to guard against the blows.
Now you cant marry him.
Why cant I marry him?
Because he's dead.
Dead?
Yes. I killed him.
He (Quentin) couldn't pass that. He

20-23 said, *Ma'am? What's that? What did you say?*
There's something in that house.
What? In that house? That will be ⟨old⟩ Clytie.
~~Yes.~~ ⟨No.⟩ Something ~~out there~~.
⟨living in it.⟩ It has been there a long time, living hidden in that house.

30-34 said, "Ma'am? What's that? What did you say?"
"There's something in that house."
"In that house? It's Clytie. Dont she—"
"No. Something living in it. Hidden in it. It has been out there for four years, living hidden in that house."

²This pasted-in slip covers the following passage written on the page as it originally stood:
"Because he's dead."
"Dead."
"Yes. I killed him."
He could not pass it. He was not even listening to her; he said, *"Ma'am? What was that? What did you say?"*
"Some~~body~~ ⟨thing⟩ ~~out there~~ in that house."
"What?" ~~Quentin said.~~ ~~"Out there~~ in that house?"
"Yes. There is some~~body~~ ⟨thing⟩ out there. [Two crossed-out illegible words] ~~in that house.~~ It has been out there a long time, living hidden in that house."

CHAPTER VI

Page 80 [79]

Page 173

1-2	[1-19 PASTED IN: There was no snow on Shreve's ungloved square blond hand red and raw from the cold, going away, vanishing: and now on the table before Quentin, intervening[?] the open	1-3	There was snow on Shreve's overcoat sleeve, his ungloved blond square hand red and raw with cold, vanishing. Then on the table before Quentin, lying on the open
2-3	white still square of envelope,	4	white oblong of envelope,
3	blurred sharp and mechanical	5	blurred mechanical
6	cigar,	10	cigar-smell,
9-10	almost a week and	15	*almost two weeks and*
14	*well and*	21-22	*well. And*
15	*a sudden confounding[?] slow*	23	*a slow*
16-17	*with what it has over a long period of bewilderment and dread been taught*	23-25	*with that which over a long period of bewilderment and dread it has been taught*

Page 174

19	*of 45 years has been companionship and bread and*]	3-4	*of forty-three years has been companionship and bread and*
20-28	*either—*	4-6	*either——*

No he will have to say *Neither aunt cousin nor uncle Rosa, Miss Rosa, Miss Rosa Coldfield, an old lady that died young of outrage in 1866 one summer* and Shreve *You mean she was no kin to you, that there was no kin to you at all, that there was actually one Southern Bayard or Guinevere that wasn't any kin to you at all, then what did she die for* and that not Shreve's first time, no first time to hear such as that in Cambridge since September; *Tell about the South, what's it like there, what do people do there, why do they live there, why do they live at all, why do they bother to die:* and he down again along that road in the moonless September dust, in the light buggy behind the fat horse

————————————

—that very September p.m. itself

——the letter bringing with it that very September evening itself

MANUSCRIPT

BOOK

32-33 Tell about the South, what's it like there, what do they do there, why do they live there, why do they live at all, why do they bother to die.)—

13-15 *Tell about the South. What's it like there. What do they do there. Why do they live there. Why do they live at all)—*

35-36 listening now too since there was something which he too had not been able to pass:

18-19 listening, since he had something which he still was unable to pass:

36 young face

20-21 youthful face

38 the cast

23-24 the rest of the cast

38-40 commencement; the two of them, the brother and the sister standing breast to breast and hurling at one another with ~~ten then a dozen words, hurling 12 words~~ 12 or 14 words. [MARGIN: and most of these the same ones said 2 or 3 times, so that when you boiled ~~them~~ ⟨it⟩ down, they did it with just 10. and ~~that's a record on anybody's dice~~]—And she had

24-30 Commencement, the sister facing him across the wedding dress which she was not to use, not even to finish, the two of them slashing at one another with twelve or fourteen words and most of these the same words repeated two or three times so that when you boiled it down they did it with eight or ten.

And she (Miss Coldfield) had

40-41 known, and the ~~black~~ bonnet (black once tho faded long since to that fierce hushed green

31-32 known she would, and the bonnet (black once but faded now to that fierce muted metallic green

Page 175

41 bag, con-
Page 81 [~~81~~ 80]
1 [1–31 PASTED IN: taining

1-2 bag containing

2 be opened by

4 be solved by

3 for and used with, like

6 for like

4 general ~~air to breathe and~~ weight of air to [MARGIN: displace] breathe

8-9 general weight of air to displace and breathe

5-6 oblivious [MARGIN: biding] earth to support their weight—; that p.m. the 12 miles ~~in the moonless September dust~~ behind the fat horse, in

9-11 oblivious biding earth to bear their weight—That evening, the twelve miles behind the fat mare in

6-7 road, the entire ⟨~~arboreal~~⟩ circum-adjacence ~~of~~ arboreal and inferential[?], did not rise but squatted like

11-12 road not rising soaring as trees should but squatting like

8 of fowls, heavy with 40 days

13-14 of panting fowls, heavy with sixty days

9-10 like submarine masses

17 like masses

13 foot to

23 foot of dust to

MANUSCRIPT		BOOK	
		Page 176	
21-22	the grim implacable small figure smelling of heat-distilled old woman-flesh and heat-distilled camphor from the old fold-creases in the shawl, feeling himself like an electric bulb since	2-6	the implacable doll-sized old woman clutching her cotton umbrella, smelling the heat-distilled old woman-flesh, the heat-distilled camphor in the old fold-creases of the shawl, feeling exactly like an electric bulb, blood and skin, since
23-25	him, produced not enough movement in him to cause his skin to sweat, thinking Good Lord yes, let's dont find him or it, dont try to find him or it, dont risk disturbing him or it (and Shreve again now: "Wait.	7-10	him with motion, created not enough motion within him to make his skin sweat, thinking *Good Lord yes, let's dont find him or it, try to find him or it, risk disturbing him or it:* (then Shreve again, "Wait.
30	in 45 years	17-18	in forty-three years,
31-42	at night to prove if she was right or not and she was right?" "Yes," Quentin said. ~~"Wait then" Shreve said. Wait. Wait."~~)]	20-23	at midnight to see if she was right or not?" [closing parenthesis omitted] "Yes," Quentin said. "That this old dame that grew

~~Faustus brother-in-law came back home and so she became engaged to him.~~ That she grew up in a household like an overpopulated mausoleum, with nothing to need to do and no claim on her time except the hating of her father and aunt and her sister's husband in peace and comfort and wait for the day to come when they would prove not only to everybody else (not her: she didn't need it) but to themselves that she was right, and so sure enough one night the aunt slid down the rainpipe with a mule trader and fixed that: and then her father nailed himself up in the attic to keep from being drafted into the Rebel army and starved to death and fixed that except for the unavoidable possibility that when the moment came for him to tell himself that she had been right he couldn't hear himself speak or there was no one there to tell it to: and now there was [illegible word] this Faustus, this brother-in-law who seemed to be impervious not only to her and public opinion but to justice too only Providence had not forgot her, one p.m. this Jones rides

181

BOOK

up on a borrowed mule and sits in the
street hollering [illegible word] to
her that her nephew has just killed
his sister's fiance and it even looks
like that is fixed

Page 82 [81]

1-2   That this dame, this Aunt Rosa—"
        "Miss Rosa,"—Quentin said I tell
        you," Quentin said. "All right, all
        right [MARGIN: all right,"] Shreve
        said. "—who grew

3   no claim or call on her time except   24-25   no call or claim on her time but the
        the

4-16   would each of them prove not only to   27-30   would prove not only to themselves
        everybody else but to themselves that   but to everybody else that she had
        she had been right, and so one night   been right. So one night the aunt slid
        the aunt slid down a rainpipe with a   down the rainpipe with a horse trader,
        mule trader   and she was right about the aunt so
        that fixed that: then her father nailed
        himself up

---

and so she was right about the aunt
and that fixed that: and then one day
her father nailed himself up in the
attic and starved h to keep from being
drafted into the Rebel army and died
starved to death and that fixed that
except for the unavoidable possibility—
life and death being what they are—
that when the instant came to admit
to himself that she was right he may
not have been able to hear himself
speak or may not have had anyone
there to tell it to, and she was right
about the father because if he hadn't
made General Lee and Jeff Davis mad
he would not have had to shut himself
up in the attic and so die and leave
her an orphan and a pauper—and right
about the brother/in/law and so would
not have had to go out to Sutpen's
Hundred

---

and so left her at the mercy of a man
who would disregard all his responsi-
bilities to her to the extent of nailing
himself up in an attic for a principle
and so that fixed that: she was right
about the aunt and that fixed that:
and then one day her father shut himself

CHAPTER VI

MANUSCRIPT

BOOK

17-19   starved ~~and so left her an orphan and a pauper~~ to death and that fixed that save for the unavoidable possibility— life ~~being wh~~ and death being what they are: the one a delusion in its own right and the other an illusion of the first—that when the instant came to admit

32-33   starved to death, so that fixed that except for the unavoidable possibility that when the moment came for him to admit

Page 177

20   have ~~had~~ been able to hear himself speak or

1-2   have been able to speak or

20-21   to and she right about the father be- cause if

2-3   to: so she was right about the father too, since if

22-23   and so die and leave her orphan and pauper ~~who would~~ and so situated and rendered[?] susceptible

5-6   and die and if he hadn't died he wouldn't have left her an orphan and a pauper and so situated, left sus- ceptible

23-24   she might have received the outrage and affront which she received:

7   she could receive this mortal affront:

24-41   had not been a demon he could not have begot two half demon children ~~who would~~ to consume and destroy one another's posterity and his own and so she would never have had occasion to go out there and try to save the one which remained as she had promised her dying sister and so be betrayed by the old meat ~~to more than acquiesce, to more than recon- cile: to compound~~ to remain[?] ~~no longer the Cassandra~~ until this Faustus remains[?] no longer the widowed Agamemnon to her Cassandra but became instead the ancient Pyramus to her untried but eager Thisbe, she more than acquiescent, more than reconciled even to this unbidden April's ~~compound of demonry~~ compounded demonry. And so laid liable to the suggestion that she breed herself to him for test and sample as tho she were a horse or a cow and so that not fixed at all, doomed never to be fixed forever and ever: ~~since~~ and she blown as it were back home [MARGIN: on the identical blast of that horror and outrage] to

8-28   hadn't been a demon his children wouldn't have needed protection from him and she wouldn't have had to go out there and be betrayed by the old meat and find instead of a widowed Agamemnon to her Cassandra an ancient stiff-jointed Pyramus to her eager though untried Thisbe who could approach her in this unbidden April's compounded demonry and suggest that they breed together for test and sample and if it was a boy they would marry; would not have had to be blown back to town on the initial blast of that horror and outrage to eat of gall and wormwood stolen through paling fences at dawn. So this was not fixed at all and forever because she couldn't even tell it because of who her successor was, not because he found a successor by just turning around, and no day's loss of time even, but because of who the succes- sor was, that she might conceivably have ever suffered a situation where she could or would have to decline any office which her successor could have been deemed worthy, even by a

183

CHAPTER VI

eat ga of gall and wormwood stolen
thru paling fences at dawn and-it
since it was never to be fixed forever since now she could never be
justified herself or see him con-
demned since she could not tell it
and could not bear to have it known
because of who and what her successor was: not the fact that he found a
successor apparently by merely
turning around and apparently without a day's loss or falter in his
stride, but because of who the successor was [MARGIN: , that she might
ever have been forced, to refuse
suffered the affront situation in which
to decline any office which her successor should could have been deemed
worthy to fill;] no help for her now
seeing his daily wrongs and wrong-
ing[?] and knowing that the wrong-
doing[?] was his innoculation and
guarantee forever from even having
to admit it because-at-the-moment-of
admitting-he-would-be-dead-too, that
even the satisfaction of knowing that
Clytie had to watch the present
wrong-doing[?] with despair probably,
with rage and impotence surely, with
impotence surely[?] surely no com-
pensation for the fact that he himself
never would have to admit because

demon, to fill; this not fixed at all
since when the moment came for him
to admit he had been wrong she would
have the same trouble with him she
had with her father, he would be dead
too

Page 83 [82]

1   [1-17 PASTED IN: at that moment he
           would be dead too

2-3   affront to her just as the hammer and   30-31   affront like the hammer and nails in
       the nails had been in her father's af-   her father's business—
       fair—

                                                  Page 178

4-5   doorway as tho to smooth the very   1-2   doorway to smooth the path for
       path of brute coupling—   rutting—

5   each recurrent day's   2-3   each successive day's

6   or glass bead out of his and Jones'   3   or cheap bead for the (how
       store for the—how

7   it?—to walk in, from beyond   4-5   it?) to walk in—that scythe beyond

7-8   even tho when earth itself had re-   5-6   even when earth itself declined any
       fused any

MANUSCRIPT	BOOK
9-10 from somewhere or something, some instant and flashy glare of his ~~own Master's~~[?] creditor's	10 from some momentary flashy glare of his Creditor's
10-11 endurance, fled as she thot at first hiding and scuttling	11 endurance, hiding, scuttling
11-12 rockpile but which she realized later to be not hiding at all, not wanting to hide, but enjoyed merely in some final furious frenzy of evil and harm[?] before	12-15 rockpile, so she thought at first, until she realized that he was not hiding, did not want to hide, was merely engaged in one final frenzy of evil and harm-doing before
13-15 suddenly and without warning among them with a pistol and 20 lesser demons and acquired 100 square miles of land from some ignorant Indians nobody knew by what compound of intimidation and violence and skullduggery and built	16-19 suddenly one Sunday with two pistols and twenty subsidiary demons and skulldugged a hundred miles of land out of a poor ignorant Indian and built
16-18 and departed with 6 wagons and returned with the crystal tapestries and the Wedgwood chairs to furnish it and nobody knew if he had robbed another steamboat or had just dug up a little more of the] old loot from where he had buried it; who as soon as the house was finished hid	19-23 and went away with six wagons and came back with the crystal tapestries and the Wedgwood chairs to furnish it and nobody knew if he had robbed another steamboat or had just dug up a little more of the old loot, who hid
19-41 chose himself a wife (bought her, out-traded his father-in-law, wasn't it?) as tho with apparent deliberation, to ~~cense~~ ⟨as tho⟩ with cold and calculated intent to consolidate himself in hiding[?], in security, ~~choosing her with shrewd~~ as tho with shrewd forethought after ~~foll~~ based on 3 years of scrutiny and weighing and comparing, ⟨choosing⟩ (not from one of the local ducal houses but from a lesser baronage whose principality was so far decayed that there would be no risk of his wife bringing him for dowry delusions of grandeur before he ~~was eq~~ should be equipped for it yet not so far decayed but that she might keep them both from getting lost among the knives and forks when that day should arrive) a wife who not only could and would consolidate and guarantee his position but apparently could and	24-33 chose (bought her, outswapped his father-in-law, wasn't it) a wife after three years to scrutinize, weigh and compare, not from one of the local ducal houses but from the lesser baronage whose principality was so far decayed that there would be no risk of his wife bringing him for dowry delusions of grandeur before he should be equipped for it, yet not so far decayed but that she might keep them both from getting lost among the new knives and forks and spoons that he had bought—a wife who not only would consolidate the hiding but could
	Page 179
	1-33 would and did breed him two children to fend and shield both in themselves and in their progeny the brittle bones and tired flesh of an old man against the day when the Creditor would run him to earth for the last time and he

would breed to [*sic*] and so give him
children who both in themselves and
in the person of their progeny would
in turn fend and shield the ~~impotent
bones and flesh of an old man~~ [MARGIN:
~~and brittle~~] brittle and tired bones
and flesh of an old man against that
~~inescapable~~ ⟨inevitable⟩ hour when
the creditor should run him to earth
once more and for the last time and
he would not be able to escape; who
begot the 2 children, the son and the
daughter and saw them grow up and
the daughter fall in love in her natural
female course (promising[?]: the
brother, the son, the actual agent for
the forwarding of that which would
have provided him with that living
bulwark on which he ~~could~~ ⟨might⟩
have depended ~~for security~~ until the
son should marry in his turn and so
insure him doubly yet who intervened
himself to prevent the wedding, dis-
solved it so thoroughly that he drove
not only the fiance but the son too
from the house and so corrupted (con-
jured: what did she say?) the son
who had repudiated him for the
fiance's sake that the son himself was
to serve his father's aim when the
crisis arrived, even to the extent of
killing the fiance to prevent the
marriage which the father did not
want and in order to espouse which
the son, the murderer[?], had abjured
his very blood; who returned from the
war and should have found accomplished and waiting and complete the
situation for which he had apparently
~~striven~~[?] worked: son vanished now
for good, since he had his sister's
husband's blood on his hands, and the
daughter doomed to spinsterhood for
at least as long as he lived to watch
her and prevent, yet who almost
before his foot was free of the stirrup
set

couldn't get away: and so sure enough
the daughter fell in love, the son the
agent for the providing of that living
bulwark between him (the demon) and
the Creditor's bailiff hand until the
son should marry and thus insure him
doubled and compounded—and then
the demon must turn square around
and run not only the fiance out of the
house and not only the son out of the
house but so corrupt, seduce and
mesmerize the son that he (the son)
should do the office of the outraged
father's pistol-hand when fornication
threatened: so that the demon should
return from the war five years later
and find accomplished and complete
the situation he had been working for:
son fled for good now with a noose
behind him, daughter doomed to
spinsterhood—and then almost before
his foot was out of the stirrup he
(the demon) set out and got himself
engaged again in order to replace
that progeny the hopes of which he
had himself destroyed?"

"Yes," Quentin said.

"Came back home and found his
chances of descendants gone where
his children had attended to that, and
his plantation ruined, fields fallow
except for a fine stand of weeds, and
taxes and levies and penalties sowed
by United States marshals and such
and all his niggers gone where the
Yankees had attended to that, and you
would have thought he would have
been satisfied: yet before his foot
was out of the stirrup he not only set
out to try to restore his plantation to
what it used to be, like maybe he was
hoping to fool the Creditor by illusion
and obfuscation by concealing behind
the illusion that time had not elapsed
and change occurred the fact that he
was now almost sixty years old, until
he

Page 84 [83]

1-20   out and got himself engaged again, ?.?

Page 180

1-15   could get himself a new batch of

~~"Yes,"~~ ~~Quentin said.~~ as tho by deliberate intent to replace and restore that ~~which~~ progeny which he had himself destroyed, as tho by deliberate intent to ~~surround and entertain his~~ ~~old age~~ entertain and divert his old age by surrounding himself with a new batch of children to frustrate and destroy?" "Yes," Quentin said.

"That he took for his purpose the last woman on earth on whom he might have hoped to prevail: this Aunt R——" "——" "All right, all right, all right, all right."—who hated him, who had always hated him, yet whom he chose from a kind of outrageous bravado as tho a sort of despairing conviction of his irresistibility or imperviousness[?] were a part of the price for which he had sold his soul and did it so well that she was not even aware that she was being beseiged, thot that he was not even conscious that she was there, and he almost before his foot was clear of the stirrup undertaking the impossible task of restoring that place to what it had been as tho it were an actual complete repetition[?] with which he wanted to divert his old age, as tho he hoped to fool the creditor himself by illusion and obfuscation by concealing behind the illusion that time and change had not occurred the fact that he was now almost sixty years old; who proposed to her and was accepted, who within the actual 6 months between proposal and insult had yet no reason to believe that he was to fail to restore his lost grandeur (if that, that despair[?] could have been reason for what he did)—yet who approached her one day as you ~~ask for~~ might suggest to a neighbor that you and he breed two dogs and suggested that they try first to have a child and ~~if it ear~~[?] ~~If~~[?] ~~they would~~ be then when it was born they would be married.—But wait,"

children to bulwark him, but chose for this purpose the last woman on earth he might have hoped to prevail on, this Aunt R——all right all right all right.—that hated him, that had always hated him, yet choosing her with a kind of outrageous bravado as if a kind of despairing conviction of his irresistibility or invulnerability were a part of the price he had got for whatever it was he had sold the Creditor, since according to the old dame he never had had a soul; proposed to her and was accepted—then three months later, with no date ever set for the wedding and marriage itself not mentioned one time since, and on the very day when he established definitely that he would be able to keep at least some of his land and how much, he approached her and suggested they breed a couple of dogs together, [*sic*] inventing with fiendish cunning the thing

MANUSCRIPT

BOOK

he cried; "wait!" leaning forward
into the lamp, his torso ~~gleaming~~
~~baby-s~~ pink-gleaming and baby-
smooth, ~~and almost hairless~~ cherubic,
almost hairless, the twin moons of
his spectacles glinting against his
moonlike rubicund face: "——Wait!
Because not that, not even that: who
said to her the one thing, invented
with fiendish cunning the one thing

21-22	thing which without harming her
	would ~~blast the little dream woman~~
	not

17-18	thing that without harming her or
	giving her grounds for civil or tribal
	action would not

22 the ~~nest~~ dovecote

19 the dovecote

23 husbanded [MARGIN: —and hence[?]
himself already cuckold before she
can catch breath—] with

20-21 husbanded (and himself, husband or
fiance, already safely cuckolded before she can draw breath) with

23-24 revenge; ~~who was free now who was~~
~~free now, and it not even that~~ who
said it and was free, free now forever of any threat

22-23 revenge. He said it and was free now,
forever more now of threat

24 anyone who had eliminated

23-24 anyone since he had at last eliminated

25-41 family, and it was not that; ~~sister/~~
~~in/law~~ son vanished, and it not that;
sister-in-law swept back to town on
that wave of outrage and mortal
[illegible word], and it not that:
daughter doomed to spinsterhood for
as long as he lived he knew and
actually forever (and he knew that
too, being a demon)—who would live
in that rotting house and care for
him and feed him, raising chickens
and swapping the eggs for the clothes
for her and himself and Clytie which
she and Clytie could not make and ~~he~~
~~not only mad old man demon now but~~
~~mad old man who had realized at last~~
demon now but a mad impotent old
man who realized at last that his
dream of restoring his place to what
it used to be was not only vain itself
but that the place would never again
~~even feed~~ in his lifetime even feed
him and ~~his family~~ hence safe there
too forever more, and that not it
either because the Aunt Rosa had not

25-33 family, free now: son fled to Texas
or California or maybe even South
America, daughter doomed to spinsterhood to live until he died, since
after that it wouldn't matter, in that
rotting house, caring for him and
feeding him, raising chickens and
peddling the eggs for the clothes she
and Clytie couldn't make: so that he
didn't even need to be a demon now
but just mad impotent old man who
had realized at last that his dream
of restoring his Sutpen's Hundred
was not only vain but that what he
had left of it would never support

Page 181

1 him and his family and so running his
little

MANUSCRIPT   BOOK

been a year at home before, with her
before her successor was already
installed?" "'Yes,' Quentin said.
hence safe there too forever more
and that not all either and he not only
demon now but mad impotent old man
who doubtless had realized now that
his dream of restoring his place to
what it had been was not only vain but
that the place itself would not even
feed himself and his family yet refused to relinquish it; who now ran a
little country store crossroads store
with a stock of plowshares and hame
strings and calico and coal oil and
cheap gauds and a clientele of freed
slaves and (What is it? White what?—
Yes, trash) white trash and Jones to
help him,—Jones who lived with the
granddaughter in the abandoned fish-
ing shack belonging to Sutpen and the
rusty scythe which Sutpen had loaned
him to cut the weeds before the door
with leaning already against

Page 85 [84]

1-3   he not only demon now but mad old
        ~~man~~ impotent old man who doubtless
        had realized now that his dream of
        restoring that shell to what it used to
        be was not only vain but that the
        plantation itself would never again
        feed himself and his family yet re-
        fused to relinquish the dream, who
        now ran a little

4   and coal oil and cheap   2-3   and kerosene and cheap

5   freed slaves and   4   freed niggers and

5-17   Yes: trash) and Jones to help him   4-27   Yes, trash) with Jones for clerk and
        and who knows what illusions of   who knows maybe what delusions of
        making money with it to rebuild   making money out of the store to re-
        Sutpen's Hundred? and the old dame,   build the plantation; who had escaped
        the Aunt Rosa, back in town now who   twice now, got himself into it and
        had come out there in good faith,   been freed by the Creditor who set
        sent by that fierce blood-conscious-   his children to destroying one an-
        ness of the provincial South, to succor   other before he had posterity, and he
        a bereaved kinsman in his sorrow and   decided that maybe he was wrong in
        found bereavement but no sorrow,   being free and so got into it again and
        none to be succored save herself and   then decided that he was wrong in
        she not knowing that she was in   being unfree and so got out of it

danger until too late and saved by no efforts of her own but wafted, blown rather, back to safety on the initial blast of purely[?] reflex amazed and unbelieving outrage, living on her stolen turnips, her purloined worm-wood and watching from that distance the demon [MARGIN: , the Faustus,] whom she had escaped, who had him-self escaped twice now, who had got himself into it and had been freed by his creditor who had set his children to destroying his posterity before he had it and had decided apparently that perhaps he was wrong in being free and so got into it again and then de-cided apparently that he was wrong in becoming unfree again and so freed himself this time—and then must turn around and get right back into it again?" "Yes," Quentin said.

"The mad impotent old demon, almost-60 60 years old now and knowing, realizing that there must be a limit even to Faustus' capabilities for harming, who must have seen his situation now like that of

again—and then turned right around and bought his way back into it with beads and calico and striped candy out of his own showcase and off his shelves?"

"Yes," Quentin said. *He sounds just like father* he thought, glancing (his face quiet, reposed, curiously almost sullen) for a moment at Shreve leaning forward into the lamp, his naked torso pink-gleaming and baby-smooth, cherubic, almost hairless, the twin moons of his spectacles glinting against his moonlike rubicund face, smelling (Quentin) the cigar and the wistaria, seeing the fireflies blowing and winking in the September dusk. *Just exactly like father if father had known as much about it the night before I went out there as he did the day after I came back* thinking *Mad impotent old man who realized at last that there must be some limit even to the capabilities of a demon for doing harm, who must have seen his situation as that of* [italics continued to page 187, l. 6, with the exception of p. 185, l. 1]

	MANUSCRIPT		BOOK
17-18	who knows that	27	*who realizes that*
18	prances to is not from horn and fiddles and drums but comes from	28	*prances comes not from horn and fiddle and drum but from*
20	recoil and so looks about	31-32	*recoil, who looked about*
21	and sees son	33	*and saw son*
21	him than if he were dead	33 Page 182 1	*him now than if* *the son were dead*
21	(if he still	1	*(if the son still*
22	name will be	1-2	*name would be*
22-23	outcropping [MARGIN: Sutpen blood] he might sow upon the	3	*outcropping of Sutpen blood the son might sow on the*
23	woman it will be will do them[?] evil under	4-5	*woman would therefore carry on the tradition, accomplish the hereditary evil and harm under*
24-25	will have never heard the right one: and the daughter doomed to spinster-	6-8	*will never have heard the right one; daughter doomed to spinsterhood who*

MANUSCRIPT	BOOK

MANUSCRIPT

hood and who had chosen spinsterhood before

25-26 in sorrow and bereavement found

27-28 coffin to bury Charles Bon in and
that she

28-29 aunt was there and the 3 of them wove
their own clothes and

30 lived [MARGIN: with his granddaughter]
in

30 camp which belonged to Sutpen, ~~he~~
~~ane~~[?] with

30 rotting gallery against

31-41 the ~~scythe~~ rusting scythe which Sutpen
~~had-loaned~~ ⟨was to loan⟩ him, ~~forced~~
⟨force⟩ him to borrow to cut the weeds
from the door with leaned ~~already~~
~~against-already-leaned~~ would lean for
two years before being used: and
would still after ~~the aunt's indignation~~
~~had-swept her-back-to-town-and the~~
~~aunt too-watching-him-from-that~~
~~distance//the demon-and-Jones~~
~~watching from her-distance-as-the~~
~~daughter~~ [MARGIN: ~~the two-daughters:~~
~~Clytie-and-Judith too~~] ~~who-had-not~~
~~been-bereaved and did not-mourn~~
~~watched-from hers and-that-she-wore~~
~~during the-next-2-years while-and-for~~
~~the next-two years-while the-3 of~~
~~them//the aunt-and-the two-daughters~~
the aunt's indignation had swept her
back to town and the aunt watching
too from her distance as the daughter
(the two daughters, Clytie and Judith
both) who had not been bereaved and
did not mourn ~~w~~ watched from theirs:
~~and-wore-for the next-2-years and~~
~~wore-on-that-Sunday night-3-years~~
~~later-when-they brought the-demon's~~
~~body-home-in a-wagon-bed-with his~~
~~neck-almost severed-by the-scythe~~—
the old demon the ancient varicose
~~and-despairing~~ ⟨and despairing⟩
Faustus flinging his last ~~despairing~~
main with the creditors hand already
on his shoulder

BOOK

had chosen spinsterhood already
before

9   in bereavement and sorrow found

12-13   coffin and which she

13-14   aunt lived there and the three women
wove their own garments and

16   lived with his granddaughter in

17   camp with

17   rotting porch against

18-21   the rusty scythe which Sutpen was
to lend him, make him borrow to
cut away the weeds from the door—
and at last forced him to use though
not to cut weeds, at least not
vegetable weeds—would lean for two
years) and wore

CHAPTER VI

MANUSCRIPT   BOOK

Page 86 [85]

1   the door with would lean for two
       years yet before being used, and wore

2   stolen vegetables and   22   *stolen garden truck and*

3   daughters, the negro woman and the   24   *daughters negro and white and*
       white, and

8   using [MARGIN: out of his stock] the   32   *using out of his meager stock the*

                                                Page 183

12   hand (~~and~~ did you say delivered too?) 6   *hand (and maybe delivered too)*

12   candy and beads   7   *candy beads*

13-14 fashion ~~into a~~ dress [*sic*] to walk in 9-10 *fashion a dress to walk past the*
       past the lounging men,   *lounging men in,*

14-15 her ⟨~~incre~~⟩ ~~size began to embarrass~~ 10-11 *her increasing belly taught*
       ~~her~~ increasing distortion ~~began to~~
       ~~embarrass her // blind Jones who~~
       ~~probably (must have seen) still saw~~
       taught

17-18 and the fish and the vegetables on   14-15 *and fish and vegetables on which the*
       which the ~~demon~~ seducer-   *seducer-*

18-19 remaining negro,   16   *remaining servant, negro,*

19   door without it) depended to   17-18 *door with what he brought) depended*
                                                      on to [*sic*] [see "on," l. 15 above]

20   suddenly ~~order all and~~ curse ~~a~~ the 19-20 *suddenly curse the*

23   the box the   23   *the showcase the*

24   Sunday p.m.'s which   26   *Sunday afternoons of monotonous*
                                                      peace which

25   yard, ~~the demon in the hammock and~~   27-28 *yard, the demon lying in the hammock*
       ~~Jones~~ the demon had lain in the ham-   *while Jones squatted*
       mock while Jones had squatted

26   pour from the demijohn or the   28-29 *pour for the demon from the demijohn*
                                                      and the

26-27 fetched afoot from a spring   30   *fetched from the spring*

27   away and then squat again   30-31 *away then squatting again,*

27-28 Mister John' each   31-32 *Mister Tawm' each*

28-29 not sitting either now but reaching   33   *not lying down*
       after the first 2 or 3 drinks   *Page 184*
                                                1   *now nor even sitting but reaching*
                                                      after the third or second drink

29-30 rise [MARGIN: swaying] [30-37   3   *rise, swaying and*
       PASTED IN: and

31   so late   5   *so too late*

192

C H A P T E R   V I

MANUSCRIPT		BOOK	
31	'Kill them! Kill them like	5-6	*'Kill them! Shoot them down like*
32	sho Kernel' and	7	*sho now' and*
33	him home and	8	*him to the house and*
34-35	Europe (and the daughter holding the door open for him and with no change, no alteration in that calm and frozen face which she had worn for 4 years now) and	10-12	*Europe which Judith held open for him to enter with no change, no alteration in that calm frozen face which she had worn for four years now, and*
36-37	bed and then lie himself (Jones) on the floor beside it tho not to sleep because before dawn the man on the bed would groan and stir and Jones would say, 'Hyer I am, Kernel. Hit's all right. They aint whupped us yit,]	13-17	*bed like a baby and then lie down himself on the floor beside the bed though not to sleep since before dawn the man on the bed would stir and groan and Jones would say, 'Hyer I am, Kernel. Hit's all right. They aint whupped us yit,*
38	regiment and while the	18	*regiment when the*
39	was looking after Kernel's place	19	*'was lookin after Major's place*
42	period during which	25-28	*period while the demon believed he*
Page 87 [86]			*could restore by sheer indomitable*
1-2	the demon apparently believed that he could rebuild and restore the Sutpen's Hundred which he remembered and had lost by sheer indomitable willing; and with		*willing the Sutpen's Hundred which he remembered and had lost, labored with*
3-4	who must have almost been the agent of the⟨ir⟩ 3 year liaison—blind Jones who apparently saw still in ~~the furious wreck that furious~~ that furious	30	*who apparently saw still in that furious*
5-7	domain ~~both~~ ⟨two⟩ boundaries of which ~~at no point could the eye see~~ the eye could ~~see from no point.~~ not see from any point.?" "Yes," Quentin said.	32-33	*domain two boundaries of which the eye could not see from any point*
	"And so that Sunday came and he (the demon) is out early and Judith	*Page 185*	
		1-3	"Yes," Quentin said.
			So that Sunday morning came and the demon up and away before dawn, Judith
7-8	why because that a.m. the black stallion that he rode ~~all the way~~ to Virginia	3-4	*why since that morning the black stallion which he rode to Virginia*
8-9	born [MARGIN: on his wife Penelope:] but it is not that foal that the demon has ~~gone~~ gotten up	5-6	*born on his wife Penelope, only it was not that foal which the demon had got up*
9-11	at: and it is almost a week before they find, catch, the old negress, the midwife that the demon had sent to the	6-8	*at and it was almost a week before they caught, found, the old negress, the midwife who was squatting beside*

193

	MANUSCRIPT		BOOK
	fishing camp and who was squatting at the fire beside the quilt pallet that a.m. while Jones sat on the veranda where		*the quilt pallet that dawn while Jones sat on the porch where*
12	demon came in and	10	*demon entered and*
12	pallet [MARGIN: with the riding whip in his hand] and	11-12	*pallet with the riding whip in his hand and looked down at the mother and the child and*
13	Penelope, then	13	*Penelope. Then*
14	out: and that she sat there quite still and heard them, the voices; ~~heard~~ and Sutpen said, 'Stand	14-15	*out and the old negress squatted there and heard them, the voices, he and Jones: 'Stand*
15	Wash' and Jones said, 'I'm	16	*Wash.'—'I'm*
15-17	whip tho ~~but she didn't hear the scythe // as always that whic~~h not the scythe, no whistling wind, nothing, as always that which consummates	17-18	*whip too though not the scythe, no whistling air, no blow, nothing since always that which merely consummates*
17	cry: that	19	*cry while that*
17-18	silence: and	19-20	*silence. And*
18	they fetched him home in the bed of a wagon	20-21	*they finally found him and fetched him home in a wagon*
19	showing [MARGIN: in his parted beard (the beard which was hardly grizzled tho his hair now was almost white)] in	22-23	*showing in his parted beard (which was hardly grizzled although his hair was almost white now) in*
19	of lanterns and blazing pine	23-24	*of the lanterns and the pine*
19-20	steps with that stone-faced and tear-less daughter holding the door this time for him	24-25	*steps where the tearless and stone-faced daughter held the door open for him*
20	to drive fast to church and rode	25-26	*to like to drive fast to church and who rode*
21-23	never arrived since the daughter, the woman of 30 now, ~~the spinster,~~ and looking older not as the weak grow older either enclosed in a static ballooning of already lifeless flesh or thru a series of stages of gradual collapsing whose particles adhere not to some iron still impervious framework but to one another, ~~with~~ in	27-33	*never reached the church, since the daughter decided that he should be driven into that same Methodist Church in town where he had married her mother, before returning to the grave in the cedar grove. Judith was a woman of thirty now and looking older, not as the weak grow old, either enclosed in a static ballooning of already lifeless flesh or through a series of stages of gradual collapsing whose particles adhere, not to some iron and still imper-*

MANUSCRIPT

BOOK

1   *vious framework but to one another,*
       as though in

26-27   concealed; the spinster in homemade
       ~~garm~~ and

6-7   *concealed. The spinster in homemade*
      and

28-30   furrow, who decided that he should be
       driven in to ~~the Episcopal Church in~~
       ~~Jefferson~~ that same Baptist Church in
       Jefferson where he had been married
       before ~~going~~ returning to his grave
       in the cedar grove as her mother had
       done, who borrowed two young half-
       wild mules to draw the wagon for that
       purpose: and so he rode fast as far

8-10   *furrow, borrowed two half-wild young*
      mules to pull the wagon: so he rode
      fast toward church as far

31-32   gauntlets until the young mules bolted
       and ran away and turned the wagon
       over ~~in a ditch~~ and

11-12   *gauntlets, until the young mules*
       bolted and turned the wagon over and

33   and brot him

14   *and fetched him*

34   bereavement yet whether

15   *bereavement this time too, whether*

36-37   field ~~(Jones was gone now~~ where she
       and Clytie now did most of what
       plowing that was done,

19-20   *field since she and Clytie now did all*
      the plowing which was done,

37-38   too, having followed the demon within
       12 hours on that same Sunday (tho not
       probably to the same destination) by
       women and children with buckets and
       baskets,

20-33   *too. He had followed the demon within*
      twelve hours on that same Sunday (and
      maybe to the same place; maybe They
      would even have a scuppernong vine
      for them there and no compulsions
      now of bread or ambition or fornica-
      tion or vengeance, and maybe they
      wouldn't even have to drink, only they
      would miss this now and then without
      knowing what it was that they missed
      but not often; serene, pleasant, un-
      marked by time or change of weather,
      only just now and then something, a
      wind, a shadow, and the demon would
      stop talking and Jones would stop
      guffawing and they would look at one
      another, groping, grave, intent, and
      the demon would say, 'What was it,
      Wash? Something happened. What
      was it?' and Jones looking at the
      demon, groping too, sober too, saying,
      'I dont know, Kernel. Whut?' each
      watching the other. Then the shadow
      would

CHAPTER VI

MANUSCRIPT	BOOK

BOOK column:

Page 187

1-4   *fade, the wind die away until at last Jones would say, serene, not even triumphant: 'They mought have kilt us, but they aint whupped us yit, air they?) She would be hailed by women and children with pails and baskets,*

MANUSCRIPT	**BOOK**
39 store, open it,	5 *store, unlock it,*

39-43   return and then sold the store at last and spent the money for a tombstone: And that how one day, you told me—you and your father were hunting quail, wasn't it?— How you came to the ditch, like this, wasn't it? The ditch too steep for the horses to cross it tho the dogs already over were making a long cast up the old field, visible only by a steady furrowing of the wet sage grass and you and your father dismounted and what's his name? the nigger? Dan— Dan came up on the mule and took the reins

5-7   *return: until she sold the store at last and spent the money for a tombstone.*

    ("How was it?" Shreve said. "You

Page 88 [88 86 87]

1-2   ~~Of course his men would have had the courage to demote him.~~ money for a tombstone—(How was it? You

| 2   father hunting quail, | 8   father shooting quail, |

3-4   the horses to—what was his name? the nigger? Dan.—Dan to lead around the ditch and you and your father crossed it ~~and~~ and then the rain

10-13   the reins to—what was his name? the nigger on the mule? Luster.—Luster to lead them around the ditch") and he and his father crossed just as the rain

5-7   again [MARGIN: gray and solid and slow like a cloud and making no sound] and you not completely aware of just where you were because of the rain, because of riding with your head down to keep the rain off, until you looked up and saw the wet ~~sedge~~ yellow sedge dying upward

13-17   again gray and solid and slow, making no sound, Quentin not aware yet of just where they were because he had been riding with his head lowered against the drizzle, until he looked up the slope before them where the wet yellow sedge died upward

8-9   drawn with ink on a wet blotter and beyond the cedars, beyond the fields beyond would

20-21   drawn in ink on a wet blotter—the cedars beyond which, beyond the ruined fields beyond which, would

9-11   rotting ⟨deserted (so you thot)⟩ house in the middle of it and your father stopped to look back at Dan riding the

22-25   rotting deserted house half a mile away. Mr Compson had stopped to look back at Luster on the mule, the

196

CHAPTER VI

mule now with the tow sack that he had been using for saddle over his head now and his knees

towsack he had been using for saddle now wrapped around his head, his knees

12-15 cross and your father said, better to go on and get under the cedars,/even tho Dan would not come with until the rain was over, since Dan would not come within 100 yards of them you could not pay Dan enough to come within 100 yards of them: and you went into the cedars and it dark there, the light more dark than gray and the quiet

26-33 cross. "Better get on out of the rain," Mr Compson said. "He's not going to come within a hundred yards of those cedars anyway."

They went on up the slope. They could not see the two dogs at all, only the steady furrowing of the sedge where, invisible, the dogs quartered the slope until one of them flung up his head to look back. Mr Compson gestured with

Page 188

1-3 his hand toward the trees, he and Quentin following. It was dark among the cedars, the light more dark than gray even, the quiet

16-17 candles and you looked at the old graves, the two vaulted ones beneath heavy flat slabs and the 3 plain headstones of the other three leaning awry and with here

5-7 candles on the marble: the two flat heavy vaulted slabs, the other three headstones leaning a little awry, with here

18-19 legible by some touch of wet gleams where where the by the faint gleams which light

8 legible in the faint light

19-20 released and the both the slabs cracked across by

10-14 released; now the two dogs came in, drifted in like smoke, their hair close-plastered with damp, and curled down in one indistinguishable and apparently inextricable ball for warmth. Both the flat slabs were cracked across the middle by

21-22 in the smooth path of some animal, possum you said, generations of possums you said, since there had been nothing to feed on in them in years and years) tho the

15-19 in was a smooth faint path worn by some small animal—possum probably—by generations of some small animal since there could have been nothing to eat in the grave for a long time) though the

22-23 *Coldfield. Wife of Thomas Sutpen. Born*

19-20 *Coldfield Sutpen. Born*

23 *1862* [MARGIN: :not beloved wife of: just *Ellen Coldfield Sutpen*;] and

20 *1863* and

24 *Died June 29, 1869* and that, the date, added later obviously, crudely

22 *Died August 12, 1869:* this last, the date, added later, crudely

197

MANUSCRIPT		BOOK	
25-27	born: and you looked at it and said how you wouldn't have thot they would have had the money to buy marble with in 1869, and your father ~~said~~ told you how the demon himself had bought it, bought the 2 of them while he was with the regiment in Virginia,	24-29	born. Quentin looked at the stones quietly, thinking *Not beloved wife of. No. Ellen Coldfield Sutpen* "I wouldn't have thought they would have had any money to buy marble with in 1869," he said. "He bought them himself," Mr Compson said. "He bought the two of them while the regiment was in Virginia,
28	dead; ordered	30-31	dead. He ordered
29	his own with the date left ~~off~~ blank— this	32	his with the date left blank: and this

Page 189

30-31	electing its regimental officers anew each year (and ~~beeause of~~ ⟨thru by⟩ which custom he	2-3	electing a new set of regimental officers each year (and by which system he
31	moment profiting, since	3-4	moment entitled to call himself colonel, since
31-32	and ~~his immediate su~~ the old colonel voted	4-5	and Colonel Sartoris voted
33	received the chances were that he would be already	6-7	received he might be already
34	earth: or lacking that, he might very possibly be a corporal or even a private soldier—	8-9	earth, or lacking that he might be a second lieutenant or even a private—
36-37	them ~~sent thru to him~~ thru a seacoast so tightly blockaded	12-13	them past a seacoast so closely blockaded
37	cargo save ammunition {Jesus, You can see them:	14-15	cargo except ammunition—" It seemed to Quentin that he could actually see them:
38	gaunt ~~desperate calm~~ powder-blackened	16	gaunt powder-blackened
39	shoulders—the ~~desperate~~ ⟨glaring⟩ eyes	17-18	shoulders, the glaring eyes
39-40	indomitable ~~despair~~ ⟨desperation⟩ beyond even hope—toward ~~a~~ the dark	18-19	indomitable desperation of undefeat watching that dark
40	across ~~sp~~ which ~~sped a dark~~ grim	19-20	across which a grim
40-41	hold 4000 precious pounds-space occupied by bombastic and inert carven stone which	20-23	hold two thousand precious pounds-space containing not bullets, not even something to eat, but that much bombastic and inert carven rock which
42	the ~~retreat~~ campaign which culminated at Gettysburg and ~~was~~ fell back, moving behind his regiment	23-25	the regiment, to follow it into Pennsylvania and be present at Gettysburg, moving behind the regiment

MANUSCRIPT		BOOK	
43	by some ~~body servant~~ negro body servant, ~~with~~ thru swamp	25-26	by the demon's body servant through swamp

Page 89 [~~87~~ 88]

1	starved and ragged men	28	starved gaunt men
1-2	icy water or	29	icy mud or
3-6	and the Tennessee mountains and down into Mississippi ~~and put it one of them on his wife's grave and stored the other one in the smokehouse~~ where the daughter waited ~~who was to be widowed tho apparently not bereaved and put one of the stones on his wife's grave and stored the other in the smokehouse and rode back to the War again all in 24 hours~~ and whose	32-33	and down through the Tennessee mountains, traveling at night to dodge Yankee patrols, and into

Page 190

		1-2	Mississippi in the late fall of '64, where the daughter waited whose
6	had forbidden and	2	had interdict and
7	be widowed tho apparently	2-3	be a widow the next summer though apparently
7-9	son vanished, self-excommunicated— where to apparently he did not know and was not to see again even tho it was that son who was to estopp [*sic*] forever[?] that marriage which he had only pronounced against, and put	4-5	son self-excommunicated and -banished, and put
9-10	and stored the other in the smokehouse and ~~rode back departed for the war again all in 24 hours~~ drank	6-12	and set the other upright in the hall of the house, where Miss Coldfield possibly (maybe doubtless) looked at it every day as though it were his portrait, possibly (maybe doubtless here too) reading among the lettering more of maiden hope and virgin expectation than she ever told Quentin about, since she never mentioned the stone to him at all, and (the demon) drank
11-19	coffee which Clytie and Judith prepared for him and kissed Judith on the forehead and departed for the war again all in 24 hours: and you looked at the other headstones the 3 small ones, ~~and said how that didn't explain them; that they must have cost something too, and your father told you looked at you and said, 'Who would have: the one that said Charles Etienne Saint Velery Bon: Born in New Orleans, Louisiana. Died at~~	12-25	coffee and ate the hoe cake which Judith and Clytie prepared for him and kissed Judith on the forehead and said, 'Well, Clytie' and returned to the war, all in twenty-four hours; he could see it; he might even have been there. Then he thought *No. If I had been there I could not have seen it this plain.* "But that dont explain the other three," he said. "They must have cost something too."

~~Sutpen's-Hundred,-Mississippi,~~
~~April-19-April-19,-1864~~ ~~and-the-one~~
~~that-said~~ and said how that didn't
explain them, that they must have
cost something too, and your father
looked at you and said: 'Who would
have paid for them? Think.' and you
looked again at the three identical
stones with their ~~β~~ identical lettering, weathered and faintly slanting in
the soft loamy decay of accumulated
pine needles: ~~at~~ the one that said
Charles ~~Etienne-Saint/Velery~~ Bon.

19-24   *Mississippi, April 19, 1864. Aged*
29 years and 5 months and you said
(and your father watching you) 'She
did it. When she sold the store' and
your father said, 'Yes' and you looked
at the next one, the one that said
Charles Etienne Saint-Valery Bon.
~~Born~~ *1858-1884.* and your father
watching you and saying 'Think' and
you already looking at the third one,
~~the-one-that-said-Judith-Sutpen-the-one~~
~~that-said-Judith-Coldfield-Sutpen~~
second ~~other~~[?] date was 1884 too and
you said, 'It

24   time because ~~the-store~~ she

24-27   in '71 and besides 1884 is the same
year ~~that-she~~ that's on hers—' and
your father told you about that (and
~~how~~ this would have been terrible
sure enough for her if she had happened to want to put *Beloved Husband*

"Who would have paid for them?"
Mr Compson said. Quentin could
feel him looking at him. "Think."
Quentin looked at the three identical
headstones with their faint identical
lettering, slanted a little in the soft
loamy decay of accumulated cedar
needles, these decipherable too when
he looked close, the first one: *Charles*
Bon.

26-33   *Mississippi, May 3, 1865, Aged 33*
years and 5 months. He could feel
his father watching him.

"She did it," he said. "With that
money she got when she sold the
store."

"Yes," Mr Compson said. Quentin
had to stoop and brush away some of
the cedar needles to read the next
one. As he did so one of the dogs
rose and approached him, thrust-

Page 191

1-10   ing its head in to see what he was
looking at like a human being would,
as if from association with human
beings it had acquired the quality of
curiosity which is an attribute only
of men and apes.

"Get away," he said, thrusting
the dog back with one hand while with
the other he brushed the cedar needles
away, smoothing with his hand into
legibility the faint lettering, the
graved words: *Charles Etienne*
Saint-Valery Bon. 1859-1884 feeling
his father watching him, remarking
before he rose that the third stone
bore that same date, 1884. "It

11-12   time," he said. "Because she

12-30   in '70, and besides 1884 is the same
date that's on hers" thinking how it
would have been terrible for her sure
enough if she had wanted to put
Beloved Husband of on that first one.

"Ah," Mr Compson said. "That

of on that first stone since tho women's deaths are not important to them, since

was the one your grandfather attended to. Judith came into town one day and brought him the money, some of it, where she got it from he never knew, unless it was what she had left out of the price of the store which he sold for her; brought the money in with the inscription (except the date of death of course) all written out as you see it, during that three weeks while Clytie was in New Orleans finding the boy to fetch him back, though your grandfather of course did not know this, money and inscription not for herself but for him.''

"Oh," Quentin said.

"Yes. They lead beautiful lives—women. Lives not only divorced from, but irrevocably excommunicated from, all reality. That's why although their deaths, the instant of dissolution, are of no importance to them since

28	make of any spartan man a puling and cringing boy,	32-33	make the most spartan man resemble a puling boy,

Page 192

29	spurious ~~nor~~ immortality	1	spurious immortality

30-43 importance: and he told you about that cousin or aunt or something of yours who died at a time when her nearest female kin was a woman between whom and herself there had been for years one of those ~~fond and~~ bitter and (to the man mind) inexplicable amicable enmities which occur between women of the same blood, who was taken quite ill and was faced with a serious operation from which she (without hysteria) believed she would not survive and whose sole worry was to get rid of a certain brown dress which she owned and had never liked and which must not be given away but must be burned in the back yard beneath the window where she could see it done by being held up—and suffering excruciating pain during the operation—to the

2-33 importance. You had an aunt once (you do not remember her because I never saw her myself but only heard the tale) who was faced with a serious operation which she became convinced she would not survive, at a time when her nearest female kin was a woman between whom and herself there had existed for years one of those bitter inexplicable (to the man mind) amicable enmities which occur between women of the same blood, whose sole worry about departing this world was to get rid of a certain brown dress which she owned and knew that the kinswoman knew she had never liked, which must be burned, not given away but burned in the back yard beneath the window where, by being held up to the window (and suffering excrutiating [*sic*] pain)

window because she was convinced
that as seen as ⟨when⟩ she died the
kinswoman, the logical one to take
charge, would bury her in it:/ about
that summer and you said, 'And did
she die?' and your father said No,
that she stood the as soon as the dress
was destroyed she began to mend and
stood the operation and recovered
and outlived the kinswoman by several years and then one p.m. she died
peacefully of no particular ailment and
was buried in her wedding dress.)—
about that summer ⟨1870 [*sic*]⟩
when one of the 5 graves—tho there
were just 3 then—became actually
watered by tears and your grandfather actually there to actually see
it, he the one who had attended to the
selling of the store for Judith and
rode out there again tho he did not
know about the visitors, the pageant,
bereavement's ⟨ceremonial⟩ widowhood's tranquil and dramatic pag-
eantry;

Page 90 [89]

1-8   didn't know how she came to be there,
how Judith could have known to send
for her since Bon would not have told
her surely and Henry, when she saw
him again after his trip to New
Orleans, only said 'Now you can't
ever marry him' and fled. But there
she was, with the 10 year old boy and
it must have been fine, like a garden
scene in Oscar Wilde; late p.m. the
dark cedars, the sun, the very light
just right and the graves, the 3
pieces of marble like they had been
cleaned and polished and arranged by
the scene shifters, presently to be
struck and carried, hollow fragile
and without weight, back to the store-
house until they would be needed
again—and the pageant, the scene,
entering the stage—the magnolia-
colored ⟨faced⟩ woman a little plump
now, in a soft voluminous [MARGIN:
languid and in a costume which] a

she could see it burned with her own
eyes, because she was convinced that
after she died the kinswoman, the
logical one to take charge, would bury
her in it."

"And did she die?" Quentin said.

"No. As soon as the dress was
consumed she began to mend. She
stood the operation and recovered
and outlived the kinswoman by several years. Then one afternoon she
died peacefully of no particular ailment and was buried in her wedding
gown."

"Oh," Quentin said.

"Yes. But there was one afternoon in the summer of '70 when one
of those graves (there were only
three here then) was actually watered
by tears. Your grandfather saw it;
that was the year Judith sold the store
and your grandfather attended to it
for her and he had ridden out to see
her about the matter and he witnessed
it: the interlude, the ceremonial
widowhood's bright dramatic pag-
eantry. He didn't know at the time
how the octoroon came to be here,
how Judith could even have known
about her to write her where Bon

Page 193

1-15   was dead. But there she was, with
the eleven-year-old boy who looked
more like eight. It must have re-
sembled a garden scene by the Irish
poet, Wilde: the late afternoon, the
dark cedars with the level sun in
them, even the light exactly right and
the graves, the three pieces of marble
(your grandfather had advanced Judith
the money to buy the third stone with
against the price of the store) looking
as though they had been cleaned and
polished and arranged by scene
shifters who with the passing of
twilight would return and strike them
and carry them, hollow fragile and
without weight, back to the warehouse
until they should be needed again;

MANUSCRIPT	BOOK
woman created ~~for darkness~~ of by and for darkness ⟨whom Beardsley himself might have dressed⟩ in a soft voluminous gown	the pageant, the scene, the act, entering upon the stage—the magnolia-faced woman a little plumper now, a woman created of by and for darkness whom the artist Beardsley might have dressed, in a soft flowing gown

8-9	bereavement but	16	bereavement or widowhood but
9-10	of [MARGIN: slumbrous and fatal insatiation, of] passionate and ~~inexorable insatiation of the flesh~~ inexorable hunger of the flesh, [MARGIN: ~~that Beardsley might have drawn,~~] walking	17-18	of slumbrous and fatal insatiation, of passionate and inexorable hunger of the flesh, walking
11	smooth faintly coffee-colored sexless	22	smooth ivory sexless
12	mother [MARGIN: gave the negress the parasol and] took the cushion ~~from the negress~~ and knelt and spread her	23-24	mother handed the negress the parasol and took the cushion and knelt beside the grave and arranged her
14	of ~~prison lighted by perpetual~~ silken	27	of silken
14	perpetual candles and breathing	27-28	perpetual shaded candles, breathing
15-16	seen probably little	29-30	seen little
16-17	woman who, ~~had not~~ not bereaved, did not need to mourn, who stood	31-33	woman, Judith (*who, not bereaved, did not need to mourn* Quentin thought, thinking *Yes, I have had to listen too long*) who stood

Page 194

17-18	the ~~calico shapeless~~ calico gown and	1	the calico dress and
18	shapeless, the still cold face	2	shapeless—the calm face
19	her, ~~waiting, perhaps not even watching.~~ ⟨waiting⟩ standing	4	her, standing
20-24	waiting ~~but perhaps not~~ and patient and probably not even watching: and then the negress ~~returned~~ came and handed her a crystal bottle to smell and then handed her back the parasol and took the cushion and, with the magnolia in front again and holding her skirts from the graves, they returned to the house ~~(the old formal front steps now crumbling[?] rotted away now and replaced by narrow plank ones unpainted plank ar[?] cramped[?] plan unpainted house[?]~~ and ~~past~~ ⟨beneath⟩ the tall	5-12	waiting, probably not even watching. Then the negress came and handed the octoroon a crystal bottle to smell and helped her to rise and took up the silk cushion and gave the octoroon the parasol and they returned to the house, the little boy still holding to the negress' apron, the negress supporting the woman with one arm and Judith following with that face like a mask or like marble, back to the house, across the tall
25-26	the cornbread and the eggs on which she and Judith probably lived, and	13-15	the eggs and the corn bread on which she and Judith lived.

MANUSCRIPT	BOOK

MANUSCRIPT

~~then back to New Orleans again~~ she
spent the rest

26-27 room whose bed still wore linen
sheets (and most of that week in bed
in

28-30 lilac shade of mourning/—that room
airless and impregnated behind its
closed sagging blinds against the light
of day with ~~heavy fainting scent and
eau~~ the smell of heavy fainting scent
~~and eau/de/cologne fr~~ from her flesh
and garments and of eau-de-cologne

31 bed in the intervals of going to the
door to take the trays

32-33 carrying which Judith made her,
compelled[?] her or not, who must
have perceived quicker than any
white would that ~~haven[?], the stair~~
it was

34-35 as (so your ~~grandf~~ father said your
grandfather said) she would find that
little strange boy ~~in his esoteric half
Fauntleroy clothes~~ sitting alone on

36 dim [MARGIN: and shadowy] and un-
used parlor with

36-43 esoteric half Faunt- ~~leroy clothing
and give him what might have been
cookies but was coarse bread spread
with coarse as coarse molasses~~
leroy clothing who regarded [MARGIN:
with a kind of aghast [illegible word]
terror] the inscrutable woman who
gave him what might have been cookies
but was the coarsest bread spread
with ~~the~~ as coarse molasses (and this
surreptitiously: not that his mother
or the negro companion would have
objected but that the household did
not contain[?] food to be eaten between meals) with a ~~grim vengeful~~
cold[?] vengeful restraint and who
one p.m. driven[?] by a child's bore-
dom[?] and neglect wandered away
from the house and fell into stiff[?]
play with a small negro boy in the
road behind the house and was dis-

BOOK

"She stayed a week. She passed
the rest

16-17 room in the house whose bed had
linen sheets, passed it in bed, in

18-21 lilac of mourning—that room airless
and shuttered, impregnated behind
the sagging closed blinds with the
heavy fainting odor of her flesh, her
days, her hours, her garments, of
eau-de-cologne

23-24 bed between trips to the door to receive the trays

25-27 carrying as Judith made her, who
must have perceived whether Judith
told her or not that it was

28-31 as she would quit the kitchen from
time to time and search the rooms
downstairs until she found that little
strange lonely boy sitting quietly on

31-32 shadowy library or parlor, with his

33 esoteric Fauntleroy clothing who
Page 195

1-14 regarded with an aghast fatalistic
terror the grim coffee-colored woman who would come on bare feet to
the door and look in at him, who gave
him not teacakes but the coarsest
cornbread spread with as coarse
molasses (this surreptitiously, not
that the mother or the duenna might
object, but because the household did
not have food for eating between
meals), gave it to him, thrust it at
him with restrained savageness, and
who found him one afternoon playing
with a negro boy about his own size
in the road outside the gates and
cursed the negro child out of sight
with level and deadly violence and
sent him, the other, back to the house
in a voice from which the very

MANUSCRIPT BOOK

covered there not by mother or by
nurse but by Clytie and stood
surprised and mesmerized while
Clytie

Page 91 [90]

1-3   ~~vio~~ cursed the negro boy from sight
with ~~unbelievable deadly~~ level and
deadly violence and then sent the
other, the city child, to the house in
a voice the very absence from which
of vituperation made it seem but the
more terrible and cold—Clytie who
stood [MARGIN: impassive] beside the
wagon ~~at~~ on

3-4   ceremonial with the cushion and the
smelling bottle to the grave, when

15-17   ceremonial to the grave with the silk
cushion and the parasol and the
smelling-bottle, when

4-5   and nurse ~~retu~~ departed for New
Orleans, and your grandfather never
knew what she knew or exactly what
she did, whether it

17-18   and duenna departed for New Orleans.
And your grandfather never knew if
it

6   the moment to

19-20   the day, the moment, to

7-8   winter (it was 1873) and she returned,
who

23   winter, that December of 1871—Clytie
who

8   Jefferson yet who made the trip alone

24-25   Jefferson in her life, yet who made
that journey alone

9   child of 12, in one of the ~~$~~ Fauntleroy
but

26-28   child, the boy of twelve now and looking ten, in one of the outgrown
Fauntleroy suits but

11   not have said either) and with what

30-31   not say either) over it and what

11-16   handkerchief—that child with a face
not old but without age, as tho he had
had no childhood not in the sense that
the old dame, this Aunt Rosa claimed
that she never had any childhood but
as tho he were not human exactly,
born without agency[?] of no man or
woman ~~but produced complete and
subject to no microbe in that cloyed
and scented maze of shuttered silk
and relief,~~ orphaned by no human
being (your father said how your
grandfather said how you

32-33   handkerchief—this child who could
speak no English as the woman could
speak no French, who had found him,
hunted

Page 196

1-7   him down, in a French city and brought
him away, this child with a face not
old but without age, as if he had had
no childhood, not in the sense that
Miss Rosa Coldfield says she had no
childhood, but as if he had not been
human born but instead created without agency of man or agony or woman
and orphaned by no human being.
Your grandfather said you

CHAPTER VI

MANUSCRIPT

BOOK

16   not care—death or elopement, who would

8-9   not even care: death or elopement or marriage: she would

17-18   metamorphosis (dissolution or adultery) to another with all the old accumulated years which we ~~called~~ call

9-11   metamorphosis—dissolution or adultery—to the next carrying along with her all the old accumulated rubbish-years which we call

18   I, dragged along but as a butterfly

12   *I,* but changing from phase to phase as the butterfly

18-19   cleared, ~~leaving nothing of what is behind~~ carrying nothing of what *was* into what *is,*

13-14   cleared, carrying nothing of what was into what is,

19-20   but merely[?] vanishing[?] complete and ~~imp~~ intact and impervious into the next one ~~as the magnolia~~ [MARGIN: as the overblown magnolia or rose] itself vanishes[?] from

14-16   but eliding complete and intact and unresisting into the next avatar as the overblown rose or magnolia elides from

21   dead ~~first~~ ⟨pristine⟩ soulless

18   dead pristine soulless

22   earth) but produced

19   earth. The boy had been produced

23-24   sumbol, ~~of the page~~ immortal page of the old immortal Lilith—who entered the actual world with the delicate

22-24   symbol, immortal page of the ancient immortal Lilith, entering the actual world not at the age of one second but of twelve years, the delicate

25   that ~~uniform and reg~~ burlesque

26   that burlesque

26-27   Ham:—~~and how your grandfather also did not know it was to first told~~ [*sic*] ~~him that he was a negro would have to be a negro nigger~~ a slight

28   Ham—a slight

28   the life which he

29-30   the only life he

29-30   and ~~dre~~ feared yet could not flee as tho [illegible word], as tho hypnotized like a bird or an animal, held immobile and helpless in that state

31-32   and learned to dread and fear yet could not flee, held helpless and passive in a state

31   of dread and trust since

33   of horror and trust, since

Page 197

31-38   even speak to her [MARGIN: a child, making that week's steamboat journey (in the steerage downstairs, sleeping and eating with negroes, who could not even tell his companion when he was hungry or when he had to relieve himself] and so could not have known where he was being taken, could have known nothing save that all which

1-17   even talk to her (they made, they must have made, that week's journey by steamboat among the cotton bales on the freight deck, eating and sleeping with negroes, where he could not even tell his companion when he was hungry or when he had to relieve himself) and so could have only suspected, surmised, where she was taking him,

206

he had known and believed in up to now was vanishing about him like so much smoke and so back to that house which he had seen one time, where the woman-lived-who-had-come-and got-him,-and grim startling[?] violent woman lived who had come and got him, and the other woman, the cold calm one who was not even violent, who was not anything save cold and calm, who doubtless for him had not even a name yet was so closely connected with him as to the[?] be the obvious and apparent owner and proprietor of the one spot on earth in the ⟨entire⟩ world on which he had ever known his mother to weep.—who crossed that threshold,-entered strange irrevocable threshold, crossed that irrevocable demarcation not

could have known nothing certainly except that all he had ever been familiar with was vanishing about him like smoke. Yet he made no resistance, returning quietly and docilely to that decaying house which he had seen one time, where the fierce brooding woman who had come and got him lived with the calm white one who was not even fierce, who was not anything except calm, who to him did not even have a name yet, but who was somehow so closely related to him as to be the owner of the one spot on earth where he had ever seen his mother weep. He crossed that strange threshold, that irrevocable demarcation, not

39	gaunt household with which his	19	gaunt and barren household where his
39-40	silken clothes, and his	20	silken remaining clothes, his
40-41	and thin shoes vanished, fled from his arms and legs as tho they had been woven of chimaeras—who slept on the trundle bed beside Judith's own, beside	21-24	and shoes which still remained to remind him of what he had once been, vanished, fled from arms and body and legs as if they had been woven of chimæras or of smoke.—Yes, sleeping in the trundle bed beside Judith's, beside
42	the savage	26-27	the fierce ruthless

Page 92 [91]

1	suppressed ruthless		
1	who with a kind of	27-28	who, with a sort of
2-3	pallet put outside the door in the hall and the child lying there between them ⟨between them⟩ aware-of-this, aware unasleep in some immobile hiatus of immobile and hopeless	28-30	pallet on the floor, the child lying there between them unasleep in some hiatus of passive and hopeless
4	seemed to-become-lifeless at	32-33	seemed at
5	all life and warmth	33	all warmth

Page 198

5-6	with a cold and implacable antipathy and	1	with cold implacable antipathy, and

CHAPTER VI

MANUSCRIPT		BOOK	
6	the floor upon	2	the pallet upon
7-10	wild animal [MARGIN: (and your ~~grand~~ father said how your grandfather said, 'Suffer little children to come unto Me,' and said what did He mean by that? How, if he meant that little children should need to be suffered to approach him, what sort of world had He created; that if they had to suffer in order to approach Him, what sort of Heaven did He have?)] who crouched from his entrance ⟨into the cage⟩ in some hopeless and desperate similitude of ferocity might look upon the human creature who feeds it, who fed him, thrust food [MARGIN: (food which he himself could discern to be the choicest of what they had, food which he realized was prepared for him by deliberate sacrifice)] at him with that ~~ferocious and constant~~ curious blend of ferocity and pity, of ~~hatred and~~ yearning and hatred ~~thinking, projecting toward him, filling the thunderous solitude of his loneliness with louder than speech~~; who dressed	3-15	wild beast crouched in its cage in some hopeless and desperate similitude of ferocity look upon the human creature who feeds it (and your grandfather said, 'Suffer little children to come unto Me': and what did He mean by that? how, if He meant that little children should need to *be* suffered to approach Him, what sort of earth had He created; that if they had to *suffer* in order to approach Him, what sort of Heaven did He have?) who fed him, thrust food which he himself could discern to be the choicest of what they had, food which he realized had been prepared for him by deliberate sacrifice, with that curious blend of savageness and pity, of yearning and hatred; who dressed
10-11	into a tub of water too hot yet	15-16	into tubs of water too hot or too cold yet
11	dared not cry out and	17	dared make no outcry, and
11-12	soap and sometimes scrubbing him	18	soap, sometimes scrubbing at him
12-13	faint olive[?] from his skin and skeleton[?], as	19-20	faint tinge from his skin as
13	a brick wall	20	a wall
14-15	obliterated, thinking, projecting about him, filling the thunderous ~~solitude~~ solitude of his despair and unsleeping loneliness louder than speech would:	21-25	obliterated—lying there unsleeping in the dark between them, feeling them unasleep too, feeling them thinking about him, projecting about him and filling the thunderous solitude of his despair louder than speech could:
15	*me where thru no fault, no willing*	25-26	*me, where through no fault nor willing*
16-17	*on the floor with me where thru no fault, no willing of your own you* ~~*must be*~~ *must and will be not*	27-28	*on this pallet floor with me, where through no fault nor willing of your own you must and will be, not*

MANUSCRIPT		BOOK	
18	*cannot just as we will and wait for what must be:—And*	29-30	*cannot.* "And
19-20	negro, who could neither have heard or known the term nigger in its ~~Mississippi~~ rural ⟨North⟩ Mississippi sense, who actually had	31-33	negro. He could neither have heard yet nor recognized the term 'nigger,' who even had
21	knew, who had grown up in a sort of padded and silken cell	33	knew
			Page 199
		1-2	who had been born and grown up in a padded silken vacuum cell
23	shades and in which the	5	shades, where the
24-25	as his digestive processes; ~~⫫~~did	8	as the digestive processes. Your grandfather did
25	was driven, sent	9	was sent
25-26	bed or returned of his own accord and wishes—if	9-10	bed at last or if he quitted it by his own wish and will; if
26	when his [illegible word] youthful [two illegible words joined by *and*] of his loneliness became	11	when his loneliness and grief became
27-31	it by the 2 [illegible word] of beings[?]—the cold lifeless white one or the hard fierce restrained brown one—whose every gesture and ~~move toward him~~ office regarding[?] that ruthless and constant attention to his physical well being were rife with cold antipathy on the one part and that ~~yearning desire to physically hurt him on the other~~ savage and sadistic yearning on the other yet never with antagonism; did not know if it were himself who elected to sleep in the hall where Clytie slept (and not	12-14	it, to sleep in the hall (where Clytie had likewise moved her pallet) though not
32-34	elevated again, as tho not at Judith's decree or behest but elevated above herself by the negress' ~~implacable~~ same fierce inexorable spurious humility) and who (and still none to know just why nor when) next slept in the attic itself—the cot moved there, the few garments (the rags	14-19	elevated still and perhaps not by Judith's decree either but by the negress' fierce inexorable spurious humility. And then the cot was moved in the attic, and the few garments hanging behind a curtain contrived of a piece of old carpet nailed across a corner, the rags
35	the crude jeans	19-20	the harsh jeans
35-37	women made for him or exchanged	20-23	women bought and made for him, he

MANUSCRIPT		BOOK	
	eggs ⟨for⟩ at the store which Judith had once owned and he accepting it, with no comment, no thanks, asking for and himself making		accepting them with no thanks, no comment, accepting his garret room in the same way, asking for and making
37	in the spartan arrangements until that year when he turned 14 and	23-24	in its spartan arrangements that they knew of until that second year when he was fourteen and
38-39	beneath the cell's mattress the shard of mirror which they had not yet missed:	25-26	beneath his mattress the shard of broken mirror:
39	tearless despair he	27	tearless grief he
39-41	it/ examining himself with the door closed and barri barricaded behind him, examining himself in the delicate tatters which he had outgrown and in which	28-29	it, examining himself in the delicate and outgrown tatters in which
42	incomprehension) hanging from nails behind a curtain contrived of a section of old carpet nailed across a corner and	30-33	incomprehension. And Clytie sleeping in the hall below, barring the foot of the attic stairs, guarding his escape or exit as inexorably as a Spanish duenna, teaching him

Page 93 [92]

1-2	Clytie sleeping still on the pallet in the hall below and guarding his exit and escape from the attic as inexorably as a Spanish duenna, who taught him		

Page 200

2-3	strength (his resiliency rather, since he would never be other than light in the bone and almost delicate)—	1-3	strength increased. His resiliency rather, since he would never be other than light in the bone and almost delicate—
4	and light hands	3	and womanish hands
5-6	the steel-and-wood savage steel and wood symbol male symbol, turning ⟨ripping from⟩ the prone rich female earth for corn	7-9	the savage steel-and-wood male symbol, ripping from the prone rich female earth corn
7	both and the negress watching, never	9-10	both. While Clytie watched, never
7	unflagging care,	10-11	unflagging jealous care,
8-9	anyone, white or black, stopped at the fence as tho to wait for him to complete the row and pause and ⟨to⟩ speak to him, sending him on	11-14	anyone white or black stopped in the road as if to wait for the boy to complete the furrow and pause long enough to be spoken to, sending the boy on
9-10	the cold and level vituperation	15-16	the level murmur of vituperation

MANUSCRIPT   BOOK

10-13   the stranger or neighbor away: and so it was not Clytie ⟨and Judith⟩ ~~who watched-him-as-tho-he-were-a-Spanish virgin-and-it-was-not-Judith,-who eould-have-refused-to-let-him-sleep-in the-white-child's-bed-in-her-room-at any-time,-who,-granted-he-was-still young-enough-when-he-eame-to-need that-sort-of-care-at-night,-could-have forced-Clytie-to-take-him-into-another bed-with-her,-who-drove-him-to-do what-he-did-do~~ who would

16-26   the passerby on. So he (your grandfather) believed that it was neither of them who was responsible for his going with negroes. Not Clytie, who guarded him as if he were a Spanish virgin, who even before she could have even suspected that he would ever come there to live, had interrupted his first contact with a nigger and sent him back to the house; not Judith who could have refused at any time to let him sleep in that white child's bed in her room, who even if she could not have reconciled herself to his sleeping on the floor could have forced Clytie to take him into another bed with her, who would

14   monk of him, a celibate, tho not

27   monk, a celibate, of him, perhaps yet not

14-20   for white, for foreigner, yet certainly would not have driven him (Clytie who ~~watched~~ ⟨guarded⟩ him as tho he were a Spanish virgin, [MARGIN: , who, even before he came there to live, before he could have believed that he ever would, had broken[?] into his first contact with a nigger and sent him back to the house] and Judith who could have refused to let him sleep in that white child's bed in her room at any time, who granted he was still young enough when he came to need that sort of care at night, ~~eould-have forced-Clytie-to-take-him~~ granted that she could not have acquiesced to his sleeping on the floor, could have forced Clytie to take him into another bed with her) to consort with negroes—and this too your

28-30   for a foreigner, yet who certainly would not have driven him to consort with negroes. Your

Page 201

22   about 10 years and whom ~~Clytie~~ ⟨Judith ~~and-Clytie~~⟩ watched constantly and his presence not

1   about twelve years, whose presence was not

22-27   and the county since they wondered only why and where and how Clytie had contrived to hide him and believing doubtless that ~~Sutpen-himself had-got-the-child-on-Clytie-before-he~~

2-14   and county since they now believed they knew why Henry had shot Bon. They wondered only where and how Clytie and Judith had managed to keep him concealed all the time,

211

CHAPTER VI

MANUSCRIPT   BOOK

MANUSCRIPT

~~went away~~ and only ~~a few of them to join~~[?] ⟨Bon and Judith had not waited to be married after all and that it had been a widow who had buried him⟩ ~~your grandfather's incredulous memory~~[?] ~~thot that the man could have known or cared~~[?] ~~enough about who Clytie was to~~ join your grandfather's ~~in his~~ incredulous and ~~horrified~~ shocked speculation [MARGIN: to believe that the child might be Clytie's and not Judith's and] that ~~Sutpen~~ ⟨the demon⟩ might have ⟨deliberately⟩ got the child on his own daughter— a little boy seen much about the house

BOOK

believing how that it had been a widow who had buried Bon, even though she had no paper to show for it, and only the incredulous (and shocked) speculation of your grandfather (who, though he had that hundred dollars and the written directions in Judith's hand for this fourth tombstone in his safe at the time, had not yet associated the boy with the child he had seen two years ago when the octoroon came there to weep at the grave), to believe that the child might be Clytie's, got by its father on the body of his own daughter. A boy seen always near the house

27-28 plow a mule and

15 plow and

28-29 too: and it soon known with what cold and unflagging alertness she intercepted any

16-18 too and it soon well known with what grim and unflagging alertness she discovered and interrupted any

29-31 him and it only your grandfather to have coupled the ~~child~~ boy with that child who came with the octoroon that summer to weep at Bon's grave: and it was your grandfather's office that Judith came to that day and he

18-22 him, and there was only your grandfather to couple at last the boy, the youth, with the child who had been there three or four years ago to visit that grave.
[quotes omitted] It was your grandfather to whose office Judith came that afternoon five years later, and he

32 and the faded bonnet in which he had seen her last, ~~the same~~ who

24 and faded sunbonnet, who

33-34 down and who despite the impenetrability[?], the calm cold mask of a face, emanated a sort of terrible and desperate urgency; she would not even sit down to tell him but insisted that they walk on toward the courthouse and the justice's court while she ~~told him~~ talked: and how they entered the courthouse and found him there, handcuffed to an officer and with his hand tied up where the doctor had already treated him and how your grandfather gradually found out what had happened, or as much as he could, since they could

25-33 down, who despite the impenetrable mask which she used for face emanated a terrible urgency, who insisted that they walk on toward the courthouse while she talked, toward the crowded room where the justice's court sat, the crowded room which they entered and where your grandfather saw him, the boy (only a man now) handcuffed to an officer, his other arm in a sling and his head bandaged since they had taken him to the doctor first, your grandfather gradually learning what had happened or as much of it as he

212

MANUSCRIPT

not get very much from the witnesses, the ones who had fled and ~~the
ones who had fought him~~ sent word
for the sheriff and the ones (excepting that one whom he had injured too
badly to be present) with whom he
had fought—a ceremony of some sort
in a negro church in that neighborhood—wedding or perhaps [illegible
word] or ~~sociable~~ social—something,
and he came in, whom they did not
know ~~and~~ save by the country grape-
vine hearing[?] and ~~believed to be a
white man~~ they, the negroes, not the
ones who started it, who merely
questioned this white man's right to
be there and the stranger quiet
enough for a while: and at this point
all ~~fact,~~ ⟨truth⟩ evidence vanished,
bearing out the fact that the stranger
had started the trouble, had burst
suddenly and for no reason that was
ever divulged at the hearing from the
observer's back seat where he had
been sitting and became at once

Page 94 [93]

1-6   the focal point of a moiling knot of
black ~~heads~~ ⟨hands⟩ and arms ~~and~~
⟨clutching⟩ sticks and razors and the
stranger himself using a knife which
he produced from somewhere,
clumsy, with obvious lack of skill
and practice yet with deadly earnestness ~~a puzzling~~[?] ~~strength~~ and a
~~strength~~ strength which his slight
build denied—a strength as tho composed of sheer desperate will and
imperviousness to the punishment,
the blows and slashes which he took
in return and did not seem to feel:
and none to know exactly what happened, what he said ~~about which—~~
curses, ejaculations—which might
have indicated what drove him and
only

6   grope toward and perhaps grasp

6-7   protest against the inevitable, that
indictment of ~~heaven~~ ⟨doom⟩, that

BOOK

Page 202

1-26   could since the Court itself couldn't
get very much out of the witnesses,
the ones who had fled and sent for
the sheriff, the ones (excepting that
one whom he had injured too badly
to be present) with whom he had
fought. It had happened at a negro
ball held in a cabin a few miles from
Sutpen's Hundred and he there,
present and your grandfather never
to know how often he had done this
before, whether he had gone there to
engage in the dancing or for the dice
game in progress in the kitchen
where the trouble started, trouble
which he and not the negroes started
according to the witnesses and for no
reason, for no accusation of cheating,
nothing. And he made no denial,
saying nothing, refusing to speak at
all, sitting there in court sullen,
pale and silent: so that at this point
all truth, evidence vanished into a
moiling clump of negro backs and
heads and black arms and hands
clutching sticks of stove wood and
cooking implements and razors, the
white man the focal point of it and
using a knife which he had produced
from somewhere, clumsily, with
obvious lack of skill and practice,
yet with deadly earnestness and a
strength which his slight build
denied, a strength composed of sheer
desperate will and imperviousness to
the punishment, the blows and slashes
which he took in return and did not
even seem to feel. There had been
no cause, no reason for it; none to
ever know exactly what happened,
what curses and ejaculations which
might have indicated what it was that
drove him, and there was only

27   grope, grasp

27-28   protest, that indictment of heaven's
ordering, that gage

MANUSCRIPT   BOOK

~~aftermath~~ ⟨denial⟩ of the black blood
within him, that gage

9   the ~~very~~ walls and stones[?] in   31   the walls in

10   the very air which he had ⟨once⟩   32-33   the air which he had once walked in
     ~~breathed~~ once walked in and breathed   and breathed until that moment when
     up to the moment which his [sic]   his

Page 203

11-16   that because the others, the justice   2-9   that protest, because the justice and
        and the officers and the spectators   the others present did not recognize
        did not yet recognize him, did not yet   him, did not recognize this slight
        associate ~~him~~ with the woman (as   man with his bandaged head and arm,
        much a stranger to some of them as   his sullen impassive (and now blood-
        the prisoner himself) who had come   less) olive face, who refused to
        in with your grandfather the slight   answer any questions, make any
        man with his bandaged head and his   statement: so that the justice (Jim
        sullen impassive face, who refused   Hamblett it was) was already making
        to answer any questions, make any   his speech of indictment when your
        statement; and the justice, [illegible   grandfather entered, utilizing oppor-
        word] Hamblett[?], then[?] Jim)   tunity and audience to orate, his eyes
        already making his speech when your
        grandfather came in, finding his
        chance and taking it to ~~rate~~ orate,
        with his daily[?] listeners all lis-
        tening and his eyes

17-18   the heel of its tyrant conqueror, when   12   the iron heel of a tyrant oppressor,
                                                         when

19   the tool, which we have to use, depend 14-15   the tools which we have to use, to
        on, is the   depend on, are the

21-22   grandfather already trying to push   18-20   grandfather trying to reach him, stop
        his way thru the crowd, elbowing[?]   him, trying to push through the
        [illegible word] saying, 'Jim. Jim   crowd, saying 'Jim. Jim. *Jim!*' and
        Jim Jim!' and it too late, as if the   it already too late, as if Hamblett's
        justice's own   own

22-23   fingers to wake him: and he   22   fingers under his nose and waked
                                                         him, he

24-25   turned with his to look at the pale   25-27   turned toward the prisoner as
        expressionless prisoner: ~~a~~   Hamblett cried, *'What are you? Who*
        ~~white~~ ----------- then the justice cried: *and where did you come from?'*
        'What are you? Who and where did   "Your
        you come from?'—And how your

26-27   talked to the man himself[?], ~~telling~~ 30-33 talked to him while Judith waited in
        ~~him to go away;~~ [MARGIN: 'You're   the anteroom. 'You are Charles
        Charles Bon's son.' and the other   Bon's son,' he said. 'I dont know,'
        said, harsh and sullen, 'I dont know.'   the other answered, harsh and sullen.
        and your grandfather said, 'You dont   'You dont remember?' your grand-

MANUSCRIPT		BOOK	
	remember?' and the other said nothing and your father [*sic*] said for him to go away, disappear,] giving him the money to go on, saying, 'Whatever		father said. The other did not answer. Then your grand-
		Page 204	
		1-2	father told him he must go away, disappear, giving him money to go on: 'What ever
29	her?' and	5	her?' And
29	stop now, and he	6	stop; he
29-30	at the other face	6	at that still face
30	expression in it than Judith's— nothing of hope nor pain—	7-8	expression than Judith's, nothing of hope nor pain:
31-32	down a little while the delicate parchment colored fingers held the money; /*/Miss Ju* and your	8-10	down at the calloused womanish hands with their cracked nails which held the money while your
32	say Miss Judith to∅ him, since	11	say 'Miss Judith,' since
32-33	ever, and then he thot, I dont even know if he wants to hide it or not: and so he said Miss Sutpen:	12-13	ever. Then he thought *I dont even know whether he wants to hide it or not.* So he said Miss Sutpen.
34	are of course, because I will not know myself, but	14-15	are going of course, because I wont know that myself. But
35	out there to	17	out to
36	Judith and Clytie met him and	18	Judith, and Clytie came to the door and
36-37	Judith and your grandfather thot *I will not have to tell either of them* and he did not. Judith	20-22	Judith, and grandfather waited in that dim shrouded parlor and knew that he would not have to tell either of them. He did not have to. Judith
38-40	you ~~wont~~ ⟨cant⟩ tell me where' and your grandfather said, 'Yes. But it is not the promise now that would stop me. But he has money; he should be—' and he stopped there, with	23-26	you wont tell me.' —'Not wont, cant,' your grandfather said. 'But not now because of any promise I made him. But he has money; he will be——' and stopped, with
40	there 15 years ago with the blue overall	27	there eight years ago with the over- all
43-44	child ~~in the~~ wearing now in place of the lingering tatters of his dead and vanished life that parchment colored rope[?] and hair ~~mantle~~[?] ⟨shirt⟩ of his ancient curse, and your	32	child in his parchment-and-denim hairshirt, and your
Page 95 [94]		*Page 205*	
1-2	*dead; better if he had never lived* and then what	2	*dead, better that he had never lived:* then thinking what

MANUSCRIPT		BOOK	
2	recapitulation after the fact that	3	recapitulation that
3	it, changing	4-5	it, thought it, changing
3	and ~~tense~~ number; and how he returned to town and now,	5-6	and number. He returned to town. And now,
4	it—by means of that	7	it: by that
5	Velery	8	Valery
5	already (not home: returned) again before	9	already returned (not home again; returned) before
6	back, with	10-11	back, appeared, with
6	brought home by	12	brought back by
7-9	not move[?] alone but returned on a spavined and worthless mule with the wife walking beside it and holding him in the saddle and so up to the house where he apparently	13-16	not even hold himself on the spavined and saddleless mule on which he rode while his wife walked beside it to keep him from falling off; rode up to the house and apparently
9-10	that grim and uncalculating despair with	17-18	that invincible despair with
10	in the church and none	18-19	in the dice game. And none
10-11	behind the year of his absence, ~~and~~ which	19-20	behind that year's absence which
11-12	woman, still even after the year [MARGIN: and after their son was born] in that ~~aghast and trancelike~~ aghast	21-22	woman, who, even a year later and after their son was born, still existed in that aghast
12	she arrived did not, possibly could not, tell but	23-24	she had arrived, did not, possibly could not, recount but
13	and ~~in~~ ⟨by⟩ terrific [crossed-out illegible word] ⟨excretion⟩ like the sweat of some incredulous [crossed-out illegible word] amazement.—how	24-26	and by a process of terrific and incredulous excretion like the sweat of fear or anguish: how
14-15	whatever ~~backwater~~ secure[?] two dimensional backwater [MARGIN: and the very name of which she either had never known or the shock of her exodus from it had driven the name from her mind and memory] her mentality was capable of [illegible word] with and	26-31	whatever two dimensional backwater (the very name of which, town or village, she either had never known or the shock of her exodus from it had driven the name forever from her mind and memory) her mentality had been capable of coercing food and shelter from, and

Page 206

| 16-17 | none even knew if she did know for | 1-2 | none knew even now if she knew for |

216

CHAPTER VI

MANUSCRIPT		BOOK	
17	the slave	2-3	the dilapidated slave
17-18	renting some land from Judith), ~~how he had spent something like a year~~ how	3-4	renting his parcel of land from Judith); how
19	broken film ~~in~~ which	6	broken cinema film, which
19-20	back [MARGIN: recovering from the maulings he received] in ~~a fr~~ frowzy	7-8	back recovering from the last mauling he had received, in frowzy
21	reasonless ~~progress~~ moving,	11	reasonless moving,
21-22	and shapes thru which the white colored man	12-13	and bodies through which the man
24-25	ritual—the white colored [MARGIN: apparently hunted out in order to flaunt] ~~man who would seem to flaunt~~ fling the charcoal and apelike ~~face~~ ⟨body⟩ of his consort in	16-18	ritual. The man apparently hunting out situations in order to flaunt and fling the ape-like body of his charcoal companion in
25	on boats or	19-20	on steamboats or
26-27	more when he said he wasn't and would eject him; the white men who when	21-22	more strongly when he denied it; the white men who, when
27-28	negro believed only that he lied to save his skin or thru sheer besotment ~~with~~ of perverse lust, and the result in either case being[?] the same—the ~~light-boned~~ man	22-25	negro, believed that he lied in order to save his skin, or worse: from sheer besotment of sexual perversion; in either case the result the same: the man
29	girl's meddling[?] them first, usually unarmed and regardless of	26-27	girl's giving the first blow, usually unarmed and heedless of
30	to punishment,	28-29	to pain and punishment,
30-31	laughing. And how he	29-30	laughing. "So he
31-32	the dilapidated cabin	31	the ruined cabin
33	house: and nobody	33	house. And there was nobody
		Page 207	
34	such they had not had to burn for food and warmth or to heat	3-4	such which they had not had to chop up and burn to cook food or for warmth or maybe to heat
36	a negro, who had not [illegible word] to his	7-8	a hereditary negro concubine, who had not resented his
37-39	himself would have done it. Because there was love, your grandfather said; there was that letter, ~~wh~~ the one she gave your grandmother to	11-20	himself might have done it. (*Because there was love* Mr Compson said *There was that letter she brought and gave to your*

217

keep and which your father showed
you that night, and who

grandmother to keep. He (Quentin)
could see it, as plainly as he saw the
one open upon the open text book on
the table before him, white in his
father's dark hand against his linen
leg in the September twilight where
the cigar-smell, the wistaria-smell,
the fire-flies drifted, thinking *Yes.
I have heard too much, I have been
told too much; I have had to listen to
too much, too long* thinking *Yes,
Shreve sounds almost exactly like
father: that letter. And who*

40	house that night,	22	*house, that room, that night,*

Page 96 [95]

1-4	now and the head bare now with the once black hair ~~turning iron gray~~ streaked with iron gray while he faced her, standing; he would not have sat, perhaps she would not have asked him to sit since it would be too delicate for that, and the cold level voice no louder than the lamp's flame itself: 'I	26-30	*now, the head bare now, the once coal-black hair streaked with gray now while he faced her, standing. He would not have sat; perhaps she would not even have asked him to, and the cold level voice would not be much louder than the sound of the lamp's flame: 'I*

Page 208

7	will dare bring it up, anymore than any other prank of wild young men. And	2-4	*will anymore dare bring it up than any other prank of a young man in his wild youth. And*
9	Clytie can... No. I.	7-11	*Clytie will...' watching him, staring at him yet not moving, immobile, erect, her hands folded motionless on her lap, hardly breathing as if he were some wild bird or beast which might take flight at the expansion and contraction of her nostrils or the movement of her breast: 'No: I.*
10	worry; ~~H~~we	13	*worry. We*
14-15	the calm still sullen inscrutable thin face, ~~a~~ and she ~~looking at him~~ immobile in the chair, looking at him and her voice	19-20	*the still expressionless thin face, she watching him, not daring to move, her voice*
16	still not moving, not moving so	22-23	*still without moving, not stirring so*
17	which waited, not	24-25	*which she knew was watching her though she could not see it, not*
17-18	terror but in that restive incorrigibility of the free and she	26-28	*terror or even alarm but in that restive light incorrigibility of the*

MANUSCRIPT

BOOK

free which would leave not even a
print on the earth which lightly bore
it and she

18-19 could actually have touched the
creature; her voice soft still, filled

29-30 *could have actually touched it but*
instead just speaking to it, her voice
soft and swooning, filled

20-21 Charles' and he probably not
answering this time, turning, going
out: and she sitting there still, not
moving and still

32-33 *Charles')* Yes, who to know if he
said anything or nothing, turning,
going out, she still sitting there, not
Page 209
1 moving, not stirring, watching him,
still

21 penetrating the walls and the darkness

1-2 penetrating walls and darkness

21-22 lane toward the cabin where his
wife waited, ~~treading moving~~[?]
treading the rocky[?] path

3-5 lane between the deserted collapsed
cabins toward that one where his
wife waited, treading the thorny and
flint-paved path

24 it. But your grandfather did not
know this for certain; he knew

8-9 it.
"Not your grandfather. He knew

25 the little strange boy [MARGIN: whom
Clytie watched and had taught to
farm,] who had become the battered
~~man~~ prisoner in the justice court, ~~no~~
who had

10-14 the strange little boy whom Clytie
had used to watch and had taught to
farm, who had sat, a grown man,
in the justice's court that day with
his head bandaged and one arm in a
sling and the other in a handcuff,
who had

27-28 it well and in a solitary and unflagging fury in which his limbs,
arms and legs and body, still looked

16-18 it pretty well, with solitary and
steady husbandry within his physical
limitations, the body and limbs
which still looked

29 he had restored, who

20 he rebuilt and where his son was
presently born, who

29 neither black nor white and who

21-22 neither white nor black (Clytie did
not watch him now; she did not need
to) and who

30 next 10 years and that to appear,
~~about the negro part of the store~~
~~district~~ be

24 appear, be

30-31 who actually feared either him or
Clytie or Judith perhaps, in the
negro store district blind drunk,
where ~~Ann~~[?] your

24-26 who seemed to fear either him or
Clytie or Judith, as being either
blind or violently drunk in the negro
store district on Depot Street, where
your

32-33   away, or if he were too drunk, if he were drunk enough to become violent the officers, and hold him and presently the wife, the black gargoyle, would come ~~in the wagon~~ with nothing

34-36   and ~~her~~ strong hands, and load him into the wagon bed and take him home: and so when he did not and could not come to town again they did not know it: it was the County medical officer who told them that he had small pox and how Judith had had him moved to the

36-44   and how the doctor had tried to force Judith to desist[?] and she would not: and how he finally notified Miss Coldfield herself but it was too late then: because Judith died before he did: And that you looked at the third stone and you thot how whoever had buried Judith must have been afraid that the other dead might catch the small pox from her because it was on the opposite side of the enclosure from the 2 Bons and so your father did not have to ~~th~~ say 'Think' this time, ~~and even before you read what was carved~~ because you knew who had bot this one even before you read the inscription, and your father was already talking again about what careful printed directions Judith must have roused herself to write down for Clytie when she knew that she was going to die because the Charles Etienne Saint Velery Bon one was the newest one, the last one to be put there: and what Clytie must have done during the 12 or 15 years it

Page 97 [96]

1-6   took [MARGIN: while she raised the child that had been born in the cabin and ~~saved~~ earned and saved) ~~her to earn and save~~ the money to buy the stone with like Judith had written on the paper for her and brot the money to your grandfather and had him

27-30   away (or if he were too drunk, had become violent, the town officers) and keep him until his wife, the black gargoyle, could hitch the team back into the wagon and come, with nothing

31-33   and hands, and load him into it and take him home. So they did not even miss him from town at first; it was the County Medical Officer who told your grandfather

Page 210

1-2   that he had yellow fever and, [*sic*] that Judith had had him moved into the

2-33   and now Judith had the disease too, and your grandfather told him to notify Miss Coldfield and he (your grandfather) rode out there one day. He did not dismount; he sat his horse and called until Clytie looked down at him from one of the upper windows and told him 'they didn't need nothing.' Within the week your grandfather learned that Clytie had been right, or was right, now anyway, though it was Judith who died first."

     "Oh," Quentin said—*Yes* he thought *Too much, too long* remembering how he had looked at the fifth grave and thought how whoever had buried Judith must have been afraid that the other dead would contract the disease from her, since her grave was at the opposite side of the enclosure, as far from the other four as the enclosure would permit, thinking *Father wont have to say 'think' this time* because he knew who had ordered and bought that headstone before he read the inscription on it, thinking about, imagining what careful printed directions Judith must have roused herself (from delirium possibly) to write down for Clytie when she knew that she was going to die; and how Clytie must have lived during the next twelve years while she raised the child which had been born in the old slave

MANUSCRIPT

BOOK

order the stone; and you looking at
the third one, the one that said
Judith Coldfield Sutpen ~~Spinster~~
Daughter of Ellen Coldfield. ~~Born~~
Born October 3rd, 1841. ~~Died~~
~~February 12, 1884.~~ *Suffered the*
Indignities and Travails of this
World for 42 years, 4 Months and
9 Days and Went to ~~her~~ ⟨*Eternal*⟩
Rest ⟨*at last*⟩ *February 12, 1884.*
~~Pause-Stranger and Weep for her.~~
~~Remember Death~~ [MARGIN: Pause,
Mortal, Remember Vanity and Folly
and Beware] and you did not need to
ask who had invented that, put that
one up, and maybe not even listening
to your father's voice: 'They had
beautiful lives—women do.

cabin and scrimped and saved the
money to finish paying out for the
stone on which Judith had paid his
grandfather the hundred dollars
twenty-four years ago and which,
when his grandfather tried to refuse
it, she (Clytie) set the rusty can full
of nickels and dimes and frayed
paper money on the desk and walked
out of the office without a word. He
had to brush the clinging cedar
needles from this one also to read it,
watching these letters also emerge
beneath his hand, wondering quietly
how they could have clung there, not
have been blistered to ashes at the
instant of contact with the harsh and
unforgiving threat.

Page 211

1-9   *Judith Coldfield Sutpen. Daughter of*
       Ellen Coldfield. Born October 3,
       1841. Suffered the Indignities and
       Travails of this World for 42 Years,
       4 Months, 9 Days, and went to Rest at
       Last February 12, 1884. Pause,
       Mortal; Remember Vanity and Folly
       and Beware thinking (Quentin) *Yes.*
       I didn't need to ask who invented that,
       put that one up thinking *Yes, too*
       much, too long. I didn't need to
       listen then but I had to hear it and
       now I am having to hear it all over
       again because he sounds just like
       father: Beautiful lives women live—
       women do.

8   and ~~death~~ bereavement,

9-10   one. ~~She dreamed that head~~ She

11   will because Mr Coldfield

11   estate save the house and what
       remained of the store, and so

12   himself doubtless out of some body
       of

12-13 affairs after she returned from
       Sutpen's Hundred when the marriage
       fell thru—the same

11   *and bereavement,*

15   *one. She*

16-17 *will since Mr Coldfield*

17-18 *estate except the house and the rifled*
       shell of the store. So

18-19 *himself probably out of some con-*
       clave of

20-23 *affairs and what to do with her after*
       they realized that nothing under the
       sun, certainly no man nor committee
       of men, would ever persuade her to
       go back to her niece and brother-
       in-law—the same

14-18   night and which she consumed and made no thanks for even tho she recognized the dish, the plate and pans which contained the food and the napkins which covered it—the plates and pans and napkins which she never washed but returned soiled to the baskets and set the baskets too empty on the step as tho to carry out that illusion that they had never existed or that she herself had never touched, emptied, them, had not come out and taken them up with that air which had nothing of furtive-ness ~~in t in it~~ in it

24-30   *night, the dishes (the plate containing the food, the napkins which covered it) from which she never washed but returned soiled to the empty basket and set the basket back on the same step where she had found it as if to carry completely out the illusion that it had never existed or at least that she had never touched, emptied, it, had not come out and taken the basket up with that air which had nothing whatever of furtiveness in it*

19   food, commented to herself on it, chewed

31-32   *food, criticized its quality or cooking, chewed*

20   all the senses tell her

33   *all*
Page 212
1   *incontrovertible evidence tells her*

21   admit the fact that the store had willed her something—that

2-3   *admit that the liquidation of the store had left her something, that*

22-23   pauper—who would not accept money from Judge Benbow but would accept the money's value in

4-7   *pauper, she would not accept the actual money from the sale of the store from Judge Benbow yet would accept the money's value (and after a few years, over-value) in*

23   use stray negro boys, stop them and command them

7-8   *use casual negro boys who happened to pass the house, stopping them and commanding them*

24-25   pay but that Judge Benbow would pay it—would enter the stores and command things from the counters exactly as she commanded that ~~$1000.00~~ ⟨500.00⟩ headstone, who with

10-16   *pay from her, that they would not even see her again though they knew she was watching them from behind the curtains of a window, but that Judge Benbow would pay them. She would enter the stores and command objects from the shelves and show-cases exactly as she commanded that two hundred dollar headstone from Judge Benbow, and walk out of the store with them—and with*

26   napkins to prevent evidence, declined

17   *napkins from the baskets she de-clined*

27   have felt that the sums she had indirectly received

18-19   *have known that the sums which she had received*

CHAPTER VI

MANUSCRIPT

BOOK

28-29 ago balanced ~~whatever the store had brot.~~ (he, Benbow, had a portfolio, a fat one; it had Estate of Goodhue Coldfield [MARGIN: . Private] written on it in indelible ink. After the ~~died~~ Judge died, Percy Coldfield showed it to me. It

19-21 *ago overbalanced (he, Benbow, had in his office a portfolio, a fat one, with Estate of Goodhue Coldfield. Private written across it in indelible ink. After the Judge died his son Percy opened it. It*

30 forms [MARGIN: and cancelled betting tickets] of horses which ran at the

23-25 *forms and cancelled betting tickets on horses whose very bones were no man knew where now, which had won and lost races on the*

30 a tabulation in his own hand,

25-26 *a ledger, a careful tabulation in the Judge's hand,*

31-45 another showing how he put each winning and ~~the sum of each~~ an amount equal to each loss to that mythical account.) whatever the store

28-31 *another one showing how for forty years he had put each winning and an amount equal to each loss, to that mythical account) whatever the store had brought.*
　　But you were not listening, be-cause

had brot—and you not listening be-cause you knew it all already, had learned, absorbed it without the medium of speech somehow from having been born and lived near it, as children will and do ~~you had heard how before~~ so that what your father said did not tell you anything so much as ~~the~~ it struck, word by word, the resonant strings of what you already knew; ~~because~~ you had been here before, seen these graves probably more than once in those rambling expeditions more than just hunting game which country-bred boys make; you had known about it and about the house too which as boys you had seen, come deliberately to see tho not to enter since it was haunted—the gray rotting shell with its (scaling columns and) sagging blinds and wind-battered windows and vanished steps—and none of you knowing just when it became haunted and what ghost lived there nor for sure if anyone had ever seen the ghost there: but it was haunted because it had to be, and that was enough; possibly there had never been any ghost in it and that the repellant, the

223

guardian[?], was not a spook but that
guardian[?] (and the countryside,
black and white, knew about this too)
which the old woman whom you did
not know then was named—had once
been named—Clytie who lived in one
of (the only remaining one) the
cabins in the old quarters behind it
with a boy ~~about your size~~ (a little
bigger than you) and the same color
~~you~~ she was, who (the old woman: or
not old; you saw her once, her face
was as black as it ever was and
then[?] she did not look old

Page 98 [97]

1	had brot—' and you not listening because		

2-3	and lived near it, as children will and do, so that what your father said did	33	*and living beside it, with it, as children*

Page 213

		1	*will and do: so that what your father was saying did*

3	strings of what you already knew who had	2-3	*strings of remembering. You had*

5	game which country-bred boys make, just	5	*game, just*

5-8	would ~~look//the rotting shell with its scaling portico and missing steps and sagging shutters and plank~~ shuttered[?] windows//~~before you even saw it, were big enough to go out there and dare the ghost, because it was haunted.~~ before you even saw it, were big enough to go out there with 4 or 5 ~~boys~~ other boys	6-8	*would look before you even saw it, became large enough to go out there one day with four or five other boys*

10	there so for 26 years but no one had met the ghost until the wagon load of strangers moving from ~~Alabama~~ ⟨Arkansas⟩ tried	10-12	*there empty and unthreatening for twenty-six years and nobody to meet or report any ghost, until the wagon full of strangers moving from Arkansas tried*

11-13	happened, what they did not or could not tell but which caused them to leave it in a hurry and not stop until they had almost reached Jefferson— the rotting shell with its scaling portico and vanished steps, its sagging	13-19	*happened before they could begin to unload the wagon even. What it was they did not or could not or would not tell but it had them back in the wagon, and the mules going back down the drive at a gallop, all in about ten minutes, not to stop until*

CHAPTER VI

MANUSCRIPT   BOOK

*they reached Jefferson. You have
seen the rotting shell of the house
with its sagging portico and scaling
walls, its sagging*

13   windows on land which   19-20   *windows, set in the middle of the
domain which*

14-23   bought and sold and sold again except   21-33   *bought and sold and bought and sold
for the parts on which the house sat
and which included the old grave
yard: and then the dogs came in out
of the rain too now, disappearing
like smoke into the gloom under the
cedars, and you looked up and sure
enough Dan had stopped the two
horses and the mule in the rain
about 100 yards away and sat there,
his knees drawn up to his chin and
the towsack and the 3 animals all
streaming in the rain, and your
father said, 'Come on up out of the
rain, Dan. I wont let the old Colonel
hurt you' and Dan said, 'Yawl come
on and less go home. Aint no more
hunting today.' and your father said,
'We'll get wet. I'll tell you what:
we'll ride on over to that old house
and keep dry': and Dan sat in the
rain and invented reasons not to
go—that the house would leak or
that you would all catch cold with no
fire or that you would all get so wet
before you got there that the best
thing to do was to go right on home:
and your father laughing at Dan and
you not laughing so much because
even if you were not black like Dan
was you were not any older and you
and Dan had*

*again and again and again. No, you
were not listening; you didn't have
to: then the dogs stirred, rose; you
looked up and sure enough, just as
your father had said he would, Luster
had halted the mule and the two
horses in the rain about fifty yards
from the cedars, sitting there with
his knees drawn up under the towsack
and enclosed by the cloudy vapor of
the streaming animals as though he
were looking at you and your father
out of some lugubrious and painless
purgatory. 'Come on in out of the
rain, Luster,' your father said. 'I
wont let the old Colonel hurt you'—
'Yawl come on and less go home,'
Luster said. "Aint no more hunting
today'—'We'll get wet,' your father
said. 'I'll tell you what: we'll ride
on over to that old house. We can
keep good and dry there.' But Luster
didn't budge, sitting there in*

Page 214
1-7   *the rain and inventing reasons not to
go to the house—that the roof would
leak or that you would all three catch
cold with no fire or that you would
all get so wet before you reached it
that the best thing to do would be to
go straight home: and your father
laughing at Luster but you not laughing so much because even though you
were not black like Luster was, you
were not any older, and you and
Luster had*

24-25   day, the 5 of you, 5 boys all daring   7-8   *day when the five of you, the five
boys all of an age, began daring*

25-26   you got to it, and how you came up   9-10   *you reached it, coming up from the
from the back and so up the old
street*

rear, into the old street

MANUSCRIPT	BOOK
27-28 what were once logs and shingles and chimneys rising from among the undergrowth except that one, and you came up to it and you didn't see her at all	11-14 *what had once been log walls and stone chimneys and shingle roofs among the undergrowth except one, that one; you coming up to it; you didn't see the old woman at all*
28-29 hulking blabber-mouthed coffee colored	15 *hulking slack-mouthed saddle-colored*
31 until you all started	19 *until all of you started*
31-34 you—~~a little woman in a headrag and a shawl, her bare feet set on the round of the chair tilted back against the cabin wall~~ in a chair tilted back against the wall of the cabin—the woman whom you did not know then was named—had once been named— Clytie, who didn't look much bigger than a monkey, smoking a pipe and watching you with two eyes like shoe	20-25 *you from a chair tilted back against the cabin wall—a little dried-up woman not much bigger than a monkey and who might have been any age up to ten thousand years, in faded voluminous skirts and an immaculate headrag, her bare coffee-colored feet wrapped around the chair rung like monkeys do, smoking a clay pipe and watching you with eyes like two shoe*
36-38 woman's voice: 'What do you want?' and you said 'Nothing' and after a while you were all running without knowing who began to run first nor why you ran, since you were not scared: yet you did run, until after a time you crossed the old rotting snake fence and	28-33 *woman's: 'What do you want?' and after a moment one of you said 'Nothing' and then you were all running without knowing which of you began to run first nor why since you were not scared, back across the fallow and rain-gutted and brier-choked old fields until you came to the old rotting snake-fence and crossed it, hurled yourselves over it, and*
	Page 215
39-40 again?'' ''Yes,'' Quentin said. ''And that was the one, ~~the James~~ ⟨Jim⟩ Bond that Dan was talking about now and	2-4 *again* ''Yes,'' Quentin said. ''And that was the one Luster was talking about now,'' Shreve said. ''And
40-41 again and you had not heard the name before, had not thot of [*sic*] he might have had a name when you saw him there in the vegetable patch that day, and you saying,	5-8 again because you hadn't heard the name before, hadn't even thought that he must have a name that day when you saw him in the vegetable patch, and you said,
41 and Dan said, 'Das him. ~~Boy whut stay~~ Bright	8-9 and Luster said, 'Das him. Bright-
42 said, '~~Jim Bond?~~ Spell it.' and Dan said,	10-11 said, 'Spell it' and Luster said,

MANUSCRIPT   BOOK

Page 99 [98]

1	father and	16	father. And
2	either but he would not have cared,	17-18	either, he wouldn't have cared:
2	touched [MARGIN: and then vanished from] what	19	touched and then vanished from what
3	have started any reaction either	20-21	have set up any reaction at all, either
4-5	or sorrow?" "Yes," Quentin said.	22-24	or grief?" "Yes," Quentin said.
5	woman [MARGIN: who must be more than 70 now but who did not look old,] who	25-26	woman who must be more than seventy now yet who
6	under the headrag that day and whose	26-27	under that headrag, whose
6	instead as tho she	27-28	instead like she
7	do and then had stopped and	29	do, then had stopped, and
8-9	into millions of tiny ~~wrinkles~~ wrinkles and her whole body seemed to grow smaller	31-32	into a million tiny cross-hair wrinkles and her body just grew smaller
9-12	heads—~~the two of them living out there behind that house which nobody had entered in the 26 years except the transient~~[?] ~~family which did not stay, tho no one else had actually seen the ghost and it generally believed that there was no ghost, and that the repellant~~[?]~~, the guardian~~[?] ~~was no spook repellant~~[?]~~, the guardian~~[?]~~, might well be Clytie~~ who	33 *Page 216* 1	heads —who
13	was needed, if anyone were interested enough in it to prowl around it, which	1-3	was ever needed, if anybody ever had so little else to do as to prowl around the house, which
14-15	protect, which there was not too, or if there could have been anyone left of them to hide or need concealment, which there was not?~~" "Yes"~~ ~~Quentin said.~~ //And	4-6	protect from prowlers, which there was not; if there had been any one of them left to hide or need concealment in it, which there was not. And
15-24	there ~~and you said it was Clytie or Jim Bond and she said No and you went out there and you found Clytie and James~~ ⟨Jim⟩ ~~"And yet this old aunt told you there was, and you believed her, or at~~	8	there and you

227

least you drove her out there, 12
miles in the dark in a buggy, to
look and see. And you did look and
you did see, and someone was?"
"Yes," Quentin said.
Bond and you knew it was not this
and she still (this Aunt Rosa) still
said No: and you went on, and there
    "Wait then," Shreve said. "For
God's sake wait.") was?"

Bond and you said You see? knew it
could not be Clytie or Jim Bond
because they were not hidden and you
said, You see? but she still said No:
and you went on, and there was?"
"Yes," Quentin said.
    "Wait then," Shreve said. "For
God's sake wait.")
and you

27   both and so you knew it was not there   13   both in it and you said
          and you said

27-29   and you went on: and there was?"   14-17   and so you went on: and there was?"
          "Yes," Quentin said.   "Yes."
              "Wait then," Shreve said. "For   "Wait then," Shreve said. "For
          God's sake wait.") [for opening   God's sake wait."
          parenthesis, see 88/2]

CHAPTER VII

Page 100 [99]

1   ~~There~~ "So he just wanted a ~~son~~ ⟨grandson⟩," Shreve said. "That's all he was after." There was no snow on his arm

2-3   hand which had come back into the lamp and taken a

3   them and filled it and lit it: and so

8   "So that's it. Jesus,

9-10   it."
         "Yes" Quentin said. He

10-15   open book on which the letter lay, the oblong of paper folded across the center and open, or half open, 3/4 open, whose bulk had raised half of itself from the old crease in weightless and levitation paradox, and lying at such an angle that, regardless of this added distortion, he could not have deciphered the writing even if there were need, even if he had not already ~~done it~~ learned the contents. But he was not trying to read it. He just faced it, immobile, his face lowered and looking almost sullen a little, brooding. "He told Grandfather about it, that

15-17   escaped, tried to, tried to escape ⌈MARGIN: into the river hollow⌉ and return to New Orleans and he—"
         ("The

17-19   little dreamlike yet with that faint suggestion of bemused sullenness, of smoldering outrage still evident, so that Shreve, still too looking in the spectacles

20   be completely naked), like a baroque effigy created in colored

Page 127

1   There was no snow on Shreve's arm

3   hand coming back into the lamp and taking a

4-5   them, filling it and lighting it. So

14-15   "So he just wanted a grandson," Shreve said. "That was all he was after. Jesus,

17-18   it."
          Quentin did not answer. He

19-25   open text book on which the letter rested: the rectangle of paper folded across the middle and now open, three quarters open, whose bulk had raised half itself by the leverage of the old crease in weightless and paradoxical levitation, lying at such an angle that he could not possibly have read it, deciphered it, even without this added distortion. Yet he seemed to be looking at it, or

Page 218

1-3   as near as Shreve could tell, he was, his face lowered a little, brooding, almost sullen. "He told Grandfather about it," he said. "That

3-5   escaped, tried to escape into the river bottom and go back to New Orleans or wherever it was, and he——" ("The

7-9   little dreamy yet still with that overtone of sullen bemusement, of smoldering outrage: so that Shreve, still too, resembling in his spectacles

11-12   be stark naked) a baroque effigy created out of colored

229

CHAPTER VII

MANUSCRIPT		BOOK	
20-21	a pretty horrible affinity	12-13	a faintly nightmarish affinity
22	grandfather and a few others	15	grandfather,'' Quentin said, ''and some others
23	and put him to earth	17	and made him take earth
23-24	later; the second summer that was, when they had just finished the bricks and	18-19	later. That was in the second summer, when they had finished all the brick and
25	and the architect	20	and one day the architect
25	the niggers	22	the wild niggers
27-28	girl. And ~~you told me that~~ I think you said that the	25-26	girl. You said the
28	but one.'' But Quentin	26	but two.'' Quentin
29	that strange repressed calm voice as tho to ~~his~~ the	28-29	that curious repressed calm voice as though to the
29-30	it or his hands on	29-30	it or the letter upon the book or his hands lying on
30-31	right from the middle of all of them.	32	right out from the middle of twenty-one people.

Page 219

32	didn't know that it	1	didn't think it
33	them, and so I reckon they never	4	them all day. So I reckon the niggers never
33-34	was supposed	5	was there for, supposed
34	was, whether human or not, so	6	was, so
35	he vanished, jumped	8	he did, jumped
36	vest and pink coat and his Fauntleroy tie and probably carrying his hat	9-10	vest and Fauntleroy tie and a hat like a Baptist congressman and probably carrying the hat
38	didn't see it and didn't even miss	13	didn't even miss
39	to borrow	15	to get out and borrow
39	he needed them, with	16	he would have needed dogs, with

Page 101 [100]

1-2	young too then, I tell you) brot some champagne with him: and the men began	19-21	young then too) brought some champagne and some of the others brought whiskey and they began
2-4	there that night, in that naked house he hadn't even nailed the walls on yet because they didn't sleep Grandfather said, they just sat up with the	21-28	there a little after sundown, at Sutpen's house that didn't even have walls yet, that wasn't anything yet but some lines of bricks sunk into the

230

champagne and the whiskey around
the fire and the dogs curling[?] up
too until daylight and the dogs
struck[?] quickly because had

ground but that was all right because
they didn't go to bed anyhow, Grandfather said. They just sat around the
fire with the champagne and the
whiskey and a quarter of the last
venison Sutpen had killed, and about
midnight the man with the dogs came.
Then it was daylight and the dogs
had

5   run about a mile of the trail out
already just

29-30   run out about a mile of the trail just

5-9   last, with the dogs in the bottom with
the wild niggers and most of the men
on their horses following along the
edge of the bottom, the hills, but
Grandfather and Sutpen staying[?]
in the bottom with the dogs, in case
the wild niggers found the architect
before the dogs could get there: and
so Gran he and Grandfather had to
walk a lot, sending one of the wild
niggers around-t to lead the horses
around the bad places before they

31-33   last, the dogs and the niggers in the
bottom and most of the men riding
along the edge of it where the going
was good. But Grandfather and
Colonel Sutpen

Page 220

1-5   went with the dogs and the niggers
because Sutpen was afraid the
niggers might catch the architect
before he could reach them. He
and Grandfather had to walk a good
deal, sending one of the niggers to
lead the horses on around the bad
places until they

11   November: and

8   November. And

11-24   about it.
    "It was in West Virginia, in the
mountains; he was born there—("Not
in West Virginia," Shreve said.
"—What?" Quentin said. "Because
there wasn't any West if he was in
Mississippi in 1833 and 25 years old
in Mississippi in 1833, he must have
been born in 1808. And there wasn't
any West Virginia in 1808 because—"
"All right," Quentin said. "—West
Virginia wasn't admitted—" "All
right, all right," Quentin said.
"—into the United States until—"
"All right all right all right,"
Quentin said) "—in a cabin; there
wasn't anything there but a few other
cabins where hunters and squatters
lived and the only colored folks were
Indians and you only looked down at
them over a gun barrel and so nobody

9-10   about himself.
    "Sutpen's trouble

looked down on you because nobody
had any more than you had and he
didn't know that there were people
who had because everbody had just
what they could take and no sane man
would go to the trouble to take more
than he could eat or buy powder and
whiskey with. And so he didn't even
know that there was more than that
to have or that there were people that
had it, had other people, niggers, to
do what no man wanted to do, like
handing him a bottle[?] of drink or
pulling off his boots
    "His trouble

	MANUSCRIPT		BOOK
27	himself again, never live wh with what all the folks that	13-15	himself for the rest of his life, never live with what all the men and women that
27-28	on, and all the other dead ones still waiting to see if he did it right, fixed things so that the ones that would come after him eo he	16-18	on, with all the dead ones waiting and watching to see if he was going to do it right, fix things right so that he
28	but the ones	19	but all the living ones
28-29	after he was one	19-20	after him when he would be one
33	Quentin said. "Because if he was 25 "Not in West Virginia. ⟨"Shreve said,"⟩ Because	27-28	Quentin said. "Not in West Virginia," Shreve said. "Because

Page 221

	MANUSCRIPT		BOOK
37	cabins overrun[?] with	2	cabins boiling with
38	or did lay in front of the fire while	4	or lay before the fire on the floor while
38-39	forth over them to cook the food, where	5-6	forth across them to reach the fire to cook, where
40-41	land which people actually owned and did nothing but ride over it or sit on	9-10	land divided neatly up and actually owned by men who did nothing but ride over it on fine horses or sit in fine clothes on
42	objects to want which there were to want	14-15	objects to be wanted which there were, or that the ones who owned the objects

Page 102 [101]

	MANUSCRIPT		BOOK
1	and where the ones who had all the objects		
2-3	who had an equal number of objects but by the very human beings who	17-19	who owned objects too but by the very ones that were looked down on

MANUSCRIPT		BOOK	
	were looked down upon. Because in the life that he knew the land		that didn't own objects and knew they never would. Because where he lived the land
6	take and only	24-25	take and keep, and only
6-7	or need to buy powder and whiskey with.	26-27	or swap for powder and whiskey.
8	color they were and	29-30	color their skins happened to be and
		Page 222	
10	offices [MARGIN: —like transferring[?] to his hand from the table or pouring[?] the bottle[?] of drink or like pulling his boots off to go to sleep—] which all	1-3	offices, such as pouring the very whiskey from the jug and putting the glass into a man's hand or pulling off his boots for him to go to bed, that all
11	themselves daily since	3-4	themselves since
12	ever any more thot of avoiding than	6-7	ever thought of evading anymore than
12	of avoiding the	7	of evading the
13	chewing or breathing.	7-8	chewing and swallowing and breathing.
13	was young, a child, he did not listen	8-9	was a child he didn't listen
13-14	splendor which penetrated the mountains because he	9-10	splendor that penetrated even his mountains because then he
14	people meant,	11	people who told about it meant,
15-16	he did not listen to them because he saw nothing to compare them and gauge them by nor any chance that he ever would (certainly no belief or thot that someday he might) and because he was too busy with the things	12-16	he didn't listen to them because there was nothing in sight to compare and gauge the tales by and so give the words life and meaning, and no chance that he ever would understand what they meant because he was too busy doing the things
17-18	itself made him exhume the old tales and speculate about them, he ~~probably just thot~~ was	17-18	itself exhumed the tales which he did not know he had heard and speculated on, he was
20	it, or maybe he called lucky 'rich')	22	it)
21	little of the choosing and	23-24	little to do with the choosing and
21-22	regret, because (he told Grandfather this too) it	24	regret because it
23	down on the others	26-27	down at others, any others.
24	was: they	29	was. They
25	come as tho by sheer	30-33	come (when the ship from the Old Bailey reached Jamestown probably),

MANUSCRIPT   BOOK

                                                        tumbled head over heels back to
                                                        Tidewater by sheer

                                                        Page 223

25-27   had had (he said something to Grand-   1-3   had had on the mountain had broken.
        father about his ~~wife~~ ⟨mother⟩ dying   He said something to Grandfather
        about time [*sic*], ~~daughter of a family~~   about his mother dying about that
        ~~already established there when Sutpen~~   time and how
        ~~came, who died, he~~⫽⁇ (~~"The demon,"~~
        ~~Shreve said. "Yes," Quentin said)~~ did
        ⨍"⫽~~did not remember when~~ and how

29-31   father that far West) on the mountain   5-13   father even that far West. And now
        had broken and now the whole   the whole passel of them from the
        family[?] of them ranging from the   father through the grown daughters
        father thru the grown daughters to   down to one that couldn't even walk
        one which could not yet walk, sliding   yet, slid back down out of the moun-
        down out of the mountains and [MARGIN: tains, skating in a kind of acceler-
        skating in a kind of accelerating and   ating and sloven and inert coherence
        sloven ~~inertia~~ and inert coherence   like a useless collection of flotsam
        like some useless ~~piece~~ collection of   on a flooded river, moving by some
        flotsam on a river moving by some   perverse automotivation such as
        perverse automation[?] such as in-   inanimate objects sometimes show,
        animate objects sometimes show,   backward against the very current
        backward against the stream] back   of the stream, across
        across

31-33   James. He didn't know why they   14-17   James River. He didn't know why they
        moved, or didn't remember it if he   moved, or didn't remember the
        ever knew—whether it was optimism,   reason if he ever knew it—whether
        hope on the part of his father or   it was optimism, hope in his father's
        nostalgia, since he did not know   breast or nostalgia, since he didn't
                                                         know

33-34   from, if the part of the country to   18-19   from, whether from the country to
        which they returned was it, or even   which they returned or not, or even
        if his father ~~knew~~ himself knew,   if his father knew,

34-35   again—whether somebody had   20-21   again. He didn't know whether some-
                                                         body, some traveler, had

36   warm in the way he had to do it, or   23-24   warm in the mountain way, or if
        if perhaps somebody he knew once   perhaps somebody his father knew
        or who knew him once   once or who knew his father once

38   it and had   26   it, had

40   kinship; in his own ~~primary and~~   29-30   kinship and in his own inertia and in
        ~~profound~~ inertia or in

41-43   it was not. But he——" ("The demon,"   31-32   it were not. But all he remem-
        Shreve said. "Yes," Quentin said).   bered——" ("The demon," Shreve
        "——didn't know, or remember,   said) "——was that
        whether he had even heard, been

MANUSCRIPT   BOOK

    told, the reason or not. All he knew
    was that

43   and ~~they shut~~ somebody ~~threw~~   33   and some-
Page 103 [102]   *Page 224*

1-13 wrapped up the baby and somebody   1-2   body wrapped up the baby and some-
    else threw water on the fire and   body else threw water on the fire
    shut the door and they walked down   and they
    the mountain; and after a while they
    had two mules and a cart and he (he
    was 10 then, the two older boys had
    left home some years before and had
    not been heard of since) driving the
    cart, since as soon as they acquired
    it his father ~~began to~~ formed the habit
    of ~~performing that portion~~ accom-
    plishing that portion of the translation
    devoted to movement flat on his back
    in the cart and snoring with alcohol.
    That was how he told it to Grand-
    father; he didn't remember if it was
    weeks they travelled or months or a
    year, whether it was ~~some season's~~
    ~~completed cycle which overtook and~~
    ~~passed them on the road~~ that winter
    and spring and then summer over-
    took them in turn and passed them or
    whether they overtook and passed
    winter and then spring into the sum-
    mer as they descended; a period
    alternating between a kind of furious
    inertia and hopeless immobility
    [MARGIN: while his father drank him-
    self insensible] and phases[?] of
    dreamy and pointless[?] ~~progress~~[?]
    ⟨loco⟩motion [MARGIN: after they got
    his unconscious form[?] into the
    ~~cart again~~ cart again] ~~upon~~[?] ~~the~~
    [two crossed-out illegible words]
    ~~cart~~ behind the plodding mules,
    during which they did not progress
    at all themselves but hung suspended
    while the earth changed, broadened
    and flattened out of the mountain
    gorge[?] where he had been born,
    mounting, rising about them and
    flowing past, separating[?] like a
    [illegible word] and bringing into
    the gran[?] ~~and astonished~~ sober and
    astonished country

wrapped up the baby and somebody
else threw water on the fire and shut
the door and they

	MANUSCRIPT		BOOK
14-15	existed: and they had a lopsided cart and two spavined oxen and he told Grandfather that he	3-4	existed. They had a lopsided two wheeled cart and two spavined oxen now. He told Grandfather he
15-17	got them, and he (he was 10 then: the 2 older boys had left home some years before and had not been heard of since) driving the cart since almost as soon as they got it his father started ⟨began⟩ the	5-8	got it. He was ten then; the two older boys had left home some time before and had not been heard of since. He drove the oxen, since almost as soon as they got the cart his father began the
20	traveled [MARGIN: (except that one of the older girls who had left home unmarried was still unmarried when they finally stopped, tho she had become a mother before they had lost the last blue mountain range),] whether	14-17	traveled, except that one of the older girls who had left the cabin unmarried was still unmarried when they finally stopped, though she had become a mother before they lost the last blue mountain range. He didn't remember whether
24	or ending; —maybe	25-26	or a definite ending. Maybe
24-25	inertness and hopeless imm and patient immobility while	27-28	inertness and patient immobility, while
27-28	again, behind the plodding mules and	32	again, and
28	to move at all progress	33	to progress
28-29	just hung suspended	33	just to hang
			Page 225
		1	suspended
29	mountain valley cove	2	mountain cove
30	strange faces filled with harsh rough faces	3-4	strange harsh rough faces
31	or they were just fetching him back out was	5	or was
32	out [MARGIN: (and this one time by a huge bull of a nigger, the first black man ⟨and slave⟩ they had ever seen, who emerged with the old man over his shoulder like a sack of meal and his (the nigger's) mouth loud with laughing and full of whi teeth like tombstones)] swam	6-10	out (and this one time by a huge bull of a nigger, the first black man, slave, they had ever seen, who emerged with the old man over his shoulder like a sack of meal and his— the nigger's—mouth loud with laughing and full of teeth like tombstones) swam
32	as tho the mules and the cart moved on a treadmill/ (and it now	11-12	as if the cart moved on a treadmill. And it was now

CHAPTER VII

MANUSCRIPT

35-37 them ~~could have~~ ([illegible word] the usually insensible or impotent father who it seems made one stage of the trip in the state of delirium tremens toward which he had apparently been striving) could have ~~found his way ba~~ led them back to) bringing

38-39 now hamlets: hamlets now villages, villages now towns and

39-40 working on them and men with a different look than mountain men, on fine horses now about the taverns where already now the old

41 not permitted to

41-42 ejected now before he had had time to get drunk good, and now not to laughter and jeers even if they had been

Page 104 [103]
2-3 men ~~that did not went further than~~ ⟨was not measured by⟩ the lifting of an anvil or gouging an eye or

3 drink and stand up. That is, he had

4 that but he was not aware of it yet; he

5 how; lucky or not lucky, and

5-6 any credit for it, feel

6 luck; that they would ~~anything~~[?] feel if anything more ⟨ab⟩ tender

7 them; he was to find that

7-8 he did that, found that out, because that was when he discovered the innocence; it was not the moment that

BOOK

16-20 them could have led the way—excepting possibly the usually insensible father who made one stage of the journey accompanied by the raspberry-colored elephants and snakes which he seems to have been hunting—bringing

22-24 now become hamlets, hamlets now become villages, villages now towns, and

25-28 working in the fields while white men sat fine horses and watched them, and more fine horses and men in fine clothes, with a different look in the face from mountain men about the taverns where the old

28-29 not even allowed to

30-32 ejected before would have time to get drunk good (so that now they began to make really pretty good time) and no laughter and jeers
Page 226
1 to the ejecting now, even if the laughter and jeers had been

6-7 men, not to be measured by lifting anvils or gouging eyes or

7-8 drink then get up and walk out of the room. He had

8-9 that without being aware of it yet. He

10-11 how; whether you were lucky or not lucky; and

12-13 any advantage of it or credit for it, or to feel

14-15 luck; and he still thought that they would feel if anything more tender

16-17 them. He was to find all that

17-19 he found it out, because that was the same second when he discovered his innocence. It was not the second, the moment, that

MANUSCRIPT		BOOK	
10	before; he	23-24	before on the road; he
11-13	the difference between the need for shoes and the need for them[?] to no longer occurred while they were remained in one place (that a cowshed where the sister's baby was born and, as he told Grandfather, for all he could remember, locate in elapsed time, conceived too). They were stopped at last.	24-29	the gradual difference in comfort between the presence and absence of shoes and warm clothing occurred in one place: a cowshed where the sister's baby was born and, as he told Grandfather, for all he could remember, conceived too. Because they were stopped now at last.
14	time, a few of the first days or weeks or months the	30	time, during the first days or weeks or months, the
14-15	had inherited or had acquired from the land where he grew up or which perhaps had	31-32	had acquired from the environment where he grew up or that maybe had

Page 227

16	as far as the Mississippi River once, had left to him	1-2	as far West as the Mississippi River one time—the instinct bequeathed him
16	wornout garments	2-3	worn-out buckskin garments
17	they had left in the cabin when they departed for good and	3-4	they left in the cabin when they departed the last time for good, and
17-18	by the boy's practice, kept	5	by boy's practice at small game and such—kept
18	have returned to the cabin.	6-7	have (so he said) found his way back to the mountain cabin in time.
18-19	now, the point at which the last knew exactly	7-8	now, behind him the moment when he last could have said exactly
19-20	born now weeks and months behind (maybe the year, since that was when he	9-10	born. He was now weeks and months, maybe a year, since he
20-22	out, must not have known during all that winter while his regiment pulled and hauled those 2 tombstones at the last[?] of a campaign whether or not one of the stones lied) So	11-13	out again, so that he told Grandfather that he did not know within a year on either side just how old he was. So
23-24	them, despite the help ⟨efforts⟩ of the unwed sister	16-17	them was decreasing, thinning out, despite the efforts of the unmarried sister
24-25	decreasing and thinning out because of the climate, the warmth and the dampness) living in a cabin another cabin a cabin which was	19-20	decreasing because of the climate, the warmth, the dampness) living in a cabin that was

238

MANUSCRIPT   BOOK

27-28   backward, ~~where niggers with armed~~   23-24   backward, where
        ~~white men beside~~[?] ~~them planted~~
        ~~things which he had never seen~~ where

29   where ~~niggers arm~~ ⟨regiments⟩ of   25-26   where regiments of niggers with
        niggers with armed white   white

30-31   heard of (the old man did something   27-28   heard of. The old man did something
        too, something besides drink now; at   besides drink now, at least, he would
        least he would be gone right after   leave the cabin after

31   supper and he fed them somehow) and   29-30   supper, and he fed them somehow.
        the man who owned all of the   And the man was there who owned
                                                               all the

32-33   apparently even the armed white men   31-33   apparently the white men who
        who did nothing but watch the niggers   superintended the work, and who
        work lived in the biggest house he   lived in the biggest house he had
        ever saw and spent   ever seen and who spent

                                                       Page 228

34   watch him) in a stave   2   watch the man) in a barrel stave

34   trees with his shoes off and a nigger   3-5   trees, with his shoes off, and a
        [MARGIN: who wore ⟨every day⟩   nigger who wore every day better
        better clothes than he or his father   clothes than he or his father and
        and sisters had ever owned and per-   sisters had ever owned and ever
        haps would ever own,] who   expected to, who

35   drinks; and   6   drinks. And

36-37   that year was lost irrevocably) lying   8-10   that he had irrevocably lost count of
        there all p.m. while one of the sisters   his age) would lie there all afternoon
        would come to the door from time to   while the sisters would come from
        time and   time to time to the door of the cabin
                                                               two miles away and

37-38   who was not only ~~rich~~ ⟨lucky⟩ enough   11-12   who not only had shoes in the sum-
        to have shoes in summer too but was   mertime too, but didn't even
        so fortunate he did not even

39   "But still he did not envy   14   "But he still didn't envy

40   a ~~bright-colored~~ broadcloth monkey   16   a broadcloth monkey to hand him the
        to hand him the jug, and   jug and

40-41   and the water into the house for   17   and water into the cabin for

Page 105 [104]
1   it; maybe he even realized, felt the   19-20   it. Maybe he even realized, under-
                                                               stood the

2-3   the nigger ones but   23   the ones the nigger slaves lived in
                                                               but

4   on, because   26   on. Because

MANUSCRIPT		BOOK	
4-5	he had it.	27	he possessed it.
5	to have a	29	to own a
6	rifle and he would have even supported	30	rifle, but he would himself have supported
6-7	its possession but he	31-32	its ownership because he
7-8	gave him the rifle rather than another to say to the other, 'Because	33	gave the rifle to him
		Page 229	
		1	rather than to another as to say to other men: *Because*
8-9	*yours'* except in a fight	3	*yours* except as the victorious outcome of a fight
10-12	did? ~~He didn't even know that he was still innocent that day when he took the message went to the big house with the message from his father~~ // didn't even know he was still innocent that day when his old man sent	7-8	did? He didn't even know he was innocent that day when his father sent
13	message—didn't	9	message. He didn't
13-15	apparently still did not know for sure what his father did, what work (or maybe supposed to do) the old man had in connection with the plantation— a boy	10-13	apparently he still didn't know exactly just what his father did (or maybe was supposed to do), what work the old man had in relation to the plantation. He was a boy
16	and ~~disearded~~ ⟨worn out⟩ and which one of the sisters had ⟨patched and⟩ cut down to fit him and he no	15-16	and had worn out and which one of the sisters had patched and cut down to fit him, and he was no
16-17	of this, of the ~~fact~~ possibility that any one ~~would~~ else would be, than	17-18	of his appearance in them or of the possibility that anyone else would be than
19	portico, thinking	22	portico, the front door, thinking
19	he would see inside	22-23	he was going to see the inside
20	to have who	24	to own who
20-21	hand his liquor to him and pull off the shoes for him that he did not even have to wear,	24-26	hand him his liquor and pull off his shoes that he didn't even need to wear,
21-22	pleased and proud to	27	pleased to
22-23	as the owner of the fine rifle would have been to show the shot pouch[?] and powder horn that went with it.	27-29	as the mountain man would have been to show the powder horn and bullet mold that went with the rifle.
23	without knowing that	30	without being aware that

MANUSCRIPT		BOOK	
24	nigger had	31-32	nigger who came to the door had
25	him rush back over the two years during which they	33	him turn and rush
		Page 230	
		1	back through the two years they
25-26	room just[?] once and	2	room fast and
26	and then you happen to turn and go back and look at the objects	3-4	and you turn and go back through the room again and look at all the objects
27	out that you had not seen them before—a dozen	4-6	out you had never seen them before, rushing back through those two years and seeing a dozen
27-28	happened during the 2 years—a certain	6-7	happened and he hadn't even seen them before: the certain
28-29	other women of the same kind had of looking at the niggers,	8	other white women of their kind had of looking at niggers,
29	of alert [illegible word] antagonism	10	of speculative antagonism
30-31	inherited, the awareness of it passing between the woman at the cabin door and the nigger who passed in the road and which had nothing was	11-14	inherited, by both white and black, the sense, effluvium of it passing between the white women in the doors of the sagging cabins and the niggers in the road and which was
32	of a dare but	16	of dare or taunt but
32	were oblivious	17	were apparently oblivious
33	it (you could str knew that you could strike them,	18	it. You knew that you could hit them,
33-34	not resist.	19	not hit back or even resist.
34-36	they were not it, the right thing, not what you wanted to strike; [MARGIN: Because you d] that you would be just striking a balloon, a balloon slick and m with a face on it, a balloon slick and smooth and without weight painted	20-23	they (the niggers) were not it, not what you wanted to hit; that you knew when you hit them you would just be hitting a child's boy balloon with a face painted
36-37	distended and about to and about break into mirth and	23-24	distended and about to burst into laughing, and
38	have heard the mirth)—of talk	26-27	have stood there in the loud laughing. He remembered talk
39	had gone visiting to	28-29	had themselves gone visiting after supper to
40-42	into some running recapitulation regarding[?] his old life in the	32-33	into harsh recapitulation of his own worth, the respect which his own

mountains, his worth and physical prowess and the boy knowing that the men and the women were both talking about the same thing which had

        physical prowess commanded from his fellows, and

Page 231

1-3   the boy of either thirteen or fourteen or maybe twelve knowing that the men and the women were talking about the same thing though it had

43   siege or about sickness without naming the epidemic—of one p.m. when

5-6   siege, about sickness without ever naming the epidemic. He remembered one afternoon when

Page 106 [105]

1   [1-10 PASTED IN: along the road and he heard the carriage and stepped aside and then he realized

7-9   along the road and he heard the carriage coming up behind them and stepped off the road and then realized

2-3   very way she carried her head and the bucket of milk in her hand and he shouted to her:

11-12   very angle of her head and he shouted at her:

3-4   and the horses rearing and [illegible word] in it and the harness buckles and the wheelspokes glinting; he saw two parasols and

12-14   and rearing horses and glinting harness buckles and wheel spokes; he saw two parasols in the carriage and

5-6   gone, the carriage and the dust and the two faces under the

16   gone: the carriage and the dust, the two faces beneath the

7   on and knew now as the monkey dressed butler spoke to him that it was not the nigger

18-20   on. He knew now, while the monkey-dressed nigger butler kept the door barred with his body while he spoke, that it had not been the nigger

8-9   wheels and just that vain—of one night, his father came, blundered, in late; he

22-24   wheels, and just that vain. He thought of one night late when his father came home, blundered into the cabin; he

9-10   even still dulled with broken sleep, and his father's voice with that [illegible word] of fierce exultation, vindication in it: 'We whupped one of Pettibone's niggers tonight']

24-27   even while still dulled with broken sleep, hearing that same fierce exhultation, vindication, in his father's voice: 'We whupped one of Pettibone's niggers tonight'

11   that and asked which one and

28   that, asking which one of Pettibone's niggers and

11-12   know, ~~if he had even heard or not~~ even had

29   know, had

13   nigger'—how without knowing it then since

31-33   nigger.' He must have meant the question the same way his father meant the answer without knowing it then, since

MANUSCRIPT

BOOK

Page 232

14-15 innocence he must have meant the questions the same way his father meant the answers; ~~that he seemed to see them~~ there no actual nigger, no living flesh

1-2 innocence: no actual nigger, living creature, living flesh

16-17 out; he could seem to see them, the white men and the nigger's balloon face. Maybe the nigger's hands were tied

2-6 out. He could even seem to see them: the torch-disturbed darkness among trees, the fierce hysterical faces of the white men, the balloon face of the nigger. Maybe the nigger's hands would be tied

18-19 and twist[?] for freedom, not the balloon face; it poised among them, weightless and slick with its paper thin distension, then somebody struck the

7-10 and writhe for freedom, not the balloon face: it was just poised among them, levitative and slick with paper-thin distension. Then someone would strike the

20 and going

12-13 and passing and going

21 of the ~~bursted~~[?] ⟨mellow⟩ laughter, merry[?] terrifying and ~~loud.~~ loud.—

14-15 of mellow laughter meaningless and terrifying and loud.

22 the dressed up monkey nigger standing in it, barring it, ~~and~~ looking at

16-17 the monkey nigger barring it and looking down at

24 because probably that was one

19 because that would be one

24 sisters kept hidden good—who had

20 sisters would keep hidden good. He had

25 that ~~nigger~~ monkey nigger who ~~had maybe~~ thru no

22 that monkey nigger, who through no

26 being ~~bred-in~~ housebred in Richmond perhaps looking—" ("Or

23-24 being housebred in Richmond maybe, looking— [*sic*] ("Or

28 him [MARGIN: even before he had time to say what he came for] to never come

27-28 him, even before he had had time to say what he came for, never to come

29 [29-38 PASTED IN: "He did not even

30 "He didn't even

30 He was not even mad: he

32-33 He wasn't even mad. He

Page 233

31 could think in quiet. So he

1-2 could be quiet and think, and he knew where that place was. He

32 there, to a place he knew, would play in—where a game trail of some sort[?] went into a canebrake

3-4 there—a place where a game trail entered a canebrake

33 oak log had

4-5 oak tree had

CHAPTER VII

MANUSCRIPT

BOOK

34   sometimes; he said that he crawled back into his cave and thot.

7-8   sometimes. He said he crawled back into the cave and sat with his back against the uptorn roots, and thought.

36   was trying to think out of all he had

12   was seeking among what little he had

37   he could find nothing.

13-14   he couldn't find anything

37-39   door, who had come from a land where houses had no back doors but only windows and only these windows to enter or escape unseen and then, and he] houses had no back doors but only windows and where anyone

14-17   door even before he could state his errand, who had sprung from a people whose houses didn't have back doors but only windows and anyone

41   all people accepted.

20   all men accepted.

41   eat, since

21-22   eat a meal since

Page 107[106]

1   the

1-2   days; but he perhaps he did not even expect to be asked into the house.

23-24   days; perhaps he had not expected to be asked into the house at all.

3-4   and which at the time he says he may not have even comprehended, was certainly connected with the land which supported

27-29   and maybe at the time (he said) he might not even have comprehended, was certainly connected somehow with the plantation that supported

5-6   stockings in which the monkey nigger stood to

31-32   stockings the monkey nigger stood in to

6-8   could state his errand. He was not mad. He was just thinking, trying because he knew that something had to be done about it; he would have to do something about it in order to live for the rest of his life, and he could It

33   could even state the business. It

Page 234

8   a little lump

1   a lump

9   few made bullets

1   few molded bullets

9-12   man had told him to place the bullets on a certain stump say, and not come even close enough to see the rifle. He was not mad. He insisted on that to Grandfather. He was just
    "Because

3-6   man came to the door and told him to leave the bullets on a stump at the edge of the woods, not even letting him come close enough to look at the rifle.
    "Because

12   thinking because he knew that something had to

7-8   thinking, because he knew that something would have to

14   was [MARGIN: because of his ⟨that⟩

10-13   was because of that innocence which

244

MANUSCRIPT		BOOK	
	innocence. which he had just dis- covered he had, ~~bu~~ which have to compete with] He		he had just discovered he had, which (the innocence, not the man, the tra- dition) he would have to compete with. He
14	the standard of the rifle	14	the rifle
18	ask: and there was not, the first[?] one: *But*	20-22	ask. But there was not, there was only himself, the two of them inside that one body, arguing quiet and calm: *But*
18-19	nigger; it	23	nigger. It
19-20	had whipped that night; the nigger was just another of the balloon faces slick	24-26	had helped to whip that night. The nigger was just another balloon face slick
21-22	him ~~and his clothes and his bare~~ ~~splayed feet~~ for that instant before he knew it something	28-29	him from within the half-closed door during that instant in which, before he knew it, something
22-24	to shut the eyes of it—was looking thru the balloon as the man whom the laughter it held barricaded and pro- tected turned from whatever place he happened at the time to be, at the boy before the door	30-33	to close the eyes of it—was looking out from within the balloon face just as the man who did not even have to wear the shoes he owned, whom the laughter which the balloon held barricaded and protected from
		Page 235	
		1-3	such as he, looked out from whatever invisible place he (the man) happened to be at the moment, at the boy outside the barred door
24-25	feet and thru and beyond the boy; he himself seeing his father and brothers and sisters as (not the nigger) the owner must	3-6	feet, looking through and beyond the boy, he himself seeing his own father and sisters and brothers as the owner, the rich man (not the nigger) must
27	with a brute and	9	with brutish and
29-30	given them free, and for heritage the expression on the balloon	14-15	given the garments free, with for sole heritage that expression on a balloon
30	looked at some unremembered and nameless ancestor who	16-17	looked out at some unremembered and nameless progenitor who
32	*him*: and the other:	19	*him*: he argued with himself and the other:
32-35	the ~~first~~⟨other⟩: I dont know: and the first: But I can shoot him. I could slip right up thru them bushes and *lay there until he comes out to* *lay in the hammock* (it was just	21-23	the other: *I dont know:* and the first: *But I can shoot him. I could slip right* *up there through them bushes and lay* *there until he come out to lay in the* *hammock and shoot him:*

before dinner when he went to the
house and the man was not in the
hammock. That was when he had
gone to the door) *and shoot* him:

36   first: *What shall we do then?*   24-25   first: *Then what shall we do?*

38-39   see it in the tops of the oak and   28-29   see sun in the tops of the trees
cypress trees around him even if his   around him. But his stomach had
stomach had not told him   already told him

39   home: and   30-31   home. And

Page 236
42   but merely set   4   but just set

Page 108 [107]
1-3   leanto ~~kitchen~~ room which they used   5-7   lean-to room which they used for
for kitchen which was fine in good   kitchen and which was all right be-
weather because it did not even   cause in good weather it didn't even
matter that ~~the chi~~ it had no chimney   matter that it had no chimney since
and which they did not attempt to use   they did not attempt to use it at all
at all

3   washtub, her   9   washtub in the yard, her

4   and an old pair   10   and a pair

4-5   and her beam as broad as   11   and broad in the beam as

5   very work which she   12   very labor she

6   labor reduced   14   labor, toil, reduced

9-10   do and had spent excuse for was not   21-23   do was not done, and had sent the
done—granted that was what the   excuse for—granted that that was
errand had been for, ~~and~~ which   what his errand to the house had been,
which

11   not there and so   24-25   not at home yet. So

13   not doing it because he was still   28-30   not hearing her, paying any attention
thinking, then his old   to her because he was still thinking.
Then the old

15   supper and he went and lay on   32-33   supper nor when he went and lay down
on

Page 237
17   he would lie or not, because he said   3-4   he was going to lie or not. Because,
that the terrible   he said to Grandfather, the terrible

17-18   yet; ~~he just lay on his back~~ he   5   yet, he

18   argued, the first one and the other/   6   argued inside of him, speaking
~~But~~ speaking

19-20   *him. No. That wont do no good* ~~while~~   8-10   *him.—No. That wouldn't do no good—*
~~his central thinking went quickly~~[?]   *Then what shall we do about it?—*

246

MANUSCRIPT

BOOK

	~~on~~ and he just a listener, not especially interested he		*I dont know:* and he just listening, not especially interested, he
21	listening, because	11	listening. Because
21	he had not asked for, it	12	he hadn't asked for. It
23-24	think of it as a man would—	16	think it out straight as a man would,
25	*he wont*	17-18	*he* (not the nigger now either) *wont*
25-26	*much and*	20	*much for what he set that nigger to do and*
26-27	*wouldn't let me even tell him, warn him* and	22	*wouldn't even let me tell him, warn him.* And
27	something saying it	23-24	something shouting it
28-29	father and the 2 youngest in the bed and the room thick with the old man's alcohol snoring. *He*	25-26	father in the bed with the two youngest and filling the room with alcohol snoring, to hear too: *He*
29-30	*it. Never even give me a chance to say it* and now it was too fast, too mixed up to be thinking even, all	27-28	*it:* it too fast, too mixed up to be thinking, it all
30	once, *He*	28-29	once, boiling out and over him like the nigger laughing: *He*
32	*any word and*	31	*any message and*
32	*matter ~~to~~ even to Pap let alone to him; I*	32	*matter, not even to Pap; I*
33	*to come and tell*	33	*to tell*

Page 238

36-37	nothing, not even any trash or refuse; just a kind of limitless ⟨flat⟩ solitude with the shape of his intact innocence rising above it and the innocence telling him	4-7	nothing, no ashes nor refuse; just a limitless flat plain with the severe shape of his intact innocence rising from it like a monument; that innocence instructing him
40	*wouldn't you?* and he said yes. *But*	15	wouldn't it?' and he said Yes. 'But
40-42	*rifles, so to combat* ~~him~~ ⟨them⟩ *you got to have what he* ~~has~~ ⟨they've[?]⟩ *got that made* ~~him~~ ⟨them⟩ *do what he did.* ~~You got to combat him with land and niggers and a house where a monkey dressed nigger can go to the door and tell a man or a boy to go around to~~ *You*	16-17	rifles. So to combat them you have got to have what they have that made them do what the man did. You

Page 109 [108]

1	*with.* He left	18-19	with. You see?' and he said Yes again. He left

MANUSCRIPT		BOOK	
1	and left just	20	and departed just
2	by getting up from	20-21	by rising from
2-7	of them again.	22-30	of his family again.

MANUSCRIPT 2-7:

of them again.

"He left that night" Quentin said. "He got up ⟨waked⟩ before day and left just like he went to bed; by getting up from the pallet and tiptoeing out of the house. He never saw any of them again."

"He went to the West Indies," Quentin said. He had not moved; he sat as before, his face turned a little, his hands lying before him on the table, on either side of the open text book and the letter lying on the book, one half of the creased page tilting upward without support as tho it had learned the secret of levitation. "That was how he said it. The He

BOOK 22-30:

of his family again.

"He went to the West Indies." Quentin had not moved, not even to raise his head from its attitude of brooding bemusement upon the open letter which lay on the open textbook, his hands lying on the table before him on either side of the book and the letter, one half of which slanted upward from the transverse crease without support, as if it had learned half the secret of levitation. "That was how Sutpen said it. He

MANUSCRIPT		BOOK	
9-10	he could not have escaped and which he had mounted because they cou[?] found the sapling with his suspenders fastened around one	32-33	he (the architect) could not have escaped yet which he had undoubtedly mounted because they found the
		Page 239	
		1	sapling pole with his suspenders still knotted about one
10-11	to get climb the tree tho they could not understand why the suspenders at first and	2-3	to climb the tree, though at first they could not understand why the suspenders, and
11	before Grandfather said they discovered what ⟨how⟩ the	4	before they comprehended that the
11-12	architecture to	5	architecture, physics, to
14	had picked that	9	had chosen that
14	that sapling up	10	that pole up
16	have done and he traveled from tree to tree from there on for about a half mile; it took 3 hours	12-15	have crossed and traveled from there on from tree to tree for almost half a mile before he put foot on the ground again. It was three hours
17-18	come to earth again.	17	come down.
18-19	the whiskey	19	the rest of the whiskey
19-20	more while he and Grandfather waited. So he	20-22	more of it while they waited. "He
21	ships went from to get there,	24	ships departed from to go there,

CHAPTER VII

MANUSCRIPT		BOOK	
21-22	one. [MARGIN: nor how he liked the sea nor about the hardship and it must have been hardship indeed for him, a boy of 14 or 15 ~~going to sea in 1823,~~ who never saw water before, going to sea in 1823.] He	25-29	one, nor how he liked the sea, nor about the hardships of a sailor's life and it must have been hardship indeed for him, a boy of fourteen or fifteen who had never seen the ocean before, going to sea in 1823. He
24	now and with money	33	now,
		Page 240	
		1-2	even though they were a little soiled and worn with three years of war, with money
25-27	make up a man reach and he can say I did what I set out to do and I could stop if I wanted to and [illegible word] the instant that Fate	4-7	make a man reach, where he can say *I did all that I set out to do and I could stop here if I wanted to and no man to chide me with sloth, not even myself*—and maybe this the instant which Fate
27	you but the peak something[?] so good and fine to see that	8	you, only the peak feels so sound and stable that
28-29	he copied it	11	he had aped it
29-30	not learn it too out of the same book he taught himself ~~to read out of and to speak the~~ the words, the bombastic phrases in which	12-14	not perhaps learn it too from the same book out of which he taught himself the words, the bombastic phrases with which
30	a light for	14	a match for
31	and nothing of vanity, nothing funny in it either, Grandfather	15-16	and there was nothing of vanity, nothing comic in it either [*sic*] Grandfather
33	pity, or ~~commendation, not~~ not	20	pity; not
34	aside/ [MARGIN: like kings used to do:] I	22-23	aside like eleventh- and twelfth-century kings did: 'I
35	adjunctive nor forwarding to	24-25	adjunctive or incremental to
36	same way while	26	same tone while
36	log and waited for	27	log waiting for
37-43	winter' (he	30-32	winter, enough to have learned something about them, to realize that they would be most suitable to the expediency of my requirements.' He didn't

didn't recall how he came to be sent, just what might have entered his father's mind, what nebulous shape not of ambition for him but perhaps the same revolt against his lot which the son had and which in the father was perchance merely en[?] vindic-

249

tive envy [MARGIN: toward one or two
men] while with the son it was for
vindication and revenge upon an entire system.] He just remembered
that he went, an adolescent boy with
a good deal of the mental and moral
equipment of a grown man, in a
class of children 3 or 4 years younger than he and 3 or 4 years more
advanced. He must have been almost
as big as and probably a good deal

Page 110 [109]

1-10   a good deal stronger of will than the
teacher, who must have brot into the
cramped single room which contained the entire school his countryman's[?] grim and alert reserve and
a certain intractibility ⟨latent⟩, possibly a ⟨an in⟩subordination which he
was not even aware of nor that the
teacher himself never dared take
issue with it, because it was not
intractibility but mountain man's
pride pride inherited from those
mountain solitudes where some of
his blood at least had come from.]—
an [crossed-out illegible word]
[MARGIN: a quality] which forbade
him to condescend to the memorizing
of dry lines and sums but which listened to the reading of history and
tales of esoteric events with profound attention

---

didn't remember how he came to go
to school. That is, why his father
decided to send him, what notion
might have entered his old man's
mind, what nebulous shape that wasn't
ambition probably nor any desire to
see the boy better himself for his
own sake; it was probably some instant of blind revolt against

---

—(he didn't

10   go.   33   go to the school.

Page 241

1   nebulous vision or shape

10-11 nebulous shape

MANUSCRIPT		BOOK	
12	sake but probably some instant of blind revolt	5-6	sake, probably not even some blind instant of revolt
13-14	a 100 such families which lived under it	7-8	a hundred families like his which had come and lived beneath it
14-15	crockery which the son revolted at, except that with the older man it was probably just vindictive	9-10	crockery, but was probably mere vindictive
15-17	men where with the boy it was from ~~vindication~~ revenge against one man but vindication toward a whole system. Anyway, he went for	10-12	men, planters, whom he had to see every now and then. Anyway, he was sent to school for
20	sober and watchful ~~country re~~ mountain reserve	19-20	sober watchful mountain reserve
20-21	of insubordination too that	20	of latent insubordination that
21-22	aware that the teacher was afraid of it because it would not be intractibility ~~but~~ and	21-23	aware of any more than he would be aware at first that the teacher was afraid of him. It would not be intractibility and
22-23	either but maybe ⟨the⟩ self-reliance ~~inherited from~~ of mountains and solitude since	23-24	either, but maybe just the self-reliance of mountains and solitude, since
23-24	least had been ~~born~~ bred in them, but which anyway was probably what forbade	25-28	least (his mother was a mountain woman, a Scottish woman who, so he told Grandfather, never did quite learn to speak English) had been bred in mountains, but which, whatever it was, was that which forbade
24-25	listen to the reading)— 'where I	30-31	listen when the teacher read aloud.— Sent to school, 'where,' he told Grandfather, 'I
25-26	that a good deal of the things which men have done are already done and are to be learned	32-33	that most of the deads, good and bad both, incurring opprobrium or plaudits or reward either, within the scope of man's
		Page 242	
		1	abilities, had already been performed and were to be learned
27	that a good deal of the time he resorted to reading only	3-4	that on most of these occasions he resorted to reading aloud only
28	and walking out of the room.	6	and leaving the room.
28-29	us, and I anyway listened—tho I did not then know	6-7	us and I anyway listened, though I did not know

MANUSCRIPT		BOOK	
31	would ever serve	12	would someday serve
34-35	that, ~~the school of necessity would~~ if it were ~~included~~ to be taught in the school of energy and will, I should learn—;	17-19	that, if it were to be learned by energy and will in the school of endeavor and experience, I should learn.
35-36	when the day was over, waited	20	when school was out and waited
36-38	him (he was a smallish man who always looked dusty) ~~looked as if tho if you were to strike him there would be no resulting outery~~[?] ~~but just the sound of the blow and a puff of dust like when you strike a rug)~~ and stepped out; I	21-23	him; he was a smallish man who always looked dusty, as if he had been born and lived all his life in attics and store rooms. I
38	back and how	23-24	back when he saw me and how
40	dust to fade in the air like when you strike a rug; and asked him if it were true.	26-29	dust in the air as when you strike a rug hanging from a line. I asked him if it were true, if what he had read us about the men who got rich in the West Indies were true.
42	read;	33	read my own name;
Page 111[110]		*Page 243*	
2	the irrevocable courses of actions which he [MARGIN: his weak senses and intellect] cannot	6-7	the subsequent irrevocable courses of resultant action which his weak senses and intellect cannot
3	take, ~~else he will not sur~~ in order	8-9	take, will have to take in order
4	that and not I which caused me to hold him by the arm ~~and~~ as he drew back, glaring	9-17	that instinct and not I who grasped one of his arms as he drew back (I did not actually doubt him. I think that even then, even at my age, I realized that he could not have invented it, that he lacked that something which is necessary in a man to enable him to fool even a child by lying. But you see, I had to be sure, had to take whatever method that came to my hand to make sure. And there was nothing else to hand except him) glaring
5	know [MARGIN: (I did not actually doubt him; I think that even then at the moment I realized that he could not have invented it, would have lacked that something which is necessary in a man ~~in~~ to enable him to	18-19	know—saying,

BOOK

mock[?] even a child by lying.)⁄ But
you see, I had to be sure, had to take
whatever method which came to my
hand to make sure. And there was
nothing else.)]—saying

7	came that I realized that ~~above all things I should re~~ to	21-22	came when I realized that to
7-8	need money first and above all things, I	22-24	need first of all and above all things money in considerably quantities and in the quite immediate future, I
10-11	and so he stopped talking now. ~~They ate and~~ He	29-30	and Sutpen stopped talking for a while. He
12-16	dogs (they ~~dragged them away from the tree~~ had to drag them away from the tree but especially from the sapling pole with the architect's suspenders tied to the end of it, as tho it was not only that it was the last thing which the architect had touched but it was the thing that his exultation when he saw another chance to escape had touched too and it was not only the man but the exultation too that the dogs smelled and which made them wild) made casts in all directions, getting further and further away until about the middle of the p.m. one	32-33	dogs made casts in all directions. They had to drag the dogs away from the tree, but especially away from the sap-

Page 244

		1-7	ling pole with the architect's suspenders tied to it, as if it was not only that the pole was the last thing the architect had touched but it was the thing his exultation had touched when he saw another chance to elude them, and so it was not only the man but the exultation too which the dogs smelled that made them wild. The nigger and the dogs were getting further and further away until just before sundown one
18-19	shirt that he had come out of the mud and washed himself off and put on when he saw that	10-12	shirt he had put on when he came out of the mud and washed himself off after he realized that
19-20	talking while	13-14	talking himself and maybe not even listening while
20	politics and poured the whiskey, just	15	politics, just
24	book, and	23	book. And
25	have suffered to make it, since naturally it would have been hard but he believed that all he needed was	24-25	have had to endure to make it. But then he believed that all that was necessary was
27	him since at that time he could probably have not believed	30-31	him, because at that time, Grandfather said, he probably could not have believed

MANUSCRIPT		BOOK	
28	found the trail where	33	found where
			Page 245
31	not seem to intend to resume it; then it began to get late and	3-4	not appear to intend to resume. Then the sun went down and
32	town and so they	5	town; they
32	more, so	6	more. So
33	home and two	8-9	home, and he and Sutpen went on until the light failed. Two
33-34	were 15 miles from camp now) went back to get blankets and some more grub, and they went on; and then	9-11	were thirteen miles from Sutpen's camp then) had already gone back to get blankets and more grub. Then
35	could because now they	13	could now since they
36	dark; that	14-15	dark to keep from traveling in a circle. That
37	shining and	17-18	shining in the torch light and
38	their flanks and shoulders where the light of the torch touched them) and	19	their shoulders and flanks) and
39	pants now and then) with the torches	20-21	pants here and there) with the pine torches
41	glass and	24	glass or china and
41	they made bigger than	25	they cast taller than
42	one minute and gone	25	one moment then gone
42	one second and	26-27	one moment and
Page 112[111]			
2	breathed: and	30	breathed. And
3	realized what it was: and Grandfather said he thot how there	32-33	realized that this was some more of it, and he said how he thought there
			Page 246
6	a lapel or a sleeve:	5	a sleeve or a lapel:
7	for ~~simple~~ platform drama and ~~blood-shed innocent heroies~~ ⟨childlike⟩ heroic simplicity just	7-8	for platform drama and childlike heroic simplicity, just
8-9	broadcloth and linen that you might see on 10,000 men anywhere which he wore in the office that p.m. 30 years afterward had	8-11	broadcloth uniform which you could have seen on ten thousand men during those four years, which he wore when he came in the office on that afternoon thirty years later, had
9-10	he ~~said the both the simplest and the most outrageous things~~ stated calmly with	13	he stated calmly, with

MANUSCRIPT		BOOK	
12-13	things; Sutpen telling some more of it, already into what he was telling without telling just how he got there or how what he was now in (crouching	16-21	things. He was telling some more of it, was already into what he was telling yet still without telling how he got to where he was, nor even how what he was now involved in came to occur (he was obviously at least twenty years old at the time he was telling about, crouching
13	dark now and firing the rifles thru it	21-22	dark and firing the muskets through it
14	him) came to occur, getting	23	him), getting
14	into it as	23-24	into that besieged Haitian room as
15	there—this memory[?], ~~no~~ this anecdote no ~~continu~~ deliberate	26	there. This anecdote was no deliberate
17-18	happened ~~since that day~~ during the 6 years since that day when he, a boy of 14 who knew no language but English and not much of that, had	29-30	happened during the six years between that day when he had
18	Indies and this	31-32	Indies and become rich, and this
19	French planter, he should be barricaded in	32-33	French sugar planter, he was barricade [sic] in
19	family (and	33	fam-
		Page 247	
		1	ily. And
21	me.'') ''——that he	4-5	me. Just go on.'') ''——woman whom he
21-22	years later that he found to be unsuitable	5-6	years afterward he had found unsuitable
22-30	aside—tho providing for her) and a few frightened half-breed servants which he had to turn from the window and kick and curse into ~~lea~~ helping the girl load the rifles which he and the planter shot then thru the window: ~~into the Haitian darkness where the insurrecting niggers crept and hid howled~~[?] ~~and sang.~~[?] ~~and I recall~~[?] ~~Grandfather was saying 'Wait, wait, for Christ's sake wait' about like you were: so that they decided they had gone~~ far enough and they made camp and ate and got out the whiskey again and he and Grandfather sat before the	6-12	aside, though providing for her and there were a few frightened half-breed servants with them who he would have to turn from the window from time to time and kick and curse into helping the girl load the muskets which he and the planter fired through the windows. And I reckon Grandfather was saying 'Wait, wait

fire and the [illegible word] stopped,
the sitting, [two illegible words]
drinking[?] some too tho it was still
not clear since he was still not telling
about himself, his connected life, not
bragging at all, just telling a story
about an adventure story, a man's
story that would still have been just
as good told about any man over
whiskey at night

And I reckon Grandfather saying
'Wait wait

30-31	did slow stop
36	story; he
36-38	something that he a man n he had done but just telling something that a man named Thomas Sutpen did once and that would still have just [*sic*] as good a story if the man had not had any name at all, told
38-41	night.

'Not how he got there, happened
to be there, at all. The only mention
he ever made of the 6 or 7 years that
had occurred somewhere he had
existed in, proved this, accomplished
somewhere and somehow
"That

| 41-42 | down, but still not enough to clarify it much, he still not telling about the career of Thomas Sutpen, about how yet[?] came to be there; the only mention Grandfather said that he |
| 43 | patois and |

Page 113 [112]

1	which he had to learn to oversee the plantation he oversaw, and
1-2	to be married but certainly in order to
2-3	he already had her—how he told

13	did stop
23	story. He
24-27	something he had done; he was just telling a story about something a man named Thomas Sutpen had experienced, which would still have been the same story if the man had had no name at all, if it had been told
28-29	night. "That
29-32	down. But it was not enough to clarify the story much. He still was not recounting to Grandfather the career of somebody named Thomas Sutpen. Grandfather said the only mention he

Page 248

1-2	patois he had to learn in order to oversee the plantation, and
3-4	to get engaged to be married, but which he would certainly need to be able to
5-6	he had already got her—how, so he

MANUSCRIPT		BOOK	
	Grandfather that he had believed courage		told Grandfather, he had believed that courage
4-5	lore, when he realized that all people did not talk the same tongue and that	9-10	lore when he discovered that all people did not speak the same tongue and realized that
5	skill but he	11	skill, he
6	language or that design to which he referred would die still-born / and Grandfather So	12-13	language, else that design to which he had dedicated himself would die still-born. So
8	the fire on	17	the firelight on
11	You probably will not	21-22	You will probably not
14	eyes and saying:	27	eyes, saying,
14	dont do-me-the hold	27	dont hold
16	I should not believe it. Yet I	30	I shouldn't believe it. But I
17	girl just that shadow who could load a rifle but	32-33	girl, just that shadow which could load a musket but

Page 249

18-19	(or during the 7 or 8 nights while they were besieged and watched the barns	1-2	(or the seven or eight nights while they huddled in the dark and watched from the windows the barns
21	had made the	7	had created the
23	he knew why now and but he asked to	10-11	he (Grandfather) knew why now but he asked anyway to
24	had never been actually afraid until the granaries and fields were	12-13	had not been afraid until after the fields and barns were
24-25	had forgotten about the sugar smell but	13-14	had even forgot about the smell of the burning sugar, but
27	the rifles—	18	the muskets—
27-28	face, [MARGIN: —a single cheek and chin for an instant beyond a curtain of fallen hair—] a white slender arm raised, a hand delicate hand holding a ramrod, and that was all; no-more of no more of detail or information as to how	18-22	face, a single cheek, a chin for an instant beyond a curtain of fallen hair, a white slender arm raised, a delicate hand clutching a ramrod, and that was all. No more detail and information about that than about how
29	house than	23-24	house when the niggers rushed at him with their machetes, than
30-31	said, more incredible to him than the first had been because the first did infer years, time, a space the get-	25-28	said, was more incredible to him than the getting there from Virginia, because that did infer time, a space

MANUSCRIPT

BOOK

ting thru ~~of~~ which inferred something of leisure, since

the getting across which did indicate
something of leisureliness since

33 time ~~into violence which was its own
measure~~ which ~~became~~ ⟨was⟩ the

32-33 time which was the

Page 250

34 that clear pleasant

1 that pleasant

35 it ~~(even the Grandfather said here
that (a,~~ was apparently impressed by
it even despite that

2-4 it, was impressed by it through detached and impersonal interest and
curiosity which even fear (that

36-37 it—not only, Grandfather said, because of this but actually because
this was all it was to him since

6-10 it) failed to leaven very much.
Because he was not afraid until after
it was all over, Grandfather said,
because that was all it was to him—
a spectacle, something to be watched
because he might not have a chance
to see it again, since

38-41 terrified

12-21 terrified; did not even know that he
had found the place where money was
to be had quick if you were coura-
geous and shrewd (he did not mean
shrewdness, Grandfather said. What
he meant was unscrupulousness only
he didn't know that word because it
would not have been in the book from
which the school teacher read. Or
maybe that was what he meant by
courage, Grandfather said) but where
high mortality was concomitant with
the money and the sheen on the
dollars was not from gold but from
blood—a spot

—that land, earth, which would require 10,000 years of equatorial
heritage to bear it—a little island
which was not even the halfway point
between the jungle they came from
and the civilization ~~they were doomed
for~~ ⟨which⟩ the black blood, the
⟨black⟩ arms and hands and bones
and thinking and remembering and
hopes and desires; halfway between
civilization which had expected

Page 114[113]

1 —a spot

1-2 said, for ~~the last furious~~ violence

23 said, as a theater for violence

2-3 of greed and ~~cruelty~~ human cruelty,
for the last ~~furious~~ despairing fury
of all the doomed—a little island
which was the halfway point between
~~jungle~~ what

24-27 of human greed and cruelty, for the
last despairing fury of all the pariah-
interdict and all the doomed—a little
island set in a smiling and fury-
lurked and incredible indigo sea,
which was the halfway point between
what

4 inscrutable land from

29 inscrutable continent from

6 doomed; halfway between the

32 doomed, the

Page 251

7 and ~~the~~ set it homeless ~~on the sea~~
and

2 and set it homeless and

MANUSCRIPT		BOOK	
7-8	the sea—a little	2-3	the lonely ocean—a little
8-9	bear it, a soil ~~watered~~ ⟨riched[?]⟩ with black blood by 200 years	4-6	bear its climate, a soil manured with black blood from two hundred years
9-11	exploitation and injustice so that it sprang with an incredible fierce paradox of peaceful greenery, of trees and vines and crimson flowers, where cane grew three times the height of a man as tho nature held a balance and offered	6-11	exploitation until it sprang with an incredible paradox of peaceful greenery and crimson flowers and sugar cane sapling size and three times the height of a man and a little bulkier of course but valuable pound for pound almost with silver ore, as if nature held a balance and kept a book and offered
11-12	of man and nature watered	12-13	of nature and man too watered
13	vain or out	15	vain, out
13	blue water, along	16	blue sea, along
13	vain cry	16	vain despairing cry
14	which that old ⟨unsleeping⟩ blood which had	18-19	which the old unsleeping blood that had
15-16	for ~~revenge~~ vengeance—and he ~~riding~~ overseeing, riding over it peacefully on his horse as he	20-21	for vengeance. And he overseeing it, riding peacefully about on his horse while he
16-17	which ~~men's secret~~ the little surface corners of	22-23	which the little surface corners and edges of
18	spirit first cried and	25-26	spirit cried for the first time and
19	tremble at	28	tremble and throb at
21	was just something	32	was merely something
		Page 252	
22	it from	1	it, making his daily expeditions from
22	came: and	2	came. And
22-23	that came about, the steps that led up	3	that day happened, the steps leading up
23-35	said apparently he did not even know what he must have been seeing	4-5	said he apparently did not know, comprehend, what he must have been seeing every day

every day because of that innocence [two crossed-out illegible words] ~~about; just~~ a pig's bone, a few chicken feathers, a stained dirty rag in which a few pebbles were tied up, found on the [crossed-out illegible word] old man's pillow one night and nobody

259

knew how it came there because all
the servants, the halfbreeds, fled
from the house and he did not know
until the old man told him that the
stains on the rag were not grease
and dirt but blood: and he still not
at all alarmed but just curious and
doubtless quite interested because he
doubtless still looked on even the
planter and the daughter (he told
Grandfather how even during the
siege he had not thot to remember
her name, recall if he had ever
heard it. He also told Grandfather
that the ~~mother~~ planter's wife had
been a Spanish woman and so it was
Grandfather and not Sutpen who realized that until the siege began he had
probably never seen her a dozen
times) as foreigners—~~did not believe~~
~~there was anything serious in it until~~
~~he found the servant, one of the half~~
~~breeds~~—then one of the servants, one
of the half breeds, which he found
himself, hunted for 2 days and could
not find and then on the 3rd day
found what was left of the half breed
in a place which[?] he could not
understand how he had overlooked
and missed before

---

every day

36	knew how	9-10	knew (least of all, the planter himself who had been asleep on the pillow) how
37	they found at	11	they learned at
37-38	half breeds, had vanished and	12	half breeds, were missing, and
38-41	were not grease and dirt but blood nor that what ~~the old man~~ he considered the old man's gallic rage was actually fear and alarm; ~~because he~~ ~~did not yet believe that the old man~~ ~~and the daughter would be harmed by~~ ~~the blacks even if the blacks were~~ dangerous[?] ~~because to him~~ and he ~~not at~~ just	13-15	were neither dirt nor grease but blood, not that what he took to be the planter's gallic rage was actually fear, terror, and he just
41-42	looked on the planter and the daughter	16-18	looked upon the planter and the

MANUSCRIPT

BOOK

both ⟨he told Grandfather how ~~even during the siege he had not~~ until

daughter both as foreigners. He told Grandfather how until

43   he ~~had~~ did not know her given name,

19   he did not know the girl's Christian name,

43-44   this ~~into the story like you might push a pebble aside with your toe without even actually knowing that it had been~~ there

21   this into

Page 115[114]
1   into

1-2   joker aside from a pack of cards you were dealing without being able to say later if you had ~~come to the~~ found a joker in the pack or not, that

21-23   joker out of a pack of fresh cards without being able to remember later whether you had removed the joker or not, that

3-5   the siege he had not seen the girl probably 12 times) as foreigners— the body of one of the half breeds found at last (he found it, hunted for it 2 days ~~and~~ without even knowing that what he was meeting with was a blank wall of ~~silence~~ black

25-29   the attack he had possibly not seen the girl as much as a dozen times. The body of one of the half breeds was found at last; Sutpen found it, hunted for it for two days without even knowing that what he was meeting was a blank wall of black

5-6   anything ~~would to~~ could happen and, as he found later, almost anything did, and

30-32   anything could be preparing to happen and, as he learned later, almost anything was, and

6-7   body in a place where he could not have missed it on the first day

32-33   body where he could not possibly have missed it during the first hour of the first day

Page 253

7   there: and he sitting there on

1-2   there. All the time he was speaking he was sitting on

8   with, whom Grandfather himself had seen fighting naked and chest

3-4   with, the man Grandfather himself had seen fight naked chest

8-9   niggers, ~~and no bones about the fi who still fou~~ before the camp fire while the house

4-5   niggers by the light of the camp fire while his house

10   by lanterns in

6   by lantern light in

10   had a wife and children and no bones about

7-9   had got at last that wife who would be adjunctive to the forwarding of that design he had in mind, and no bones made about

11   while he put the shirt back on because

10   while he washed the blood off and donned his shirt because

11   be lying flat

11   be flat

	MANUSCRIPT		BOOK
12	and one of the others throwing water on him; this man sitting there and telling Grandfather that at	12-13	and another nigger throwing water on him. He was sitting there on the log telling Grandfather how at
12-16	halfbreed, and that he (Sutpen) had seen as much as most men and had done as much as most and some that he did not boast about, but that there were some things that a man who pretended to be civilized saw when[?] he had to but which he did not care to talk about, so he would just say that he found the half-breed at last and so began	14-15	half breed, and so began
17	them—the man and the daughter, two servants	17	them—the planter, the daughter, two women servants
17-18	the smell of the burning	18-19	the smoke and smell of burning
18	smoke on the sky and the air sharp and trembling	19-20	smoke of it on the sky and the air throbbing and trembling
19-20	vacuum where no succor could	22-23	vacuum into which no help could
21	forth without hope of freshness, burdened still with the forlorn[?] weary	25	forth across it and burdened still with the weary
21-22	children on the sea which sur[?] isolated it—while the girl two	26-27	children homeless and graveless about the isolating and solitary sea—while the two
22	whose first name	28	whose Christian name
22-23	the rifles which	29	the muskets which
23-24	the ⟨Hataiean [sic]⟩ night itself, the sugar-scented saccharine and blood smeared and putrid darkness lancing	30	the Haitiean [sic] night itself, lancing
24-25	the saccharine sugar-weary and blood-smeared and throbbing	31-32	the brooding and blood-weary and throbbing
25-26	and hope of rain and how on the 9th night they ran out of water and something had to be done and so he put the rifle down	33	and any hope of rain. And he told how
		Page 254	
		1-2	on the eighth night the water gave out and something had to be done so he put the musket down
26-27	them: that	3	them. That
29	'Yes, but	8	'Yes. But
30	it; he	9	it. He

MANUSCRIPT		BOOK	
31	the rifle down and had them unbar	11	the musket down and had someone unbar
33	flesh should stand);	16-17	flesh should be asked to stand);
34	themselves ~~flee~~ turning	17-18	themselves turning
34-35	theirs [MARGIN: and from which blood could be made to run as it could from theirs] and containing ~~some~~ that indomitable	19-21	theirs and from which blood could be made to spurt and flow as it could from theirs and containing an indomitable
35	fire as theirs but	22	fire which theirs came from but
35	not have ⟨been⟩ he	23	not possibly have. He
36	which by the way, Grandfather	24	which, Grandfather
37-38	too) and then daylight came and there were no drums in it and the sugar fields had stopped smoking now and ~~m~~ they went out (probably	25-27	too. And then daylight came with no drums in it for the first time in eight days, and they emerged (probably
38	sun on it as tho nothing	28-29	sun shining down on it as if nothing
39	incredible solitude	30	incredible desolate solitude
39-40	him home:	31-32	him to the house:
40	engaged. ~~And then he stopped~~ Then	32	engaged. Then
Page 116 [115]		*Page 255*	
2	you," Shreve said. "Stopped	3	you. Stopped
4	niggers shooting at it.	6-7	niggers surrounding it.
5	he thot he	9	he decided he
7	said. Still he	12	said. He
7	letter, the book on	13-14	letter lying on the open book on
8	again; it	15	again. It
9	ash particles fanning out ~~upon~~ from the bowl onto	16-17	ashes fanning out from the bowl, onto
10	support ~~himself~~ and hug himself with since, altho it was only 11 oclock, the	18-20	support and hug himself, since although it was only eleven oclock the
11	to chill toward	20	to cool toward
12-13	tho Shreve [MARGIN: he would not perform his deep-breathing in the open window tonight at all] had not yet gone into the bedroom to return with first his robe on and next with his overcoat above[?] the robe.	22-26	though (he would not perform his deep-breathing in the open window tonight at all) he had yet to go to the bedroom and return first with his bathrobe on and next with his overcoat on top of the bathrobe and Quentin's overcoat on his arm.

263

MANUSCRIPT		BOOK	
13	married, and	27	married'' [*sic*] Quentin said, ''and
14	stopped, flat	28	stopped, Grandfather said, flat
15-16	was,'' Quentin said, his face lowered, speaking still in that curious, almost grim flat voice which	31-33	was.'' His (Quentin's) face was lowered. He spoke still in that curious, that almost sullen flat tone which

Page 256

16-17	the start with that intent	1	the beginning with intent
18	created. ''He just	4-5	created. ''Sutpen just
19	to start early tomorrow; we may catch	6-7	to get an early start tomorrow. Maybe we can catch
22	river this time and he	11-12	river. But he
22-23	calculation and the dogs and the niggers ~~bayed~~ and the niggers making the racket now ~~and~~ (Grandfather	12-14	calculation this time so the dogs and the niggers bayed him and the niggers making the racket now as they hauled him out. Grandfather
24-25	meat, ~~and that now~~ had offered the gambit which they had	16-17	meat, had voluntarily offered the gambit by fleeing, which the niggers had
26-27	same name of sportsmanship and	20-21	same spirit of sport and sportsmanship and
27	side) and they hauled him and (~~most~~ ⟨all⟩ of the men	22	side. All the men
29-30	race had started)—hauled him out: a little man with ~~his clothes ruined with water and mud frock coat ripped up the his hat~~ one sleeve ~~ripped~~ missing from the frock	25-27	race started, Grandfather said. So they hauled him out of his cave under the river bank: a little man with one sleeve missing from his frock
31-32	mud and one leg of his pants ripped down where he had tried to tie up his hurt leg with his shirt tail	28-30	mud where he had fallen in the river and one pants leg ripped down so they could see where he had tied up his leg with a piece of his shirt tail
32-33	swollen and his hat completely gone; they did not find that and it was Grandfather that gave him a new ~~one~~ [MARGIN: frock coat and hat] the day he left; he in Grandfather's	31-33	swollen, and his hat was completely gone. They never did find it so Grandfather gave him a new hat the day he left when the house was finished. It was in Grandfather's

Page 257

34-35	and then burst into tears;—a little harried man with a 2 days' stubble on his face, who came out fighting	2-4	and burst into tears.—a little harried wild-faced man with a two-days' stubble of beard, who came out of the cave fighting

MANUSCRIPT		BOOK	
35-36	all, and the dogs and niggers	4-5	all, with the dogs barking and the niggers
36-38	and ~~happy pleasure~~ merry anticipation like they ~~thot that~~ were under the impression ~~they wouldn't even have to~~ that if the chase had lasted longer than 24 hours ~~they would~~ the rules would not require them to wait	6-9	and merry anticipation, like they were under the impression that since the race had lasted more than twenty-four hours the rules would be automatically abrogated and they would not have to wait
38-39	beat them and dogs and all away from him, and him standing there not	10-11	beat niggers and dogs all away, leaving the architect standing there, not

Page 117 [116]

1	[1-14 PASTED IN: and Grandfather said a little sick in the face where the niggers had wrenched[?] his leg by accident, and made them	12-14	and Grandfather said a little sick in the face where the niggers had mishandled his leg in the heat of the capture, and making them
3	it and it	16	it. But it
4-6	but that he was already moving toward the architect with the bottle out and the architect stopped talking and looked at the bottle and Grandfather saw his eyes	19-22	but he (Grandfather) was already approaching the architect, holding out the bottle of whiskey already uncorked. And Grandfather saw the eyes
7	that 30 hours	24-25	that fifty-odd hours
8	go, ~~yet~~ no hope to get there; ~~just hope and despair~~ just a dream and foreknowing	26-27	go and no hope of getting there: just a will to endure and a foreknowing
9-10	and lifted the other and	29	and raised the other hand and
10-11	gone and then flung his hand	31	gone, then flung the hand

Page 258

14	sitting on their horses in a circle and watching him and then took ⟨not only⟩ the first drink of neat whiskey he ever took in]	4-5	sitting their horses in a circle and looking at him, and then he took not only the first drink of neat whiskey he ever took in
15-16	he must have believed he would never take just as the Brahmin believes that that situation ~~will never~~ cannot conceivably	6-8	he could no more have conceived himself taking than the Brahmin can believe that that situation can conceivably
17	Now Quentin stopped; at	9	Quentin ceased. At
17-18	stopped now; just go on'' but Quentin did not—the flat curiously	10-11	stopped talking now; just go on.'' But Quentin did not continue at once—the flat, curiously
18	body not moving except	12	body not stirring except

MANUSCRIPT

BOOK

19 [19-22 PASTED IN: to breathe, both young, born within the same year the

13-14 to breathe, both young, both born within the same year: the

20-22 joined after a fashion even before birth by that River which is the geologic [illegible word] of half of the western world altho one of them had never seen it, who 4 months ago had never laid eyes on one another yet who since had slept in the same room and eaten side by side of]

16-25 joined, connected after a fashion in a sort of geographical transubstantiation by that Continental Trough, that River which runs not only through the physical land of which it is the geologic umbilical, not only runs through the spiritual lives of the beings within its scope, but is very Environment itself which laughs at degrees of latitude and temperature, though some of these beings, like Shreve, have never seen it—the two of them who four months ago had never laid eyes on one another yet who since had slept in the same room and eaten side by side of

23 books to study from to recite

26 books from which to prepare to recite

24 fragile trivial pandora's box of envelope paper

28 fragile pandora's box of scrawled paper

25-26 snug sleeve of what we call the best of dreamy and heatless best of thought. ⟨coign, this⟩ ⟨monastic⟩ coign

30 snug monastic coign,

28 said. "That was when he told any

33 said. "It was
Page 259
1 thirty years before Sutpen told Grandfather any

28 busy, all

2 busy. All

29 for talking

2 for spare talking

29 that 'design which I had in mind,' and the only

3-4 that design which he had in mind, and his only

30-31 stable while the men would come up from the back and hitch their horses and traps[?] in the pasture and walk up to the stable so they couldn't see them from the house because he was married

4-7 stable where the men could hitch their horses and come up from the back and not be seen from the house because he was already married

32-33 and a wife and two children he already arrested and freed for having stolen it and then freed and so that was all settled, and a

7-9 and he already arrested for stealing it and freed again so that was all settled, with a

266

MANUSCRIPT		BOOK	
33-34	planted (Grandfather loaned him the seed corn and cotton for the first planting) and he getting	10-11	planted with the seed Grandfather loaned him and him getting
37	work they are smart and when they do not work you	16-17	work you were smart and when they dont you
38	and seen his	19	and watched his
39-40	that sam very same thing all the time only	21-22	that very same thing all the time, only
40	him, and then Sutpen	23	him. Then Sutpen

Page 118 [117]

| 1-3 | didn't and Mr Coldfield let him; father said because Mr Coldfield did not believe they would get away with it and when it failed he (Mr Coldfield) would take his half of the blame be able to get it out of his mind then; and father said that Mr Coldfield would have insisted on taking | 25-31 | didn't. And Mr Coldfield let him. Father said it was because Mr Coldfield did not believe it would work, that they would get away with it, only he couldn't quit thinking about it, and so when they tried it and it failed he (Mr Coldfield) would be able to get it out of his mind then; and that when it did fail and they were caught, Mr Coldfield would insist on taking |
| 3-4 | as expiation for having been tempted all | 32-33 | as penance and expiation for having sinned in his mind all |

Page 260

4-5	it had worked, was going to work, all he could do the least he	1-2	it was going to work, had worked, the least thing he
5	his half of	3	his share of
7	had produced his conscience and which offered	5-6	had created his conscience and then offered
8	created; hated	7-8	created, which could do nothing but decline; hated
8	it getting into a	9-10	it drifting closer and closer to a
10-11	hardship before the South was even aware that he was opposed to it, of his hatred of it, and so he picked out the only	13-17	hardship, and so he would not be present on that day when the South would realize that it was now paying the price for having erected its economic edifice not on the rock of stern morality but on the shifting sands of opportunism and moral brigandage. So he chose the only
11-12	his disapprobation on the great number of people who would outlive the fighting,"—"Sure,"	18-20	his disapproval on these who should outlive the fighting and so participate in the remorse—" "Sure,"

MANUSCRIPT   BOOK

12-14 now," "—Yes," Quentin said. "The
design.")—getting richer and richer,
and it must have looked clear and
fine ahead for him now—his house
finished and bigger

21-24 now."
    "Yes," Quentin said. "The
design.—Getting richer and richer.
It must have looked fine and clear
ahead for him now: house finished,
and even bigger

15 nigger had told

25-26 nigger came in his monkey clothes
and told

15 even, to cull

27-28 even, which the man who lay in the
hammock with his shoes off didn't
have, to cull

15-16 and raise and train him

29 and train him

17 it (only father said that was not it

31-32 it. Only Father said that that wasn't
it

Page 261

20 against; time, shortening time ahead
of him that wou could

5 against: time shortening ahead of
him that could

22 door was not it, that that was

9 door wasn't it because the boy-
symbol was

23 again have to

11 again need to

24 for shelter

12-13 for mere shelter

24 whatever stranger,

13-14 whatever nameless stranger,

25 himself behind

14 himself forever behind

25 the light

15-16 the still undivulged light

26-27 even remember his name (the boy's)
name would not even know that they
had ever been once been riven forever free from beasthood ⟨brutehood⟩
just as his own (Sutpen's) children
should)—the two children,

17-33 even ever hear his (the boy's) name,
waited to be born without even having
to know that they had once been riven
forever free from brutehood just as
his own (Sutpen's) children were—"
    "Dont say it's just me that sounds
like your old man," Shreve said.
"But go on. Sutpen's children. Go
on."
    "Yes," Quentin said. "The two
children" thinking *Yes. Maybe we
are both Father. Maybe nothing ever
happens once and is finished. Maybe
happen is never once but like ripples
maybe on water after the pebble
sinks, the ripples moving on, spread-
ing, the pool attached by a narrow
umbilical water-cord to the next pool
which the first pool feeds, has fed,*

MANUSCRIPT   BOOK

did feed, let this second pool contain
a different temperature of water, a
different molecularity of having seen,
felt, remembered, reflect in a differ-
ent tone the infinite unchanging sky,
it doesn't matter: that pebble's
watery echo whose fall it did not
even see moves across its surface
too at the original ripple-space, to
the old ineradicable rhythm thinking
Yes, we are

Page 262
1-4   *both Father. Or maybe Father and*
I are both Shreve, maybe it took
Father and me both to make Shreve
or Shreve and me both to make
Father or maybe Thomas Sutpen to
make all of us.
    "Yes, the two children,

28-29	too; ~~to grow~~ by character ~~and~~ mental	6	too, by character mental
30	there was when	9	there must have been when
31	to the design which he had in mind:— and	11-12	to the forwarding of the design. And
32-33	after the 30 years and told him, how his conscience had hurt him at first	13-15	after thirty years and told him how his conscience had bothered him somewhat at first
33-34	argued with his conscience and so settled that just	15-16	argued calmly and logically with his conscience until it was settled, just
34-35	about leaving home that night without telling anyone and settled that—how	17-19	about his and Mr Coldfield's bill of lading (only probably not as long here, since time here would be pressing) until that was settled—how
35-36	as it was possible by being above-board; that he could have deserted her and the child without telling them but he did not,	21-24	as lay in his power by being above-board in the matter; that he could have simply deserted her, could have taken his hat and walked out, but he did not:
37-38	what anyone would have admitted to be a good and valid claim ~~not only~~ ⟨if not⟩ to the whole place ~~because~~[?] ⟨which⟩ he alone had save [*sic*] it and the lives	24-26	what Grandfather would have to admit was a good and valid claim, if not to the whole place which he alone had saved, as well as the lives
38	it, certainly to	27	it, at least to
38	which was specifically stated in	27-28	which had been specifically described and deeded to him in

MANUSCRIPT		BOOK	
39	origin while	30-31	origin and material equipment, while
40	been what was more than reservation, actual misrepresentation in theirs and	31-32	been not only reservation but actual misrepresentation on their part and
41	a serious nature as to ⟨not only⟩ have voided	33	such a crass nature as to have not only voided

Page 263

MANUSCRIPT		BOOK	
41	his knowledge the very central	1	his knowing it the central
41	design but would have	2	design, but to have
42-43	suffered and all that he could have ever accomplished toward the design afterward—	3-4	suffered and endured in the past and all that he could ever accomplish in the future toward that design—
43-44	all which he might have had and	6	all he might have claimed and
44	another would	7	another man in his place would
44	keeping ~~and been supported in it by the law and the opinion of~~	8-10	keeping and (in which contention) would have been supported by both legal and moral sanction even if not the delicate

Page 119 [118]

1-3	~~and which, injustice or no, many another might have insisted upon and been supported in the taking by public opinion by both jurisprud the~~ opinion ~~both of~~ and (in which contention) been supported by both legal and ~~human~~ ⟨moral⟩ sanction even if not ~~moral,~~ the delicate		
3-4	now ~~but saying, 'Conscience? -My God, man: - you did not need conscience to warn you~~ because	11	now because
7	out—he sitting there in the office trying to explain ~~patien~~ with that patient ~~recapit~~ amazed recapitulation not	16-17	out.—Yes, sitting there in Grandfather's office trying to explain with that patient amazed recapitulation, not
9	it—trying to explain as tho to circumstance, fate itself the	20-21	it, but trying to explain to circumstance, to fate itself, the
10-11	of the history which both he and Grandfather knew as tho he had to explain it to some intractible and unpredictable and patient child:	23-25	of his history (which he and Grandfather both now knew) as if he were trying to explain it to an intractible and unpredictable child:
12	mind; whether	26	mind. Whether
12	the question: the question	27	the point; the question
12-13	it, what ever[?] did I make in it, whom injure	28-29	it, what did I do or misdo in it, whom or what injure
13	extent that this ~~demand~~ would	29-30	extent which this would

CHAPTER VII

MANUSCRIPT		BOOK	
15	anyone; I risked	33	any man. I even risked

Page 264

MANUSCRIPT		BOOK	
18	mind, I even entered into the agreement as one	6	mind, as one
18-19	expected out of his own ignorance of gentility to do in dealing with gentle-born people; I did not demand, I	7-9	expected to do (or at least be condoned in the doing) out of ignorance or gentility in dealing with gentle-born people. I did not demand; I
20	explaining about myself, yet they withheld	10-12	explaining fully about myself and my progenitors: yet they deliberately withheld
22	me, and I did not learn this fact until	14-15	me—a fact which I did not learn until
22	hastily; I	16	hastily. I
23-24	years which would not put me the not only the amount of that stopped time behind but	17-19	years which would now leave me behind with my schedule not only the amount of elapsed time which their number represented, but
24	time which	20-21	time represented by their number which
25	had now reached, but	22	had reached and lost. But
26	child should ever be incorporated in my plan design and, as	24-25	child be incorporated in my design, and following which, as
26-27	to keep that which I had earned keep	25	to keep
28	declined this	28-29	declined and resigned all right and claim to this

Page 265

MANUSCRIPT		BOOK	
31-33	30 years during which I had been led to believe // and Grandfather not saying Wait now but saying, years after	1-2	thirty years after
33	done harm or injustice I	3	done an injustice, I
34-36	saying Wait now but saying 'Conscience? Conscience? Good God, man what else did you expect?--Didn't the knowledge of things you must have drawn in with your mother's milk teach you better than that? Good	4-5	saying 'Wait' now but saying, hollering maybe even: 'Conscience? Conscience? Good
36-37	very intuition and instinct for misfortune which anyone who a man who spent	6-7	very affinity and instinct for misfortune of a man who had spent
37-38	had spent that many years as you spent them,	8-9	had lived that many years as you lived them,

271

MANUSCRIPT		BOOK	
38-39	the very ~~instinct and~~ dread and fear of them which you must have drawn in with that primary	10-11	the dread and fear of females which you must have drawn in with the primary
40-41	virginity?'~~//~~ What conscience that you could have traded with and have[?] believed that	13-15	virginity? what conscience to trade with which would have warranted you in the belief that
41	her with ~~just niggers and money and land//nothing for coin pay save justice?~~ for no exchange but justice?'—" ~~It was now that Shreve went into the bedroom and put on his robe. He did not say wait a moment, he just rose and~~	16-18	her for no other coin but justice?'—" It was at this point that Shreve went to the bedroom and put on the bathrobe. He

Page 120 [119]

1	[1-13 PASTED IN: It was now that Shreve went into the bedroom and put on the robe. He		
1-2	Wait a minute, he just got up and	18	Wait, he just rose and
5	discharged ~~30~~ ⟨25⟩ years ago. Go on."—"Yes," Quentin said. "He even probably	25-26	discharged twenty-eight years ago. Go on." "Yes," Quentin said. "Father said he probably
6-7	would have; that	29	would have. That
7	the trading, the cleaning	29	the cleaning
8	had not been sick; he	32	hadn't been sick (or maybe engaged); he

Page 266

11	which probably would	5	which would
11-12	name nor that of its grandfather,	6-7	name or that of its maternal grandfather,
13-14	woman; he chose the name himself, Grandfather said, just as he named them all—the Charles Goods and the Clytem] nestras	8-11	woman and so give his son an authentic name. He chose the name himself, Grandfather believed, just as he named them all—the Charles Goods and the Clytemnestras
14	dragon teeth, as father called it. And father said ~~how he~~ how he	12-28	dragons' teeth as father [*sic*] called it. And Father said—" "Your father," Shreve said. "He seems to have got an awful lot of delayed information awful quick, after having waited forty-five years. If he knew all this, what was his reason for telling you that the trouble be-

tween Henry and Bon was the octoroon woman?''

"He didn't know it then. Grandfather didn't tell him all of it either,
like Sutpen never told Grandfather
quite all of it."

"Then who did tell him?''

"I did." Quentin did not move,
did not look up while Shreve watched
him. "The day after we—after that
night when we——"

"Oh," Shreve said. "After you
and the old aunt. I see. Go on. And
father [*sic*] said——"

"——said how he

16   about to come up the drive and ~~they did~~ that maybe ~~after~~ even after

30-31   about all fall to come up the drive, and that maybe after

17-18   irony where it became just harmless coincidence, and then they did and Henry said 'Father, this is Charles' and he saw

33   irony beyond which it became
Page 267
1-6   either just vicious but not fatal horseplay or harmless coincidence, since Father said that even Sutpen probably knew that nobody yet ever invented a name that somebody didn't own now or hadn't owned once: and they rode up at last and Henry said, 'Father, this is Charles' and he——" ("the demon," Shreve said) "——saw

20   around ~~it and~~ the unscathed child and

9-10   around the unscathed head and

21-22   together and in the fury of the strug-gle for ~~that emot~~[?] ⟨the fact⟩ called gain or loss, victory or defeat, not to speak of the preservation[?] of the risked arms and legs and neck, nobody

10-11   together, and in the fury of the strug-gle for the facts called gain or loss nobody

24   nameless lost child

15-16   nameless and homeless lost child

25   to bar the door

17   to come to the door

28   debris: and

23   debris. And

29   not find himself

26   not discover himself

30   to ~~father~~ Grandfather, not to excuse, but

26-27   to Grandfather, not to excuse but

31   a legal) mind to examine—not moral retribution, you

28-30   a legally trained) mind to examine and find and point out to him. Not moral retribution you [*sic*]

MANUSCRIPT		BOOK	
32	possessed and the	31-32	possessed, the
		Page 268	
35	to come ~~to pass the~~ into existence the	4	to bring about the
36	of ~~doubt but the~~ any	5	of any
37	mistake and so he	7-8	mistake and until he discovered what that mistake had been he
38-39	vacation ~~he~~ (only it didn't take that long; ~~he had already had Henry's letter about Bon and him at school~~ father	11	vacation (only it didn't take that long; Father
39-40	Bon engaged from the minute she saw Bon in the house) he watched Bon and Henry and Judith, and Bon and Judith, already knowing about	12-16	Bon already engaged from the moment she saw Bon's name in Henry's first letter) he watched Bon and Henry and Judith, or watched Bon and Judith rather because he would have already known about
41	school; and he did nothing. Henry	17-18	school; watched them for two weeks, and did nothing. Then Henry
42	forth between	20	forth each week between
42	letters for	21-26	letters to Judith now that were not
Page 121 [120]			in Henry's hand (and that not neces-
1-2	[1-25 PASTED IN: Judith now and it not Henry's hand on the envelope: and that not necessary either father said with Mrs Sutpen telling not only him but the whole town and county about an engagement that father said didn't exist yet; and still he did nothing, apparently not until Henry		sary either, Father said, because Mrs Sutpen was already covering the town and county both with news of that engagement that Father said didn't exist yet) and still he did nothing. He didn't do anything at all until spring was almost over and Henry
3	went on home. And then	28	went home. Then
4	Orleans: whether	28	Orleans. Whether
4	time to have Bon and the mother together nobody	29-31	time to go in order to get Bon and his mother together and thrash the busi- ness out for good and all or not, nobody
5	not, tried	32-33	not while he was there, if she received him or refused to receive him; or if she did and he tried
		Page 269	
7	logic could [*sic*] be bought off with cash too; and it didn't work tho it	4-7	logic would believe that she could be placated with money too, and it didn't

MANUSCRIPT		BOOK	
	may have been Bon himself now who refused tho nobody		work; or if Bon was there and it was Bon himself who refused the offer, though nobody
9-10	Rosa says Sutpen started and ~~would have to pay~~ had	11	Rosa said Sutpen had started and had
10-11	white. But it didn't work and then the next	12-13	white both. But it didn't work evidently, and the next
12	Bon and that whether Bon wanted revenge or was ⟨just⟩ caught	15-16	Bon and whether Bon wanted revenge or was just caught
13	Henry (father	17-18	Henry that Christmas eve just before supper time (Father
14	know that it would do no good	20-21	know it wouldn't do any good
14	Henry and he	21	Henry. And he
17	mistake and he	27	mistake. So he
18-19	calm enough he	30	calm enough and alert enough he
19	it, and he	31-32	it. And he
		Page 270	
20	himself and then	1	himself. Then
21	do too; he may have known all the time that Henry	3-5	do; maybe (being a demon—though it would not require a demon to foresee war now) he even foresaw that Henry
23-24	roster and where the company was ~~before it was brigaded with~~ ⟨into⟩ ~~the regiment that Grandfather was colonel of~~ was included into the regiment that Grandfather was colonel of until	7-9	roster, some way of knowing where the company was even before Grandfather became colonel of the regiment the company was in until
24	Landing where Bon did and	10-11	Landing (where Bon was wounded) and
24-25	get well and Sutpen came home with the tombstones	11-12	get used to not having any right arm and Sutpen came home in '64 with the two tombstones
25-26	before they both went back] to the war; that the day and he [*sic*] knew where	13-15	before both of them went back to the war. Maybe he knew all the time where
27	where ~~he could watch~~ Grandfather could watch over them after a fashion	16-17	where Grandfather could look after them in a fashion
30-31	just as his father had that time ~~30 years~~ more	23	just like his father had that time more

275

MANUSCRIPT		BOOK	
31	maybe turned fatalist like Bon and was giving	24	maybe even turned fatalist like Bon now and giving
31-32	whole thing by	25	whole business by
32	or maybe both	26	or both
32	part, since it	27	part because it
33	that they would	28	that the South would
34	much, that would be worth protesting	30-31	much, worth getting that heated over, worth protesting
35-36	for—that the day, his one day of leave at home and he came home with the two tombstones and Judith	32-33	for. That was the day he came to the office, his——" ("the demon's," Shreve said) "——one day of leave at home,

Page 271

		1	came home with his tombstones. Judith
39	came and he	7	came so he
39	writes that he is coming to you you	7-8	writes you that he is coming, you
41	the tombstones on Ellen and set the other one on edge in the smokehouse and	10-11	the stones on Ellen's grave and set the other one up in the hall and
42	could find that	13	could discover that
42-43	the cause of his problem;—sitting	14	the sole cause of his problem, sitting
44	had the a plume by all means; he might have been without the saber but	16-17	had the plume by all means. He might have had to discard his saber, but

Page 122 [121]

1	frayed, with	18-19	frayed and soiled, with
1	street and	19	street below and
4-5	peace and he even after he became dead would become dead still	26	peace, and he, even after he would become dead, still
6	springing up along[?] his mud[?] as	28	springing as
6	still the fine figure of a man even	28	still, even
7-8	him before the time came when Wash had to would have to kill him for seduction and breach of promise or anyway breach of expectations, now fogbound	30	him, but not now. Now fog-bound
9-10	while Rome and Jericho crumbled and faded, that	32-33	while (Grandfather said) Rome vanished and Jericho crumbled, that

MANUSCRIPT		BOOK	

13	about ~~anymore than Grandfather be~~ because	7	about because
14	knew what he was talking about be-cause	8	knew because
15	it (and	9	it. And
17	it, ~~not even to his son of another marriage save as the last resort,~~ not	13	it, not
18	confidence he	13-14	confidence and discretion he
19	life's plan, except	16	life's attainment and desire, except
20	had got out without asking for or	19	had extricated himself without asking or
20	anyone;	20	any man;
21-23	anyone imposed on to the same.) ~~and so he (Grandfather) believed that he knew all that Sutpen could know knew: that Bon might decide at any moment to defy Henry and come to Judith, and that when he did so Judith would marry him half brother or no~~ —sitting	20-21	imposed upon do the same.—Sitting
27	Grandfather's hand and rode away—	28-29	Grandfather's left hand and rode away;
29	all that he	32	all he

31	answer, ~~since apparently he either believed~~ who	3	answer, who
32	[32-36 PASTED IN: taken, and vin-dication and justification	4	taken, and justification
32	ago and he	5-6	ago. And he
33	he might not have acquired	7	he had acquired
36	will to ~~st~~ make a third]	13	will and strength to make a third
38	[38-41 PASTED IN: for pity and not for help because Grandfather said he had never learned how to ask any-body for help and	15-17	for pity and not for help because Grandfather said he had never learned how to ask anybody for help or any-thing else and
39	with it if	18	with the help if
39-40	him: but just with that earnest and quiet	19	him, but came just with that sober and quiet

277

MANUSCRIPT		BOOK	
41	on that he himself]	23	on, which he himself
42	with ~~changing~~[?] ~~bettering~~[?] ~~a~~ ~~mistake~~ condoning	24	with condoning
43	knowledge ~~and~~ ~~which~~ ~~meant~~ ~~the~~ ~~absolute~~ ~~negation~~ in the process	25	knowledge during the process
43	design and	26	design, which

Page 123 [122]

1	which		
2	in the pursuit of which I had incurred the ~~danger~~[?] ~~to~~ ~~it~~ ~~from~~[?] negation of it.	28-29	in pursuit of which I had incurred this negation.
4	I did than	32	I chose than
4-5	second choice the curious quality of which	33	second necessity to

Page 274

1			choose, the curious factor of which
6	choice to have arisen but	2-3	choice should have arisen, but
6	I take leads to the same result:—to destroy	3-5	I might make, either course which I might choose, leads to the same result: either I destroy
7	trump, or do nothing and see the design	6-8	trump card, or do nothing, let matters take the course which I know they will take and see my design
9	who came to that	11	who approached that
11-12	an arrangement, an agreement which	15-16	an agreement, an arrangement which
13	toward, so that it	19-20	toward, concealed it so well that it
14-15	discovered (and this by chance, accident) that that factor existed.'——" It was cold now, the heat almost	20-32	discovered that this factor existed'——" "Your old man," Shreve said. "When your grandfather was telling this to him, he didn't know any more what your grandfather was talking about than your grandfather knew what the demon was talking about when the demon told it to him, did he? And when your old man told it to you, you wouldn't have known what anybody was talking about if you hadn't been out there and seen Clytie. Is that right?" "Yes," Quentin said. "Grandfather was the only friend he had." "The demon had?" Quentin didn't

MANUSCRIPT

BOOK

answer, didn't move. It was cold in
the room now. The heat was almost

Page 275

	MANUSCRIPT		BOOK
16	renewal; it	1	renewal. It
17	rung for eleven	2	rung eleven.
17	He sat at his side of the table, hugging himself into the bathrobe as	3-4	He was hugging himself into the bathrobe now as
18	himself into his pink naked almost hairless skin. "He chose lechery. Go on." So	4-5	himself inside his pink naked almost hairless skin. "He chose. He chose lechery. So
19-21	on." [20-23 PASTED IN: But it was a rise out of Quentin that Shreve was trying to get (and it probably was not; his remark ‹if from any source— een[?] born of that	6-7	on." His remark was not intended for flippancy nor even derogation. It was born (if from any source) of that
21-24	levity) he did not get it, for Quentin merely sat as before, who for almost 3 hours had no scarcely altered his position, immobile in the chair, his face bent a little and his hands lying on either side of the open book and the open letter which] he had not finished reading. "He rode away that night; Grandfather	9-14	levity—to which, by the way, Quentin paid no attention whatever, resuming as if he had never been interrupted, his face still lowered, still brooding apparently on the open letter upon the open book between his hands. "He left for Virginia that night. Grandfather
25	gaunt horse, the black stallion, swaggering still in his un erect in the faced	16	gaunt black stallion, erect in his faded
26	with the broken plume cocked a little tho not as much	17	with its broken plume cocked a little yet not quite so much
26-27	days just as (Grandfather	18	days, as if (Grandfather
28	chastened or spent or even	20-21	chastened by misfortune or spent or even
28	riding in the world's view[?] he	22	riding he
28-30	in that state where he tried to encountered by a turmoil of unpredictable and unreasoning human beings he still clung to his that state where he tried to hold	22-23	in that state in which he struggled to hold
31	and hardship for posterity,	25-26	and striving to establish a posterity,
31-32	morality, while his formula of	26-27	morality, his formula and recipe of
32-33	product refused to flout swim or even float—saw	28-29	product declined, refused to swim or even float. Grandfather saw

CHAPTER VII

MANUSCRIPT   BOOK

33   McCaslin that buried Charles Bon,   30   McCaslin and two
      and two

34   and halt him and he sitting the horse   30-31 and stop him, he sitting the stallion
      and   and

34-35 raised Grandfather said yet   32   raised, Grandfather said, yet

35-37 oratorical: then he went on and   33   oratorical.
       Grandfather did not know ~~if he rode~~   *Page 276*
       if he rode straight on toward the   1-4   Then he went on. He could still
       Atlantic Ocean, or if he went to   reach Sutpen's Hundred before dark,
       Sutpen's Hundred first and he ~~and~~   so it was probably after supper
       ~~Judith to face one another again and~~   than [*sic*] he headed the stallion
       ~~he not saying 'If I can stop it I will'~~   toward the Atlantic Ocean, he and
       ~~and she not saying 'You cannot stop~~   Judith facing one another again for
       ~~it can stop it cant stop it but and~~   maybe a full minute, he
       ~~maybe not even goodby~~e and Judith
       facing one another for maybe a full
       minute again and he

39-41 can' but maybe, probably just good-   6   can' but just goodbye, the kiss
       bye: and that right enough[?] too—
       ~~her~~[?] saddled warhorse[?] , south
       portico, ~~un~~ faded gray and all: the
       kiss

41-42 tears; the word, the master's word   7-16 tears; a word to Clytie and to Wash:
       to slave and retainer: 'Well, Clytie;   master to slave, baron to retainer:
       well, Wash. I'll send you both a   'Well, Clytie, take care of Miss
       piece of Lincoln's coat tail from   Judith.—Wash, I'll send you a piece
       Washington [MARGIN: and Wash saying,   of Abe Lincoln's coat tail from
       [illegible word] ~~when~~ under the   Washington' and I reckon Wash
       scuppernongs and he pouring from   answering like it used to be under
       the jug and then the bucket: 'Sho,   the scuppernongs with the demijohn
       Kernel; ~~shoot~~ kill ever one of the   and the well bucket: 'Sho, Kernel;
       varmints!']—that would be correct[?]   kill ever one of the varmints!' So
       and right; he would insist on   he ate the hoecake and drank the
Page 124 [123]   parched acorn coffee and rode away.
1-2   that the same as on the plume. And   Then it was '65 and the army (Grand-
       that was '63 and then it was '64 and   father had gone back to it too; he was
       the army (Grandfather had got well   a brigadier now though I reckon this
       and had gone back too; he was a   was for more reason than because
       brigadier now) had   he just had one arm) had

3-5   knew that it could not be very much   17-24 knew it wouldn't be very much longer
       longer now: and Grandfather didn't   now. Then one day Lee sent Johnston
       know what had happened, whether he   some reinforcements from one of
       (Sutpen) had found out that Bon and   his corps and Grandfather found out
       Henry had come to terms, that   that the Twenty-third Mississippi was
       Henry's conscience had succumbed at   one of the regiments. And he (Grand-
       last as his (Sutpen's) had   father) didn't know what had happened:

280

CHAPTER VII

BOOK

whether Sutpen had found out in some
way that Henry had at last coerced
his conscience into agreement with
him as his (Henry's) father had

6-7   had to happen,

28   had to be done, had to happen,

7   know: he

29   know. He

7-8   ridden into ~~father's~~ Grandfather's
old regimental h.q. the night before
and

30-31   ridden up to Grandfather's old regiment's headquarters and

8-11   Henry in what was left of the
Virginian company and then rode
away before midnight.
     "So he played that last trump
card that he had told Grandfather
about and then it was '65 and it was
over and he came home and found
what he must have known that he
would find, that he didn't need any
word about even if Judith

31-33   Henry and did speak to him and then
rode away again before midnight."
Page 277

1-16   "So he got his choice made, after
all," Shreve said. "He played that
trump after all. And so he came
home and found——"
     "Wait," Quentin said.
     "——what he must have wanted to
find or anyway what he was going to
find——"
     "Wait, I tell you!" Quentin said,
though still he did not move nor even
raise his voice—that voice with its
tense suffused restrained quality:
"I am telling" *Am I going to have to
have to hear it all again* he thought
*I am going to have to hear it all
over again I am already hearing it
all over again I am listening to it all
over again I shall have to never listen
to anything else but this again forever
so apparently not only a man never
outlives his father but not even his
friends and acquaintances do* —he
came home and found that at least
regarding which he should have
needed no word nor warning even if
Judith

12-15   him word and acknowledgment that
she was beaten: ~~and Grandfather said
not her, not Judith, anymore than she
would have waited for him and met
him with~~ who neither sent him word
that he had beat her anymore than she
waited (who Miss Rosa said had not
even been bereaved) ~~for h~~ for him
and met him with the fury and despair

17-22   him acknowledgment that she was
beaten, who according to Mr Compson
would no more have sent him acknowledgment that he had beat her than
she waited (whom [*sic*] Miss Coldfield said was not bereaved) and met
him on his return, not with the fury
and despair perhaps which he might
have expected even though knowing

CHAPTER VII

which ~~anyone~~ ⟨even he⟩ might have
expected, ~~granted that they had been~~
~~tuve~~[?] knowing

16   as ~~Grandfather said~~ father said he
had—the kiss

                                23-25 as Mr Compson said he had, yet
certainly with something other than
the icy calm with which, according
to Miss Coldfield, she met him—
the kiss

17-22 brow, the saddled steed and the
portico[?], the sabre sheathed at
last but not surrendered, the gray
ready to be laid temporarily[?] away
among the moths until he should ride
that last time just to church in it—
the voice, the speech, quiet, contained
gentleman[?] and gentlewoman[?]:
'And——?'' 'Yes. Henry killed him'
and the brief burst of tears and no
need to say 'And Henry?' because
the whole house[?], the tears, the 3
faces all answered that—the 'Ah,
Clytie; ah, Rosa; ah, Wash. I didn't
have time to take[?] those coattails
I promised you' and Wash: the
guffaw

26-33 brow; the voices, the speeches, quiet,
contained, almost impersonal:
'And——?' 'Yes. Henry killed him'
followed by the brief tears which
ceased on the instant when they began, as if the moisture consisted of
a single sheet or layer thin as a
cigarette paper and in the shape of
a human face; the 'Ah, Clytie. Ah,
Rosa.—Well, Wash. I was unable to
penetrate far enough behind the
Yankee lines to cut a piece from that
coat tail as I prom-

Page 278

1   ised you'; the (from Jones) guffaw,

22   which father says outlasts

2-3 which, Mr Compson said, outlasts

23   defeats too:

3   defeats both:

23-25 they ~~whupped~~ ⟨kilt⟩ us but they aint
~~kilt~~ ⟨whupped⟩ us yit, air they?'
Because his problem now was haste,
time, the need for haste. He wasn't
concerned about the courage and the
will and even the shrewdness now;
he

4-8 they kilt us but they aint whupped us
yit, air they?': and that was all. He
had returned. He was home again
where his problem now was haste,
passing time, the need to hurry. *He
was not concerned,* Mr Compson
said, *about the courage and the will,
nor even about the shrewdness now.
He*

26-28 time enough to do it in/ ~~the~~ and he
not wasting any of it either—the will
and the shrewdness too ~~so that Miss~~
~~Rosa~~ and the opportunity waiting to
his hand and Miss Rosa engaged to
him before she knew it—Miss Rosa,

11-18 *time sufficient to do it in, regain his
lost ground in. He did not waste any
of what time he had either. The will
and the shrewdness too he did not
waste, though he doubtless did not
consider it to have been either his
will or his shrewdness which supplied
waiting to his hand the opportunity,
and it was probably less of shrewdness and more of courage than even*

MANUSCRIPT

BOOK

*will which got him engaged to Miss
Rosa within a period of three months
and almost before she was aware of
the fact—Miss Rosa,*

29-31 object, engaged to him before she
knew he was home again almost—
the will but mainly[?] the shrewdness
and father said his[?] the shrewdness
of all that 50 years suddenly retroactive or suddenly ~~sprouting and~~
sprouting

19-24 *object (even though not victim), engaged to him before she had got
accustomed to having him in the
house—yes, more of courage than
even will, yet something of shrewdness too: the shrewdness acquired
in excrutiating [sic] driblets through
the fifty years suddenly capitulant
and retroactive or suddenly sprouting*

31 clod, since he

25 *clod. Because he*

32-36 house where he greeted them all and
dragged Wash out to the ~~fallow fields~~
brier-choked fields and the tumbled
fences all in one breath, the one
weak spot, the one vulnerable spot
which was possible for him[?] and
to assault and carry her in a single
stride; assault and carry her in more
than that sense only assault not the
right word, and father said how
then[?] the shrewdness failed him
again, broke down and vanished

26-33 *house which was an unbroken con-
tinuation of the long journey from
Virginia, the pause not to greet his
family but merely to pick up Jones
and drag him on out to the brier-
choked fields and fallen fences and
clap ax or mattock into his hands,
the one weak spot, the one spot
vulnerable to assault in Miss Rosa's
embattled spinsterhood, and to
assault and carry this in one stride,
with something of the ruthless tacti-
cal skill of his old master (the
Twenty-third Mississippi*

Page 279

1-2 *was in Jackson's corps at one time).
And then the shrewdness failed him
again. It broke down, it vanished*

36-40 morality that had betrayed him before: and he said what day it might
have been, what furrow or fence panel
he might have stopped dead in or held
in his hand when he realized that
there was more to it than just lack
of time but some kind of superdistillation of its lack: that he was now
past 60 years old and that possibly
he could not get but one more son,
that he had but the one more son in
his loins just as

3-11 *morality which had betrayed him before: and what day might it have
been, what furrow might he have
stopped dead in, one foot advanced,
the unsentient plow handles in his
instantaneous unsentient hands, what
fence panel held in midair as though
it had no weight by muscles which
could not feel it, when he realized
that there was more in his problem
than just lack of time, that the problem contained some superdistillation
of this lack: that he was now past
sixty and that possibly he could get
but one more son, had at best but one
more son in his loins, as*

MANUSCRIPT	BOOK

40-41 So he said, suggested what he did to

12-13 *So he suggested what he suggested to*

Page 125 [124]

1-2 morality that had all the parts and even ran[?] but did not move; it was a garden scene too, even the horse was there; the proposal, the ~~indigna-tion~~ the outrage and the unbelief;

15-17 *morality which had all the parts but which refused to run, to move. Hence the proposal, the outrage and un-belief;*

3-5 anger and she vanishing, ~~from his sight~~ rushing from sight with her skirts spread upon it chip-light and her bonnet (maybe one of Ellen's that the Yanks didn't find but she did) put fast onto her head and ~~trembling yet rigid with~~ rigid and precarious with rage; and him standing

17-21 *anger upon which Miss Rosa vanished from Sutpen's Hundred, her air-ballooned skirts spread upon the flood, chip-light, her bonnet (possibly one of Ellen's which she had prowled out of the attic) clapped fast onto her head rigid and precarious with rage. And he standing*

5-7 arm and maybe something almost like smiling just inside his beard and maybe even his eyes smiling to him-self[?] at Rosa but it would not be smiling but crinkles from thinking—

22-24 *arm, with perhaps something like smiling inside his beard and about the eyes which was not smiling but the crinkled concentration of furious thinking—*

9 worse//~~the fact that~~ only

27-28 *worse; only*

10-12 for another spotting shot and then a full-sized one—the fact that ~~that~~ the thread of thinking, shrewdness un-fortunately ran onto the same spool that the thread of his days ran onto and the spool near enough for him tc almost reach his hand out and touch it but no concern yet since

28-33 *for both a spotting shot and then a full-sized load—the fact that the thread of shrewdness and courage and will ran onto the same spool which the thread of his remaining days ran onto and that spool almost near enough for him to reach out his hand and touch it. But this was no grave concern yet, since*

Page 280

14-15 exist—" (Now Shreve said Wait again; Wait: "Let

4-5 *exist.*
"No," Shreve said; "you wait. Let

15-16 while. Now Wash. Him standing there with the horse and all, and all lost save dishonor, and then the ~~faithful~~ voice ~~carrying out of the wings~~ of

5-9 while now. Now, Wash. Him (the demon standing there with the horse, the saddled charger, the sheathed saber, the gray waiting to be laid peaceful away among the moths and all lost save dishonor: then the voice of

17 they whupped

11-12 they mought have whupped

18 they?'——meaning no harm by this since it too

12-13 they?'——" This was not flippancy either. It too

MANUSCRIPT		BOOK	
19	Quentin too spoke,	15	Quentin also spoke,
19-20	Quentin's musing[?] savagery: the rapidity[?], the strained	16-17	Quentin's sullen bemusement, the (on both their parts) flipness, the strained
20-21	not, ~~back-to-back-now-and-embattled in-the~~ [MARGIN: in the] cold room (it was quite cold in the room now) dedicated [MARGIN: ~~set aside-for-it~~ ~~and~~ (and set aside for it since here more than any other place it could do the least amount of harm)] to	18-19	not, in the cold room (it was quite cold now) dedicated to
21-22	which was a good deal like the morality of Sutpen's[?] and Miss Coldfield's so-called demonizing account[?] to Quentin's father—this	19-21	which after all was a good deal like Sutpen's morality and Miss Coldfield's demonizing—this
23	here more than any	22	here above any
24	back and saying No to Quentin's shadow who	24-25	back as though at the last ditch, saying No to Quentin's Mississippi shade who
25-26	morality and who ~~dead-rose somehow above-it-still-remained-somehow potent-and-more-alive-and-not-only sup-indifferent~~ dying had escaped it and dead	27	morality, who dying had escaped it completely, who dead
27-28	alive: and no harm taken because Quentin did not even stop. ~~He took Shreve-up in-stride~~ He	29-31	alive. There was no harm intended by Shreve and no harm taken, since Quentin did not even stop. He
28-30	stride (and neither of them to know if Shreve had ~~anticipated him altered~~[?] ~~him and~~ reined him aside and put words into his mouth or if he (Shreve) had merely anticipated him) without [for opening parenthesis, see 125/14]	32	stride without
		Page 281	
32-33	hand; maybe it was the string of beads just out of the little store he and Wash ran, where	2-4	hand. Maybe it was the first string of beads out of his and Wash's little store where
33-34	customers, the trash and niggers and the haggling over dimes and quarters and turn	4-5	customers, the niggers and the trash and the haggling, and turn
34-35	blind, cursing Lincoln and Sherman[?], until Wash carried him home	6-7	blind. And maybe Wash delivered the beads himself, Father said,

in a wagon and maybe Wash deliver-
ing the beads himself father said,

36	day and after	8	day, that after

37-38 he did believe it; ~~Grandfather said~~
        ~~how~~ father's mother said how at first
        the Sutpen niggers heard about it and
        they

11-12 he even believed it. Father's mother
        said how when the Sutpen niggers
        first heard about what he was saying,
        they

39 him live in [MARGIN: , where the
     granddaughter (she was about 8 then)
     lived]; there

14-15 him and the granddaughter (she was
        about eight then) live in. There

39-40	even risk trying and	17	even try to, risk trying to: and

41 laughing, saying 'Who

19-20 laughing, asking one another (except
        it was not one another but him):
        'Who

41-42 niggers?' and then laughing and he
        rushing at them

21 niggers?' and he would rush at them

43 laughing; and he was still carrying
     fish and things he killed ⟨or maybe
     stole⟩ and

23-24 laughing. And he was still carrying
        fish and animals he killed (or maybe
        stole) and

Page 126 [125]

1-2 [1-16 PASTED IN: would not let him
      come into the kitchen with the basket
      even, saying, 'Stop right ~~d~~[?] ⟨there⟩,
      white man. ~~You aint never crossed~~
      Stop

26-28 would not let him come into the
        kitchen with the basket even, saying,
        'Stop right there, white man. Stop

2	crossed these steps while	28-29	crossed this door while
4	like he might say to himself	33	like (Father said) he might have

                                                  Page 282
                                                  1   said to himself

5 *it* ~~*is I aint going to give any black*~~
    ~~*nigger the chance*~~ *aint that*

1 *it aint that*

6-7 *cant but that I aint going to force*
      ~~*Kernel to have (he called him Kernel*~~
      ~~*even then)*~~ *Mister Thomas to have to*
      cuss a nigger on my account And they

2-4 *cant but because I aint going to force*
      Mister Tom to have to cuss a nigger
      or take a cussing from his wife on
      my account. But they

7 together on the Sunday p.m.s and

4-5 together under the scuppernong arbor
      on the Sunday afternoons, and

8-9 it) ~~galloping about the plantation~~
      ~~and~~ ⟨—⟩ they were about the same
      age father said—on the fine figure of
      the black stallion) galloping about the
      plantation and father said that for

7-8 it) on the black stallion, galloping
      about the plantation, and Father said
      how for

MANUSCRIPT		BOOK	
10	and it seeming to him that the world in which niggers,	9-10	and that maybe it would seem to him that this world where niggers,
14-15	thinking how the Book said too that	18	thinking maybe, Father said, how the Book said that
15-16	anyway, and so he would tell himself look at Sutpen and think 'A fine proud man. If God Himself was to come down and ride the natural]	20-22	anyway, looked the same to God at least, and so he would look at Sutpen and think *A fine proud man. If God Himself was to come down and ride the natural*
17	like.';—delivered those first beads himself probably, and father	23-24	*like.* Maybe he even delivered the first string of beads himself, and Father
18-19	fast after the early fashion of her kind, or anyway knowing each	26-27	fast like girls of that kind do; or anyway he would know and recognize each
19-20	got it or not since he had been seeing them in the showcase which	29	got it, which
20	not since she would know	29-30	not, since she would be bound to know
21-22	and so knew them just as the other men, the white and the black who would stand or squat along the gallery of the store and watch her pass not	31-33	and would have known them as well as he knew his own shoes. And not only he knew them, but all the other men, the customers and the
		Page 283	
		1-2	loungers, the white and the black that would be sitting and squatting about the store's gallery to watch her pass, not
22-23	cringing/ at once bold and	3	cringing and
23	ribbons but almost; at once bold sullen and fearful: and Grandfather father	4-5	ribbons and the beads, but almost; not quite any of them but a little of all: bold, sullen and fearful. But father [*sic*]
24	dress and she telling [MARGIN: and spoke about it, probably grave now and watching her secret defiant frightened face while she told] him	7-9	dress and spoke about it, probably only a little grave now and watching her secret defiant frightened face while she told him
25	her make it, and perhaps realizing all	10-11	her to make it: and Father said maybe he realized all
26-29	they had ⟨already⟩ known something ⟨that⟩ which he had just thot that they were thinking/ but still his heart quiet, not alarmed: just grave and thotful, answering maybe if he	13-16	they already knew that which he had just thought they were probably thinking. But Father said his heart was still quiet, even now, and that he answered, if he

287

a̶n̶s̶w̶e̶r̶e̶d̶ ̶a̶t̶ ̶a̶l̶l̶,̶ ̶s̶t̶o̶p̶p̶e̶d̶ ̶t̶h̶e̶ ̶p̶r̶o̶t̶e̶s̶-
t̶a̶t̶i̶o̶n̶s̶ yet his heart still quiet, not
concerned yet, and he answering
af [*sic*] he

30	them'—; not alarmed yet, just	19	them.'—Not alarmed, Father said: just
31	Grandfather stopped at the store to speak to Sutpen and	20-21	Grandfather rode out to see Sutpen about something and
31-32	the store and	22	the front of the store and
32	out when	22-23	out and go up to the house when
32	voices and	23-24	voices from the back and
32	toward the back and	24	toward them and
33-34	before they heard him call, and heard Wash speak of the dress and heard Sutpen say: 'What about it?' And Grandfather couldn't see them yet, he hadn't got far enough back for them to even hear him yet but	25-28	before he could make them hear him calling Sutpen's name. Grandfather couldn't see them yet, he hadn't even got to where they could hear him yet, but
35	knew almost exactly how they would be—Sutpen already	28-29	knew exactly how they would be: Sutpen having already
35	jug down probably and	29	jug out and
36-37	Wash said and then	32	Wash was saying, then
37	and all of a sudden sort of reared back and up looking	33	and then all of a sudden kind of reared back

Page 284

		1	and flinging his head up, looking
39	and W̶a̶s̶h̶'̶s̶ ̶v̶o̶i̶c̶e̶ [MARGIN: it was Sutpen's voice that was short and sharp t̶h̶o̶ ̶n̶o̶t̶ ̶r̶a̶i̶s̶e̶d̶, ⟨and⟩ not Wash's; that Wash's] was ⟨just⟩ flat	4-5	said it was Sutpen's voice that was short and sharp: not Wash's; that Wash's voice was just flat
39-40	slow: a̶n̶d̶ ̶i̶t̶ ̶w̶a̶s̶ ̶S̶u̶t̶p̶e̶n̶'̶s̶ ̶t̶h̶a̶t̶ ̶w̶a̶s̶ s̶h̶a̶r̶p̶,̶ ̶s̶h̶o̶r̶t̶ ̶t̶h̶o̶ ̶n̶o̶t̶ ̶l̶o̶u̶d̶ ̶e̶i̶t̶h̶e̶r̶: '̶W̶h̶a̶t̶ ̶a̶b̶o̶u̶t̶ ̶t̶h̶e̶ ̶d̶r̶e̶s̶s̶?̶'̶ ̶I̶ I've knowed	6	slow: 'I have knowed

Page 127 [126]

4	one minute or day of	18-19	one second or minute or hour of
8-9	sharp and father said that Grandfather said he thot then[?] or sensed just what father was thinking but	26-27	sharp, and Grandfather said he reckoned, thought just about what he imagined Wash was thinking. But
9-10	jug' and that Wash said, 'Sho, Kernel.'; "And so	28-29	jug.'—'Sho, Kernel,' Wash said. "So

MANUSCRIPT		BOOK	
11	married; it	31	married. It
11-12	and father said that he was expecting one of his mares to	32	and he was expecting his mare to
12-13	stallion and that when he left the house that dawn Judith thot ~~perhaps~~ that it was that mare that he was going to see, who knew what and how	33	stallion, so when he left the house before day that morn-
		Page 285	
		1-2	ing Judith thought he was going to the stable. What Judith knew and how
14-15	known since everyone else white and black	4-6	known (may have or may not have told her, whether or no) since everybody else white or black
15-16	girl in the ribbons and beads that they all recognized from the store, how	7-8	girl pass in the ribbons and beads which they all recognized, how
16-17	to learn during the time when she helped the girl (father said she actually	8-10	to discover during the fitting and sewing of that dress (Father said Judith actually
17	for more than one day in	11-12	for about a week in
18-19	about, and the girl's sullen defiant secret face answering	13-15	about while the girl stood around in what she possessed to call underclothes, with her sullen defiant secret watchful face, answering
19-20	to in return, nobody knew) make the dress out of the cloth Sutpen gave her, nobody knew—so that ~~when he did not return~~ it	16-17	to, nobody knew). So it
21	he did not return at	17	he failed to return at
21	stable to see about him and found that tho the mare	18-19	stable and found that the mare
22	night, her father was not there; and	19-20	night but that her father was not there. And
23	the fish	21	the old fish
24	cabin [MARGIN: where the scythe had rested for 2 years now that Sutpen had made Wash borrow to cut the weeds which he had never cut,] where the girl and the child lay on the pallet and saw	23	cabin and saw
25	lying ~~th~~ in the weeds and	24-25	lying in the weeds which Wash had not yet cut, and
26	him: ~~"Wait," Shreve said;~~ "wait" and about	26-27	him. Then about

BOOK

	MANUSCRIPT		BOOK
26-27	they found, caught, the old nigger midwife that Sutpen had sent there and she said how she did not know	27-28	they caught the nigger, the midwife, and she told how she didn't know
27-28	all and how Sutpen, she heard the horse and then his feet	28-29	all that dawn when she heard the horse and then Sutpen's feet
28	and she said how he stood	30	and stood
28-31	the mother and child lay and ~~he said,~~ ~~'Griselda (that was the mare) foaled~~ ~~this a.m.' and the old nigger said~~ ~~the girl did jerked his riding crop~~ ~~toward the pallet and said, 'Well?~~ ~~What is it?' and the~~ said, 'Griselda (that was the mare) foaled this a.m. A ~~damned fine colt horse~~ A damned	30-32	the girl and the baby were and said, 'Penelope——' (that was the mare) '——foaled this morning. A damned

Page 286

	MANUSCRIPT		BOOK
33	jerked his riding crop toward	2	jerked the riding whip toward
33	hide: well?' and	3-4	hide: horse or mare?' and
34	riding crop against his legs and	5-6	riding whip against his leg and
36	eyes, watched them and she saw his teeth then inside his beard and she said that	8-9	eyes and then his teeth inside his beard and that
37	then but she could not: she just anchored there and heard him say 'Well,	10-12	then only she couldn't, couldn't seem to make her legs bear to get up and run: and then he looked at the girl on the pallet again and said, 'Well,
38-39	and turn and go out and she could not move yet and she did not even know that Wash was there, she	14-15	and turned and went out. Only she could not move even yet, and she didn't even know that Wash was outside there; she
40	and Wash then, his	17	and then Wash, his
40	reach the house:	18	reach her:
40-41	Kernel' and Sutpen saying again 'Stand back, Wash' and	18-19	Kernel': and Sutpen again: 'Stand back, Wash!' sharp now, and
41	whip and she did not know	19-20	whip on Wash's face but she didn't know
41-42	because she found that she could move then and she jumped out the door and into the weeds, running——" "Wait,"	21-23	because now she found out that she could move, get up, run out of the cabin and into the weeds, running——" "Wait,"

Page 128 [127]

	MANUSCRIPT		BOOK
1-6	yet he ~~would have~~ still——" "yes, sat there all that day in that	24-33	yet still he——" "——walked the three miles and

little window, ever since he had walked the 3 miles and back in the dark to fetch the nigger midwife ~~and~~ yet father said that his heart must have been quiet enough[?] then, even tho he knew now what they would be saying behind his back on the gallery of the store and in the cabins just as he ~~knew~~ had known before, during the 4 or 5 months while his grand-daughter's condition ~~could no longer be mistaken~~ that he had never tried to conceal could

back before midnight to fetch the old nigger, then sat on the sagging gallery until daylight came and the granddaughter stopped screaming inside the cabin and he even heard the baby once, waiting for Sutpen. And Father said his heart was quiet then too, even though he knew what they would be saying in every cabin about the land by nightfall, just as he had known what they were saying during the last four or five months while his granddaughter's condition (which he had never tried to

Page 287

1   conceal) could

6-7	*It took him 20 years to do it in, but*	2	*It taken him twenty years to do it, but*

7-8   *squeal*; that's how father said it must have been: him waiting outside where

4-5   *squeal* That's what Father said he was thinking while he waited outside on the gallery where

8-9   out of the house, standing there may-be [MARGIN: ~~and holding the reins of the stallion after Sutpen dismounted and entered the house~~] by

6   out, standing there maybe by

9-10   scythe leaned rusting for 2 years that Sutpen had made him borrow to cut the weeds away from the door and he had not done it yet, while his granddaughter's ~~voice~~ ⟨screams⟩ came

7-8   scythe had leaned rusting for two years, while the granddaughter's screams came

10   now and his heart

9   now but his own heart

11   alarmed: and father said how out of the fumbling and the groping

10-11   alarmed; and Father said that maybe while he stood befogged in his fum-bling and groping

12   was like

12   was a good deal like

12-13   else) ~~there broke suddenly free in midgallop~~ that was now somehow

13-14   else) which had always been somehow

13-14   hoofs until there broke suddenly free in mid-gallop the fine proud figure of the man on the fine stallion, so that

15-22   hoofs even during the old peace that nobody remembered, and in which during the four years of the war which he had not attended the galloping had been only the more gallant and proud and thunderous—Father said that maybe he got his answer; that maybe there broke free and plain in mid-

BOOK

			gallop against the yellow sky of dawn the fine proud image of the man on the fine proud image of the stallion and that
15	broke free too and clear, not	22-23	broke clear and free too, not
18	*he fought for*	28	*he fit for*
18	*has brought him*	29	*has brung him*
19	*store; bigger than the denial which it held to*	30-31	*store for his bread and meat; bigger than the scorn and denial which hit helt to*
20	*lived near to*	32	*lived nigh to*

Page 288

21	*was dragged along*	1	*was drug along*
22	*do it and*	2	*do hit and*
22	*do.;* [MARGIN: standing there and holding the stallion's reins after Sutpen dismounted and entered the house,] hearing	3-5	*do;* and maybe still standing there and holding the stallion's reins after Sutpen had entered the cabin, still hearing
23	galloping figure merge	6	galloping image merge
25	sky the color of thunder;	10	sky in color like thunder;
25-26	house say what he said and then father	11-13	house speak his single sentence of salutation, inquiry and farewell to the granddaughter, and Father
26-27	earth itself under his feet, watching Sutpen come out of the house again with the riding crop in his hand and (Wash) thinking	14-16	earth under his feet while he watched Sutpen emerge from the house, the riding whip in his hand, thinking
27	*I cant*	16	*I kaint*
28-29	*I know I cant;* thinking *'It was that colt then. That was what got him up. It aint me and mine; it wasn't even hisn[?] that got him out of bed;* may-be	17-19	*I just know I kaint* thinking *That was what got him up. It was that colt. It aint me or mine either. It wasn't even his own that got him out of bed* maybe
29	stability yet,	20	stability, even yet,
30	face [MARGIN: (the face of the man who in 20 years he (Sutpen) had no more known to make any move save at command than he had the stallion which he rode)] and stopped, flung[?] back: 'You	21-24	face (the face of the man who in twenty years he had no more known to make any move save at command than he had the stallion which he rode) and stopped: 'You
30-31	a good stall in the stable',	24-25	a decent stall in the stable,'

MANUSCRIPT		BOOK	
31-32	must have, ~~because he~~ must have heard something since he answered something and that right: 'I'm	27-28	must have heard that because he answered it: 'I'm
33	whip: only	29-30	whip. Only
34	on his face that night; maybe they knocked him to the ground, maybe	31-32	on Wash's face that night. Maybe the two blows even knocked him down; maybe
		Page 289	
35-36	he——" "——yes, sat all that day in that little	2-3	he——" "——sat there all that day in the little
37	house and maybe	5	house where maybe
37-38	asked him what it was and he saying 'Whut?	6-7	asked querulously what it was and he answered, 'Whut?
38-39	meat which he had brot from the store Saturday night/ ~~maybe tried to te~~ or	8-9	meat he had probably brought home from the store Saturday night or
40	sack and maybe ate himself and	11	sack, and maybe ate and
41	weeds beneath and watch the road because	13-14	weeds below, and watch the road. Because
41 *Page 129* [128] 1	boy ~~that~~ came around the corner and saw him: and father said how he must have known then/ ~~how he~~ ⟨that⟩ it	14-16	boy came around the corner of the house whistling and saw him. And Father said he must have realized then that it
2	dark, that	17	dark when it would happen; that
4	to get nearer	21	to approach nearer
5	battle, who maybe also had signed	23-24	battles, who might also possess signed
6	first of	25	first and foremost of
7-8	grief: and that they whom he would be expected	28-29	grief; these it was whom he was expected
9	be merely fleeing one	31	be fleeing merely one
		Page 290	
13-14	and father said it probably seemed to him for the first time how it was that Yankees or any other living[?] armies ~~could~~ had managed to whip them—	5-8	and Father said that maybe for the first time in his life he began to comprehend how it had been possible for Yankees or any other army to have whipped them—
15	to carry courage	9	to bear the courage

CHAPTER VII

	MANUSCRIPT		BOOK
15-16	pride;—and it would probably be near sunset	10	pride. It would probably be about sunset
16	now: and father	11	now; Father
17	voices, the stable[?] ⟨lethargic[?]⟩ murmuring of tomorrow and tomorrow beyond	13-14	voices, the murmuring of tomorrow and tomorrow and tomorrow beyond
18-19	*had Sutpen where Sutpen would have to tear meat or squeal but Sutpen fooled him* and then he maybe	16-17	*had him, but old Wash Jones got fooled* and then maybe
20-21	querulously to him and	19-20	querulously again and
22	him without	22	him easy, without
22	asked ⟨or wanted⟩ nothing	23-24	asked or wanted nothing
23	said *I*	26	said to myself *I*
25	Brave'—and maybe loud again, forgetting again: 'Better	28-29	Brave' (and maybe it would be loud again, forgetting again) 'Brave! Better

Page 291

28-29	*fire.* And then they rode up—he	1-2	*fire* Then they rode up. He
29	been hearing them: the dogs and horses,	2-3	been listening to them as they came down the road, the dogs and the horses,
29	lanterns—and	4	lanterns since it was dark now. And
30-32	Wash: he just drew his pistol and called and Wash answered, spoke his name, and de Spain told him to come out, and that Wash's voice was quite quiet when he answered and told them in just	6-10	Wash nor know that he was there until Wash spoke his name quietly from the window almost in his face: 'That you, Major?' De Spain told him to come on out and he said how Wash's voice was quite quiet when he said he would be out in just
32-33	much so that for the time de Spain said he did not realize that it was too calm:	11-12	much too quiet and calm that de Spain said he did not realize for a moment that it was too calm and quiet:
34	out.' and Wash 'Sho, Major. In	14-15	out.' 'Sho, Major,' Wash said, [*sic*] 'In
34-35	waited and	15-16	waited in front of the dark house, and
35-36	a 100 ⟨dozen⟩ men who remembered about the 5 gallons of kerosene he had brot home too Sunday night, and there were 100 of them who remembered about the butcher	16-17	a hundred that remembered about the butcher

MANUSCRIPT

BOOK

37-38   his ~~sloven life~~ sloven life that he had ever taken pride in—only by that time it was too late. They

18-20   his sloven life that he was ever known to take pride in or care of— only by the time they remembered all this it was too late. So they

38   about, they

21   about. They

38   moving in the room and heard

21-22   moving inside the dark house, then they heard

39   Grandpaw' and him saying 'That wont

24   Grandpaw' then his voice: 'Hit wont

39   honey. That wont

24-25   honey. Hit wont

40   minute' and then de Spain said,

25-26   minute' then de Spain drew his pistol and said,

40   and he didn't answer, still murmuring to

26-27   and still Wash didn't answer, mur- muring still to

41   Where would

28-29   Where else would

41-42   it——' and now de Spain said, 'Jones' and was already running toward the door when

29-30   is——' then de Spain said, 'Jones!' and he was already fumbling at the broken steps when

Page 130 [129]

1-5   claimed to have heard Wash when he picked up the kerosene and dumped it into the fire, only that was too late then too because they said how the whole rotting flimsy[?] house ex- ploded: a blue glare and Jones run- ning against it and still running against it when they got the horses stopped and turned, with the scythe above his head and de Spain saying 'Jones! Stop! Stop or I'll kill you. Jones! Jones! [quotation mark omitted] They said he never made a sound.''
        "Wait,"

31-33   claimed that they heard the knife on both the neckbones, though de Spain didn't. He just said he knew that Wash had come out

Page 292

1-13   onto the gallery and that he sprang back before he found out that it was not toward him Wash was running but toward the end of the gallery, where the body lay, but that he did not think about the scythe: he just ran back- ward a few feet when he saw Wash stoop and rise again and now Wash was running toward him. Only he was running toward them all, de Spain said, running into the lanterns so that now they could see the scythe raised above his head; they could see his face, his eyes too, as he ran with the scythe above his head, straight into the lanterns and the gun barrels, making no sound, no outcry while de Spain ran backward before him, saying, 'Jones! Stop! Stop, or I'll kill you. Jones! Jones! *Jones!*' ''
        "Wait,"

MANUSCRIPT		BOOK	
5	mean, he	13	mean that he
7	"Yes," Quentin said. "Sitting	16	"Yes. Sitting
7-8	that p.m. ~~and telling him about how he never found out until after~~ Ben ~~was born that the mother that they had told him was a Spaniard had some nigger blood. Yes. Sitting there~~ with	16	that afternoon, with
10	was a son. That ~~seemed to me~~ seems	19-20	was just a son. Which seems
10	look around at my contemporary scene, little enough to demand, to ask——' "	20-22	look about at my contemporary scene, no exorbitant gift from nature or circumstance to demand——' "
12	that ~~after~~ with the son lying	23-24	that with the son he went to all that trouble to get lying
15	Let's ~~get in bed. This damn room is like an ice box~~ get out of this ⟨damn⟩ ice box and ~~get in bed.'~~ go to bed."	29-30	Let's get out of this damn icebox and go to bed."

CHAPTER VIII

Page 131 [130]			*Page 293*		
4	Henry and Henry		7-8	Henry," Shreve said. "And Henry	
6	room and		12	room. And	
12	Shreve's voice ceased; he (he stood at the table; ~~bigger~~[?] ~~in~~ in		20-21	Shreve stood beside the table, facing Quentin again though not seated now. In	
13	stared quietly at		23	stared at	
15	surface) sitting hunched		25	surface)	
			Page 294		
			1	who sat hunched	
15-16	hands now thrust into his pockets as he apparently tried to hug himself between		1-2	hands thrust into his pockets as if he were trying to hug himself warm between	
16	and wan in the lamp's rosy glow		3-4	and even wan in the lamplight, the rosy glow	
17	of coziness, warmth, in it/ and both		4-5	of warmth, coziness, in it, while both	
20	[20-22 PASTED IN: was one of those people whose correct actual age		10-11	was one of those people whose correct age	
21-22	that but is only taking advantage of appearances· and so you can never		13-14	that because he or she looks too exactly that not to take advantage of the appearance: so you never	
22	or which in desperation they]		15-16	or that which in sheer desperation they	
24	[24-26 PASTED IN: Not 2 of them in a New England college sitting room		18-19	Not two of them in a New England college sitting-room	
26	or two decorating		23	or so decorating	
26	desk behind]		24	desk, behind	
28-29	sense the son would remember later how he saw thru		27-28	sense, Henry would recall later how he had seen through	
29	window behind the father's		28	window beyond his father's	
30-31	head turned and the lover's bent above it [31-34 PASTED IN: ~~above hers~~ while		30-31	head bent with listening, the lover's head leaned above it while	
31	which the heart		31-32	which not the eyes but the heart	
32	for not the eyes, and disappeared slowly		33	for, to disappear slowly	

MANUSCRIPT		BOOK	
32	bush starred	33	bush or shrub
		Page 295	
		1	starred
34	and did not know altho	3-4	and never seen although
34-35	first that became tempered and nourished] them—and it not mattering here that the time had been winter there too and	4-7	first which became tempered to nourish them. It would not matter here in Cambridge that the time had been winter in that garden too, and
36-37	seen at it since gauged by subsequent events that hour[?] had been night ~~too~~ also.	8-9	seen there since, judged by subsequent events, it had been night in the garden also.
38	anyway who could ~~quit~~[?] ~~room and table~~ without moving, as free of	11-12	anyway, who could without moving [*sic*?], as free now of
38-39	who stated and	12-13	who decreed and
39-40	who ⟨acquiesced, accepted, withdrew: what?⟩ and	14-15	who acquiesced, the beloved who was not bereaved, and
40-41	garden (granted the garden) to saddle, he already clattering ~~along the~~ over	15-16	garden to saddle, who could be already clattering over
41	December dawn, that	17	December night and that Christmas dawn, that
Page 132 [131]			
1	but 4 riding the 2 horses ~~in~~ thru that old iron darkness and	19-20	but four of them riding the two horses through the iron darkness, and
2	by not mattering either so	22	by so
3-4	recent ~~blood~~ intransient blood that held ~~love~~ ⟨honor⟩ above slothy unregret and ~~honor~~ ⟨love⟩ above	23-25	recent intransient blood which could hold honor above slothy unregret and love above
6	said ~~'I dont believe it~~ 'It's	28	said 'It's
		Page 296	
11-12	doing, how she might have passed the time,	5-6	doing all that time,
12-13	receipted and saw	7	receipted, so he thought, and saw
13	wind, but	9-10	wind; never once wondered about this but
14-15	it, tracked him down, could have and would have wanted to? So she wouldn't have told him; maybe the reason was that she knew that he—	10-13	it, could have and would have wanted to track him down? So it wasn't her that told Bon. She wouldn't have wanted to, maybe for the reason that she knew he—

MANUSCRIPT		BOOK	
16	a born[?] son who	15-16	a lone child out of her own body who
16-17	told about it.	16-17	told how she had been scorned and suffered.
17-18	words and maybe by the time he could understand what was said to him she had said it	18-20	words and so by the time he was big enough to understand what was being told him she had told it
19	to and maybe she had got to where	22-23	to make sense to her, and so she had got to the point where
20-22	and unforgetting. ~~Or maybe she was grooming him for the day and the hour when she would say to him,~~ Or maybe she didn't tell him deliberately. Maybe	25-26	and the unforgetting. Or maybe she didn't intend for him to know it then. Maybe
22-23	would come some	28	would arrive some
23	to come or	29	to arrive or
23	would do	29	would have to do
24	breathed, when he would	30-31	breathed—the moment when he (Bon) would
24	father **and** so that fate	32	father where fate

Page 297

25	could even have invented it or	1	could have invented or
28	the child's fun in	5-6	the other child's fun and diversion and needs in
29	dozen to do it with	8	dozen or bought a hundred to do it for her with
29	money, the mazuma that he had	8-9	money, the jack that he (the demon) had
29-30	repudiated too to balance his moral ledger with but like the millionaire that could	10-11	repudiated to balance his moral ledger: but like the millionaire who could
30-31	horse and the one moment,	12	horse, the one maiden, the one moment,
31	the instant, and ⟨himself⟩ patient	13-14	the one instant: and himself (the millionaire) patient
32	the horsesweat and the stable muck, hurrying him	15-16	the sweat and the stable muck, and the mother bringing him
33	down for God to finish it—pistol	18	down and let God finish it: pistol
37	with love,	25-26	with (what passed at least with him for it) love,
37	knees and the face	26-27	knees, the face

MANUSCRIPT		BOOK	
28-29	stomach and warmth and fun and security swooping	28-29	stomach and entrails, of warmth and pleasure and security, swooping
39	immobility and he	30	immobility: he
40	just a mere natural phenomenon of ~~in the course of childhood~~ existence,	31-32	just another natural phenomenon of existence;
41	fever [MARGIN: (not bitterness and despair: just implacable will for revenge)] as	33	fever (not bitterness
		Page 298	
		1	and despair: just implacable will for revenge) as
41	love;—he not	2-3	love—and he not knowing
Page 133 [132]			
1-2	~~comprehending and not caring, just curious, creating for himself without help since who to help him his own not~~ not knowing		
2	about since he	3	about. He
2	to sift any	3-4	to curry any
6	didn't anyway)	11-12	didn't intend to, anyway)
6-7	there and that maybe	12	there (and maybe
8	a desire to go back there; which you	15-16	a wish to go back there). You
9	left it except that you escaped,	16-17	left but only that you had escaped,
9-10	power ~~(this mostly the devil/ avaunting[?] skill and fortitude and foresight of your mother by the way)~~ had	17	power had
11-12	likewise (this mostly due to the devil-avaunting[?] and despising[?] skill and fortitude and foresight of your mother by the way) had also got	18	likewise got
13	in ~~peace~~ quiet and monotony tho not exactly what you would call peace,	20-21	in quiet and monotony (though not exactly in what you would call peace);
13-14	God that you did not remember anything about it and yet	21-22	God you didn't remember anything about it yet
14-15	it; that couldn't even know that he did not know that he was being held in (not back: in) ~~and~~ not even	23	it—he not even
16-17	so ~~was~~ and being	26-29	so from whatever harmless pursuit in which you were not bothering anybody or even thinking about them, by someone because that someone was bigger than you, stronger than you, and being

MANUSCRIPT		BOOK	
18	fierce affection and pride and vin-dictiveness and jealous love was ~~not~~ ~~a~~ a part of childhood and all	30-32	fierce yearning and vindictiveness and jealous rage was part of child-hood which all
19	had caught it, had it transmitted in turn	32	had received in turn

Page 299

20	in and so when	2	in. So that when
24	calculable intervals out	8	calculable moments out
26	ambiguous and eluded	12	ambiguous eluded
30	at one another	20	at each other
30	a ~~young boy~~ ⟨youth⟩ and	20	a youth and
31	and profound and ~~intent~~ naked	21	and naked
33	"And then	25	"Then
34	her (and him both maybe) and	26-27	her (despite him too maybe; maybe the both of them) and
34	care; he	27	care. He
36-40	that he had been wrong[?] and maybe he believed that she had tricked him and didn't care about that too because ~~nra~~[?] probably the only way she could have pinched him and made him hold back would have been with the money, the mazuma and he knew, found out, she wouldn't dare to that [*sic*] because he had found out soon[?] that she was grooming him even if he didn't know for what and maybe he even buys[?] her off	30-33	that she had been shaping and tem-pering him to be the instrument for whatever it was her hand was im-placable for, maybe came to believe (or saw) that she had tricked him into receiving that shape and temper,

Page 300

| | | 1-11 | and didn't care about that too because probably by that time he had learned that there were three things and no more: breathing, pleasure, darkness; and without money there could be no pleasure, and without pleasure it would not even be breathing but mere protoplasmic inhale and collapse of blind unorganism in a darkness where light never began. And he had the money because he knew that she knew that the money was the only thing she could coerce and smooth him into the barrier with when Derby Day came, so she didn't dare pinch him there and she knew he knew it: so that maybe he even blackmailed her, bought her off |
| 40 | jack and I wont ask what for' yet' and so she wouldn't dare refuse him or | 12-13 | jack as I want it and I wont ask why or what for yet.' Or |

301

CHAPTER VIII

41	she forgot about the money now like she never had remembered it anyway[?] for the hating	14-16	she never thought of the money now, who probably never had had much time to remember it or count it or wonder how much there was in the intervals of the hating

Page 134 [133]

1-2	all ~~the~~ ⟨to⟩ check him, rein[?] him up about the money was the lawyer and he had maybe learned	17-18	all to check him up about the money would be the lawyer. He (Bon) probably learned
2-3	anytime like the millionaire's race-horse knows that he has	20-21	anytime, like the millionaire horse has
4	jock;—that lawyer with a private mad female millionaire that probably	22-24	jock. Sure, that's who it would be: the lawyer, that lawyer with his private mad female millionaire to farm, who probably
5	them at all when	26	them when
5-6	lawyer that maybe Bon's mother was plotting	26-27	lawyer who, with Bon's mother already plotting
6-8	remember and even if she didn't [7-11 PASTED IN: know it or whether she knew it or not or would maybe have cared or not, up to the day when he would be translated quick into that much rich and rotting dirt, the lawyer had	28-29	remember for that day when he should be translated quick into so much rich and rotting dirt, had
9-10	and his mother both since before he could remember as tho he already was—that lawyer; maybe he even had	30-32	and the mother both as if he already was—that lawyer who maybe had

Page 301

11-12	code: ~~he~~ *Today he finished taking 100 square*] *miles of virgin land away from a drunk Indian, val. 25,000. At 2:31 p.m. today he came*	1-3	code: *Today Sutpen finished robbing a drunken Indian of a hundred miles of virgin land, val. $25,000. At 2:31 today came*
13	*with the last plank for his house.*	4	*with final plank for house.*
13	*land 35,000. At 7:52*	4-5	*land 40,000. 7:52*
14	[14-19 PASTED IN: *threat value minus nil. unless quick buyer could be found which not*	5-6	*threat val. minus nil. unless quick buyer. Not*
18-19	*100% increase yearly for each child plus intrinsic val. plus liquid assets plus working acquired credit and maybe here with the date]*	12-14	*100% times increase yearly for each child plus intrinsic val. plus liquid assets plus working acquired credit and maybe here with the date*
20	maybe have	15	maybe even have

CHAPTER VIII

MANUSCRIPT		BOOK	
21-22	still and then backing	18	still then, backing
24	spending from	22-23	spending on his whores and his champagne from
25	[25-40 PASTED IN: what his mother had ~~and~~ already and	23	what his mother had, and
26	be ripe—would think about	25-26	be good and ripe—thinking about
26-27	on the fine horses	27	on his horses
28	did; maybe he would have had	30	did even if it had been any secret; maybe he even had
28-29	in her bedroom like he did in Sutpen's even if it had been a secret; maybe	31-32	in the bedroom like he seems to have had in Sutpen's; maybe
29-30	her, maybe he even said like you would about a dog: *He's rambling*	32-33	her, said to himself like you do about a dog: *He is beginning to ramble.*
30	*block. Not to be tied:*	33	*block. Not a tether:*

Page 302

MANUSCRIPT		BOOK	
30-31	*cant go thru fences)* and him trying to check the money as much as he dared and	1-3	*cant get inside of anything that might have a fence around it)* and only him to try to check it, or as much as he dared, and
31-32	because that was probably the first thing Bon learned: that he only had to go	3-4	because he knew too that all Bon had to do was to go
33	jock was careful, a new jock thrown in—	6	jock wasn't careful, a new jockey too—
33-34	he ~~netted a month maybe against what would be left of it~~ ⟨wo⟩ would	7	he would
34-36	years against what it looked like would be left of it in that time to net out of, crucified between his two problems: ~~whether to wash his hands of the Sutpen angle and clean up what was left and go to Texas maybe~~ whether	8-9	years, and meanwhile crucified between his two problems: whether
37	and hit for Texas except whenever he thot about that	11-12	and light out for Texas. Except that whenever he thought about doing that
39-40	or 5 or even last year and so maybe at night ~~he~~ while he would lie and wait for the window to get light again he would be like the Aunt Rosa and have	14-18	or five years ago or even last year he would have made more: so that maybe at night while he would be waiting for the window to begin to turn gray he would be like what Aunt Rosa said she was and he would have

303

CHAPTER VIII

MANUSCRIPT		BOOK	
40-41	he ~~could~~ didn't)	18-19	he didn't)
41	Year's;—rising	20-21	Year's—the water backing up from the stick and rising
42-43	in misfortune or	23-24	in human misfortune and folly or

Page 135 [134]

3-4	that ~~had~~ could occur to try to anticipate, and	31	that could occur; and
5	[5-22 PASTED IN: him without showing him the moving people anymore than	33	him without showing him the moving people

Page 303

		1	than
8	the fleas and lice of	6	the lice and fleas of
9	another, their voices (it	8	another. It
10	them ~~of~~ not of tone	10-11	them (differences not in tone
11	words, it might have been either and	12	words), it might have been either of them and
11-12	both, both thinking the same thing, the voice speaking it only the thot become	13-14	both: both thinking as one, the voice which happened to be speaking the thought only the thinking become
13	talking people ~~whose shadows were not~~ who probably had	16-17	talking, people who perhaps had
15	Shreve) ~~shadows too~~ shades too)	20	Shreve) shades too
18	told ~~the law~~ you or the lawyer or anybody else what	24-25	told you or the lawyer or Bon or anybody else probably what
21-22	yet but she would have just let herself go in the sense that you keep the engines clean and oiled and the best of]	30-32	yet, but she would have just let herself go in the sense that you keep the engines clean and oiled and the best of

Page 136 [135]

Page 304

2	go a little on the outside: not fat,	1-2	go on the outside. Not fat;
3	chewing but the having	4	chewing; having
4-7	clothing but having the old garments wear out and having to choose new ones just another nuisance like the having to take them off to sleep and having to put them back on to get up another nuisance: and no pleasure in the fine figure that he ~~(Bon) out~~—" neither of them said Bon. It was not necessary "—cut, the fine	5-8	clothing; having the old wear out and having to choose the new just another nuisance: and no pleasure in the fine figure he——" neither of them said 'Bon' "——cut in the fine
8	shoulders or that	9	shoulders nor in the fact that
8	and red wheeled	10	and yellow-wheeled

304

MANUSCRIPT		BOOK	
9	others, but all that just an unavoidable nuisance too that	11-12	others did, but all that too just an unavoidable nuisance that
10	of to do any good for her just as he had had to	13-14	of before he could do her any good just like he had to
11	the too-light bones before he could do her any good);—	14-15	the light boy's bones in order to be able to do her any good)—
14	she got upset and	20-21	she would begin to itch for news and
14	report about	21-22	report, the communique about
14-15	him in Texas or Tennessee or Missouri or maybe California and we	22-25	him (Sutpen) in Texas or Missouri or maybe California (California would be fine, that far away; convenient, proof inherent in the sheer distance, the necessity to accept and believe) and we
15-16	and dont worry and so	26-27	and so do not worry. So
16-17	lawyer and bust on[?] i̶t̶ in	28	lawyer, busting in
17	a piece of	29	a section of
17-18	hat, just a shawl over her head and a̶l̶l̶ the only thing missing the mop	30-31	hat but just a shawl over her head, so that the only things missing would be the mop
19	be' meaning not like the Aunt Rosa meant, where did they find or invent a bullet that could kill him but, How can he be allowed to die without having to admit that I̶ ̶a̶m̶ ̶r̶i̶g̶ he was wrong and suffer and regret it: and so in that two	33 *Page 305* 1-3	be,' not meaning what the Aunt Rosa meant: *where did they find or invent a bullet that could kill him* but *How can he be allowed to die without having to admit that he was wrong and suffer and regret it.* And so in the next two
21-22	him [MARGIN: (he would show her the actual letter, the writing, i̶n̶ ̶t̶h̶e̶ E̶n̶g̶l̶i̶s̶h̶ ̶w̶h̶i̶c̶h̶ ̶s̶h̶e̶ ̶c̶o̶u̶l̶d̶n̶'̶t̶ ̶r̶e̶a̶d̶] get so close t̶h̶a̶t̶ to him	4-11	him (he—the lawyer—would show her the actual letter, the writing in the English she couldn't read, that had just come in, that he had just sent for the nigger to carry to her when she came in, and the lawyer done practised putting the necessary date on the letter until he could do it now while his back would be toward her, in the two seconds it would take him to get the letter out of the file)—catch him, get so close to him
22-24	alive, so close indeed that probably (not absolutely, mind; just possible and with the limitations of the natural	12-15	alive; so close indeed that he would be able to get her out of the office before she had sat down and into the

	MANUSCRIPT		BOOK
	unpredictability of human events, possible) and so get her out again and she would return home and among		carriage again and on her way home again where, among
24-25	camisoles look still like	16	camisoles, she would still look like
26-27	even new, holding, clutching the paper, the letter in the English that she could not read [MARGIN: and maybe the only word she could recognize would be the Sutpen] (he had maybe practiced putting the right date onto it while he would be getting it out of the file until he could do it quick) in	18-21	even when it was new five or six years ago, holding, clutching the letter she couldn't read (maybe the only word in it she could even recognize would be the word 'Sutpen') in
28	the paper like	23	the letter like
29-30	it so-you-could like she un knew that she	24	it as if she knew she
30	in after her eyes touched it before	25-26	in, only a second for it to remain intact in after her eyes would touch it, before
30-31	and would not be perused but consumed and her sitting	27-28	and so would not be perused but consumed, leaving her sitting
31-33	crumbling carbon ash in her hand. And him——" neither of them said Bon now either "——there watching her, that had got old enough to find out that what he had thot was	28-32	crumbling black carbon ash in her hand. "And him——" (Neither of them said 'Bon') "——there watching her, who had got old enough to have learned that what he thought was
			Page 306
35	boy and new again at the point where he	3	boy, new again when he
35-36	man, between a woman that he	4-5	man; created between a lawyer and a woman whom he
37	pleasure until	7	pleasure because he was himself, until
37	him she	8	him at all she
38-39	yet and even the woman had never seen and who	10-11	yet, whom even she had never seen yet, who
39-40	dynamite that wrecks ⟨destroys⟩ the	12	dynamite which destroys the
41	chem-	16-20	chemicals that had rather be still and dark in the quiet earth like they had been before the meddling guy with ten-power spectacles came and dug them up and strained, warped and
Page 137 [184 136]			
1-3	[1-10 PASTED IN: icals that had rather be still and dark in the quiet earth like they had been before the		

MANUSCRIPT

BOOK

meddling guy with ten-power spectacles came and dug them up and strained and twisted[?] and kneaded them, and a hired lawyer—the woman that since

kneaded them—created between this woman and a hired lawyer (the woman who since

4-5 he must have seen that he would be little more to her than so much rich and rotting dirt, and the lawyer that he must have realized now had

23-25 he saw that to her he would be little more than so much rich rotting dirt; the lawyer who since before he could remember he now realized had

6-7 and fertilizing[?] and harvesting him since before he could remember too as if he already was;—him watching

26-27 and manuring and harvesting him as if he already was) and Bon watching

7 the odor

28 the harem incense odor

8-10 the paper, having known for years that she was up to something and not even caring what because he already knew the hating and so not even thinking '*I am looking at my mother naked* because if the hating was the nakedness,

30-31 the letter, not even thinking *I am looking upon my mother naked* since if the hating was nakedness,

10-11 to be the same as clothes, like they say that modesty]¹ can be, is——"

32-33 to do the office of clothing like they say that modesty can do, does——

Page 307

12 [12-17 PASTED IN: "And so

1 "So

12 school.

1-2 school at the age of twenty-eight.

12-13 either—which one of them it was nor why nor how because he didn't care just like he had known all along that

3-5 either: which of them—mother or lawyer—it was who decided he should go to school nor why, because he had known all the time that

14-15 about what that was to try to find out and so it was not from having tried to find out that he knew

7 about what either of them was to try to find out, who knew

15 [MARGIN: and he didn't care about that either because maybe by now he knew that his mother didn't know and would not know what she wanted and

---

¹This pasted-in slip covers the following passage written on the page as it originally stood:

seen now had been plowing and harvesting him since before he could remember too as if he already was;—him watching her, lounging there against the mantel (maybe in the fine clothes and ~~with~~ ⟨in⟩ the ~~oder~~ odor of what you might call the easy sanctity watching her read the paper and not [illegible word] and not caring what it was because he already knew the hating [?], not thinking I am looking at my mother naked because ~~she had~~ if the hating was the nakedness she had worn it long enough now for it to be the same as clothes like they say that modesty can be, is;——the old ~~Sabine~~ [illegible crossed-out word] and ~~maybe it was the last one, the one she had been waiting for~~

MANUSCRIPT   BOOK

so he couldn't beat her (and maybe
he had learned from the octoroon
that you couldn't beat women anyway
and that if you]

	MANUSCRIPT		BOOK
17	lawyer, it would be fine with the lawyer if the mother	10-11	lawyer if his mother
17	wanted provided that he (the]	11	wanted, provided he (the
18-19	time; he went away to school, he told said 'All right' and the octoroon good said	13	time. He went away to school; he said
19-20	school that not in all the 26 [the *6* is written over a *3*] years	14-15	school, who not in all the twenty-eight years
20-21	at 8:00 oclock tomorrow	16-17	at nine a.m. tomorrow
21	was the octoroon that they used— the light block ⟨(not tether)⟩ that the	17-19	was even the octoroon whom they (or the lawyer) used—the light block (not tether) which the
22	from running thru fences, ⫽getting inside fences—maybe	20-21	from getting inside of something which might be found to have a fence around it later. Maybe
23	and the ceremony and the child and	22	and the child and the ceremony and
23-24	believe) who only considered Bon dull but not a fool—then finding out about it and sending for him and him coming and lounging against	23-25	believe, who considered Bon only dull, not a fool) and sent for him and he came and lounged against
25	maybe he knew what was up, what it was before	25-26	maybe knowing what was up, what had happened before
26	that, it was just something that you	28	that but just something you
27	see thru and her watching	29	see through or past, and she watching
28	any paper of rep[?] writing now	32	any letter now

Page 308

	MANUSCRIPT		BOOK
29-30	it down because she had not told him yet and now she would not dare risk it down because she	1	it down since she
30-31	betrayal since she had not told him yet and now she did not dare risk it—him looking	2-3	betrayal because she had not told him yet, and now, at this moment, she would not dare risk it—he looking
32	see thru and saying	5-6	see beyond, saying,
33	have . . . . And it not	7-8	have . . . . It's not
34-35	she could because she did not dare	9-11	she would because she had put off too

MANUSCRIPT

BOOK

say what she would: 'But you. But this

long now saying what she could: 'But you. This

35-36   it; he would know ~~just as he knew~~ because

11-12   it. He would know because

37   to ever since before he could remember ~~or love~~ or take

14-15   to since before he could remember, since before he could take

38-39   one that I know, get along with, who makes no trouble for me.

17   one whom I know, who makes me no trouble.

Page 138 [137]

1   my ⟨*little* portion of⟩ ~~*portion of hurt or harm to dead*~~ *hurt or harm to dead);*

23-24   *my little portion of hurt and harm to, dead;*

1   of ~~black~~ negro

24   of negro

2   and the fear before going away,

25-26   and fear, then to depart,

3   the first desperate

27-28   the desperate

4   that: and maybe

28   that; maybe

5   *shawl, and so*

30   *shawl. So*

5-7   *know if I cared to know:* ~~*Hand so maybe by night they did tell him:*~~ and maybe that night he did know, maybe before that if they ~~could~~ managed to find where he was, because she went to the lawyer, and

31-33   *know—if I cared to know.* Maybe by night he did, maybe before that if they managed to find him, get word to him, because she went to the lawyer. And

7   the alley; maybe before she got

33   the

Page 309

1   lawyer's alley. Maybe before she even got

8   glow glared up like turning up a wick,

2-3   glow began like when you turn up a wick;

9   been it all

5-6   been the lawyer's trouble and worry and concern all

10   he wouldn't tell Bon he

7-8   he would never tell Bon who his father was, he

11-12   maybe if he told Bon himself he might believe it or not but anyway he would go and tell her that

9-11   maybe he knew that if he were to tell Bon, Bon might believe it or he might not, but certainly he would go and tell his mother that

12-13   him: and then he would be sunk if for no other reason than breaking the agreement, the promise; maybe

11-15   him and then he (the lawyer) would be sunk, not for any harm done because there would be no harm, since this could not alter the situation, but for

309

MANUSCRIPT

BOOK

having crossed his paranoiac client. Maybe

14-15 had done already a long time ago maybe paid Bon the compliment

18-19 had probably a long time ago paid Bon that compliment

15 dull to

19-20 dull or too indolent to

16 to carry it thru once somebody showed him the next move;

21-22 to take advantage of it once somebody showed him the proper move;

19-20 would have to either find it out or somebody—such as the mother—would have to tell him: and so

28-30 would either have to find it out himself, or where somebody—the father or the mother—would have to tell him. So

20 good [MARGIN: or at least as soon as he had ~~time to look at the~~ had time to look at the old reports and make sure that it was the University of Mississippi that Henry was at] before

30-33 good—or at least as soon as he had had time to open the safe and look in the secret drawer and make sure that it was the University of Mississippi that Henry attended—before

Page 310

21-22 showed/, ~~Two children.--Say 20 years.--Increase~~ and

2 showed—and

22 date too: *1858.*

2-3 date here too: *1859.*

25 period and ~~d~~ lined out the *Credible* and wrote *Certain* and underlined it.

7-8 period, lining out the *Credible,* writing in *Certain,* underlining it.

26 didn't even care about that too. [MARGIN: ; he said 'All right.] Because

9-10 didn't care about that too; he just said, 'All right.' Because

30-31 [30-35 PASTED IN: wanted was just the money and so if he did not make the mistake of believing that he could beat all of that, if he was just quiet about it and alert about it he

15-17 wanted was just the money; and so if he just didn't make the mistake of believing that he could beat all of it, if he just remembered to be quiet and be alert he

31-32 it; and so he just said 'All right' and ~~packed the fine clothes and the linens in the bags~~ let

18 it.—So he said, 'All right' and let

32-33 bags and maybe he lounged in the

19-20 bags and trunks, and maybe he lounged into the

35 all and maybe watching from behind the smiling while the]

25-26 all; watching from behind the smiling while the

37-38 and ~~how he would get that quick and better in this particular school~~ how

29 and how

40 high class) college—and he——" neither of them said Bon; never

33 high class, high class) college—and he——" (neither of them

310

MANUSCRIPT

1   said 'Bon.' Never

41   any question as to who Shreve meant by he "——listening polite and courteous

1-3   any confusion between them as to whom Shreve meant by 'he') "——listening courteous

Page 139 [138]

1   [1-25 PASTED IN: behind that expression that was not smiling but just something you were not supposed to see thru, asking

3-4   behind that expression which you were not supposed to see past, asking

2   affable [MARGIN: ; nothing of irony, nothing of sarcasm] 'What

5-6   affable—nothing of irony, nothing of sarcasm—'What

2-3   elbow here for him to look at while the lawyer would be shuffling the papers to find one he could read the name from that he

7-9   elbow motion here while the lawyer would shuffle through the papers to find the one from which he could read that name which he

4   he talked to the mother the first time:

10   he first talked to the mother:

5-6   "——Oxford," Quentin said. About 40 miles." "—— "—— 'Oxford,' [*sic*] and the papers being allowed to settle back again and him talking now, about how there would be a small college that wasn't but 10 years

12-15   "Oxford," Quentin said. "It's about forty miles from——" "—— 'Oxford.' And then the papers could be still again because he would be talking: about a small college only ten years

7-8   him there and about how wisdom herself in a sense would be virgin or at least not very hard used and

16-17   him from his studies there (where, in a sense, wisdom herself would be a virgin or at least not very second hand) and

8-10   and provincial section of that land in which his destiny as the man he was and the financial power which he would represent after his mother passed on was rooted; and B he

18-24   and a provincial section of the country in which his high destiny was rooted; (granted the outcome of this war which was without doubt imminent, the successful conclusion of which we all hoped for, had no doubt of) as the man he would be and the economic power he would represent when his mother passed on, and he

10-11   expression that was just something you were not supposed to see thru and saying,

24   expression, saying,

11   law?' and now just for a moment

25-26   law as a vocation?' and now for just a moment

14-15   one moment when I was glad that I had': and

31-32   one occasion in my life when I was glad I had' and

MANUSCRIPT

BOOK

Page 312

16	care; maybe not even goodbye	2	care. Maybe he didn't even say good-bye
17	soft ~~abject~~ ⟨despairing⟩ magnolia colored	4	soft despairing magnolia-colored
18	above that boneless steel the expression that was	5-6	above those boneless steel gyves that expression of his which was
18-19	something you were not intended to see thru because you cant beat them, you just flee; and thanks	7-11	something not to be seen through. Because you cant beat them: you just flee (and thank God you can flee, can escape from that massy five-foot-thick maggot-cheesy solidarity which overlays the earth, in which men and women in couples are ranked and racked like nine-pins; thanks
19-20	masculine ⟨hipless⟩ tapering peg which fits but light enough ~~at best into the~~ and glib to move at best where	12-13	masculine hipless tapering peg which fits light and glib to move where
22	there and he to make	16-17	there to see him off and this not for godspeed but to make
22	boat: and	17-18	boat. And
24	bar preparing for it and he leaning on the rail,	20-21	bar, preparing for it, but not he; he alone, at the rail,
24-25	wink away	22	wink and glitter and sink away
25	boat ~~hung~~[?] ~~hanging~~ ⟨suspended⟩ immobile	23	boat suspended immobile
25	the very stars]	24	the stars
26	stacks; and	25-26	stacks. And
27	sober first[?] intent weighing	26	sober weighing
27-29	something even tho he did not ~~knew~~ (and believed that he probably never would) know what, and that the lawyer was up to something, tho he knew that that was just money and yet he knew that within his known and masculine	28-30	something; that the lawyer was up to something and though he knew that was just money, yet he knew that within his (the lawyer's) known masculine
30-31	unknown female quantity of his mother: and now this⫟—school, college—he 28 years old; and	31-33	unknown quantity which was his mother; and now this—school, college—and he twenty-eight years old. And

MANUSCRIPT	BOOK
	Page 313
31-32 college that he had never heard of before and that 10 years ago did not even exist:	1-2 college, which he had never heard of, which ten years ago did not even exist;
32-33 who chose it—what sober first[?] intent, what almost frowning, Why? Why? Why this college, this particular one?; maybe	3-5 who had chosen it for him—what sober, what intent, what almost frowning *Why? Why? Why this college, this particular one above all others?*—maybe
33-34 solitude and almost	6 solitude between panting smoke and engines and almost
34-36 of it just beyond him, the puzzle[?] inextricable and jumbled and unrecognizable yet just on the point of dropping into pattern which would show him at once like a flash of light the meaning of his whole past—	7-11 of the jigsaw puzzle picture integers of it waiting, almost lurking, just beyond his reach, inextricable, jumbled, and unrecognizable yet on the point of falling into pattern which would reveal to him at once, like a flash of light, the meaning of his whole life, past—
36-37 woman he called his mother—all (and maybe the letter itself or the mail lying somewhere	12-14 woman who was his mother. And maybe the letter itself right there under his feet, somewhere
37 deck he stood on, addressed	14-15 deck on which he stood—the letter addressed
38 Mississippi and one	17-18 Mississippi. One
39-41 glare (who had had no father and the fact that he had no visible father having created about his childhood a dark sense not of shame but of impotent and weary fury so that he believed that he had been fathered on his mother not thru that natural process in which the man is quite often	19-33 glare (showed it to him who not only had no visible father but had found himself to be, even in infancy, enclosed by an unsleeping cabal bent apparently on teaching him that he had never had a father, that his mother had emerged from a sojourn in limbo, from that state of blessed amnesia in which the weak senses can take refuge from the godless dark forces and powers which weak human flesh cannot stand, to wake pregnant, shrieking and screaming and thrashing, not against the ruthless agony of labor but in protest against the outrage of her swelling loins; that he had been fathered on her not through that natural process but had been blotted onto and out of her body by the old infernal immortal male principle of all unbridled terror
Page 140 [139] 1-2 victim[?] but had been punched[?] and blotted onto her and out of her by the old ⟨infernal and⟩ immortal male principle of all unbridled and doomed terror and darkness) and he standing in it and looking at the ⟨innocent⟩ face	

MANUSCRIPT	BOOK
	and darkness) a glare in which he stood looking at the innocent face

3-4   said *My eyes or my brow or my skull or my jaw or my shoulders* and

1   said *He has my brow my skull my jaw my hands* and

5-6   *Wait)* that he—'' it was not Bon he [6-41 PASTED IN: meant

4-5   *Wait.*
"The letter which he—'' it was not Bon Shreve meant

6   to know without

6   to comprehend without

7   record [MARGIN: and thinking 'By all means he must not know now, must not be told before he can get up there and he and the daughter'—not knowing anything about young love from his own youth and not believing it even if he had yet was willing to use that too as he would have courage and pride, thinking not of any hushed ⟨amazed⟩ importunate blood and ⟨light⟩ hands hungry for touching but of the [illegible word] fact that this Oxford and this Sutpen's Hundred should be only a day's ride apart and Henry already there and so maybe for once in his life he even believed in God:] *My dear Mr Sutpen—*

8-19   record, into the *daughter? daughter? daughter?* while he thought *By all means he must not know now, must not be told before he can get there and he and the daughter*—not remembering anything about young love from his own youth and would not have believed it if he had, yet willing to use that too as he would have used courage and pride, thinking not of any hushed wild importunate blood and light hands hungry for touching, but of the fact that this Oxford and this Sutpen's Hundred were only a day's ride apart and Henry already established in the University and so maybe for once in his life the lawyer even believed in God: *My Dear Mr Sutpen:*

9   *you or*

22   *you in person or*

10   *two people, one*

23   *two persons of birth and position, one*

11   *other, ⟨of whom,⟩ a ~~gentleman~~ young gentleman and her son,*

26   *other of whom, a young gentleman her*

11-13   *be ~~in residence with the same~~ or will shortly thereafter be ~~in residence within the same walls of learning~~, a petitioner, ~~at the same doors of knowledge as yourself~~ before*

26-27   *be as you read this, or will shortly thereafter be a petitioner before*

15-17   *county, as yourself. Indeed, better it were for me if they do not know that I wrote you at all; perhaps it had been better for me ~~if~~ had I not*

31-33   *county as it is your fortunate lot to be. Indeed, it were better for me if I had not*

18   *of ~~beseechment~~[?] ⟨humility⟩, take*

1   *of humility, take*

CHAPTER VIII

MANUSCRIPT		BOOK	
19	*gratitude to one who has*	5	*gratitude toward one whose generosity has*
19-20	*this: I am proud of it)*	6	*this; I proclaim it)*
21-22	*action ~~which~~ whose means fall behind the intention*	8-9	*action whose means fall behind its intention*
23	*he is ⟨loyal-and-grateful⟩ and ~~not what he would wish to be~~ professes*	9-10	*he is and professes*
25-26	*but (clumsy tho it be) as an introduction to a young gentleman ⟨whose position requires⟩ who needs no ~~reminder-of~~ ⟨neither detailing nor⟩ recapitulation ⟨~~nor de~~⟩ ~~of his position~~ in*	13-14	*but as an introduction (clumsy though it be) to one young gentleman whose position needs neither detailing nor recapitulation in*
30	another like to a cat—New Orleans or country[?] Mississippi;	20-22	another, like to a cat—cosmopolitan New Orleans or bucolic Mississippi:
31	gilded commodes and	23	gilded toilet seats and
31-32	old; [MARGIN: ~~about 10~~] ~~the octoroon's boudoir~~ champagne	24	old; champagne
33	country boy,	26	country youth,
33-34	his own roof (with the exception of lying fully dressed before a fire in the woods while ~~he~~ night hunting) until	27-29	his paternal house (unless perhaps to lie fully dressed beside a fire in the woods listening to dogs running) until
35-36	clothing and carriage and speech and all and (the boy) completely unaware of it, who (the boy) over the bottle one night should say, blurt—no, not blurt:	30-33	clothing carriage speech and all and (the youth) completely unaware that he was doing it, who (the youth) over the bottle one night said, blurted—no, not blurted:
36-37	groping: he (on the sofa, lounging too, in	33 *Page 316* 1	groping: and he (the cosmopolite ten years the youth's senior almost, lounging in
37-38	the boy had never seen until that fall and believed that only women wore, watching the boy blush fiery red yet face him, look	2-4	the youth had never seen before and believed that only women wore) watching the youth blush fiery red yet still face him, still look
39	blurted: 'If	5-6	blurted with abrupt complete irrelevance: 'If
39-40	he 'Ah?' and the boy:	7	he: 'Ah?' and the youth:
41	brother': and the boy 'Yes.	9-10	brother' and the youth: 'Yes.
41	standing now,]	11	standing (the youth) now,

315

MANUSCRIPT   BOOK

Page 141 [140]

| 1-2 | steady on the other's: '—Yes. | 13 | steady: 'Yes. |

6-7   them, like somebody will always have to   20-21   them, as someone always has to

7   bonfire; that   21   bonfire. That

9   of talking and listening wherein   25   of speaking and hearing wherein

11   discarding and conserving what grains seemed   29-30   discarding the false and conserving what seemed

12   might and would be   31   might be

13-14   her, even how she looked and her ~~days~~ private   33   her before he ever saw her—what she looked

                                                   Page 317

                                                   1   like, her private

14-16   world men were not supposed to see or know much about; he must have known that without having asked one question. He did not have to ask. Jesus, it must have come out, ⟨~~bold~~[?]⟩ boiled out kind of all over him; there   1-5   world that even men of the family were not supposed to know a great deal about; he must have learned it without even having to ask a single question. Jesus, it must have kind of boiled out all over him. There

16-17   him (and with no attempt to teach, to do the mentor, on   6-13   him how to lounge about a bedroom in a gown and slippers such as women wore, in a faint though unmistakable effluvium of scent such as women used, smoking a cigar almost as a woman might smoke it, yet withal such an air of indolent and lethal assurance that only the most reckless man would have gratuitously drawn the comparison (and with no attempt to teach, train, play the mentor on

19   *of chin* ⟨*and some of my thinking behind them*⟩ *and*   17-18   *of jaw and chin and some of my thinking behind it, and*

20-21   *blood* [MARGIN: *whose* ~~*blending*~~[?] ⟨*admixing*⟩ *was necessary that he* ~~*become alive, exis*~~ *exist*] ~~*out of which he was created,*~~ *is*   20-21   *blood whose admixing was necessary in order that he exist is*

23-24   *face* ~~*but on my father*~~ *whom I did not know I had and hence have never missed, but my father's* ~~*whose absence*~~ *out*   25-26   *face whom I did not know I possessed and hence never missed, but my father's, out*

25   eagerness, without   28-29   eagerness which was without

MANUSCRIPT		BOOK	
27	the trivial outer shell—thinking, *what*	31-32	the shell—thinking *what*
			Page 318
28-29	*which ~~ran in sunlight where that which he bequeathed me ran in darkness~~ sprang from* ⟨*quiet*⟩ *peace*	1	*which sprang in quiet peace*
30-31	*me ~~was given in~~ sprang in hatred and ~~rage~~ and outrage*	3	*me sprang in hatred and outrage*
31-32	*and willing clay (as that father himself could not do it)—to what shape ~~of honor and pride courage and pride~~ of what*	5-6	*and eager clay which that father himself could not—to what shape of what*
33	*blood which there was none*	6-7	*blood and none*
34-35	nonsense, could not be so, that such as this happened only in books and thinking [MARGIN: (the weariness, the fatalism, the ~~cat's aptitude~~ incorrigible cat for solitude:):] *That young clodhopper bastard: how*	9-12	nonsense, it could not be true; that such coincidences only happened in books, thinking—the weariness, the fatalism, the incorrigible cat for solitude—*That young clodhopper bastard. How*
36	days while	14	days, the afternoons, while
37	better rider, who ~~proba~~ maybe	15-16	better horseman, who maybe
39-40	speech and telling, translated, the 3 of them,	21	speech, translated (the three of them:
40-41	the girl he had never seen and did not care even yet, maybe even out of curiosity, ~~to see~~ whether he ever saw or not, into	22-23	the sister whom he had never seen and perhaps did not even have any curiosity to see) into
41	tale, where	24-31	tale in which nothing else save them existed, riding beside Henry,
Page 142 [~~142~~ 141]			listening, needing to ask no questions, to prompt to further speech in
1-16	*warn me that I was young,* feeling that same despair and shame like when you have to watch your father ~~fat~~ fail in physical courage, thinking *It should have been me that failed; me, I, not he who stemmed from that blood which we both bear before it could have become tainted and corrupted by whatever it was in mother that he could not brook;—* Wait," Shreve said. Quentin had not spoken; it was some movement, some quality ~~on~~ ⟨f⟩ his still lax and hunched ~~and attitude~~ body that presaged speech, and Shreve saying[?] Wait, Wait before he ⟨Quentin⟩ could have begun to speak:		any manner that youth who did not even suspect that he and the man beside him might be brothers, who each time his breath crossed his vocal chords was saying *From now on mine and my sister's house will be your house and mine and my sister's lives your life,* wondering (Bon)—or maybe not wondering at all—how

"Wait. / he "Because he hadn't
looked at the girl. Oh, he had seen
her all right; he had even looked Mrs
Sutpen would have seen to that: what
tete/a/tete a young country bred girl
like that was ea one thousand 14
p.m.'s of carefully arranged tete-a-
tete where maybe even she too felt
like the other one to a pair of goldfish and maybe she even began to

---

tin) could have begun to speak:
"Wait. Because he hadn't even
looked at the girl. Oh, he had seen
her all right; Mrs Sutpen would
have seen to that: 14 p.m.'s of
carefully-arranged p.m.'s p.m.'s of
arranged planned and executed
privacies where maybe even she too
felt like the other one to a pair of
goldfish

---

nothing else but them existed: and
maybe Bon thot with how with every
time Henry breathed across his vocal
chords who did not even suspect that
they were ⟨might be⟩ brothers
breathed across his vocal chords he
was saying *From now on* our [MARGIN:
mine and Judith's] *house will be your
house and mine and Judith's life
your life* and wondered (or maybe he
did not wonder at all) how

17	(Bon) still knowing what he knew or suspected,	32-33	(Bon) the scion and still knew what he suspected,
17-18	same. And he (Bon)	33	same;
		Page 319	
		1	then (Bon)
19	third one of them of Henry's	2-3	third inhabitant of Henry's
19-20	thot about her: he just listened	4	thought of her: he had merely listened
20-21	thinking *Maybe I shall see my father whom it seems that I*	5	thinking *So at last I shall see him, whom it seems I*
21	*I even learned at last to*	6	*I had even learned to*
23	instant between	9-10	instant of indisputable recognition between

CHAPTER VIII

<table>
<tr><td colspan="2">MANUSCRIPT</td><td colspan="2">BOOK</td></tr>
<tr><td>24</td><td>him know just</td><td>12</td><td>him understand just</td></tr>
<tr><td>25</td><td>I will</td><td>13</td><td>I do not expect that, will</td></tr>
<tr><td>27</td><td>even ⟨just⟩ a clodhopper <s>brother</s> bastard</td><td>16-17</td><td>even just a clodhopper bastard</td></tr>
<tr><td>28</td><td>either because</td><td>19</td><td>either. Because</td></tr>
<tr><td>31</td><td>own with and be</td><td>23</td><td>own flesh with, to be</td></tr>
<tr><td>31-32</td><td>turn <s>after</s> [MARGIN: to run hot and loud in veins and limbs after] that</td><td>23-24</td><td>turn to run hot and loud in veins and limbs after that</td></tr>
<tr><td>32-33</td><td>dead. <s>And so he did that, he went there</s>; And so he did that, he went there; he</td><td>25</td><td>dead. So the Christmas came and he</td></tr>
<tr><td>37</td><td>about thru the thinking; and Henry doubtless not</td><td>33</td><td>about from behind the more urgent thinking, and</td></tr>
<tr><td></td><td></td><td colspan="2">Page 320</td></tr>
<tr><td></td><td></td><td>1</td><td>Henry probably not</td></tr>
<tr><td colspan="2">Page 143 [142]</td><td></td><td></td></tr>
<tr><td>1</td><td>too of complete surrender—that he was used to seeing on Henry's face:</td><td>7-8</td><td>too, of complete surrender—which he had used to see on Henry's face,</td></tr>
<tr><td>3</td><td>thot too and</td><td>10</td><td>thought also: and</td></tr>
<tr><td>4</td><td>been far too</td><td>13</td><td>been too</td></tr>
<tr><td>5</td><td>spent 2 weeks there,</td><td>13-14</td><td>spent ten days there,</td></tr>
<tr><td>6</td><td>the piece of furniture, the mold</td><td>16</td><td>the object of art, the mold</td></tr>
<tr><td>8-9</td><td>have paid for him with Judith⟋or even if there had been none else among</td><td>19-20</td><td>have purchased him as and paid for him with Judith even, if there had been no other bidder among</td></tr>
<tr><td>9-10</td><td>and remain until he disappeared, he and Henry together, and</td><td>21-23</td><td>and which he did remain to her until he disappeared, taking Henry with him, and</td></tr>
<tr><td>11</td><td>days and maybe</td><td>24</td><td>days until maybe</td></tr>
<tr><td>11</td><td>remember then that she had forgot him (and</td><td>25</td><td>remember after a while that she had ever forgot him. (And</td></tr>
<tr><td>12-13</td><td>that p.m: what prayer ridden</td><td>27-28</td><td>that afternoon when they rode up the drive, what prayer, what maiden meditative dream ridden</td></tr>
<tr><td>13-14</td><td>but rather the tragic and silken Lancelot nearly 30, <s>more than</s> 10</td><td>29-30</td><td>but the silken and tragic Lancelot nearing thirty, ten</td></tr>
<tr><td>15-16</td><td>her) and then the day came to ride away again and no sign yet, and he and Henry mounted and did ride away</td><td>32-33</td><td>her.) And the day came to depart and no sign yet; he and Henry rode away</td></tr>
</table>

CHAPTER VIII

<table>
<tr><td colspan="2">MANUSCRIPT</td><td colspan="2">BOOK</td></tr>
<tr><td></td><td></td><td colspan="2">Page 321</td></tr>
<tr><td>17</td><td>might have</td><td>2-3</td><td>might (he would believe) have</td></tr>
<tr><td>18</td><td>himself and so needed no sign if</td><td>3-4</td><td>himself the truth and so would have needed no sign, if</td></tr>
<tr><td>19-20</td><td>hide that one and so there could have been no unanswered question to the eyes those eyes, yet no flicker, no sign, in them: and so he knew that it</td><td>5-7</td><td>hide it, could have seen the truth if it were there: yet no flicker in them: and so he knew it</td></tr>
<tr><td>22-23</td><td>nothing. And maybe he thot,</td><td>10-11</td><td>nothing. Maybe he even thought,</td></tr>
<tr><td>26</td><td>to even if not actual understanding, thinking</td><td>16-17</td><td>to let it be in secret even if he could not have understood why, thinking</td></tr>
<tr><td>27</td><td>me, warn me, that</td><td>19</td><td>me, that</td></tr>
<tr><td>30</td><td>become tainted and corrupt by</td><td>23</td><td>become corrupt and tainted by</td></tr>
<tr><td>35</td><td>[35-40 PASTED IN: had seen her all right, he had had plenty of opportunity for that, he</td><td>29-30</td><td>had seen her all right, he had had plenty of opportunity for that; he</td></tr>
<tr><td>36</td><td>it—14 afternoons of</td><td>31</td><td>it—ten days of</td></tr>
<tr><td>37</td><td>of generals in the military textbooks,</td><td>33</td><td>of dead generals in the textbooks,</td></tr>
<tr><td></td><td></td><td colspan="2">Page 322</td></tr>
<tr><td>38-39</td><td>the p.m.'s until maybe J planned maybe from the time Mrs</td><td>1-2</td><td>the afternoons—all planned three months ago when Mrs</td></tr>
<tr><td>39</td><td>letter about him until maybe ⟨even⟩ Judith too felt like</td><td>3-4</td><td>letter with Bon's name in it, until maybe even Judith too began to feel like</td></tr>
<tr><td>40</td><td>have done to a]</td><td>6</td><td>have found to do to a</td></tr>
<tr><td colspan="2">Page 144 [143]</td><td></td><td></td></tr>
<tr><td>1</td><td>before that didn't sooner or later smell</td><td>7-8</td><td>before who sooner or later didn't smell</td></tr>
<tr><td>2</td><td>would have to talk to the old lady on</td><td>8-9</td><td>would talk to the old dame on</td></tr>
<tr><td>3-6</td><td>other case he couldn't even make his escape until Henry would come and get him he not only wouldn't have to make the talk, he couldn't even make his own escape until Henry would come and get him: and</td><td>11-13</td><td>other he would not even be able to make his own escape but would have to wait for Henry to come and get him. And</td></tr>
<tr><td>10</td><td>tray and you tell</td><td>19-20</td><td>tray and you look at the sherbet and tell</td></tr>
<tr><td>11</td><td>you?" "Yes," Quentin said. "But it's not love."</td><td>21-22</td><td>you?"<br>"But it's not love," Quentin said.</td></tr>
</table>

320

MANUSCRIPT		BOOK	
12	not?'' Shreve said. ''Because	23	not? Because
12-13	dame told you, the Aunt Rosa, about	24	dame, the Aunt Rosa, told you about
15	it; he	28	it. He
15	be; like	29	be. Like
17	known that that would be; it	31-32	known it was going to happen. It
			Page 323
20	you did not even go on to the side-board and maybe	3-4	you didn't even go to the sideboard, maybe
21-22	dirty plates and a[?] ~~the na~~ crumpled napkins and	5-6	dirty haviland and the crumpled damask, and
22	there; it	7	there even. It
24-25	spring there by then, in the country where he never had spent a spring before, and you say North	10-11	spring then, in that country where he had never spent a spring before and you said North
25-26	than New Orleans, with dogwood and the earth	12-13	than Louisiana, with dogwood and violets and the early scentless flowers but the earth
26-27	sticky ⟨little⟩ buds ~~on the maples and~~ like the breasts of young girls on	14-15	sticky buds like young girls' nipples on
31-32	cup once that [MARGIN: it would be like a flower that] if any other hand ~~but yours~~ reached out for	22-23	cup that it would be like a flower that, if any other hand reached for
33-34	hadn't had sherbet in them but	25-26	hadn't contained sherbet but
34-35	that: it was knowing what he knew might	27-28	that. There was the knowing what he suspected might
35-36	knowing whether it was so or not: and who to say if maybe it was not the possibility of incest because	28-29	knowing if it was so or not. And who to say if it wasn't maybe the possibility of incest, because
37	encounter and not thot how ~~perhaps~~ you	32-33	encounter; who has not had to realize that when the brief all is done you
38	pleasure ~~but maybe if there was just sin~~ since the gods condone	33	pleasure, gather
Page 145 [144]		*Page 324*	
1	them but	1-6	up your own rubbish and refuse—the hats and pants and shoes which you drag through the world—and retreat since the gods condone and practise these and the dreamy immeasurable coupling which floats oblivious above the trameling and haried instant, the: *was-not: is: was:* is a perquisite only of balloony and weightless elephants and whales: but

MANUSCRIPT		BOOK	
1-2	escape, part, return." [MARGIN:—"Aint that right?"] He ceased;	8-9	escape, uncouple, return.—Aint that right?" He ceased,
3	He (Quentin) just sat as before, ~~looking curious~~ his	10-11	He just sat as before, his
3-4	pockets and his shoulders down a little and his face lowered and looking somehow curiously smaller because	11-13	pockets, his shoulders hugged inward and hunched, his face lowered and he looking somehow curiously smaller than he actually was because
5	spareness ~~and that of~~ that quality of delicacy as to bone,	14-15	spareness—that quality of delicacy about the bones,
6	last dying echo	16	last echo
8	by 20 pounds	20-21	by twenty or thirty pounds
9	who has lost that weight, that bulk, sold	22	who had that plumpness once and lost it, sold
14-15	that?"—"I dont know," Quentin said. ~~//"All right," Shreve said. "Then listen.~~ He did not move, stir.	31-32	that?" "I dont know," Quentin said. He did not move.
		Page 325	
16-17	have to ring soon now. ~~"All right," Shreve said. "Then listen.~~ "You	2-3	have rung some time ago now. "You
17-18	you?" Shreve said. Quentin did not move. "That's right," Shreve said. "Dont say it, because	3-4	you?" Quentin did not answer. "That's right. Dont say it. Because
20-21	knew then that there was a fate, a doom, on him, like what this old Aunt told you: that some things just	7-8	knew there was a fate, a doom on him, like what the old Aunt Rosa told you about some things that just
23-24	or bad by it, ~~somebody was going to have to pay for~~ he was going to have to pay for it and	13-14	or ill by it, it wasn't going to be the old man who would have to pay the check; and
24-25	was too old to pay, who should pay except his sons,	15-16	was bankrupt with the incompetence of age, who should do the paying if not his sons,
25-26	way back in the old days, and the old Abraham would be full of years and weak [MARGIN: and incapable ever of further harm] ~~and~~ when the ~~sin caught up with~~ would be caught	17-18	way in the old days? the old Abraham full of years and weak and incapable now of further harm, caught
27	the ⟨captains and the⟩ collectors would say	19-20	the captains and the collectors saying,
28	raised sons about me to bear	20-21	raised about me sons to bear
29-32	herds ~~for the comfort of mine old age that I might rest mine eyes upon~~	22-23	herds from the hand of the ravisher: that

MANUSCRIPT   BOOK

~~them and upon my descendants my~~
~~goods and upon my descendants~~
~~increased an hundred fold the~~
~~generation of my descendants~~
~~increased an hundred fold~~ that

32   goods, upon

33-37 me.' So that would be all right. He
       never[?] knew he would never have
       to worry about that: maybe he knew
       now that he had known that all the
       time and that that was the reason he
       did not have to bother to think about
       her all those 3 months between
       September and Xmas while Henry
       was saying every time he breathed
       Our 3 lives are to be one life, and
       so he did not even have to worry
       about it after

37-39 him between the first two of the 3
       times he was to see her; maybe that
       was why he didn't even bother to
       write her any letters (until that last
       one) that she would want to save,
       like your father said she didn't;
       maybe
Page 146 [145]
1   why he never actually even ~~asked~~
       proposed

1-6   for Ellen to show; never anything in
       those letters that the nigger would
       carry to Sutpen's Hundred every two
       weeks from the school that your
       father told about that even she would
       want to save. He didn't need to
       worry about that; he never had needed
       to worry about her; maybe he knew
       that now too, that he had known all
       the time just from Henry's talking
       what he did not need to have to see
       her once to know, to see her look at
       him once to know that, who had never
       seen anything ~~exec~~ like him before
       either and because the fate was on
       her too,

7   nobody wanted him in the flesh;
       maybe it was

24   goods and chattels, upon

26-32 me.' He knew all the time that the
       love would take care of itself. May-
       be that was why he didn't have to
       think about her during those three
       months between that September and
       that Christmas while Henry talked
       about her to him, saying every time
       he breathed: *Hers and my lives are
       to exist within and upon yours;* did
       not need to waste any time over the
       love after

32-33 him, why he never bothered to write
       her any letters (except that last one)
Page 326
1-2   which she would want to save, why he
       never actually proposed

2-3   for Mrs Sutpen to show around. Be-
       cause the fate was on her too:

4-14   nobody would want him in the flesh on
       any debt; maybe he didn't even have
       to wait for that Christmas to see her

to know this; maybe that's what it
was that came out of the three
months of Henry's talking that he
heard without listening to: *I am not
hearing about a young girl, a
virgin; I am hearing about a narrow
delicate fenced virgin field
already furrowed and bedded so that
all I shall need to do is drop the
seeds in, caress it smooth again,*
saw her that Christmas and knew it
for certain and then forgot it, went
back to school and did not even
remember that he had forgotten it,
because he did not have time then;
maybe it was

8	about and he stopped and told him *All*	15-16	about when he stopped and said, right quiet: *All*
9	*right* and that was all. Because	17	*right* and then forgot that too. Because

10-18 anything but time. That was it.; it
didn't need the letter he probably got
from the lawyer that spring, asking
if he had met a fellow student named
so-and-so maybe [MARGIN: and hoped
he was well and his humble servant,
etc., etc.,] since the lawyer ~~would
still believe he was the wrong kind
of not-fool~~ who had believed that he
was not a fool would believe right up
to the last that he was a the wrong
kind of not-fool. He was waiting;
maybe he thot it would be in each
mail that the nigger brot back from
Sutpen's Hundred, and Henry thinking it was the letter from her that he
was wanting, waiting for, because
they could not have been home a
whole day that Xmas before Mrs
Sutpen took Henry aside even if that
had been needed—Henry thinking it
was that that he would ~~maybe prob~~[?]
say 'Did Spen[?] [illegible word] the
horse out when he got in today[?]?'
about when what he was thinking was
Maybe

18-23 anything else but time, because he
had to wait. But not for her. That
was all fixed. It was the other.
Maybe he thought it would be in the
mail bag each time the nigger rode
over from Sutpen's Hundred, and
Henry believing it was the letter
from her that he was waiting for,
when what he was thinking was
Maybe

19	*this.' And*	25	*this' and*

MANUSCRIPT		BOOK	
19	*sheet of*	25	*sheet, a scrap of*
19-20	*'Charles' on it,*	26	*'Charles' in his hand,*
22	*what it would*	29-30	*what his hair and his finger nails would*
24-25	*of them should come back unopened, that would be a sign* and it didn't: and Henry	33	*of mine to her should come*
		Page 327	
		1-2	*back to me unopened then. That would be a sign. And that didn't happen:* and then Henry
25-26	Hundred on his way home when University[?] was out and ~~the subject~~ ~~me~~[?] the date sent for this and ~~no objection to that ea~~ the family	3-8	Hundred for a day or so on his way home and he said all right to it, said *It will be Henry who will get the letter, the letter saying it is inconvenient for me to come at that time; so apparently he does not intend to acknowledge me as his son, but at least I shall have forced him to admit that I am.* And that one did not come either and the date was set and the family
27-28	Hundred notified and no objection to that came back and he thot *It will be then; he was waiting for that* and maybe	9-11	Hundred notified of it and that letter did not come either and he thought *It will be then; I wronged him; maybe this is what he has been waiting for* and maybe
31	*demand of him what it was that my*	15-16	*demand to know of him what it was my*
31-39	*me* ~~And then~~	17	*me. So*

---

he and Henry went back, rode back
the 40 miles and into the gates, and
he knew what he would find there—
the mother that he had seen thru,
that had probably taken Henry to one
side before they had been in the
house 8 hours back during that Xmas
and so that maybe before they even
started; it would be June now and
what would it be now? The magnolias
in bloom and the mockingbirds, and
the ~~Decoration Day~~ Decoration Day
with the veterans in gray and the ~~y~~
chosen young girls in white dresses
with red sashes and the ~~veterans~~
~~would~~ band would play Dixie and all
the old guys ~~that~~ would yell that you

MANUSCRIPT   BOOK

would think never had the breath to—
⟨Yes.⟩ That's right. They hadn't
fought it then. They would have to
wait 40 years for that.—Just the
magnolias and the mockingbirds

Page 147 [146]

1   [1-25 PASTED IN: So

MANUSCRIPT	BOOK
1-2 gates again and up the drive.	**18-19** gates and up the drive to the house.
2-6 —the mother that he had seen thru at once, that had taken Henry aside before they had been in the house 8 hours th of that first day last Xmas and that Henry without knowing it probably had told him (Bon) all about what she said not before they had been back at school a full day but probably before they had got back to the school at all: so that maybe before they even started; ⟨it	**19-32** —the woman whom he had seen once and seen through, the girl whom he had seen through without even having to see once, the man whom he had seen daily, watched out of his fearful intensity of need and had never penetrated—the mother who had taken Henry aside before they had been six hours in the house on that Christmas visit and informed him of the engagement almost before the fiance had had time to associate the daughter's name with the daughter's face: so that probably before they even reached school again, and without his being aware that he had done so, Henry had already told Bon what was in his mother's mind, (who had already told Bon what was in his); so that maybe before they even started on Bon's second visit—(It

Page 328

MANUSCRIPT	BOOK
8 and finished, the Decoration	**2-3** and lost it and come back home, the Decoration
9-10 dresses ~~and~~ tied at	**6** dresses bound at
10 old men	**8** old doddering men
13 music inside	**13** music, fiddles and triangles, inside
14 swirling hoops:	**14** swirling and dipping hoops:
19-20 and act would say to me, ~~I have seen and~~ I	**23-24** and action and speech would say to me, I
21 Bon knew what he meant by that, thinking ~~(Henry)~~ telling himself (Henry) *Not*	**27-28** Bon would know what he meant, was trying to say, tell him, thinking, telling himself (Henry): *Not*
23 *I have known and*	**29-30** *I shall ever know and*
24 *time ~~dont~~ or not dont matter, I gave myself and Judith to him——"*	**31-33** *time or not does not matter, I gave my life and Judith's both to him——"*

MANUSCRIPT

"That's still not love," Quentin said.]

26-27 listen—Rode the 40 miles back to Sutpen's Hundred and into the gates and up the drive to the house, and

27-28 Sutpen was not even there. And ~~Mrs Sutpen~~ ⟨Ellen⟩ didn't

29-30 and Judith and Henry not even caring that much and

37 somber implacable woman

37-38 grim implacable man

Page 148 [147]
1 another [MARGIN: in grim and implacable armistice] after

6-7 Xmas now (didn't your old man say

7-8 trousseau or something?) and Judith ~~not~~ neither

12 *me to do it and I will;*

14-15 *is the reason he will not ask*

20-21 'What? No engagement, no troth, no ring? she

23 no spoken engagement—

26 to know, be aware.

28-30 *knows I would not have claimed that as my home; he knows I would not have to because he has already provided for me* not because

35 all became blended

BOOK

"That's still not love," Quentin said.

Page 329
1-2 listen.—They rode the forty miles and into the gates and up to the house. And

3 Sutpen wasn't even there. And Ellen didn't

6 and Henry and Judith not even caring that much, and

17 somber vengeful woman

18 grim rocklike man

20 another in grim armistice after

29-30 Christmas—didn't your father say

31-32 trousseau?—and Judith neither

Page 330
5-6 *me what to do and I will do it;*

10 *is why he will never ask*

20-21 'What?' [*sic*] No engagement, no troth, no ring?' she

23 no proposal.—

29 to comprehend.

32-33 *knows that I shall never make any claim upon any part of what he now possesses, gained at the*
Page 331
1-6 *price of what sacrifice and endurance and scorn (so they told me; not he: they) only he knows; knows that so well that it would never have occurred to him just as he knows it would never occur to me that this might be his reason, who is not only generous but ruthless, who must have surrendered everything he and mother owned to her and to me as the price of repudiating her,* not because

14-15 all seemed blended

MANUSCRIPT

BOOK

37   *again.*

Page 149 [148]

1-7   and he (Bon) thinking *All right*
thinking of the 2 of them, the implacable woman who was his mother
and the ⟨implacable⟩ man who had
looked at him with absolutely no
alteration of expression whatever,
facing one another in grim and
implacable armistice after almost
30 years in that ⟨rich⟩ baroque
charming room in that house which
he called home since apparently
everybody seemed to have to have a
home, thinking, *Yes. Yes. Even that
way. Even if he wants to do it that
way. I will promise never to see
her again, never to see him again.*

"And then he reached home and he
never knew if

7-9   He ~~hear~~[?] never knew. He ~~must
have~~ believed, yet he never knew. He
tried to find out from his mother,
who did not dare to ask, and got
nothing, and the very

10-12   of North Miss. and perhaps he had
made friends up there maybe would
be but further proof that ~~Sutpen had
not been in New Orleans~~ his father
had not come to see his mother,
since

13-19 he ~~ha~~ believed that he had fathomed
during that past fall what the lawyer
had known all the time there could
have been nothing in the question to
~~tell~~ assure him that the lawyer ~~knew~~
had learned anything more in the
interval—who now knew that the
lawyer may have believed him to be
a fool but not the kind of fool he was
going to be.
"And he told the lawyer nothing
and the lawyer ~~did~~ probably did not

18-19 *again.* Then he reached home. And
he never learned if

19-23 He never knew. He believed it, but
he never knew—his mother the same
somber unchanged fierce paranoiac
whom he had left in September, from
whom he could learn nothing by in-
direction and whom he dared not ask
outright—the very

25-29 of that country and how perhaps—or
had he not perhaps?—he had made
friends up there among the country
families) only that much more proof
to him at that time that Sutpen had
not been there, or at least the
lawyer was not aware that he had,
since

30-33 he believed he had fathomed the
lawyer's design in sending him to
that particular school to begin with,
he saw nothing in the questions to
indicate that the lawyer had learned
anything new since. (Or what he
could have learned

Page 332

1-12 in that interview with the lawyer,
because it would be a short one; it
would be next to the shortest one ever
to transpire between them, the

MANUSCRIPT

BOOK

actually ask, who believed him to be a fool but not that kind of a fool; and the summer passed and he knew that the lawyer was watching him, and September

shortest one of all next to the last one of course, the one which would occur in the next summer, when Henry would be with him.) Because the lawyer would not dare risk asking him outright, just as he (Bon) did not dare to ask his mother outright. Because, though the lawyer believed him to be rather a fool than dull or dense, yet even he (the lawyer) never for one moment believed that even Bon was going to be the kind of a fool he was going to be. So he told the lawyer nothing and the lawyer told him nothing, and the summer passed and September

19   lawyer had not yet asked

13   lawyer (his mother too) had not once asked

20-21   return to the school, until at last he had to say himself that he intended to return and so he knew

14-15   return to the school. So that at last he had to say it himself, that he intended to return; and maybe he knew

21-22   nothing at all in the lawyer's face except an agent's

16-17   nothing whatever in the lawyer's face save an agent's

22-23   school, and Henry was there waiting (oh yes, waiting) who

18-19   school, where Henry was waiting (oh yes; waiting) for him, who

24-25   *What I and my sister have belongs to you* and maybe now he did write to Judith by that first nigger post that rode on to

20-22   *What my sister and I have and are belongs to you* but maybe he did write to Judith now, by the first nigger post which rode to

27   and inescapable on

25   and inelidable on

28-29   *back* ~~and if~~ *thinking* ~~nothing~~[?]/ ⟨maybe⟩ *if it should come back then nothing will stop me. And that fall*

27-30   *back thinking Maybe if it comes back nothing will stop me then and so maybe at last I will know what I am going to do. But it didn't come back. And the others didn't come back. And the fall*

31-33   gone hunting, he had ridden into town—something; /(this Sutpen who was not there and it Bon who knew then that he had not expected him to be ~~there~~ there, who said *It*

32-33   gone to town, he was hunting—something; Sutpen not there when they rode up and Bon

Page 333

1-2   knew he had not expected him to be there, saying *Now. Now. Now. It*

34-35   *do* and so maybe what he was doing in the garden

3-11   *do.* So maybe what he was doing that twilight (because he knew that Sutpen

MANUSCRIPT   BOOK

			had returned, was now in the house; it would be like a wind, something, dark and chill, breathing upon him and he stopping, grave, quiet, alert, thinking *What? What is it?* Then he would know; he could feel the other entering the house, and he would let his held breath go quiet and easy, a profound exhalation, his heart quiet too) in the garden
35-37	she ~~had~~ thot about that kiss last summer, *so that's it. That's the way it is* ~~a little disappointed but~~ bludgeoned	13-14	she thought about that first kiss back in the summer: *So that's it. That's what love is,* bludgeoned
38	unbowed,) because he knew that Sutpen was now in the house, ~~was—~~	15	unbowed)—maybe
Page 150 [149]			
1	maybe		
1	himself ⟨still,⟩ thinking *My God I am young* 'Maybe	16	himself *Maybe*
2-3	better: maybe he knew that it was coming, maybe he told himself *He*	17-18	better: *He*
4	*the door* so	19	*the room:* so
4-5	smiling and turned her by the elbows~~/gently~~ easy and gentle until	20-22	smiling now, and took her by the elbows and turned her, easy and gentle, until
6	day and he	24-25	day, with maybe the feel of the flat of his hand light and momentary upon her behind. And he
7-8	out and they just looked at one another for a moment with no word said and then they turned and walked together down to the stable, and maybe	26-29	out, and they looked at one another for a while with no word said and then turned and walked together through the garden, across the lot and into the stable, where maybe
9	saddled their own horses, had them saddled when the house	30-31	saddled the two horses themselves and waited until the house
10-11	saddlebags, and they mounted and rode away." He stopped talking. That	31-33	saddlebags. And maybe he didn't even say then, 'But he sent no word to me?' " Shreve ceased. That
		Page 334	
11-12	stopped, just as for	1	stopped, since for
12	begun, just as it	2	begun, since it

CHAPTER VIII

MANUSCRIPT		BOOK	
12-13	(and probably neither of them knew) which	2-3	(and possibly neither of them scious of the distinction) whic
13	talking: so	4	talking. So
14	horses ⟨thru the dark⟩ over the frozen ~~ruts~~ December ruts of that Xmas eve;	5-6	horses through the dark over frozen December ruts of that Christmas Eve:
14-19	just 2, Charles-Shreve and Henry-Quentin ~~with Henry not thinking even yet~~ *~~He must have known or at least suspected; that's why he did has acted as he has, why he did not answer my letters last summer or write to Judith; why he has never actually asked her to marry him but~~* ⟨~~with the 2 of them both thinking that Henry that~~⟩ ~~with Henry thinking~~ *He (~~meaning~~ his father) has destroyed us all; not He (meaning Bon) must have known or at least suspected* ~~all the time~~ with the 2 of them	7-8	just two—Charles-Shreve and Quentin-Henry, the two of the
24	another and then turned without a word and walked	16	another for a while without a then walked
25	saddled their horses, but believing that Henry had taken	17-18	saddled the horses, but that H had just taken
26-27	true since he now must have understood with complete despair his whole relation and attitude	19-21	true, because he must have n understood with complete desp secret of his whole attitude
27-28	moment a year and 1/4 ago when he had first seen Bon; he	21-22	moment when he had seen him and a quarter ago; he
28	not, refused to,	23	not, had to refuse to,
30-31	with branches of holly and mistletoe and bowls	27-28	with sprigs of holly thrust ben the knockers on the doors and mistletoe hanging from the ch deliers and bowls
32-33	River landing[?] to wait until the steamboat put in.	31	River and the steamboat.
		Page 335	
34-35	ball: and the 2 of them, perhaps even in the cold, standing	1-2	ball, but not for them: the two them in the dark and the cold s ing
36	that hiatus, that suspension,	4-5	that probation, that suspension
37-38	which, ~~would be like death to him to find out.~~ so	7	which, so

MANUSCRIPT		BOOK	
38	him	8	him to learn. So it was four
Page 151 [150]			
1	to find out. So it was the 4		
2	before, whose entire ~~cosmo metropolitan~~ cosmopolitan	10	before (whose entire cosmopolitan
2-3	the University, consisted	11	the school, consisted
3	one trip to	12	one or two trips to
3	father, and	12-13	father to buy live stock or slaves) and
3-5	now;—~~4 of them who sat in that dark room of baroque yet fusty magnificence which Shreve had imagined and which was probably true enough~~ Henry	13	now—Henry
6	but who [illegible word] according to Shreve and Quentin did not resist Henry for	15-16	but who, according to Shreve and Quentin, did not resist Henry's dictum and design for
7	Henry was going to do because he ~~did~~ had long before realized	17-18	Henry intended to do because he had long since realized
9	had imagined and	21	had invented and
13-14	forgetting which Shreve and Quentin had imagined and	27-28	forgetting, whom Shreve and Quentin had likewise invented and
16	with ~~my son?~~ him?' and laughing	32	with him' and then sat laughing
		Page 336	
17-30	have—	1-3	have, who did not even have to answer at all either Yes or No.—Four of them there, in that room in New Orleans in 1860, just

And Bon may have taken Henry to
call on the octoroon mistress and the
child, as Mr Compson said, but
neither Quentin nor Shreve believed
that it would have had the effect that
Mr Compson seemed to believe it
had; Quentin did not even tell Shreve
what Mr Compson thot about that,
perhaps he himself had not even been
listening when Mr Compson said
what he said about it, perhaps at that
moment on the gallery at home on
that September p.m. Quentin took
that in stride just as Shreve himself
would have taken it if Quentin had
told him, since both he and Quentin
believed—and were probably right
in this too—that the octoroon and

MANUSCRIPT   BOOK

child would have been to Henry only
something else about Bon to be, not
envied exactly, but aped if that had
been possible, if there had been time
and peace to ape it in—peace not
between men of the same race and
nation but between two ~~young
embattled spirits and and~~ young
embattled spirits and the fact with
which they were mutually embattled,
since neither Charles nor Henry
anymore than Shreve and Quentin
were not the first young men to look
upon a war as tho it had been created
for the sole aim of settling youth's
private difficulties or discontent.

---

4 of them there ~~just as it~~ in that
room ⟨in New Orleans in 1860⟩ just

	MANUSCRIPT		BOOK
31-32	have, ~~taken Henry to call on~~ probably	5	have, probably
32-33	Compson ~~believed~~ said, tho neither ~~of them belie~~ Shreve	6-7	Compson said, though neither Shreve
35-36	not even been listening when Mr Compson ~~told him~~ said what he said about the visit;	10-11	not been listening when Mr Compson related it that evening at home;
36	gallery at home that September p.m. Quentin	12-13	gallery in the hot September twilight Quentin
40	nation [The sentence—interrupted by pp. *152-153*, which were inserted during revision—is picked up at p. *154*, line 1.]	19-28	nation but peace between two young embattled spirits and the incontrovertible fact which embattled them, since neither Henry and Bon, anymore than Quentin and Shreve, were the first young men to believe (or at least apparently act on the assumption) that wars were sometimes created for the sole aim of settling youth's private difficulties and discontents.

Page 152 [150-a]

1   so now

                                    "So the old dame asked Henry that one question and then sat there laughing at him, so he knew then, they both knew then. And so now

Page 337

9	have managed to	9	have contrived to
18	know ~~to pull the do~~ make	26	know to make

MANUSCRIPT		BOOK	
20-22	[20-35 PASTED IN: fortunate young man? With most of us, even when we are lucky enough to get our revenge, we must pay for it, some-times in actual dollars. While you are not only in a position to get your revenge, clear your mother's name, but ~~you are in a position to be paid for it in cash~~ the balm	27-31	fortunate young man? With most of us, even when we are lucky enough to get our revenge, we must pay for it, sometimes in actual dollars. While you are not only in a position to get your revenge, clear your mother's name, but the balm

Page 338

MANUSCRIPT		BOOK	
25	saying 'What do you mean?' ~~because he knew~~ and	2	saying *What do you mean?* and
26-27	than that, as lagniappe is it was, this	5-6	than this, than the revenge, as lagniappe to the revenge as it were, this
27	this prairie ~~bloom~~ flower which might as well bloom for a day in	6-8	this scentless prairie flower which will not be missed and which might as well bloom in
29	would hear him moving.	10-11	would just hear the feet moving.
31	'Help! Help!' then just screaming	14-15	'Help! Help! He—!' then just screaming,
32	could wrench his fingers free of the pistol and	16-17	could free his fingers of the pistol, and
35	obeyed, to sit in the righted	21-22	obeyed, who got him back into the righted
35-36	desk] and it the	23	desk; the
36-37	but only to half lie there, ~~dabbing at his face with a handkerchief~~ nursing	24	but instead to half lie there, nursing
37-38	handkerchief ~~and saying 'I was wrong. I misunderstood. I ask your pardon~~ while Bon looked down	25	handkerchief while Bon stood looking down
39-40	lawyer sitting back a little and dabbing the handkerchief at his face and saying, 'I	28-29	lawyer, sitting back now, dabbing the handkerchief at his cheek now: 'I
40-41	misunderstood. I ask your pardon.' and Bon 'Granted. ~~Either one you like~~ ⟨As you wish⟩. I will accept an apology or a bullet, either one you prefer.' and	29-32	misunderstood your feeling about the matter. I ask your pardon' and Bon: 'Granted. As you wish. I will accept either an apology or a bullet, as you prefer' and
42	a little red still on his cheek,	32-33	a faint fading red in his cheek,

Page 153 [150-b]   *Page 339*

MANUSCRIPT		BOOK	
1-2	my ~~nr er~~ unfortunate misconception.—	2	my unfortunate misconception—

CHAPTER VIII

MANUSCRIPT

BOOK

2	not) I would

2 not) I would

3-4 not) I would still have to decline
your offer. I would

3 pistols.' and Bon, 'Nor knives or
rapiers either?' and

5-6 pistols' and Bon: 'Nor with knives
or rapiers too?' and

3 smooth, easy:

6 smooth and easy:

5 the pistol lax in his hand, thinking

9 the lax pistol, thinking

5-6 *But just with pistols and knives and
rapiers.*

10 *But only with knives or pistols or
rapiers.*

6-7 *him just as I would a snake.*

11-12 *him with no more compunction than I
would a snake or a man who cuckolded
me.*

7 he was lying in the corps hospital in
Corinth

13-15 he—he—(Listen,'' Shreve said, cried.
''It would be while he would be lying
in a bedroom of that private house
in Corinth

8-9 well and the letter ~~could come from
his mother about how the lawyer had
gone to Texas or Mexico at last~~
from the octoroon [MARGIN: (maybe
even the one that enclosed hers and
the child's picture)] finally reached
him wailing

16-19 well two years later and the letter
from the octoroon (maybe even the
one that contained the photograph
of her and the child) finally over-
taking him, wailing

10-11 Mexico at last and that his mother
had vanished also and that more than
likely the lawyer had murdered her
in order to steal the money,

20-23 Mexico or somewhere at last and
that she (the octoroon) could not find
his mother either and so without
doubt the lawyer had murdered her
before he stole the money,

11-12 to die or vanish and leave her un-
provided for.—Yes, the old dame
sitting there laughing and laughing

24-25 to flee or get themselves killed
without providing for her at all.)—
Yes, they knew now. And Jesus,

Page 154 [151] [picking up from p. *151*,
line 40]

1-6 but between two young embattled
spirits and the incontrovertible fact
which embattled them, since neither
Henry and Bon, anymore than Quentin
and Shreve, were the first young
men to believe (or at least apparently
go on the assumption) that a war had
been created for the sole aim of
settling youth's private difficulties
or discontents:
  ''So the old dame asked Henry
that one question and then sat there
laughing at him and so he knew then,
they both knew then. And Jesus,

335

MANUSCRIPT		BOOK	
7-8	know, ~~that maybe if one of the two~~ because ~~he~~ as far as he knew he had never ⟨~~tho every~~⟩ had any father [MARGIN: tho everybody else at least used to have one,] that had just been created	27-28	know, who as far as he knew had never had any father but had been created
10-11	bread as tho he had never existed, that no one had taken	31-32	bread—two people neither of whom had taken
11-13	him and no one had suffered pain in borning him, that maybe if one of the two of them had told him none	33	him or suffered pain and travail in borning him—
		Page 340	
		1-2	who perhaps if one of the two had only told him the truth, none
13-14	have happened; that there was Henry who was told it by both of them while he, Bon, was told it by neither.	2-5	have come to pass; while there was Henry who had father and security and contentment and all, yet was told the truth by both of them while he (Bon) was told by neither.
16-19	enough force and passion to blow him out of the house where he had been born and all the way to New Orleans where he had to believe and yet even tho he had to believe he still could not turn around and go back home;	8-12	enough of strength to repudiate home and blood in order to champion his defiance, and in which championing he proved his contention to be the false one and was more than ever interdict against returning home;
19	carry, that had been born	12	carry, born
20	long family of	13	long invincible line of
20	in the country in North	14	in provincial North
21	with this question of incest that all	14-16	with incest, incest of all things that might have been reserved for him, that all
21	training rebelled at, in	16-17	training had to rebel against on principle, and in
22	knew that heredity nor training either was going to help him: so	17-18	knew that neither incest nor training was going to help him solve it. So
23	streets and at last	19-20	streets that night and at last
25	days and Henry said 'You shall not! Shall not!'' and it	22	days, and Henry said, 'You shall not. Shall not' and then it
30-31	that summer and then that fall while Lincoln got elected president of the U.S. and then they held that Alabama	29-30	that winter and then that spring with Lincoln elected and the Alabama
32	and one day the ~~paper~~ telegraph	32-33	and the telegraph
		Page 341	
33-35	and Bon and Henry maybe knowing	2-5	and Henry and Bon already decided

MANUSCRIPT		BOOK	
	that they would go, would have gone anyway even if they had never laid eyes on one another but after all you dont waste a war;—		to go without having to consult one another, who would have gone anyway even if they had never seen one another but certainly now, because after all you dont waste a war—
35-36	say 'But must you do it?	6	say, 'But must you marry her?
36	me.	8	me, myself, himself.

Page 155 [152]

2	himself. If	10-11	himself. But he didn't do it. If
5	a servant	16	a nigger servant
6-7	say ~~'Yes.--I see.--But you will have to give me time to get used to it. You are my older brother; you can do that much for me.~~ But	17	say, 'But
8	her.' and Bon would say 'All	18	her' and Bon: 'All
9-10	pride about anything except love: and	21-22	pride and honor about almost anything except love, and
10	see. But	22	see. I understand. But
11	me.'; think	24	me.' Think
12	and ~~said~~ ⟨had to say⟩ he did, and Henry that knew	25-26	and had to say, pretend, he did; and Henry who knew
13	didn't, and it was Xmas again and then 1861 and ~~Judith hadn't heard~~ they	27-28	didn't. Then it was Christmas again, then 1861, and they
14	know where	29	know for sure where
15-16	they ~~were~~ had been waiting for that and so	32	they had been waiting for that. So

Page 342

17	war begins,	2	war starts,
19	at a guard rail above the churning river and	4-5	at the rail again above the churning water, and
20	dukes. There was a Lorraine	7	dukes! There was that Lorraine
22	hurt!' [MARGIN: they were still husband and wife. They were still alive.'] and then he would say again,	9-11	hurt! They were still husband and wife. They were still alive. They still loved!' then again,
25	signed into the company and	15-16	signed the company roster and
26	would come into the quarters at night	18	would steal into the quarters by night
28-31	girls goodbye, and they fell in ~~with it and went on; maybe your old man was right this time and they did think that~~	21-23	girls farewell and started for the front. "Jesus,

MANUSCRIPT   BOOK

~~maybe the war would~~ with it and
went on to the war.
    "~~Because Bon would~~ Jesus,

32-33   another. He would know; ~~he would~~   26   another. Maybe
        ~~watch~~ maybe

34-35   because he knew that he did not   27-28   because he did not know what he
        know himself what he was going to   himself was going to do, that he
        do. ~~So all he had to do~~ until   would not know until

36   all along that that's what it would 30-31   all the time what it would be, so he
        be. So   didn't have to bother about himself
                                                     and so

38   training saying *No.*   33   training
                                              Page 343
                                              1   which said *No.*

38   *not;* maybe   1-2   *not.* Maybe

38   be lying   2   be under fire now, with
Page 156 [153]
1   under fire now with

1   rushing past and exploding and them   3   rushing and rumbling past overhead
                                                      and bursting and them

2   lots that have   5-6   lots in the world who have

4   it but   8   it. But

5-6   Bon would watch him and listen to   10-11   Bon watching him and listening to
        him and think *It's*   him and thinking *It's*

6-7   *I have not decided without*   12   *I am undecided without*

8   *and say You*   14   *and tell me, You*

9   did hope that the war   15-16   did think maybe the war

12-13   now because he knew now that even   20-22   now, revenge or love or all, since he
        revenge would not and could not   knew now that revenge could not
        compensate him; maybe   compensate him nor love assuage.
                                                      Maybe

14-15   even about knowing what it was that   25-26   even that he didn't know yet what he
        he was going to do: and it   was going to do. Then it

16-19   that too, maybe without even thinking 27-31   that either, talking again as they
        about that since they didn't have time   moved along in column, the officer
        to think much about the war and Bon   dropping back alongside the file in
        didn't care about that either; moving   which the private marched and Henry
        toward Shiloh and they would talk   crying again, holding his desperate
        then too as they marched in column   and urgent voice down to undertone:
        and Henry would say 'Dont   'Dont

MANUSCRIPT		BOOK	
19-20	him with that expression that could have been smiling and say 'Suppose	32-33	him for a moment with that expression which could have been smil-
			Page 344
		1	ing: 'Suppose
22-23	panting and Bon watching him and Bon would say, 'I	4	panting while Bon watched him: 'I
23	now, going into battle I	5	now; going into battle, charging, I
24-27	Henry would say 'Stop! Stop!' and Bon would watch him, saying—'and with the artillery[?] and the musketry[?] and all, and I will be right out in front of you with my back toward you—' and Henry would say 'Stop! Stop!' panting and Bon watching him and saying—'and	6-8	Henry panting, 'Stop! Stop!' and Bon watching him with that faint thin expression about the mouth and eyes: '—and
28	might not have struck me at the exact instant or	10-11	might have struck me at the exact second you pulled your trigger, or
29	looking at	12	looking, glaring at
29-30	face, saying 'Stop!	13-14	face and the knuckles of the hand on his musket butt white, saying, panting, 'Stop!
30	Stop!' and then	15	Stop!' Then
31-32	and they had to fall back from Pittsburg Landing and after a time Bon found Henry where he lay on the ground [MARGIN: Henry saves Bon. H says 'I wish it was me here. That would settle it.' Bon suggests that Henry leave him to die to settle it.] and stooped	16-32	and the brigade falling back from Pittsburgh Landing—And listen,'' Shreve cried; ''wait, now; wait!'' (glaring at Quentin, panting himself, as if he had had to supply his shade not only with a cue but with breath to obey it in): ''Because your old man was wrong here, too! He said it was Bon who was wounded, but it wasn't. Because who told him? Who told Sutpen, or your grandfather either, which of them it was who was hit? Sutpen didn't know because he wasn't there, and your grandfather wasn't there either because that was where he was hit too, where he lost his arm. So who told them? Not Henry, because his father never saw Henry but that one time and maybe they never had time to talk about wounds and besides to talk about wounds in the Confederate army in 1865 would be like coal miners

talking about soot; and not Bon,
because Sutpen never saw him at all
because he was dead—it was not Bon,
it was Henry; Bon that found Henry
at last and stooped

32   struggled, and said 'Let

33   struggled, saying, 'Let

Page 345

33-35 want it' and Henry lying there
       struggling and Bon said 'Maybe if
       you would say you do want it, I will
       not go back to her.' and Henry lay
       there with his shirt red at the
       shoulder and his teeth

2-7   want me to go back to her' and
      Henry lay there struggling and
      panting, with the sweat on his face
      and his teeth bloody inside his
      chewed lip, and Bon said, 'Say you
      do want me to go back to her. Maybe
      then I wont do it. Say it' and Henry
      lay there struggling, with the fresh
      red staining through his shirt and
      his teeth

35-37 face and Bon held his arms and
       raised him onto his shoulder——"
            Two

8-9   face until Bon held his arms and
      lifted him onto his back——"
           First, two

38   living c̶o̶l̶d̶ chill.

11   living cold.

Page 157 [154]
1   it; Quentin

12-13 it, though not thirty feet away was
      bed and warmth. Quentin

2-5   down. Even with the coat he w̶o̶u̶l̶d̶
      (Quentin) would have felt the cold
      more than Shreve, who perhaps would
      not have been very uncomfortable in
      it with his bare arms and torso. Yet
      they both bore it as tho in some f̶l̶a̶
      deliberate flagellant e̶x̶a̶l̶t̶a̶t̶i̶o̶n̶
      exaltation of m̶i̶ physical

15-17 down. They did not retreat from the
      cold. They both bore it as though in
      deliberate flagellant exaltation of
      physical

6-7   since it was '63 and then '64 and

19-20 since it was '64 and then '65 and

8   swept ahead not

22   swept onward not

10-13 of inferior numbers and failing food
      and ammunition but because the
      generals of it d̶i̶d̶ ̶n̶o̶t̶ ̶l̶i̶v̶e̶ ̶l̶o̶n̶g̶ ̶e̶n̶o̶u̶g̶h̶
      t̶o̶ ̶l̶e̶a̶r̶n̶ either should never have
      been generals, were generals not
      thru training or competence but by
      the divine right of an absolute caste
      system, or

26-31 of superior numbers and failing
      ammunition and stores, but because
      of generals who should not have been
      generals, who were generals not
      through training in contemporary
      methods or aptitude for learning
      them, but by the divine right to say
      'Go there' conferred upon them by
      an absolute caste system; or

14   fight the massed cautious battles of
      the day and time since

32   fight massed cautious accretionary
      battles, since

MANUSCRIPT		BOOK	
		Page 346	
16	captured steamboats with	2	captured warships with
18	night would	6-7	night and with a handful of men would
19	a $1,000,000 enemy ⟨supply⟩ depot and	7-8	a million dollar garrison of enemy supplies and
20	death: and the 2 of them, according	9-10	death—two, four, now two again, according
21-22	know or care what he was going to do, and the	12	know what he was going to do, the
22	he was going to do and could not yet reconcile	13	he would have to do yet could not reconcile
24	that [MARGIN: fierce ruthless defiant convinced humbled] ~~unhappy~~ shade	15-16	that condemned and excommunicated shade
26-27	upon. So it would be like this; Shreve may have still been talking or he may not have; it would not have mattered: the two	19	upon—the two
29	ears, and Quentin,	22	ears; Quentin,
30	suitable suit which	24	suitable clothing which
31	thin for	25	thin and vain for
32-37	it:	27-29	it:

"Then it was '64; they were in Carolina ~~what was left of the army~~ and what was left of the army with nothing left now but the ability to walk backward slow and stubborn and to endure ~~shelling~~ musketry and shelling; maybe they didn't even miss the shoes and overcoats and food anymore and so that was the reason Bon could write about the captured stove polish like he did in the letter when he finally wrote to Judith, when he finally found out what he was going to do and

(——the winter of '64 now, the army retreated across Alabama, into Georgia; now Carolina was just at their backs and Bon,

Page 158 [155]

1-2	"——the winter of '63 now, and the army of the West retreated across Alabama and into Georgia, and across Georgia toward Carolina, and Bon,		
3	will ~~fall back upon Lee in front of~~ make	31	*will make*

341

MANUSCRIPT		BOOK	
4	will ~~all be annihilated~~ at least	32	*will at least*
5-6	remember how that regiment that his father was now colonel of was in Longstreet's ~~army~~ corps,	33	*re-*
		Page 347	
		1-2	*membered, how that Jefferson regiment of which his father was now colonel was in Longstreet's corps,*
8	chance: so	4-5	*chance. So*
9	he intended to do; maybe	6	*he wanted to do. Maybe*
9-10	second, *My God, I am still young: even after these 4 years I am still young* but	7-8	*second, 'My God, I am still young; even after these four years I am still young' but*
10	second he thot that because	8	*second, because*
12	*alive in order*	11-12	*alive and able in order*
13	*for ground at the best bargain moment,*	12-13	*for the largest amount of ground at its bargain price,*
15	*again':* and then it was '64 and	16	*again:' Then it was '65 and*
16	nothing left now	17	*nothing remaining now*
18	anymore and so that was the reason why	19-20	*any more now and that was why*
19-21	letter when he finally wrote to Judith, when he finally knew what he intended to do and [20-31 PASTED IN: told Henry at last and ~~maybe~~ Henry	21-22	*letter to Judith when he finally knew what he was going to do at last and told Henry and Henry*
23	the repudiation	25	*the irrevocable repudiation*
24	he even ~~qu~~ could quit	27	*he could even quit*
26-27	there but we, the 3 of us:—(remembering his father) the 4 of us' and	31	*there, but we, the three—no: four of us. And*
27-28	will be together where we all belong since ~~if~~ even	32	*will all be together where we belong, since even*
		Page 348	
29-30	memory and	2	*memory. And*
30-31	not ~~need~~ need to think about love and fornication and	3-4	*not need to remember love and fornication, and*
31	there and	5	*there. And*
31-32	this] then it	5	*this, it*
32-33	of '64 and	6	*of '65 and*
35	than that which they had come but to Bon not	9-10	*than the distance they had come; the distance between them and the end a good deal less far. But to Bon it was not*

CHAPTER VIII

MANUSCRIPT		BOOK	
36-37	regiment where his father was, between him and the hour, the moment and he thinking *He*	12	*regiment, between him and the hour, the moment: He*

Page 159 [156]

1	*again:*—⟨Then April and May in Carolina and them still⟩ Walking	15	*again.' Then March in Carolina and still the walking*
2-3	was all finished now and	18	*was finished now, and*
3	they ever expected to hear from the northward was defeat: and one	18	*they expected to hear from the North was defeat. Then one*
4	officer; maybe he knew that Lee had detached troops	19-20	*officer; he would have known, heard, that Lee had detached some troops*
5	them) he saw	21-22	*them; perhaps he even knew the names and numbers of the regiments before they arrived) he saw*
5	that time Sutpen did not see him; maybe	23-24	*that first time Sutpen actually did not see him, maybe*
7	situation: and for	26	*situation. Then for*
7-11	the grim implacable face in which he saw his own and in which he saw recognition now but absolutely no alteration of expression at all in it. And so that was all; there was nothing further now; that was all of it: and maybe his face had that expression again that you might have glanced at and called smiling and him thinking *I*	26-32	*the expressionless and rocklike face, at the pale boring eyes in which there was no flicker, nothing, the face in which he saw his own features, in which he saw recognition, and that was all. That was all, there was nothing further now; perhaps he just breathed once quietly, with on his own face that expression which might at a glance have been called smiling while he thought, 'I*

Page 349

12	now: and	1-2	*now and at last. And*
14-15	warmth anyway [15-36 PASTED IN: because	4-5	*warmth at least because*
15-16	remain eaten up, Bon said 'Henry' and he said 'It	5-6	*remain consumed, that Bon said, 'Henry' and said, 'It*
17	backward.	8-9	*backward slowly for a reason, for the sake of honor and what's left of pride.*
18	to tell us;	11	*to notify us;*
19	land or ~~any-way~~ any way to make food but	12-13	*land nor any way to make food, but*
22	to and live and flourish.	16	*to and flourish.*
23	that dont know nor care	18	*that doesn't care*

MANUSCRIPT		BOOK	
24	left still will decline	20	*left, will still decline*
24-27	die but will probably be out in the woods grubbing at roots and such' [MARGIN:—the old mindless sentient meat that dont even know any difference between despair and victory, Henry] and that was when Henry began to say *Thank God. Thank God* panting and saying *Thank God* and he said, 'Dont	21-26	*die, but will be out in the woods, moving and seeking where just will and endurance could not move it, grubbing for roots and such—the old mindless sentient undreaming meat that doesn't even know any difference between despair and victory, Henry.' And then Henry would begin to say 'Thank God. Thank God' panting and saying 'Thank God,' saying, 'Dont*
27-30	it.' and Bon said, 'You authorize me? You give me permission?' and Henry said, 'Why ask my permission? You are the oldest': and Bon said, (and he would have that expression that might have been called smiling): 'He	27-29	*it' and Bon: 'You authorize me? As her brother you give me permission?' and Henry: 'Brother? Brother? You are the oldest: why do you ask me?' and Bon: 'No. He*
31	Henry?' and Henry said, 'Write. Write': and so Bon wrote that letter,	31-32	*Henry?' and Henry: 'Write. Write.' So Bon wrote the letter,*

Page 350

| 32 | letter, they | 1 | *letter. They* |
| 35-36 | was, not the will, just the ability to endure; they walked backward in Carolina now and it got to be April and May and one night when they had stopped] | 5-8 | *was not the will but just the ability, the grooved habit to endure. Then one night they had stopped again since Sherman had stopped again, and an orderly came along the bivouac line and found Henry at last and said,* |

Page 160 [157]

1	again because Sherman had stopped again, an orderly found Henry and said,		
2-4	tent.' '' Shreve ceased again, standing bearlike and shapeless, looking at the delicate almost sullen youth who sat in the chair beyond the table, in his thin suit shaking slowly and steadily with the cold. "And	9-10	*tent.')* "And
7-8	just 45 or 50 years of ~~waiting and~~ despair, and you,	14-16	with forty-five years of hate like forty-five years of raw meat and all Clytie had was just forty-five or fifty years of despair and waiting; and you,
8	with: and	17	with. And
9-12	trouble was not ~~aur~~[?] ~~or even fidel~~[?] ~~distrust but terror, fear~~ ⫽ʋ-	18-19	trouble wasn't anger nor even distrust; it was terror,

344

MANUSCRIPT		BOOK	
	He ceased again; Quentin had not moved, still brooding[?] apparently over the open letter which by[?] lay on the open book on the table before him. distrust, but terror,		
16-17	took the from his coat the	26-27	took from his pocket the
21	and hit her like	33	and knocked Clytie down with her fist like
		Page 351	
23	of rags	3-4	of clean rags
24-25	saw that it was not rage but terror and	6-7	saw it was not rage but terror, and
26	upstairs for	9	up there for
27	the words	10	the actual words
27-28	secret, and so you didn't know how you knew but all of a sudden you knew nevertheless she told you or	11	secret; nevertheless she told you, or
30	listener; tho perhaps	14	listener. Perhaps
31	either tho doubtless he	15	either, though possibly he
32	there; they	16	there. They
32	Carolina 46 years	17	Carolina and the time was forty-six years
32-33	not 4 now but compounded further still since both	18-19	not even four now but compounded still further, since now both
33-34	were Charles Bon at one and the same time, it going like this: *It would be about 9 o'clock at night, the scattered bivouac*	19-22	were Bon, compounded each of both yet either neither, smelling the very smoke which had blown and faded away forty-six years ago from the *bivouac*
35	*the* [MARGIN: gaunt and ragged] *men*	22-23	*the gaunt and ragged men*
37	*the glow and gleam perhaps of*	26-27	*the flicker and gleam of*
Page 161 [158]			
1-2	*fires in front for each one fire in their rear and*	28-29	*fires for each Confederate one, and*
3	*outposts waited in the dark also,*	30	*outposts watched the darkness also,*
4	*the other's officers, the challenge passing on and a from picket to picket and dying*	31-32	*the challenge of the other's officers passing from post to post and dying*
		Page 352	
8	*you going?*	3	*you fellers going?*

CHAPTER VIII

MANUSCRIPT		BOOK	
11	*air waiting.*	6	*air.*
13	*and reaching the fire,*	9-10	*and so reaches the fire at last,*
14	*log at last with*	10	*log, with*
14-15	*speech: Sutpen? I'm looking for Sutpen, where one rises and says, Here; it is Henry. He*	11-12	*speech: 'Sutpen? I'm looking for Sutpen' until Henry sits up and says, 'Here.' He*
16	*because of his ~~y~~ age 4 years ago he*	13-14	*because he had not quite got his height when the four years began, he*
17-18	*by 20 pounds as he will probably be a few years after he outlives the*	15-16	*by thirty pounds as he probably will be a few years after he has outlived the*
21	*him; he walks alone, along a rutted road now,*	20-21	*him. Instead, he walks alone through the darkness along a rutted road,*
22	*have already passed over it, and*	22	*have passed over it that afternoon, and*
28	*wall, and comes*	31	*wall. He (Henry) comes*
		Page 353	
31	*it now but*	2	*it here and now, but*
31-32	*He is just facing[?]it at salute and*	2-3	*He just salutes the braided cuff and*
Page 162 [159]			
2	*tent and embrace*	7-8	*tent, where they embrace*
3	*moved, knew that he was*	8	*moved, was*
5	*between his hands,*	12	*between both hands,*
7-9	*the candle. They are alone and will not be disturbed thru the kindness of Henry's colonel. —You*	14-17	*the table, in the chairs reserved for officers, the table (an open map lies on it) and the candle between them. —You*
12	*word about it.*	23	*word somehow that Charles has written her.*
13	*natural: that*	24-25	*natural that their father should know of his and Bon's decision: that*
14	*instant in all of time.*	27-28	*instant, after a period of four years, out of all time.*
17-18	*merely looks at his father* [MARGIN: the 2 of them in leaf faded grey,]—*a* ~~crude tent~~ *a single*	32-33	*merely stares at his father—the two of them in leaf-faded gray, a single*
		Page 354	
20	*to start again: yet in a second it*	3-4	*to commence again: yet in a second tent candle gray and all are gone and it*

346

CHAPTER VIII

MANUSCRIPT

BOOK

21-23 heavy table ~~/ You are going to let him marry Judith, Henry.~~ on which sat the 3 photographs of himself and his mother and sister, his

6-8 heavy carved rosewood one at home with the group photograph of his mother and sister and himself sitting upon it, his

27 answer; it

13 answer. It

28 it ~~was~~ is victory or defeat that he

15 it be victory or defeat which he

34 food on

23 food out of but

Page 163 [160]

1 but

2-3 care about whether it was defeat or victory that

26 care if it was defeat or victory, that

3 woods grubbing ~~at r~~ up roots and such—Yes.

27 woods and fields, grubbing up roots and weeds.—Yes.

4-5 or no brother, I have decided. He

28-29 or not, I have decided. I will. I will. —He

7-8 years, and I am decided. —He

31-33 years to decide in. I will. I am going to. —He

Page 355

8-11 mother was a Spanish woman. After he was born I learned that she was not pure Spaniard but that she had some negro blood.
It might be said easily (and possibly credibly) that Henry does not remember leaving the tent, remembers nothing more until dawn. But he does. He

1-5 mother had been a Spanish woman. I believed him; it was not until after he was born that I found out that his mother was part negro.
Nor did Henry ever say that he did not remember leaving the tent. He

11 the canvas again

5-6 the entrance again

14-15 than 10 o'clock. W[?] he

10 than eleven oclock, he

20-21 chill April stars,

19 chill vivid stars of early spring,

22 do, because

21-22 do. Because

27 undernourishment, thru the

29 undernourishment; the

29 cloak, enough light for Henry to

33 cloak; enough light for him to

30 to see Henry's face

33 to dis-

Page 356

1 tinguish his face

31-33 speak, he just rises and puts the cloak about him and goes to the fire and begins to kick it into a blaze when Henry says, —Wait.

2-6 speak, demand to know who it is: he merely rises and puts the cloak about his shoulders and approaches the smouldering fire and is kicking it into a blaze when Henry speaks: —Wait.

MANUSCRIPT

34   *pauses, looks at him;*

Page *164* [161]

1   *—You are cold now. You will be cold. You have not even been to bed. Here. He*

4   *Yes. I'll*

7-9   *weary monotonous*[?] *backward walking will begin,* ~~with~~ *facing annihilation and falling back upon defeat, tho not yet; there will be a little time: and they sit side by side upon the log, the one wrapped in*

9-11   *blanket; perhaps Henry has already thot, And I knew how this would be too.*
        —So

11-12 *incest, that you cannot bear, Henry, Bon says. Henry does not answer.*

13   *word? Bon says. He did not tell you*

15   *it of me. I would have said,*

16-20 *me. He did not have to tell you that I am a nigger, Henry.*
      Now Henry speaks.
      —But not now?
      —No. What else can I do?
      —Think of her.

BOOK

7   *pauses and looks at Henry;*

9-11   *—You will be cold. You are cold now. You haven't been asleep, have you? Here.*
      He

13   *Yes. Take it. I'll*

17-19 *weary backward marching will begin, retreating from annihilation, falling back upon defeat, though not quite yet. There will be a little time yet for them to sit side by side upon the log in the making light of dawn, the one in*

21-23 *blanket; their voices are not much louder than the silent dawn itself:*
        —So

23-24 *incest, which you cant bear.*
      Henry doesn't answer

25   *word? He did not ask you*

28-29 *it, require it, of me. I would have offered it. I would have said,*

30-33 *me. He did not have to do this, Henry. He didn't need to tell you I am a nigger to stop me. He could have stopped me without that, Henry.*
      —No! Henry cries.—No! No! I will—I'll—

Page *357*

1-15   *He springs up; his face is working; Bon can see his teeth within the soft beard which covers his sunken cheeks, and the whites of Henry's eyes as though the eyeballs struggled in their sockets as the panting breath struggled in his lungs—the panting which ceased, the breath held, the eyes too looking down at him where he sat on the log, the voice now not much louder than an expelled breath:*
      —You said, could have stopped you. What do you mean by that?
      Now it is Bon who does not answer, who sits on the log looking at the face stooped above him. Henry

CHAPTER VIII

MANUSCRIPT

BOOK

says, still in that voice no louder than breathing:
—*But now? You mean you——*
—*Yes. What else can I do now? I gave him the choice. I have been giving him the choice for four years.*
—*Think of her.*

21   *have.* ⟨For 4 years. Of you and her. And of him.⟩ *Now*

16   *have. For four years. Of you and her. Now*

26-29   —*No. No. No.*
Henry does not look at Bon; it is Bon who watches Henry as he sits there in the cloak, gaunt-faced, un-shaven his face raised a little and turned toward the south; it is Bon who watches Henry with that expres-sion on his face which might be called smiling. He reaches beneath the blanket and *Henry's hand*

23-26   —*No, Henry says.*—*No. No. No.*
Now it is Bon who watches Henry; he can see the whites of Henry's eyes again as he sits looking at Henry with that expression which might be called smiling. His hand

Page 165 [162]
2-5   *now, Henry, he says.*
Henry looks at the pistol. Then he looks at Bon.
—*You are my brother, Henry says.*
—*No I'm not, Bon says. I'm*

29-33   *now, he says.*
Henry looks at the pistol; now he is not only panting, he is trembling; when he speaks now his voice is not even the exhalation, it is the suffused and suffocating inbreath itself:
—*You are my brother.*

Page 358
—*No I'm not. I'm*

6-14   *sister—unless you stop me, Henry.*
For a moment Henry looks at Bon. Then he grasps the pistol and jerks it free and springs up and stands facing Bon, the pistol in his hand, panting and panting: and Bon still was *sitting quiet on the log, still watching him with that expression that might be called smiling.*
—*Go on, Henry, he says. Do it now.*
—*No, Henry says.* He
He flings the pistol away, hurls it away; he stoops, panting, clutching Bon by both shoulders.
—*No, he says. No. No. No.*
—*You will*

2-15   *sister. Unless you stop me, Henry.*
Suddenly Henry grasps the pistol, jerks it free of Bon's hand stands so, [sic] the pistol in his hand, panting and panting; again Bon can see the whites of his inrolled eyes while he sits on the log and watches Henry with that faint expression about the eyes and mouth which might be smiling.
—*Do it now, Henry, he says.*
Henry whirls; in the same motion he hurls the pistol from him and stoops again, gripping Bon by both shoulders, panting.
—*You shall not! he says.*—*You shall not! Do you hear me?*
Bon does not move beneath the gripping hands; he sits motionless,

349

MANUSCRIPT

BOOK

with his faint fixed grimace; his
voice is gentler than that first breath
in which the pine branches begin to
move a little:
—You will

15   tried; Jesus,

16-17   tried. Jesus

17   gate; ~~and~~ side by side and it was
only then that Henry spurred

20-22   gate; side by side and it only then
that one of them ever rode ahead or
dropped behind and that only then
Henry spurred

18-21   pistol and said 'Dont you pass that
shadow, Charles' and Bon said 'I am
going to pass it, Henry' and Clytie
and Judith heard the shot and then
Henry's feet and then the door and
Henry said, 'Now you cant marry
him because I have just killed him':
and maybe

23-24   pistol; and Judith and Clytie heard
the shot, and maybe

21-23   yard then and Judith and Clytie and
Wash carried ~~him~~ Bon into the house
and up the stairs and laid him on the
bed and

25-26   yard and so he was there to help
Clytie and Judith carry him into the
house and lay him on the bed, and

24   before that closed door, holding in
her hand the metal

29   before the closed door, holding the
metal

25-26   but it had the ~~octoroon~~[?] ⟨octoroon⟩
and the boy.

31   but that of the octoroon and the kid.

Page 359

28   know. Dont you know? it was

2-5   know too. Dont you? Dont you,
huh?" He glared at Quentin, leaning
forward over the table now, looking
huge and shapeless as a bear in his
swaddling of garments. "Dont you
know? It was

30   I can say

8   I will have to say

33   this ice box and

11   this refrigerator and

CHAPTER IX

MANUSCRIPT

BOOK

4-7	it. You never could. You would have to be born there.'' "Al-right "Would		31-32	it. You would have to be born there.'' *Page 362*
			1	"Would
14	there but		13-14	there to finish up what she found she hadn't quite completed, but
16	dust; even now, the the [*sic*] chill wei pure weight		17-18	dust. Even now, with the chill pure weight
18	furnacelike)		20	furnace-breathed)
18-19	night; he could smell the old woman beside, he could smell		21-22	night. He could even smell the old woman in the buggy beside him, smell
19	which he		23	which (he
20	they reached the house that she had hidden a hatchet to break in the door.		24-25	they had reached the house) she had concealed a hatchet and a flashlight.
25	clumsy eagerness before		33	clumsy and fumbling and trembling eagerness (which he
				Page 363
			1-2	thought derived from terror, alarm, until he found that he was quite wrong) before
28	would: ''Now'' she		6-8	would, before the prescience of her desire and need could warn its consummation. "Now," she
31	"Now. This is it.'': and after the long		12-13	'Now. Now' and (as during the long
31	house it		14	house) it
32	he [MARGIN: stopped the buggy and] listened he might hear the galloping hoofs, that even so he might see		14-16	he stopped the buggy and listened, he might even hear the galloping hoofs; might even see
33	rider sweep across		16-17	rider rush across
Page 168 [165]				
2	home and found that		23	home to find that
2-3	even but with one more chance; who said At least I have life left but		23-24	even, though not absolutely all; who said *At least I have life left* but
5-6	him pass the rotting fishing camp cabin, watching him as he p from		28-29	him from
7-8	too; maybe		31	too. Maybe
9	mile to the spring and return to		33	mile and back to the spring to
				Page 364
10-11	God; this the one chance since		2-3	God—this the not-all, since

MANUSCRIPT		BOOK	
12	a while in	5	a time in
13	snow born New England air. She did	6	snowborn darkness. She (Miss Coldfield) did
13	gate; she said	7	gate. She said
16-17	do.''—''I do. Go back to town and go to bed,'' ~~He~~ he thot but did not say, looking at	10-12	do. I dont know what to do.'' ('I do,' he thought. 'Go back to town and go to bed.') But he did not say it. He looked at
17-18	gates now swung, wondering from which direction	14	gates swung now, wondering from what direction
19	pass; if some living tree that still lived or was gone now or if	16-19	pass alive; if some living tree which still lived and bore leaves and shed or if some tree gone, vanished, burned for warmth and food years ago now or perhaps just gone; or if
27	the drive	32	the tree-arched drive
		Page 365	
28	whimpered.	1	whimpered, in a kind of amazed self-pity.
33	someone else	9-10	someone or something else
34	umbrella; it	12	umbrella. It
Page 169 [166]			
1-2	could hear her breathing where she waited close against one of the gate posts while he led the horse from	12-14	could still hear her whimpering panting where she waited close beside one of the posts while he led the mare from
2-3	rein to a sapling tree in the choked and overgrown ditch.	15	rein about a sapling in the weed-choked ditch.
4-6	gate; he could hear her breathing now as they went up the rough tree-arched drive. ⟨where⟩ The darkness was intense and where she stumbled and grasped his arm. ''I	18-22	gate, still breathing in those whimpering pants as they walked on up the rutted tree-arched drive. The darkness was intense; she stumbled; he caught her. She took his arm, clutching it in a dead rigid hard grip as if her fingers, her hand, were a small mass of wire. ''I
7-8	stopped; he stopped too and turned, hearing her	24-25	stopped. He turned; he could not see her but he could hear her
8	and a rustling of cloth; then	26	and then a rustling of cloth. Then
10-11	heavy hot[?] nicked head on which his hand read rust.	29	heavy gapped rust-dulled blade.

MANUSCRIPT		BOOK	
		Page 366	
15	arm."	2	arm, I am trembling so bad."
19	place; he	9	place. He
20	child, when distances should seem long: so	10	child, a boy, when distances seem really long (so
21	long ⟨crowded⟩ mile of boyhood is less than a stone's throw: yet	11-12	long crowded mile of his boyhood becomes less than the throw of a stone) yet
23	words: *if we can just get to the house, get inside the house* telling	14-15	words: 'If we can just get to the house, get inside the house,' telling
24-25	breath: *I am not afraid. I just dont want to be here. I just dont want to know about whatever it is she keeps hidden in that house.* At last they reached it.	16-18	breath: 'I am not afraid. I just dont want to be here. I just dont want to know about whatever it is she keeps hidden in it.' But they reached it at last.
27-28	ragged section of sky with hot stars in it as tho the	22	ragged segment of sky with three hot stars in it as if the
29	tear; the dead	24	tear; now, almost beneath it, the dead
31	was hurrying beside	28	was trotting beside
31-32	yet at the same time clutching it with astonishing strength,	29	yet gripping it still with that lifeless and rigid strength;
		Page 367	
34-35	without being aware of it her own tense and alarmed[?] panting haste: ~~"Be careful~~ Wait.	1-2	without knowing it her own tense fainting haste: "Wait.
Page 170 [167]			
2	his hands and	6	his palms and
2-4	he thot, *Why, she's not afraid at all. It's something but it's not afraid,* feeling her ~~flee~~ flee	7-10	he thought, knew, said suddenly to himself, 'Why, she's not afraid at all. It's something. But she's not afraid,' feeling her flee
4	the ~~ver por~~ gallery and overtaking her where she stood now at the invisible door,	10-12	the gallery, overtaking her where she now stood beside the invisible front door,
6	hatchet."	14	hatchet. Break it."
14	the veranda, guiding himself with one hand on the wall,	25-26	the gallery, guiding himself by the wall,
16	to the first window.	28	to a window.
18	feeble woman or	31-32	feeble person—woman—or
		Page 368	
19	it.	1-2	it, that all he had to do now was to step through the vacant frame.

MANUSCRIPT		BOOK	
22	said; he did not whisper tho he	7	said. He did not whisper, though he
23	voice hollowly,	9	voice with hollow profundity,
23-24	door.'' He climbed over	10-11	door.''—'So now I shall have to go in,' he thought, climbing over
25	wall,	14	wall with his hand,
26	found a door and passed into the hall. It	15-18	found the door and passed through it. He would be in the hall now; he almost believed that he could hear Miss Coldfield breathing just beyond the wall beside him. It
28-30	He followed the wall still, past another angle; and he felt the door under his hand; it seemed to him that he could hear her whimpering	22-23	He went on; he felt the door under his hand at last and now he could hear Miss Coldfield's whimpering
30	he felt for	24	he fumbled for
30	the raked match	25	the scraped match
31	explosion; even before the puny light	25-26	explosion, a pistol; even before the puny following light
32-33	of sany[?] sanity roared silently in his head: *It's all right. If it was dang[?] ⟨danger⟩ they would not have struck the match* until he could move and turn and see	28-30	of sanity roared silently inside his skull: 'It's all right! If it were danger, he would not have struck the match!' Then he could move, and turned to see
35	one hand	33	one coffee-colored and doll-like hand
		Page 369	
35	but the match as	1	but watching the match as
Page 171 [168]			
2-3	saw the crude table then and the lamp on it as she lifted the chimney and lit the lamp.	3-6	saw then the square-ended saw chunk beside the wall and the lamp sitting upon it as she lifted the chimney and held the match to the wick.
5-6	of huge old fashioned keys,	10-11	of enormous old-fashioned iron keys,
7	entered: and	14	entered. And
8-9	said nothing to each other either, as tho Clytie had looked at Miss Coldfield and knew at once that	14-16	said no word to one another, as if Clytie had looked once at the other woman and knew that
12-13	away without pausing and	22-23	away and
13-14	he thot, *It must have been in the umbrella too with the axe*)	24-25	he thought, 'It must have been in the umbrella too along with the axe')
14-15	ran toward her again and Miss Coldfield turned on the stair and	26-27	ran after the other again, whereupon Miss Coldfield turned on the step and

CHAPTER IX

MANUSCRIPT

BOOK

16-18 would and turned and went on up the stairs. She lay on the [MARGIN: barren floor of the scaling and empty hall,] f̶l̶o̶o̶r̶, a small shapeless bundle of quite clean rags; when he stood over her he saw that her eyes were wide open and quite still; he thot *She is the one that owns the terror.*

28-33 would have, and turned and went on up the stairs. She (Clytie) lay on the bare floor of the scaling and empty hall like a small shapeless bundle of quiet [*sic*] clean rags. When he reached her he saw that she was quite conscious, her eyes wide open and calm; he stood above her, thinking, 'Yes. She is the one who owns the ter-

Page 370

1 ror.'

19-20 her, feeling some

3 her up, aware of some

24-25 done, him and Judith and me have paid it out.'' So he went up the stairs,

10-12 done, me and Judith and him have paid it out. You go and get her. Take her away from here.'' So he mounted the stairs,

26 other; he

14 other. He

28 hulking ⟨young⟩ negro man w̶i̶t̶h̶ ̶a̶ s̶a̶d̶d̶l̶e̶ ̶c̶o̶l̶o̶r̶e̶d̶ ̶b̶l̶a̶b̶b̶e̶r̶ ̶m̶o̶u̶t̶h̶e̶d̶ ̶f̶a̶c̶e̶ i̶d̶i̶o̶t̶,̶ in clean

17 hulking young light-colored negro man in clean

29 and blabber mouthed idiot face; he

19 slack-mouthed idiot face. He

29-30 remembered [MARGIN: he remembered how he thot *It's Jim Bond.*/ a̶n̶d̶ *It's the heir to the house:* and] how

19-21 remembered how he thought, 'The scion, the heir, the apparent (though not obvious)' and how

30 Miss Coldfield's

21 Mrs [*sic*] Coldfield's

32 before: the eyes wide, the face

25-26 before—the eyes wide and unseeing like a sleepwalker's, the face

32-33 tallow-colored now

27 tallow-hued now

33-34 bloodlessness: and he thot *What? What is it now? It's not just shock. And it never has been fear. Can it be triumph?;* a⟨A⟩nd

28-30 bloodlessness—and he thought, 'What? What is it now? It's not shock. And it never has been fear. Can it be triumph?' and

35 on; he

31 on. He

36 thinking *I should go with he* and

32-33 thinking, 'I should go with her' and

36-37 then *But I must see too now. I will have to. Maybe I will be sorry tomorrow, but I must see:* so that when

33 then, 'But I must see too now. I will have to. May-

Page 371

1 be I shall be sorry tomorrow, but I must see.' So when

38 he thot *Maybe my face looks like hers did, but it's not triumph)*

2-4 he thought, 'Maybe my face looks like hers did, but it's not triumph')

356

MANUSCRIPT		BOOK	

Page 172 [169]

1-2	hall, ~~the~~ sitting still on the bottom step where she had not moved. He did not overtake Miss Coldfield and Bond, it	4-7	hall, sitting still on the bottom step, sitting still in the attitude in which he had left her. She did not even look at him when he passed her. Nor did he overtake Miss Coldfield and the negro. It
2-3	them.	8-9	them ahead of him.
3-4	he thot *But she cant be afraid to show light now.*	10-11	he thought, 'Surely she cant be afraid to show a light now.'
4-5	to Bond's arm now as she had held to his when they came up the drive;	12	to the negro's arm now;
5	heard Bond's voice	13	heard the negro's voice
7	hear her	15-16	hear (or believe he did) her
7	breath: then	16	breath. Then
8-10	stopped and looking down at her patient and without interest or curiosity as he ran forward. "You, nigger!" she cried. ~~"You aint any Sutpen.--You dont~~ "Help	18-23	stopped in his tracks, looking toward the sound of the fall, waiting, without interest or curiosity, as he (Quentin) hurried forward, hurried toward the voices: "You, nigger! What's your name?" "Calls me Jim Bond." "Help
10	dont need to	24	dont have to
12	her house she	26	her gate she

Page 372

25	lot; he	15	lot. He
30	still hurried up	22	still ran, up
31	*I ought to bathe* he	24	'I ought to bathe,' he
31-32	he lay on the bed, naked, wiping at himself steadily with his discarded	24-26	he was lying on the bed, naked, swabbing his body steadily with the discarded
33-34	hand he said *I have been asleep* it	28-29	hand, he said 'I have been asleep' it
34-35	difference: he just walked down that upper hall with its scaling walls and cracked ceiling too, toward the faint light which came from a door	29-32	difference: waking or sleeping he walked down that upper hall between the scaling walls and beneath the cracked ceiling, toward the faint light which fell outward from the last door
35-36	there saying *No. No.* and then *Only I must. I have to* and	33	there, saying 'No. No' and then 'Only I must. I have to' and

MANUSCRIPT	BOOK
	Page 373
36 bare room	1 bare, stale room
36-37 too and a lamp turned low on	2 too, where a second lamp burned dimly on
Page 173 [170]	
3-15 "And you are——?" "Henry Sutpen." "And you have been ⟨hidden⟩ here——?" "Four years." "And you came home——? [*sic*] "To die. Yes." "To die?" "Yes. To die." "And you have been here——? [*sic*] "Four years." "And you are——?" "Henry Sutpen." ~~"And she waited 3 months,"~~ ~~Shreve said.~~ It	9-21 *And you are——?* *Henry Sutpen.* *And you have been here——?* *Four years.* *And you came home——?* *To die. Yes.* *To die?* *Yes. To die.* *And you have been here——?* *Four years.* *And you are——?* *Henry Sutpen.* It
15-16 chimes ~~had rung~~ ⟨would ring⟩ for one ~~some time ago and~~ ⟨any time⟩ now and the ~~air~~ ⟨chill⟩ had	21-22 chimes would ring for one any time now; the chill had
17 months," Shreve said.	24-25 months before she went back to get him," Shreve said.
20 thinking *Nevermore of peace. Nevermore of peace. Nevermore. Nevermore. Nevermore.*	29-31 thinking 'Nevermore of peace. Nevermore of peace. Nevermore Nevermore Nevermore.'
21 steps, and	32-33 steps, that it would be over then, finished, and
	Page 374
22-23 risk destroying the source of supply?" Still Quentin did not answer. "And then at last she decided to save him,	1-4 risk cutting off the supply, destroying the source, the very poppy's root and seed?" Still Quentin didn't answer. "But at last she did reconcile herself to it, for his sake, to save him,
25 Clytie must have been watching for that	7 Clytie maybe watching for just that
25-26 now and I guess your	8-9 now: and maybe even your
26-27 she ~~said~~ believed that they were coming to take Henry out and hang him	10-13 she believed it was that same black wagon for which she probably had had that nigger boy watching for three months now, coming to carry Henry into town for the white folks to hang him

MANUSCRIPT

BOOK

27-29   guess she had that closet all fixed, with the kindling and the kerosene and all, had it all fixed and ready for 3 months now——" Now

14-19   guess it had been him who had kept that closet under the stairs full of tinder and trash all that time too, like she told him to, maybe he not getting it then either but keeping it full just like she told him, the kerosene and all, for three months now, until the hour when he could begin to howl——" Now

29-30   ceased, perhaps to listen to them too, ~~thot~~ tho Quentin was not listening; he

20-22   ceased, as if he were waiting for them to cease or perhaps were even listening to them. Quentin lay still too, as if he were listening too, though he was not; he

Page 174 [171]

1   Coldfield on the front seat between the driver and another man,

27-28   Coldfield between the driver and the second man,

3   way cautiously up the rutted drive;

31-32   way gingerly up the rutted and frozen (and now partially thawed) drive;

3-4   the deputy

32-33   the howling or it may have been the deputy

Page 375

6   furious implacable woman not much bigger than

2-3   furious grim implacable woman not much larger than

8   reach the monstrous ~~tinder/dry~~ tinder-dry

6   reach the house, the monstrous tinder-dry

8-9   smoke and filled with roaring and the deputy

7-12   smoke through the warped cracks in the weather-boarding as if it were made of gauze wire and filled with roaring and beyond which somewhere something lurked which bellowed, something human since the bellowing was in human speech, even though the reason for it would not have seemed to be. And the deputy

9   driver could spring out and Miss Coldfield could stumble to the ground and

12-13   driver would spring out and Miss Coldfield would stumble out and

10   running to, onto the porch too, into the seeping smoke, screaming harshly "The

14-21   running too, onto the gallery too, where the creature which bellowed followed them, wraith-like and insubstantial, looking at them out of the smoke, whereupon the deputy even turned and ran at him, whereupon he retreated, fled, though the howling did not diminish nor even

MANUSCRIPT

BOOK

			seem to get any further away. They ran onto the gallery too, into the seeping smoke, Miss Coldfield screaming harshly, ''The
11	the deputy at	21	the second man at
14-15	draft of the opened door ~~sent the flames~~ seemed	28	draft created by the open door seemed
17	ambulance clear and returned on foot, and the	31-32	ambulance to safety and returned, the
18	glaring, at the burning house:	33-34	glaring at the doomed house:

Page 376

19	have watched constantly	1-2	have been watching the gates constantly
20	gnome face beneath the headrag,	3	gnome's face beneath the clean headrag,
20-21	fire, looking down at them perhaps [MARGIN: ~~(he could see her)~~]	4-5	fire, seen for a moment between two swirls of smoke, looking down at them, perhaps
21-24	serene as the clapboards melted and peeled away. Then her face went away, vanished; ~~he~~ they held Miss ~~Coldfield as she struggled, still making no sound and foaming a little now at the mouth. Then the whole enormous house seemed to collapse.~~ Coldfield as she struggled: he ~~had not he~~ could see her; he had	7-17	serene above the melting clapboards before the smoke swirled across it again—and he, Jim Bond, the scion, the last of his race, seeing it too now and howling with human reason now since now even he could have known what he was howling about. But they couldn't catch him. They could hear him; he didn't seem to ever get any further away but they couldn't get any nearer and maybe in time they could not even locate the direction any more of the howling. They—the driver and the deputy—held Miss Coldfield as she struggled: he (Quentin) could see her, them; he had
26-27	wild glare as the entire enormous house collapsed.	20-22	wild crimson reflection as the house collapsed and roared away, and there was only the sound of the idiot negro left.
29-30	⸢Miss Rosa.⸣ ~~And she went to bed because it was all~~ He	25	*Miss Rosa.* He
30	blinking, rigid, breathing	26	blinking, breathing
32	now. And so	28-34	now, nothing out there now but that idiot boy to lurk around those ashes and those four gutted chimneys and

MANUSCRIPT

howl until someone came and drove
him away. They couldn't catch him
and nobody ever seemed to make
him go very far away, he just stopped
howling for a little while. Then after
awhile they would begin to hear him
again. And so

Page 377

32-33 window. And now it began to emerge,
take shape in its curious,

1-4 window; then he could not tell if it
was the actual window or the window's pale rectangle upon his
eyelids, though after a moment it
began to emerge. It began to take
shape in its same curious,

34 fireflies. ~~"Jesus~~ "The

7 fireflies. "The

36-37 soon.
      "I

10-12 soon, in a moment; even almost now,
now, now.
      "I

Page 175 [172]

1 have ~~died than have~~ been 21,~~" Shreve
said.~~ than have died,"

14 have died than have been twenty-one."

2-3 finish, the sloped quizzical hand out
of Mississippi,

15-17 finish it—the sloped whimsical ironic
hand out of Mississippi attenuated,

5-6 *amazed but on the contrary she has*

20 *amazed and of not forgiving but on
the contrary has*

8 *the ~~outrage~~ ⟨anger⟩ ~~and the pity~~
hatred*

23 *the hatred*

17 it takes two niggers to get rid of
Sutpen," Shreve said; ~~his mother
and Bon~~ Charles

33 it took Charles

Page 378

19-21 Henry. And yet you have got one
nigger left. And so do you know what
I think?"
      "No,"

1-18 Henry; and Charles Bon's mother and
Charles Bon's grandmother got rid
of Charles Bon. So it takes two
niggers to get rid of one Sutpen,
dont it?" Quentin did not answer;
evidently Shreve did not want an
answer now; he continued almost
without a pause: "Which is all
right, it's fine; it clears the whole
ledger, you can tear all the pages
out and burn them, except for one
thing. And do you know what that
is?" Perhaps he hoped for an
answer this time, or perhaps he

merely paused for emphasis, since
he got no answer. "You've got one
nigger left. One nigger Sutpen left.
Of course you can't catch him and
you don't even always see him and
you never will be able to use him.
But you've got him there still. You
still hear him at night sometimes.
Don't you?"

"Yes," Quentin said.

"And so do you know what I
think?" Now he did expect an
answer, and now he got one:

"No,"

	MANUSCRIPT		BOOK
24	conquer ~~the North~~ the	22	conquer the
25	course, as	22-23	course it won't quite be in our time and of course as
25-26	again ~~so they wont show up so sharp~~ like	24	again like
27	will be Jim Bond. And	26	will still be Jim Bond; and
27-28	will have also sprung	27	will also have sprung
30-31	quickly, ~~too quickly~~ ⟨at once, immediately⟩. "I dont hate it." *I dont hate it*, he thot. ⟨panting⟩ [MARGIN: panting in the cold air, the ~~d~~ iron New England dark.] *I dont. I dont. I dont hate it. I dont hate it.*	30-33	quickly, at once, immediately; "I dont hate it," he said. *I dont hate it* he thought, panting in the cold air, the iron New England dark; *I dont. I dont! I dont hate it! I dont hate it!*

Absalom, Absalom!
_____
William Faulkner

Mississippi, 1935
California, 1936
Mississippi, 1936

Rowanoak.
31 January 1936